Ideology and the Language of Human Rights

It is crucial to apply robust analytic methods to the study of discourses deemed "ideological." This book applies the Guidelines and Procedures for ideological research presented in Verschueren's *Ideology in Language Use*, to an exciting new area of study: discourses intended to improve humanity. It analyzes the discourse of Amnesty International appeal letters, to show (contrary to what the field of critical discourse analysis often assumes) that ideological discourse can sometimes have a positive, rather than a negative, agenda. It explores how Amnesty's choice of words, sentence structures, speech acts, and other discourse elements enact its ideological meanings, functions, frames of reference, and interpretation, as well as the social, interactional, and ideological positioning of discourse participants in its reports, communications, and appeals. These findings have wider implications not only for the field of discourse analysis, but also for theories within pragmatics, such as speech act theory and (im)politeness.

GERALD DELAHUNTY is Professor of Linguistics at Colorado State University. He teaches a broad array of linguistics and applied linguistics topics, and on language, law, and justice. He has published his research on syntax, semantics, discourse analysis, pragmatics, sociolinguistics, ideology, and Irish landscapes and archaeology.

Ideology and the Language of Human Rights

Language, Text, and Ideology in Amnesty International Appeal Letters

Gerald Delahunty
Colarado State University

CAMBRIDGE
UNIVERSITY PRESS

CAMBRIDGE
UNIVERSITY PRESS

Shaftesbury Road, Cambridge CB2 8EA, United Kingdom

One Liberty Plaza, 20th Floor, New York, NY 10006, USA

477 Williamstown Road, Port Melbourne, VIC 3207, Australia

314–321, 3rd Floor, Plot 3, Splendor Forum, Jasola District Centre,
New Delhi – 110025, India

Cambridge University Press is part of Cambridge University Press & Assessment,
a department of the University of Cambridge.

We share the University's mission to contribute to society through the pursuit of
education, learning and research at the highest international levels of excellence.

www.cambridge.org
Information on this title: www.cambridge.org/9781009635615
DOI: 10.1017/9781009635622

When citing this work, please include a reference to the DOI 10.1017/9781009635622

First published 2026

A catalogue record for this publication is available from the British Library

Library of Congress Cataloging-in-Publication Data
Names: Delahunty, Gerald Patrick author
Title: Ideology and the language of human rights : language, text, and
ideology in amnesty international appeal letters / Gerald Delahunty.
Description: 1. | New York : Cambridge University Press, 2026. | Includes
bibliographical references and index.
Identifiers: LCCN 2025053475 | ISBN 9781009635615 hardback | ISBN
9781009635622 ebook
Subjects: LCSH: Amnesty International | Human rights – Discourse | Ideology
| Discourse analysis | Pragmatics | Language and languages – Political
aspects
Classification: LCC K3240 .D453 2026
LC record available at https://lccn.loc.gov/2025053475

ISBN 978-1-009-63561-5 Hardback

For Marna and Cian for many years of love and support

To the memory of Conn R. Ó Cléirigh for his support and inspiring introduction to linguistics

To Peter W. Culicover for his support and guidance on the winding road to my PhD

To Amnesty International and human rights defenders everywhere

To the Prisoners of Conscience mentioned in this book and the great many other individuals, families, and communities whose dignity and human rights have been violated

Contents

The appendices to this book are available online at: www.cambridge.org/delahunty. The appendices include an Amnesty International letter writing guide; the analyzed appeal letter corpus; and additional unanalyzed letters.

Figures

Preface

While academics interested in ideology have generally focused on ideologies that they regard as nefarious, they would generally agree that ideologies may be positive or negative or both. In contrast, people outside the academy tend to view ideologies as nefarious and Amnesty International (AI) takes the view that its activities on behalf of human rights and those deprived of them are not ideological. Using conceptions of ideology proposed in Verschueren (2012), in Eagleton (2007), and in myriad other sources, this book demonstrates that Amnesty's discourses of human rights are indeed ideological.

The book is organized according to Verschueren's Guidelines, Procedures, and Caveats for empirical ideological research and thereby presents an analysis of the discourse and language of AI documents by engaging a thoroughly thought-out framework by an important scholar in the fields of pragmatics and ideology research.

The analysis incorporates several approaches I adopted in studying the AI documents. This multiplicity of approaches is in keeping with the precept that discourse analysis is a multi-disciplinary, multi-perspectival enterprise. These approaches include studies of aspects of the AI documents: genre, speech acts and (im)politeness, ideological conflict, ideological positioning of multiple audiences, participant positioning, rhetorical moves and steps, and the re-entextualization, re-contextualization, and re-genrefication of information from other texts and genres.

I ask and answer the following questions: What ideological functions, meanings, frames of reference, and interpretation undergird the documents? What linguistic choices enact these ideological positions? How do those choices enact a specifically oppositional, and hence explicitly dialogic, genre? Can the analytic methods developed by scholars to study the discourses of nefarious ideologies to expose their hidden claims be profitably applied to the discourses of liberationist ideologies? Are the two discourse types similar and, if they are, in what ways, for example, do liberationist discourses also hide important claims?

Acknowledgements

Thank you, Jef Verschueren. Without your encouragement this project might have languished in a forgotten .doc file.

Thanks, too, to two anonymous Cambridge University Press reviewers who read the book when it was just a toddler, provided essential commentary, and later encouraged Cambridge University Press to publish it.

To Jeffrey Kaplan, for your careful reading and insightful comments on several drafts.

To my colleague Tony Becker for the KEYword analysis.

To Nora Gordon for the Move and Step analysis.

To Andreea Calude for a very enjoyable and productive research visit to the University of Waikato, New Zealand.

To Cambridge University Press' Helen Barton, Isabel Collins, Lisa Carter, Sophie Rosinke, Preethi Sekar, and their colleagues for all their help in preparing the book for publication.

To Robert Saigh of Razorsharp Communications, Inc. for the index.

To Richard Swingler for his help in obtaining permission from Amnesty International to use its webpages, emails, and appeal letters in this research.

And to Amnesty International for their permission to use the Amnesty webpages, emails, and appeal letters that constitute the data for the analysis presented in this book.

Sections of this book have appeared as published papers (Delahunty 2018a, 2018b, 2021, 2023) and as conferences presentations (Delahunty 2013, 2014, 2015, 2017).

Abbreviations

25P	25 Points of American National Socialism
ACLU	American Civil Liberties Union
AFP	Agence France-Presse
AHD	American Heritage Dictionary
AI	Amnesty International
AI USA	Amnesty International USA
An	animator
ANSP	American National Socialist Party
AR	addressed recipient
Au	author
CDA	Critical Discourse Analysis
CDHRI	Cairo Declaration on Human Rights in Islam
CIA	Central Intelligence Agency
COCA	Corpus of Contemporary American English
CP	Cooperative Principle
DRC	Democratic Republic of the Congo
EU	European Union
FTA	face threatening act
H&P	Huddleston and Pullum (2002)
HR	Human rights
HRW	Human Rights Watch
IACtHR	Inter-American Court of Human Rights
ICC	International Criminal Court
ICCPR	International Covenant on Civil and Political Rights
ICESCR	International Covenant on Economic, Social, and Cultural Rights
ICJ	International Court of Justice
IR	intended recipient
ISA	Ideological State Apparatus
LGBTQIA+	lesbian, gay, bisexual, transsexual, queer, asexual, collectively
NGO	non-governmental organization

NP	noun phrase
NSA	National Security Agency
OAS	Organization of American States
OED	*Oxford English Dictionary*
PF	philanthropic fundraising
PoC	Prisoner of Conscience
Pr	principal
R	recipient in general
RSA	Repressive State Apparatus
RT	Relevance Theory
SE	Standard English
SPLC	Southern Poverty Law Center
UAN	Amnesty International Urgent Action Network
UBCV	Unified Buddhist Church of Viet Nam
UDHR	Universal Declaration of Human Rights
UK	United Kingdom
UN	United Nations
UNHCR	United Nations High Commissioner for Refugees
UR	unaddressed recipient
US	United States
USA	United States of America
USSR	Union of Soviet Socialist Republics

1 Introduction

Donald Trump, speaking to the United Nations General Assembly on September 25, 2018, contrasted "the ideology of globalism" with the "doctrine of patriotism," thus invoking the traditional understanding of ideology as necessarily nefarious. "Doctrine," of course, is blessed by religious collocations and connotations thereby sanctifying "patriotism." This contrast is in keeping with his administration's withdrawal of the US from international human rights institutions. This withdrawal suggests that Trump regards these universal rights as elements of globalism, so we must assume that he regards them also as ideological and thus nefarious. As nationalism is just as certainly ideological as globalism, it is clear that one person's ideology may be another's sacred duty, and an ideology that is nefarious to some may be liberating to others.

Though most current scholars would claim that ideologies may be positive or negative and anything in between, most current research on ideological discourse takes as its object of study discourses that the authors find objectionable, for example, van Dijk's (1998) studies of racism in D'Souza's *The End of Racism* (1995), and his study of the denial of racism (1992) and ideology and discourse (2013); Blommaert and Verschueren's (1998) study of anti-migrant themes in Belgian public discussion and government publications; Wodak's (2007) study of the ideological constructions of the "German *Wehrmacht*" and her (2011) study of far-right populist and racist rhetoric; Verschueren's (2012) study of the coverage of the 1857–58 Indian Mutiny in late nineteenth- and early twentieth-century French and English history textbooks; to name but a very few. These studies reflect the tradition that assumes that ideologies are characteristically injurious in that they typically benefit some more or less clearly demarcated groups and disadvantage other more or less clearly identified groups: Nazi and Neo-Nazi ideologies are intended to benefit those of "pure White blood" and disadvantage all others, but particularly Jews and homosexuals (Point 4 in 25 Points of American National Socialism).[1] It is

[1] http://junkscience.com/wp-content/uploads/2012/04/neo-nazis-on-agw.pdf (accessed July 29, 2025).

much less clear who is disadvantaged by the ideologies of human rights activism: while Amnesty celebrates the release of Prisoners of Conscience (PoCs), it does not exclude representatives of governments that imprison PoCs from the protections afforded by human rights.

Besides focusing on objectionable ideologies, these studies assume that the target ideologies are hegemonic and that their goals are at least partially hidden in their texts and must be unearthed by careful linguistic analysis, employing methods from various strands of discourse analysis, linguistic pragmatics, and sociolinguistics, and informed by cognitive, historical, and sociological studies.

The analysis presented in this book departs from the usual assumptions about ideology and takes as its object elements of the discourse of human rights activism, a discourse that many would regard as positive and thus non-ideological, a position assumed in Amnesty International's *Letter Writing Guide*,[2] which directs members and volunteers not to "discuss ideology or politics" in their appeals[3] in support of human rights. Another version of this Guide is provided in Appendix 1.[4] I demonstrate in Chapter 3 that the Amnesty International (AI) documents[5] display the characteristics of ideology identified in Eagleton (2007) and Verschueren (2012) and are thus unquestionably ideological. Briefly, these documents are *normative* in that they invoke international declarations, for example, the UN Universal Declaration of Human Rights (UN UDHR);[6] international covenants, for example, the International Covenant on Civil and Political Rights[7] and the International Covenant on Economic, Social, and Cultural Rights;[8] and international enforcement mechanisms, for example, the International Criminal Court[9] and the International Court of Justice.[10] They are also designed to *unify* their addressees and readers, especially AI members and volunteers, *motivate* them to *act*, and provide them with a *universal rationale* to *naturalize* and *legitimize* their beliefs and actions.

The AI documents explicitly espouse the ideology of human rights and make it the basis for the evaluation of certain governmental and non-governmental

[2] www.amnesty.org/en/wp-content/uploads/2021/05/ORG1090612018ENGLISH.pdf (accessed March 18, 2026). A search for AI's *Guide* will return a great many, generally consistent, versions.
[3] Drafts of these appeals are included in emails to AI members; they describe a violation of human rights and ask for its redress. I use the terms "appeal," "appeal letter," and "letter" variably to refer to these documents.
[4] See also Verschueren 2000 on "metapragmatic awareness in language use."
[5] A note on my terminology: I use "text" to refer to linguistic representations and "document" to refer to representations that may incorporate text, photos, and/or other forms of representation intended to be interpreted as coherent wholes (Hodges 2018).
[6] www.un.org/en/universal-declaration-human-rights/ (accessed July 29, 2025).
[7] www.ohchr.org/sites/default/files/ccpr.pdf (accessed July 29, 2025).
[8] www.ohchr.org/sites/default/files/cescr.pdf (accessed July 29, 2025).
[9] www.icc-cpi.int/about/the-court (accessed July 29, 2025).
[10] www.icj-cij.org/en/court (accessed July 29, 2025).

actions as violative and the basis for redress of those violations. Additionally, as elements of activist resistance, of counterpower (Featherman 2015; Gee 2011), the AI documents and the discourses of human rights in general, though representing universal laws, represent the weaker party in the situations in which they operate, so that their hegemonic aspirations are held firmly in check.

This study takes as context the methodologies proposed in Verschueren (2012) for the systematic, controlled, accurate, empirical, and cross-disciplinary study of ideological discourse.[11] The study adopts Verschueren's guidelines, and where necessary, adapts, augments, and challenges them. In investigating the relations among the AI documents, the study invokes the extensive literature on the analysis of multi-modal documents (e.g., Bateman 2018; Forceville 2014, 2017; Forceville and Clark 2014; Jewitt 2009, 2014, 2016; Machin 2014; Roque 2017; Tseronis and Forceville 2017; van Leeuwen 2015).

The Amnesty International webpages, emails, and appeal letters that constitute the primary data for the analysis presented in this book are a convenience sample collected over the period 2013–16. The appeal letters came to me in emails I received from Amnesty as an active member of the organization. These emails encourage their receivers to forward the appeals to government or other officials with the power to improve the situations of the PoCs and others who are the subjects of the appeals. Amnesty members who receive the emails may edit the appeal letter or may just click a SEND button. As the appeals analyzed for the study were collected over more than a decade ago, some of the individuals on whose behalf the appeals were created have been released, others may still be imprisoned, some have died, and others may have revoked their consent for Amnesty International to campaign on their behalf.[12]

This book presents an analysis of a corpus of forty AI appeal letters[13] on behalf of "Prisoners of Conscience"[14] and other individuals and classes of individuals whose human and/or humanitarian rights have been violated, and in support of specific human and humanitarian causes, for example, freedom from torture, freedom of expression, arms control treaties, protection of LGBTQIA+ (lesbian, gay, bisexual, transsexual, queer, intersex, asexual, collectively) people, and rights to abortion.

The appeals are sent to AI members/volunteers by AI staffers, embedded in an email that provides background information on the situation that is the

[11] Verschueren's (2012) goal was to create "a package of methods in a clear methodological perspective inspired by a general theory of linguistic pragmatics, viewed as an interdisciplinary science of language use" (51).

[12] This paragraph includes language required by AI for permission to use its documents for this book.

[13] Verschueren (1999: 153) mentions "Amnesty International letter writing sessions" in his discussion of speech activity/events.

[14] https://amnesty.ca/human-rights-news/first-amnesty-international-prisoner-of-conscience-held-in-canada/ (accessed September 3, 2025).

subject of the appeal, along with links to AI webpages with further information. These appeals can also be found on AI's website embedded in webpages that are similar to the emails. Ostensibly, the appeals are to be electronically forwarded by the volunteers to their "Message Recipients," who are generally powerful government functionaries, by clicking on a button marked SEND.

The analyzed letters were collected into a single Word document (Appendix 2); a further forty letters are collected in a separate corpus (Appendix 3). These allow other researchers to compare their analyses with mine, the kind of counterscreening recommended by Verschueren (2012: 22).

Verschueren (2012) presents "pragmatic guidelines for empirical research" into ideology in language use. While Verschueren's book presents a well-organized framework for a description of an ideologically infused discourse genre, it is not, as he says, a theory. Consequently, its framework must be augmented with a broad range of linguistic, pragmatic, and discourse analytic theories in order to provide explanations for the specific phenomena encountered in the data identified by Verschueren.

Even though Verschueren's (2012) book is "designed for training purposes" - its "target audience includes … historians, sociologists, anthropologists, and political scientists, to name but a few broad categories" (xii) - Costa (2014) deems it a "major book for students and advanced scholars in pragmatics and discourse analysis" (310). The current book is organized according to Verschueren's Guidelines, Procedures, and Caveats for empirical ideological research and thereby presents an analysis of the discourse and language of the AI appeal letters by engaging a thoroughly thought-out framework by an important scholar in the study of pragmatics and ideology.

The analysis I present here is derived from several approaches I have adopted in studying the AI letters. This multiplicity of approaches is in keeping with the precept that discourse analysis is a multi-disciplinary, multi-perspectival enterprise. These approaches include initial studies of aspects of the letters: genre, speech acts and (im)politeness (Delahunty 2013), ideological conflict (Delahunty 2015), ideological positioning of multiple audiences (Delahunty 2017), participant positioning (Delahunty 2018a), rhetorical moves and steps (Delahunty 2018b), and the re-entextualization, re-contextualization, and re-genrefication of information from other texts and genres (Delahunty 2021, 2023).

Research Questions and Data

This section addresses the preliminary methodological issues Verschueren (2012) raises in his chapter 2 on "Pragmatic rules of engagement" and presents as a series of rules. These rules deal with the formulation of research questions, the selection of data, and pragmatics-derived rules for the study of ideological discourse to "*enable interpretation with due regard for what can be intersubjectively established to count as evidence*" (21, emphasis in original; footnote omitted). The research questions may be prompted by the analyst's "*involvement*" (emphasis in original) with the discourse and perhaps a sense that something is "wrong" (21) with it, characteristically, that there is a contradiction between its overt and covert messages. My initial interest in analyzing the AI letters derives not from any sense of contradiction, but from my desire to know what happened to "my" letters when I clicked the SEND button. Did they go to their Message Recipients? If so, what happened to them there? Who, if anyone, reads them? If they did not go to the Message Recipients, then what happened to them? Was clicking SEND merely a signal to AI's computer systems to send a "Thank you. Please donate" email? This puzzle about the fate of my letters led to questions about their roles in AI's activism and fundraising, which led to whether the letters were elements in an ideological discourse, and if so, by what criteria.

> ***Rule 1: Formulate researchable questions, i.e., questions to which answers can be given, supported with empirical evidence and susceptible to counterscreening. (Verschueren 2012: 22)***

Verschueren prefers "research questions" rather than hypotheses, as the latter require the articulation of "an assertion that can be verified or proven," or as Karl Popper claimed, can only be falsified (Andersen and Hepburn 2021). Analysis of ideological discourse should be "*data-driven*" and "*theoretically grounded in [a] methodology for letting the data speak*" (Verschueren 2012: 23, emphasis in original), though "*criteria for data to count as (carriers of) evidence*" are essential (23, emphasis in original). In the coming chapters, I ask and answer the following questions: What ideological functions, meanings, frames of reference, and interpretation undergird the appeal letters? What linguistic choices enact these ideological positions? How do those choices enact a specifically oppositional, and hence explicitly dialogic, genre? Can the analytic methods developed by scholars to study the discourses of nefarious ideologies to expose their hidden claims be profitably applied to the discourses of liberationist ideologies? Are the two discourse types similar and, if they are, in what ways, for example, do liberationist discourses also hide important claims?

> ***Rule 2: Before an aspect of meaning can be seen as an ingredient of ideology, it should emerge coherently from the data, both in terms of conceptual connectedness with other aspects of meaning and in terms of patterns of recurrence or of absence. (Verschueren 2012: 23)***

While this book argues that the AI appeals fulfill all the functions of ideology proposed in Eagleton (2007), here I briefly address Verschueren's more general methodological concern. I claim that human rights, "an aspect of meaning," are "an ingredient of ideology" that "emerge[s] coherently from the data." The AI letters consistently and systematically derive their evaluations of the problems they address and the solutions they propose by referring to human and/or humanitarian rights and justify their appeals for redress by reference to those rights, though it is only rarely that reference is made to specific instruments, for example, the UN UDHR; they are typically generic, for example, to "the right to life" or "human rights."[15]

The letters occasionally offer concessions to the Message Recipients that rights violations are based on competing exigencies, for example, governments' responsibilities to bring criminals to justice (#4 Al-Qahtani, Iraq),[16] which are then rebutted by characterizing the violations as local failures to meet universal and international standards (of legal procedure, and the like). This is not to say that the discourse of human and humanitarian rights is in general internally consistent, coherent, and settled (see Chen's 2015: 434–435 remarks on the "evolution" of the UDHR), merely that the AI letters adopt consistent positions on the issues they address and express these in consistent ways, thus allowing the ideological meanings of the letters to be seen to emerge coherently from the data.

In the few letters that include them, concessions are based on local, often legal, considerations. Where concessions might be made on the basis of religious ideologies, the letters are silent. For example, in the case of Raif Badawi (#18 Badawi, Saudi Arabia), who was flogged by Saudi Arabian authorities in front of a mosque after Friday evening prayers, the appeal might have acknowledged that the verdict and punishment are based in Islamic (Sharia) law. Certainly, one might reasonably infer an implicit criticism of that law and the religion it derives from. In the case of Beatriz (#8 Beatriz, El Salvador), who was denied an abortion even though continuing her pregnancy was endangering her life, the appeal might have conceded that El Salvador's absolute ban on abortion, like that of other countries, for example, Argentina, is based on Catholic tenets. The letters' appeals to universal rights avoid a direct confrontation between religious and secular values, even if one might argue that those secular values ultimately derive from religious notions of the transcendent value and dignity of individual human beings, for example, Quinlan (2011), and thus avoid inviting the response that values deriving from a god, however partial and capricious, outrank values deriving from mere human deliberations.

With a few exceptions, the letters typically also omit reference to, or discussion of, broader political contexts. In this, the letters appear to follow the

[15] According to Friedman (2011: 2), a sociocultural study of human and related rights, "'Human rights' is, unfortunately a vague and slippery phrase."

[16] The appeal letters in the corpus are numbered sequentially and given a name that briefly identifies their topic and the country involved.

AI letter-writing guidelines that explicitly prohibit politicizing an appeal, thus implying that appeals based on human rights are not political discourse. The exceptions are two letters to President Obama urging him as representative of the US government to lead "the effort to stop the unregulated flow of weapons" (#2 Arms Trade, USA) by supporting "the highest possible human rights standards within a new Arms Trade Treaty." This treaty was adopted by the UN and came into force on December 24, 2014.

Rule 2.1: Types of data must be varied horizontally and vertically. (Verschueren 2012: 26)

"*Horizontal* variation refers to *genre differences*" (26, emphasis in original). As we will see in Chapter 2, several distinct though related genres are relevant to the study of AI appeal letters. The most immediately relevant to the AI appeal genre is the email sent to volunteers in which the appeal is embedded. This email is addressed to the volunteer, provides information on the case, which is characteristically reproduced in the appeal, and urges the volunteer to SEND the embedded appeal. Other relevant documents include bulletins on AI webpages, AI reports on violative situations and the case information on which these reports are based, as well as the laws, legal decisions, treaties, covenants, and declarations that define the various rights invoked in the letters. And on a larger scale, discussion of human rights in a broader range of contexts.

Verschueren's *vertical* variation refers to levels of linguistic structure, for example, "patterns of word choice, presupposition- and implication-carrying constructions, interaction patterns, and more global constructs (such as argumentation patterns)" (Verschueren 2012: 27). In response to later guidelines, I address all of the items mentioned in Rule 2.1, and considerably more.[17]

Rule 2.2: An appropriate amount of data is required. (Verschueren 2012: 28)

For Verschueren, an "appropriate amount of data ... depend[s] on the specific nature of one's research question" (28). Clearly my corpus is far smaller than those referred to in Verschueren's book: his studies of discourses on migrants in Belgium and of discourses on colonization in English and French history textbooks from the late 1800s and early 1900s. Nonetheless, my database is sufficient to provide reliable results which can be further tested by counterscreening and by the study of relevant related genres, for example, the embedding emails from AI, AI webpage documents and reports, and

[17] Van Dijk (2013: 190–193) lists as "formal structures of discourse" relevant to ideological analysis, the lexicon and syntax, particularly word order patterns that allow for topicalizing, foregrounding, and backgrounding information, and which may be conventionally deployed in the construction of relevant genres. See Van Dijk (1995) for an earlier and somewhat more detailed version.

the legal, academic, and journalistic polemics surrounding human rights and their violations. The letters in my corpora are similar enough to each other in function, rhetorical organization, and patterns of linguistic choice for me to be confident that other researchers' analyses of the letter corpora in Appendixes 2 and 3 would be consistent with mine. Moreover, the size and generic consistency of the AI letters suggest that my analysis may avoid the risks Verschueren (2012: 28) associates with "sizable" corpora – that given corpus enough and time an analyst will "find – or construct – the 'desired' patterns of meaning."[18]

> ***Rule 2.3: Whatever is found throughout a wide corpus should also be recoverable in (at least a number of) individual instances of discourse. (Verschueren 2012: 28)***

Rule 2.3 is formulated to minimize the likelihood of researcher bias by requiring that claims about the corpus be manifested in individual instances of the target discourse. For example, Blommaert and Verschueren (1998) devote chapter 7 (162–189) "to the analysis of a single leaflet that was widely distributed by the official Belgian information bureau Inbel ..." (Verschueren 2012: 29).

> ***Rule 2.4: The quality of the data must be carefully evaluated in view of the precise research goal. (Verschueren 2012: 29)***

The goal of the current research is to develop an analysis of AI appeal letters that identifies the linguistic choices their writers make and the ways in which those choices enact the ideological formations underlying human and humanitarian rights. The AI letters fit this goal because they are written by (specialist) staffers in AI in accordance with AI guidelines and reflect AI's mission to promote human rights. They are therefore authentic representatives of the genre, even if the details of their composition are obscure. They function as directives to their addressees and enact the characteristics of ideology identified by Eagleton (2007) discussed in Chapter 3 below, and briefly re-presented here: the letters are based on a body of ideas characteristic of a particular social group, specifically AI staffers and volunteers, and, probably, staffers and volunteers of other human, humanitarian, and civil rights organizations. Because they derive from universal norms, these ideas offer legitimating epistemological and evaluative positions according to which individuals can identify themselves and others and which motivate them to act in their own and others' social interests by engaging in a discourse of power and counterpower (Featherman 2015) – they include projected "voices of dissent"

[18] Anyone seeking an even larger corpus should visit www.amnesty.org/en/get-involved/take-action/, though this site is occasionally unstable (accessed July 29, 2025).

(Verschueren 2012: 30). Their epistemological, legitimating, and evaluative functions rely on the assumption of universality undergirding the UN UDHR and of the various humanitarian conventions they invoke. Elements of these instruments are typically invoked by definite descriptions, for example, "the right to life," thus presupposing the existence of the named rights. As these instruments have the force of law, they are normative and thus allow for the naturalization of evaluations based on them, which are typically expressed as unhedged categorizations, for example, "Flogging is a flagrant violation of the right to life" (#18 Badawi, Saudi Arabia). The genre represents the direct expression of AI's ideological positions and range of interests and has remained consistent over the years I have been collecting instances.

Six Analytic Dimensions

Verschueren (2012) compares and contrasts the history textbooks he analyses across six dimensions (31–50); here, I briefly discuss these dimensions in relation to the AI letters.

(1) Language (Verschueren 2012: 31)

The language of the letters and of the embedding emails is mainly standard (American) English, for example, "authorize" (#1 Targeted Killings, USA) rather than "authorise," though occasionally a British spelling slips in, for example, "labourers" (#40 Cobalt, Apple Corp.). I have not found any clearly non-standard usages. The underlying assumption must be that the addressees (or their surrogates) speak or read English well enough to be able to understand the letters. This assumption reflects the global importance of English as a lingua franca and its predominance among the official languages of the UN and working languages of other international institutions and organizations (Crystal 2003; Hickey 2012). The literacy level required to write and read the letters ranges from requiring a graduate degree (#1 Targeted Killings, USA) to 11th grade (#11 Pussy Riot, Russia), though the readability formulas differ in their grade level assignments. The relatively high literacy levels suggest that AI staffers are highly literate and that AI assumes that its members and volunteers are equally so. This literacy level may also suggest that AI assumes that the Message Recipients or their surrogates will have similarly high levels of English proficiency, even if few if any of the letters will actually be read by their Message Recipients and that what is persuasive to them is the number of letters sent and/or received, not the sophistication of their arguments. While the letters are linguistically consistent, they occasionally display minor editing errors, for example, inconsistent punctuation and the omission of a definite article in "I am deeply concerned *that US* government's ..." (#1 Targeted

Killings, USA; emphasis added), and collocations suggestive of second language usage, for example, in (#3 Satire as Crime, Egypt), "their free expression of speech," indicating, again, that their arguments may be less important to their success than their numbers.[19]

Complementary to the readability levels of the appeals are their keywords. Keywords are those that distinguish a target corpus from a general corpus, in this case the 10,311 words of the appeal letter corpus and the 10 million words of the BNC_COCA_mixed_Sp_Wr_US_UK_10_million corpus. The analysis returned eighty-one keywords whose frequencies in the appeals and reference corpus are substantially different. As one would expect, most of these are specific to legal and human rights domains, for example, *deport*, whose various forms (*deportation*, etc.) occur seven times in the appeals corpus, which is 5,819 times more frequent than they occur in the reference corpus. The least frequent keyword listed is *execute*, which occurs 25.52 times more frequently in the appeals than in the reference corpus. The ten most frequent words and their variant forms in the appeals corpus are: *program*, *politic*, *deportation*, *meaning*, *relation*, *extrajudicial*, *detain*, *perpetuate*, *abduct*, and *defame*. While several of these are not specific to the legal and human rights domains, most are. However, when we look at the collocations of those that are not, we find them to be human rights specific, for example: "These *programs* are a violation of the human rights of people across the globe" (#23 Mass Surveillance, USA; emphasis added); "They are too often unable to make decisions about who they can love, who they have intimate *relations* with, who they marry, and about whether to have children and how many" (#33 Contraception, Burkina Faso; emphasis added).[20]

(2) Temporal Perspective (Verschueren 2012: 32)

As a genre, the AI appeal letters have a history going back to 1961, when AI was founded, though elements of that genre are clearly much older, for example, protest directives. According to an AI webpage,[21] "Over the years, human rights have moved from the fringes to centre stage in world affairs," and the categories of rights appeals have broadened from focusing on individual PoCs to include such issues as the abolition of torture and the death penalty, sexual and reproductive rights, discrimination against various categories of people, and refugee and migrant rights, among others (see Domaradzki et al. 2019; Vašák 1977). However, demands for human

[19] In contrast, AI's Urgent Action letter-writing instructions allow for English, the language of the addressee(s) if the writer has the necessary competence, or the writer's native language.

[20] The forms quoted above are lemmatized. My thanks to Tony Becker for this keyword analysis.

[21] https://amnesty.ca/who-we-are/ (accessed September 5, 2025).

rights, in their modern formulations, go back at least as far as the European Enlightenment and the American and French Revolutions. (Chapter 2 provides a brief history of AI.)

While Verschueren's history textbooks describe and evaluate events that occurred prior to, and sometimes a long time prior to, when they were published, the AI appeals deal with situations current when they are written (and, ideally, sent). As they deal with situations of considerable urgency, they direct their addressees to act immediately upon their receipt.

(3) Geographical Perspective (Verschueren 2012: 33)

AI was founded in England in 1961, and its headquarters are still there, though it has branches worldwide, with an important one in the US. Currently, AI claims to be "a global movement."[22] While the legal instruments AI appeals to were designed, negotiated, and enacted to be universally applicable, certain Muslim countries have developed analogous instruments based on Muslim (Sharia) law (e.g., the Cairo Declaration on Human Rights in Islam (CDHRI) enacted in 1990),[23] which, for example, legalize executions, though UDHR does not (UDHR Article 3).

The appeal letters in my corpus were sent to eighteen countries: Algeria, Burkina Faso, Dominican Republic, Egypt, El Salvador, Indonesia, Iraq, Malawi, Myanmar, Peoples Republic of China, Russian Federation, Saudi Arabia, South Africa, Sudan, Turkey,[24] USA, Uzbekistan, and Vietnam, as well as to Apple Corporation. Amnesty's Country Profiles includes information on AI's "research and campaigning across the world, with all the latest news, blogs, and reports," as well as a link to the current year's report on the "The State of the World's Human Rights" "during 2023 in 155 countries."[25]

(4) Size and Degree of Detail (Verschueren 2012: 33)

The letters re-entextualize, re-contextualize, and re-genrecize information in their embedding emails and in the AI webpages, reports, and case files, which may be indefinitely large, as they contain internet and other links to electronic documents which may also contain such links.

In keeping with AI's letter-writing instructions, the appeals are typically brief: they range from about a third of a page to about a page and a half and are

[22] www.amnesty.org/en/ (accessed July 29, 2025).

[23] http://hrlibrary.umn.edu/instree/cairodeclaration.html (accessed July 29, 2025).

[24] On June 1, 2022, the UN accepted Turkey's request to be known henceforth as Türkiye, the name adopted after independence in 1923. In this work, I use the form of the name as it appears in the documents I analyze.

[25] www.amnesty.org/en/documents/pol10/7200/2024/en/ (accessed July 29, 2025).

on average approximately 300 words. They typically provide only information deemed essential to their specific cases, including the names of individuals involved, what the subjects of the appeals have been accused of, the threats to their persons, liberties, and lives, and the specifics of the redress sought. The letters may also contain elaborations of the primary appeals; for example, an appeal initially on behalf of a single individual may be generalized to include all the individuals belonging to a relevant category.

(5) Coverage (Verschueren 2012: 34)

The letters vary in the amount of coverage of the case they provide. Some letters provide little coverage, just a brief description of the situation motivating the letter and a brief directive to redress that situation, but always (just) enough to state the problem and to urge its solution. Other letters may provide somewhat more detail on both elements. A very few letters include concessions and their rebuttals. Occasionally, the letters include bulleted (or otherwise displayed) lists of demands, though "demand" occurs only once in the corpus, and even there it is used impersonally and non-directively: "The revelations demand careful analysis by Congress" (#23 Mass Surveillance, USA). In contrast, the embedding emails may direct their addressees to *demand* that the letter addressees redress a wrong.

(6) Intended Audience (Verschueren 2012: 34)

Verschueren's history books were primarily designed as textbooks for primary and secondary school students, though one was for a "general audience" and another was a "general children's book" (see his Table 1, 38–39). As history texts dating from the late nineteenth century through the first two decades of the 20th, they display the tension between the ideologies of historiography as the objective presentation and explanation of facts and the more traditional excitation of uncritical patriotism, typically to the advantage of ruling elites, and their roles in identity formation.

The ostensible intended audience of the appeal letters must be the explicitly listed Message Recipients identified above the letter. These are typically important government functionaries, for example, presidents, prime ministers, defense ministers, and the like. Presumably these are individuals assumed to have the power to accede to the requests in the letters.

However, the letters are sent to AI volunteers, embedded in emails that present the problematic situation and exhort the volunteers to forward the letters by clicking a SEND button on the webpage. Certainly, the embedding email is designed to motivate the volunteers; however, the appeal letters themselves also seem to function in this way and, thus, seem to be designed for at least two audiences – the Message Recipients and potential letter SENDers. For both audiences, though especially for the former, it is important that the facts represented in the letters be accurate and AI is well-known for the care its staffers take to establish and accurately represent the facts of each case.

If we assume, as I suggest, that the AI volunteers who receive and are named in the emails are also an audience for the letters, then we need to be able to say something about who these people are. Presumably they are among the 10 million people around the globe that AI claims to represent and engage "to fight injustice all around the world."[26] I do not know how many of these 10 million are on the organization's email list, though I assume that the addressees on the email list have opted to be on it, most likely by donating to AI. However, I do not know how often that list is pruned to eliminate inactive members or people who prefer to no longer receive AI's frequent, indeed daily, emails.

As I've noted, appeals can be accessed by going to the AI webpage and clicking on the link to an ongoing case. Obviously, the netizen who accesses cases in this way is not personally identified, unlike the recipients of the AI emails, who are directly addressed by first name. Nonetheless, the email recipients and those who purposefully access AI webpages are engaged in acts of identity creation or maintenance.

Verschueren raises the issue of "objectivity" in the history texts, and here I address its relevance to the appeal letters. To do so, I distinguish between objectivity and accuracy. I address the issue of accuracy in AI documents in Chapter 2, noting that the organization, having learned from its occasional errors, is recognized for the accuracy of its characterization of situations, though ultimately these characterizations are dependent upon local witnesses who typically have been affected by the situations. Accuracy simply has to do with getting the facts right. Objectivity is a stance toward the representation of a situation. It suggests a detached, impersonal, uninvolved view of a situation in contrast to an engaged, involved view. AI's documents are accurate, personal, and involved, but not objective, in the sense I've just outlined. The letters' appeals to pathos, to the readers' empathy and sympathy, reflect this involvement and impute it to the volunteer letter SENDers. I suggest that the invocation of empathy is designed rather more for the volunteers than for the Message Recipients, whose attitudes to the cases are likely to be unsympathetic and who may respond angrily to the appeals. It is hard to imagine that a US state governor or attorney general who has refused to release a prisoner despite three court rulings to do so would be moved by appeals to their better natures (#20 Woodfox, Louisiana, USA).

[26] www.amnestyusa.org/about-us/who-we-are/ and www.amnestyusa.org/about-us/ (both accessed July 29, 2025).

As I discuss in more detail in Chapter 2, I am unclear about where my email goes when I click SEND, but I immediately receive an invitation to donate to AI, thus implicating that the letters serve at least three functions: appealing to government officials on behalf of AI's causes; engaging and motivating AI volunteers; and fundraising. This connection between misery and money is not unique to AI; for example, according to an article in ProPublica, "Inside the Red Cross, the Haiti disaster was seen as 'a spectacular fundraising opportunity,' recalled one former official who helped organize the effort."[27] See Mann and Thompson (1992) and Biber, Connor, & Upton (2007) on philanthropic fund-raising letters, and Delahunty (2018b) for a comparative analysis of AI appeals and philanthropic fund-raising letters.

Finally, it is important to note that while Verschueren's history textbooks, and presumably, history textbooks as a genre, are descriptions of prior events and reflections upon them, the AI letters and their related documents both represent current historical events and intervene in them. And just as there are "histories of history writing," there are histories of human rights activism, for example, Neier (2012) and Sikkink (2017).

Book Plan

Chapter 2 briefly discusses rights and human rights. It provides a short history of Amnesty International and a discussion of the multi-modal relations among its primary document genres: the appeal letter, which is the main focus of this book; its emails to volunteers/members and the webpage in which the appeal letter is embedded; the email it sends asking for a donation in response to a volunteer SENDing the appeal; and an AI report which documents in detail an appeal situation. The chapter provides a brief analysis of the primary document genres, paying particular attention to the linguistic and visual resonances occasioned by their mutual contextualizations and proposes a Relevance Theory explanation for the intricate relations between the documents' linguistic and visual modes and argues for the ideological study of AI documents, particularly of the appeal letters.

Chapter 3 reviews several important understandings of ideology and concludes with discussion of Verschueren's Theses 1–4, which articulate his characterization of ideology and its manifestations and roles in discourse. These theses along with the attributes identified in Eagleton (2007) provide the bases for the arguments presented throughout the book that the AI appeals and related documents are ideologically imbued genres.

Chapter 4 addresses Verschueren's Caveat 1 through his Procedure 2.3, which deal with data, its contexts, and the "lines of vision" connecting the

[27] https://reliefweb.int/report/haiti/how-red-cross-raised-half-billion-dollars-haiti-and-built-six-homes (accessed March 16, 2026).

documents with their relevant contexts. The chapter investigates the ideological relevancies of the appeals' social, political, historical, and geographical contexts; their immediate context of situation; and their linguistic contexts, guided by Verschueren's preliminary caveats, his Guidelines 1 and 2, and their associated analytic procedures. This investigation requires that Verschueren's broad guidelines be augmented by multiple discourse analytic theoretical apparatuses: deixis; speech act theory; Gricean and post-Gricean pragmatics; contextualization cues; various theories of participant roles; positioning theory; theories of argumentation; move and step analysis; epistemic vigilance; and discussion of a broad range of specifically linguistic devices.

Chapter 5 addresses Verschueren's Guideline 3 through Procedure 3.3 and associated caveats and procedures, which deal with language, social structures, processes, relations, and meaning. It investigates the "dynamics of meaning generation in relation to issues pertaining to social structures, processes, and relations" (Verschueren 2012: 117), the roles of grammatical relations and their interactions with semantic roles, particularly the identification of agents and experiencers of violative and other actions and the ideological positioning of those referents relative to human-rights-based evaluations of the actions. It also examines the topics of the appeals and the language of the rhetorical moves and steps that constitute them.

Chapter 6 addresses Verschueren's Procedures 3.4 to 3.7 and his Guideline 4. These deal with implicit meanings, tropes, sequential ordering of genre and interactional elements, and metapragmatic indications in the AI appeals. It investigates "carriers of implicit meanings" (Verschueren 2012: 166) that function as "strategies of meaning generation" (186) "pertaining to social structures, processes, and relations" (191).

Chapter 7 provides a brief reprise of the contents of the prior chapters, of the main results of the analysis, and of the analytic methods employed. It revisits ideology and ideologies from the perspective of the analyses presented in the previous chapters and briefly contrasts AI and human rights documents with a pair of US Neo-Nazi documents. It identifies a number of "unexpected findings," as directed by Verschueren (2012: 64), as well as changes to AI's communicative practices since its inception. It concludes with an invitation to readers to use the data in Appendixes 2 and 3 to counterscreen my analysis.

Permission to Use Amnesty Documents

We are happy to grant you and Cambridge University Press permission to publish our material in this case, subject to ensuring that you add a paragraph in your introduction about where the material has come from, to provide some context, which will mitigate concerns about any risks to Amnesty. We agree that the following form of words will discharge this obligation.

The Amnesty International documents that constitute the data for the analysis presented in this book are a convenience sample collected over the period 2013–2024. The appeal letters came to me in emails I received from Amnesty as an active member of the organization. These emails encourage their receivers to forward the appeals to government or other officials with the power to improve the situations of the Prisoners of Conscience who are the subjects of the appeals. Amnesty members who receive the emails may edit the appeal letter or may just click a SEND button. As the documents referred to in the study were collected over more than a decade, some of the individuals on whose behalf the appeals were created have been released, others may still be imprisoned, some have died, and others may have revoked their consent for Amnesty International to campaign on their behalf.

(Letter from Amnesty, July 21, 2025)

2 Rights, Human Rights, and Amnesty International

In this chapter, I begin with a brief discussion of rights in general and then focus on human rights as background for a discussion of the history and activities of Amnesty International.

Right(s)

The word *right(s)* is richly polysemous. The *American Heritage Dictionary* (5th ed.: 1510) devotes a little over a half column to it and distinguishes forty-one numbered and alphabetized senses, two of which are relevant to our current concerns: "**6a**. A just or legal claim or title. **b**. Something that is due to a person or governmental body by law, tradition, or nature." The Merriam-Webster's *Dictionary of Law* (2011: 431) likewise devotes considerable valuable space to *right*, distinguishing nine senses; the ones most relevant to us are:

> **2:** something to which one has a just claim: as **a :** a power, privilege, or condition of existence to which one has a natural claim of enjoyment or possession … <that all men … are endowed by their Creator with certain unalienable ~s …> – see also NATURAL RIGHT **b:** a power, privilege, immunity, or capacity the enjoyment of which is secured to a person by law … **c:** a legally enforceable claim against another that the other will do or not do a given act <the defendant may be under a legal duty … to exercise reasonable care for the plaintiff's safety, so that the plaintiff has a corresponding legal ~ to insist on that care …>

More succinctly, Wenar and Cruft (2025) characterize rights as "entitlements (not) to perform certain actions, or (not) to be in certain states; or entitlements that others (not) perform certain actions or (not) be in certain states."

However, there are substantial and long-standing arguments about the bases of rights, especially of human rights. Elements of these arguments can be discerned in the definitions above. Some scholars have argued that rights derive from a god or gods; religion (De Gaay Fortman 2011; Ghanea 2011; Witte and Green 2011; Zuber 2019); morality; human nature; tradition; laws enacted by those with authority to do so; human dignity (Habermas 2010;

Moka-Mubelo 2017; Muders 2018; Regilme 2019);[1] human agency (Gutmann 2001; Ignatieff 2001); and from a most basic reciprocal and general right – the right to justification (Forst 2012, 2016).

Our concern in this book is with human rights, and in particular with those articulated by authoritative institutions such as the United Nations, so we can limit our interest to rights based in international law and to the issues of alienability and precedence.

Human Rights

Current human and humanitarian rights are of recent vintage, originating in the declarations of the French and American Revolutions, and in nineteenth- and twentieth-century attempts to limit the carnage of war (The Hague and Geneva Conventions) and to protect people and groups from severe abuse the United Nations Universal Declaration of Human Rights (UN UDHR); the International Covenant on Civil and Political Rights (ICCPR); and the International Covenant on Economic, Social and Cultural Rights (ICESCR). These rights are deemed to be universal: the *Universal* Declaration of Human Rights, and thus applying to all people, peoples, and governments, even though some countries have not ratified these instruments and others have crafted alternatives (e.g., Cairo Declaration on Human Rights in Islam).[2, 3, 4, 5]

Human rights are fundamental rights articulated in legal instruments enacted by authoritative international bodies and are designed to protect individuals and groups "from severe political, legal, and social abuses" (Nickel and Etinson 2024). They derive from "widely cherished" values of "respect, power, enlightenment, well-being, wealth, skill, affection, and rectitude" (Chen 2015: 251–252). Human rights are currently assumed to include social, economic, environmental, civil, and political rights, as well as group protections of women, children, racial, ethnic, and LGBTIQA+ minorities

1 Discussions of the human dignity basis for human rights typically attribute the concept to Kant (Gregor 1996), often via Habermas (2010).

2 Neier (2012) provides a comprehensive history of the human rights movement from the 1970s, and in his chapter 1, synopsizes its roots in earlier human rights activities and movements.

3 See Neier (2012: ch. 5) on the history of international humanitarian law and its synergies with human rights law.

4 The Magna Carta is often cited as a more remote source.

5 Vašák (1977) distinguished three generations of human rights. The first-generation rights are civil and political rights that identify individual liberties that may not be infringed, so-called "negative" rights. The second generation are social, economic, and cultural rights that are supported by states, so-called positive rights. The third generation, just developing as Vašák was writing, are "solidarity" rights: "to self-determination, economic and social development, healthy environment, natural resources, and participation in cultural heritage" (Domaradzki et al. 2019).

(Neier 2012: 2). These values and their protections are proclaimed in the United Nations Charter, the UDHR, the ICCPR, the ICESCR, the UN Convention Against Torture, and a broad range of other such instruments. Some of these instruments are regional international agreements, for example, the European Convention for the Protection of Human Rights and Fundamental Freedoms, the American Convention on Human Rights, the African Charter of Human and Peoples' Rights, and the Arab Charter of Human Rights.[6] These rights are enforced, more or less effectively, by international tribunals such as the International Court of Justice (ICJ), the International Criminal Court (ICC), the European Court of Human Rights, the Inter-American Court of Human Rights, and the African Court of Human and Peoples' Rights.[7]

In spite of the adoption of human and humanitarian rights by the UN and other authoritative international organizations, there have been specific and general criticisms of human rights. For example, NGO Monitor[8] publishes articles critical of AI, Human Rights Watch, and other human rights organizations, especially when these organizations criticize Israeli policies and activities in relation to the Israeli/Palestinian conflict. More generally, criticisms of the human rights framework have claimed that:

- Any compilation of rights is necessarily arbitrary and derived from the horse-trading among diplomats and other representatives of governments. As Nickel and Etinson (2024) puts it, "the process of identifying human rights in the United Nations and elsewhere was a political process with plenty of imperfections. There is little reason to take international diplomats as the most authoritative guides to which human rights there are."
- Human rights activists and organizations ignore critiques of the human rights movement from conservative commentators (e.g., Devlin 2012; Mutua 1996).
- It is illegitimate to expect cultures and societies to change fundamentally to accommodate human rights, for example, changes in the relationships between, and roles of, the sexes (Tharoor 1999/2000).
- The universality claimed for human rights assumes that all human beings are essentially the same, regardless of cultural, religious, or other differences (Tharoor 1999/2000).
- Many religions claim that the only source of universal values is the divine, though the UDHR is unquestionably of human manufacture (Tharoor 1999/2000).

[6] The texts of many of these can be accessed at www.un.org/en/global-issues/human-rights (accessed July 30, 2025).

[7] Neier (2012: 17–18) lists a sample of the many individuals indicted and convicted by these and other institutions, while noting their limited capacity and power.

[8] www.ngo-monitor.org and https://ngo-monitor.org/ngos/amnesty_international/ (both accessed July 30, 2025).

- The human rights ideology and its (attempted) hegemony are thinly disguised Western imperialism, particularly as they appear to privilege the individual over community.
- Human rights as currently formulated are founded on conceptions derived from Western ideologies of individuals as separate from, and independent of, others and thus unacceptably individualistic.
- Human rights defend individuals as individuals rather than as members of national, ethnic, or religious minority groups (Chamedes 2019: 239–240).
- Human rights ignore human responsibilities and duties.
- Governments have responsibilities that override their human rights responsibilities, for example, to protect their populations or to preserve national stability or social harmony.
- Human rights entail illegitimate limitations on the sovereignty of states.

In response to the last four criticisms, Article 1 of the UDHR[9] requires individuals to "act towards one another in a spirit of brotherhood," and Article 29 specifically declares that:

(1) Everyone has duties to the community in which alone the free and full development of his [*sic*] personality is possible.
(2) In the exercise of his rights and freedoms, everyone shall be subject only to such limitations as are determined by law solely for the purpose of securing due recognition and respect for the rights and freedoms of others and of meeting the just requirements of morality, public order and the general welfare in a democratic society.

Sikkink (2017) identifies "some forgotten aspects of the history of human rights."

First, civil and political rights *and* economic and social rights coexisted in human rights law from the moment that the international protection of human rights was first endorsed by governments, with the American Declaration [of the Rights and Duties of Man] and the UDHR. Second, both rights and duties were stressed, not only in the American Declaration of the Rights and Duties of Man, but also in the African Charter on Human and Peoples' Rights [footnote omitted]. Both the American Declaration and the African Charter stressed that individual duties could complement individual rights, not conflict with them. This idea of combining individual duties and individual rights could serve as a tool for achieving more consensus on the legitimacy of human rights norms, particularly in developing nations and those outside the Global North.

(231; emphasis in original)

In response to other criticisms, Tharoor (1999/2000) makes *The Case for the Defense* (emphasis in original):

[9] The full text of the UN UDHR can be found at https://tinyurl.com/4p848dtj (accessed July 30, 2025).

- Cultures and traditions share a great many "philosophical common denominators"; most especially, concepts such as those of justice, law, and human dignity are to be found in all societies.
- Human rights derive from Christianity and liberalism, as well as from "civic republicanism, socialism, and communitarianism" (Sikkink 2017: 231).
- Cultures inevitably change over time, often in response to outside influences: there is no such thing as a "pure" culture.
- "Third World" critics of human rights often represent countries, most notably Ghana and Nigeria, that were essential to the passage or adoption of the human rights covenants.
- Many "Global South" countries, especially from Latin America, were instrumental in crafting and ensuring the ratification of the UN Charter and UDHR. In fact, the Organization of American States ratified the American Declaration of the Rights and Duties of Man in 1948 almost a year before the UN ratified the UDHR. (See Donnelly and Whelan 2017: ch. 1.1; Neier 2012: 98; Sikkink 2017: ch. 3.)[10]
- The fact that the vast majority of countries have ratified the UDHR rebuts any claims that it is merely a Western instrument of neo-colonialism.
- All too frequently, those who criticize human rights benefit from their violation, while those whose rights are violated suffer.

In addition to arguments about the bases of rights, scholars argue about their relative statuses: which rights, if any, are inalienable; which rights take precedence over others and in what circumstances; and which rights, if any, take precedence over all others.[11]

The international human rights treaties typically include provisions requiring individual state signatories to promote human rights by enacting relevant legislation or constitutional changes, by encouraging respect for human rights, and by educating their populations about them. International and state human rights agencies are aided in their educational and enforcement efforts by a number of non-governmental organizations. Prominent among these organizations are Amnesty International, Human Rights Watch, and Doctors Without Borders. These organizations are active in the identification of human rights abuses, of those responsible for them, and in advocating on behalf of the abuse victims. Many such organizations are active also in informing decision-makers about human rights situations and in influencing the development of human rights policies and legal instruments.

[10] The American Declaration of the Rights and Duties of Man was adopted by the conference of American States that created the Organization of American States (OAS) in April 1948.

[11] For a discussion of the relations between rights and respect for self and others, see Dillon (2022).

It is important to note here that the development, ratification, and adoption of human rights as currently articulated are integral components of the processes of globalization which, arguably, began with European explorations around Africa into the Indian Ocean and across the Atlantic in the fifteenth and sixteenth centuries, and which processes continue today. These processes encompass economics, politics, and culture, in addition to human rights, and typically entail relinquishing elements of national sovereignty. Such concessions were often hard-won as empires collapsed and colonialism retreated. These losses of sovereignty often elicit nationalist reactions that can be authoritarian and antidemocratic, as my quote from Donald Trump in Chapter 1 illustrates. As the discussion above of the criticisms and defenses of human rights indicates, appeals to sovereignty often seek to legitimize authoritarian repression.

The AI letters describe repressive actions such as the use of torture and the denial of freedom of expression, denial of due process, denial of protection of minorities, denial of the right to life, and denial of freedom of association. They invoke the universal attributes of the declarations, treaties, and conventions to frame and evaluate local values and exigencies, for example, by characterizing government actions as violating universal international rights/standards. The following extract demonstrates how a local contingency – the long-term solitary confinement of a prisoner in a Louisiana prison – was framed from a universal perspective reflecting Article 5 of the UDHR: "No one shall be subjected to torture or to cruel, inhuman or degrading treatment or punishment."

> Albert Woodfox has been kept in isolation for decades, in conditions that the UN United Nations Special Rapporteur on Torture condemns as torture. He has been denied meaningful social contact and access to rehabilitation programs. Such conditions violate minimum international standards for humane treatment.
>
> (#16 Woodfox, Louisiana, USA)

Because human and humanitarian rights are systematized, legitimized, and universalized in universal legal instruments, they provide "plausible explanations and justifications" (Eagleton 2007: 52) for the human rights-related evaluations and actions of AI, its members, and its volunteers.

As I discuss more fully in later chapters, some AI letters include concessions to the Message Recipients or acknowledgement of some positive action they have taken, though these are typically rebutted by reference to continuing exigencies such as the life-threatening "long and unnecessary delays" to medical treatment introduced by the italicized contrastive marker "however" in:

> I am encouraged by recent statements from Health Minister María Isabel Rodríguez that Beatriz will receive the treatment that she needs. *However*, given the long and unnecessary delays that Beatriz has already suffered, she must not be forced to wait any longer – especially not until her health deteriorates further. Each day that goes by without action brings increased danger for Beatriz.
>
> (#8 Beatriz, El Salvador)

And to the injustice of solitary confinement to "a cell the size of a parking space" and the "legal irregularities" introduced by italicized "however" in:

> Over the years, Louisiana authorities have often repeated that Brent Miller's family is due justice. I have no doubt that this is true, and I have tremendous sympathy for Officer Miller's family and friends. *However*, I do not believe that confining Albert Woodfox to a cell the size of a parking space is just – particularly in light of the legal irregularities that lead [*sic*] to his conviction. The litigation surrounding Albert Woodfox's case has spanned four decades and includes two flawed trials. His conviction has been overturned once by a state court and twice by a federal court, underscoring concerns about the fairness of the legal process. No physical evidence ties Mr. Woodfox to Officer Miller's murder.
>
> (#16 Woodfox, Louisiana, USA)

AI presents these rebuttals as "trumping" (Dworkin 1984) whatever reasons might be adduced by the Message Recipients to reject the appeal, a ranking endorsed by Chen (2015): "[i]nternational law and national law sometimes conflict, and in general it is international law that should prevail. States (and the individuals who compose the state) ought to be held to international standards. This is the essence of the supremacy of international law that is so indispensable to maintaining world order" (4).

Amnesty International

In this section, I offer a brief history of Amnesty International (AI), and its goals and activities. While AI was one of the earliest global HR organizations, it is far from alone in that field, and was preceded by more local civil liberties organizations, such as the American Civil Liberties Union in the US. These groups have different though related agendas and methods (see Chen 2015; Neier 2012; Sikkink 2017).[12]

AI is perhaps the best-known and most active NGO currently working on behalf of human rights. It claims to "campaign for a world where human rights are enjoyed by all" and to be "a global movement of more than 10 million people in over 150 countries and territories who campaign to end abuses of human rights."[13] It has offices in Africa, Australia, Asia, Europe, the Middle East, and in North and South America. It is an important non-governmental player in a movement that Neier (2012: 7–8) characterizes as "global both in its constituency and in its concerns."

AI was founded in 1961 after Peter Benenson, an English lawyer, Eric Baker, and Louis Blom-Cooper published an article, "The forgotten prisoners," in the British newspaper, *The Observer*, on behalf of two Portuguese students imprisoned by the Salazar regime for toasting to freedom. Benenson

[12] For a more complete list of HR organizations, see https://en.wikipedia.org/wiki/List_of_human_rights_organisations (accessed July 30, 2025).

[13] www.amnesty.org/en/ (accessed July 30, 2025).

"urg[ed] readers to write letters on behalf of people around the world imprisoned because they exercised their human rights."[14] This article introduced the designation "Prisoner of Conscience," currently defined as

> a person imprisoned (or otherwise detained) solely because of **who they are** (ethnic origin, sex, colour, language, national or social origin, economic status, birth, sexual orientation, gender identity or expression, or other status) **or what they believe** (political, religious or other conscientiously held beliefs), who has not used violence or advocated violence or hatred in the circumstances leading to their detention.[15]

This article was reprinted in newspapers around the globe and initiated a campaign on behalf of freedom of speech, a focus that has been substantially broadened over the years as AI has responded to a changing world. AI has also adapted to changing communications media – from hand- or type-written letters to mobile apps. It is currently represented online by a great many websites, several from each of its major regional offices.[16] The AI USA website characterizes its work as research, mobilization, and advocacy on behalf of people whose human and/or humanitarian rights have been violated, whether by governments or non-state actors. Its priorities at the time of this writing are as follows:

Priority campaigns:
- End genocide in Gaza
- Demand "Alligator Alcatraz" be shut down
- No one is above the law (Trump administration)

Priority campaigns in the U.S.:
- Return makeup artist and others illegally expelled to El Salvador
- Protect the right to protest
- Protect freedom of the press

Priority international campaigns:
- Help release Palestinian pediatrician
- Demand accountability for Russia's war of aggression
- Demand an arms embargo to protect civilians in Sudan[17]

AI's governance structure consists of an International Council, which meets every two years and is responsible for the organization's constitution, for its International Statute, and for developing its Integrated Strategic Plan. Between the International Council's meetings, the International Executive Committee assumes formal authority, and the International Secretariat oversees day-to-day matters.

[14] www.amnestyusa.org/about-us/history/ (accessed July 30, 2025).
[15] www.amnesty.org/en/what-we-do/detention/#prisonersofconscience (accessed September 5, 2025); emphasis in original.
[16] Buchanan (2002) is a history of the early years of Amnesty International.
[17] www.amnestyusa.org/take-action/#:~:text=Support%20Our%20priority%20Campaigns (accessed July 30, 2025). These were the priority campaigns on July 30, 2015, but campaigns and priorities change as exigencies arise and AI responds to them.

For its advocacy and mobilization of opinion and action, as well as its fund-raising, AI uses at least its reports on particular situations, its websites, its emails to volunteers and members, its appeal letters, and its "Thank you" fund-raising emails. I discuss these later in this chapter.

Neier (2012: 3) notes the importance of "detailed and reliable information" "in advancing the cause of the international human rights movement." AI's reports have earned a reputation for consistency of approach and accuracy in detailing human rights abuses and related situations. This reputation is based on the careful collection and multiple checking of information for its reports on specific situations and has earned it the ability to work "directly with the U.N. system while maintaining an independence that allows public criticism of U.N. shortcomings and failures" (Chen 2015: 83). AI also advises governments on issues pertaining to human rights and has been influential in the setting up of the UN High Commission on Human Rights and the ICC.

AI's reports characteristically contain an executive summary, a detailed and heavily footnoted description of the methods of information collection, background information on the situation, descriptions of the violations of international laws that elicited the report, and recommendations addressed to the relevant government, UN Security Council, and "the international community," as well as any other actors, for example, armed groups, who might be involved.[18]

Some, but not all, of AI's other genres are derived from these reports. AI's webpages, emails to members/volunteers, and appeal letters regarding a situation may contain information selected from reports and re-contextualized and re-genrefied. Because of the exigency of the situations they deal with, AI's Urgent Action[19] appeals seem to be based on more limited investigation.

In addition to text and photos regarding the situation described in the report, AI webpages also contain multiple links that allow readers to TAKE ACTION to help redress a situation. Clicking on one of these links takes the clicker to a page giving a related description of the situation and an embedded AI appeal letter. Readers are asked to electronically SEND this appeal, ostensibly to its named Message Recipients. In addition to SENDing the appeals to their intended recipients, AI tallies the SENDs and the tallies are used in AI's efforts to persuade the powerful to redress the exigent situation by weight of numbers. An email from AI on September 24, 2019 refers to "thousands … who swiftly take action and donate to help Amnesty make a tremendous impact around the world."

AI's emails, like its webpages, provide a précis of the report information on the situation and typically include photos, but unlike the webpage, they are

[18] AI's reports are available at www.amnestyusa.org/learn/reports/ (accessed July 30, 2025).
[19] www.amnestyusa.org/take-action/urgent-action-network/ (accessed July 30, 2025).

addressed to the individual member/volunteer, for example, "Dear Gerald," with a request to SEND the embedded appeal.

There have been, unsurprisingly, critical voices over the years (see Baehr 2009). One voice criticized AI's reporting on unrest in Nicaragua.[20] Another criticized AI's reporting on the Syrian civil war, claiming that it "stoked" the war.[21] In 2015, NGO Monitor criticized AI for its "Failed Methodology, Corruption, and Anti-Israel Bias."[22] There have been other controversies over the years.[23, 24] Perhaps tellingly, AI has been criticized for being both pro- and anti-Western.[25]

AI was awarded the Nobel Prize for Peace in 1977 for its "defense of human dignity against torture," and the United Nations Prize in the Field of Human Rights in 1978. It was awarded the Revolution Award in 2001 for the best use of email and a Webby award in 2021 for excellence on the internet. Its online media project, *Tear Gas: An Investigation*, was honored as the best activism website worldwide. It has also been credited with a significant role in the dramatic increase in the number of countries that have abolished the death penalty (Neier 2012: 196; Sikkink 2017, cited in Bettinger-López 2018).[26]

[20] https://portside.org/2018-06-18/former-prisoner-conscience-condemns-amnesty-international (accessed July 30, 2025).

[21] https://consortiumnews.com/2017/02/11/amnesty-international-stokes-syrian-war (accessed July 30, 2025).

[22] https://ngo-monitor.org/topics/irene-khan/ (accessed July 30, 2025).

[23] https://en.wikipedia.org/wiki/Amnesty_International (accessed July 31, 2025).

[24] The website https://en.wikipedia.org/wiki/Criticism_of_Amnesty_International lists a great many criticisms of AI; however, some are inadequately evidenced and Wikipedia asks for more balanced treatment, especially of the section on Israel (accessed July 31, 2025).

[25] A reviewer of this work posed "for consideration" two questions. The first is whether "human rights and humanitarian organizations have negative effects." Many commentators have claimed so, see e.g., essays making this argument in Hopgood et al. (2017); see also Hopgood (2013) and Posner (2014). But see the Simmons and Strezhnev article in Hopgood et al. (2017) rebutting claims of negative effects of international human rights law.

The reviewer also asked: has there "ever been an appeal that might be seen as a culturally relative rather than a universal one?" At a very general level, human rights have been criticized as Western ideology masquerading as universal values (e.g., Mutua 1996; but see Friedman 2011 for a nuanced response to this claim). One matter in which AI might be regarded as demanding a culturally relative right is access to abortion. Various international Covenants and Conventions require governments to "respect, protect, and fulfill" women's "[a]ccess to sexual and reproductive health care," but no "key international human rights instrument" recognizes a specific right to abortion (Chapman 2023). Consequently, the right to abortion might reasonably be viewed as a local rather than universal cultural option. One Amnesty appeal (#8 Beatriz, El Salvador) specifically requests that a woman "at high risk of pregnancy-related death if she continues with this pregnancy" be allowed an abortion, which was being denied because her doctors "fear prosecution under El Salvador's strict ban on abortion." The AI appeal thus pits what it presents as a universal right to abortion against a local ban on the procedure derived from Catholic teaching.

[26] For a history of AI to 2001, see Power (2001: ch. 4); for a brief history of AI to 2017, see www.amnestyusa.org/about-us/history/ (accessed April 16, 2026). Wikipedia's history of AI is mentioned above in fn. 23. Hopgood (2006) is an ethnography of AI's International Secretariat in 2002–03 and includes information on AI's history, methods, and controversies.

It is hard to estimate AI's impact. Neier (2012), Pinker (2011), and Sikkink (2017) all argue that the human rights movement, and AI specifically, have been effective in persuading governments to honor the rights of their citizens and those over whom they wield power, though estimates of how effective they have been is difficult to quantify. Whenever an individual for whom AI has campaigned is released, AI publishes and celebrates the fact, as a visit to its website Victories will attest.[27] Readers might also access AI "Wins: Impacts of the Write for Rights Campaign."[28] For a critical perspective, see: "Amnesty has lost focus on rights of prisoners of conscience."[29] And a response, "Amnesty has not lost its way."[30] AI's webpage, "About Us," claims that "Tens of thousands of people have been freed after we campaigned against their unjust imprisonment for exercising their human rights."[31]

Why Amnesty International?

As I noted in Chapter 1, I chose to analyze AI letters for a variety of reasons, which I enlarge upon here. The emails and letters that I analyze are a convenience sample: they arrived in my email box and so they were easily collected. But they also represented an ideological genre that had not been studied. The discourse type studied by discourse analysts interested in the manifestations of ideology are typically those that the analyst(s) regard as injurious; for example, Verschueren's work with various collaborators on debates about migration into Belgium and nationalist tendencies in Europe (see references in Verschueren 2012: 4–5, fn. 7), and his analysis of colonial discourse in English and French history textbooks (Verschueren 2012). These studies sought to discover and identify covert ideologies and the linguistic devices used to mask them. In contrast, I, along with many others, view AI discourses as beneficial both in specific cases and more generally in attempting to prevent abuses and create a world in which it and organizations like it need no longer exist. The AI documents present the beliefs and actions attributable to the organization and its members positively and do so overtly. In these respects, they are similar to other discourses that are presented as beneficial, if not to all of humanity, at least to the producers of the discourse and like-minded others. For example, racist discourse explicitly presents its ideological stances as positive. The *25 Demands of American National Socialism* (25P)[32] are overtly racist and

[27] AI celebrates its successes, e.g., https://www.amnestyusa.org/blog/amnesty-internationals-human-rights-wins-of-2025/ (accessed April 21, 2026).

[28] www.amnesty.org.au/wins-impacts-of-the-write-for-rights-campaign/ (accessed July 30, 2025).

[29] *Irish Times*, March 1, 2021, https://tinyurl.com/3hypzr2t (accessed July 30, 2025).

[30] *Irish Times*, March 4, 2021, https://tinyurl.com/4j6krwec (accessed July 30, 2025).

[31] www.amnestyusa.org/about-us/ (accessed July 30, 2025).

[32] www.nsm88.org/25-point (accessed September 6, 2025). This text is frequently revised. An earlier version demanded "pure White blood" as the primary prerequisite for citizenship of the "nation."

purport to benefit people of "sacred White blood," which "means the right DNA code." Item 4 in the *25 Demands* explicitly specifies that "[o]nly Whites may become citizens. Consequently, since Jews are not White, no matter what they may claim, no Jew may become a member of our nation." I briefly discuss 25P and another US Neo-Nazi document in Chapter 7.

This is not to say that human rights and racist discourses do not depend on unspoken or fallacious assumptions or inferences, such as the inference required in the quote above from the assertion that only those of "sacred White blood … may become a member of our nation" to the conclusion that Jews may not belong, which implicates that Jews may not be of "sacred White blood" or, in other versions, of "pure White blood," and that there is some criterion by which the "purity," or sanctity, or even the existence, of "White" blood can be determined.

The AI documents presuppose the existence of human rights, that these rights have been articulated and approved as universal laws by organizations such as the United Nations, and that these organizations have the authority to establish laws binding on all countries, such that these laws "trump" local laws. For example, one letter (#4 al-Qahtani, Iraq) asserts that "[t]he death penalty violates the right to life," thus presupposing that the right to life exists with no specification of any limits on that right or identification of its legal status or how that status came about. No document or communicative event is free of implicitly communicated assumptions, and those communicated by the AI appeals are an important focus of this book.[33]

The intertextual relations among AI documents and between them and other documents such as the UDHR are innumerable and this recursion seems to be typical of synoptic genres such as the AI webpages, emails, and appeal letters, though perhaps of any genre. While Verschueren does not explicitly prescribe analysis of the discursive context of target texts, he does, in his Guideline 2 and its ancillary prescriptions, require analysts to get to know the "linguistic context, the immediate context of situation, and the wider context (social, political, historical, geographical, etc.)" which is "not finite in any sense. Hence cannot be described exhaustively." But "[t]hose aspects of context may be deemed most relevant … which are actualized in the discourse" (56 ff, 201). I develop this discussion in response to Guideline 2 in Chapter 4.

AI's webpages are updated daily to bring attention to new violations of human rights and I, like other members/volunteers, receive frequent emails

[33] While discussion of AI genres would be incomplete without consideration of the genres created by other human rights organizations such as Human Rights Watch or Doctors Without Borders, attempting a comprehensive survey of the discourses of human rights organizations would be impossible given the number of such organizations. For information on the goals and activities of the most important of these organizations, see Nickel and Etinson (2024) and references therein; Forst (2012, ch. 9); Neier (2012); Chen (2015, ch. 12); Sikkink (2017).

alerting me to these new violations and asking me to click on a link to ACT NOW or HELP US STOP THIS, or other similar directives. This continuous stream of new violations suggests that human rights are more honored in the breach than in the observance. However, recent publications (e.g., Pinker 2019: 207–211, ch. 13; Sikkink 2017) have argued that in spite of appearances and recent regressions to authoritarian and repressive nationalist regimes in Europe, the USA, and elsewhere, human rights are violated less frequently than before and the number of Prisoners of Conscience has declined (Neier 2012: 196). The perception of widespread abuses may be due to the greater amount of, and access to, information and to the activist organizations' "naming and shaming" of violators. (See Sikkink 2017: 212–214 for discussion of the efficacy and desirability of this practice.)

AI Documents

Though his analysis is "almost exclusively" of the verbal aspects of his textbooks, Verschueren does remark on their illustrations (2012: 104–105, 197–198) and draws our attention to the increasing pervasiveness of multimodal discourses, which contribute "not only to the construction or generation of representational meaning … but also to what Dupret (2011) calls 'practices of truth,' as well as to multiple layers of connotation and affect." In this section, I discuss examples of the AI documents most relevant to my study, all of which, with the exception of the appeal letter, are multimodal, a property I discuss later in this chapter.

- The Appeal Letter
- The Email to AI Volunteers
- The AI Webpage
- The "Thank You" Email
- The Donation Request Email
- The AI Report[34]

The Appeal Letter

The appeal letters are typically addressed to heads of state and other government functionaries, identified as "Message Recipients." They briefly characterize the violative situation and urge the addressees to redress that violation, which they typically characterize as contravening human or humanitarian rights. They belong to the category of "hortatory discourse" as described by Longacre (1992) and closely related to philanthropic fund-raising appeals (Delahunty 2018b; Mann and Thompson 1992).

[34] www.amnestyusa.org/wp-content/uploads/2017/04/mde2420792015english.pdf (accessed July 31, 2025).

> **Message Recipients**: Presidents Putin and Assad
>
> **Subject**: End the attacks and lift the siege on Eastern Ghouta immediately
>
> Dear Presidents Putin and Assad,
>
> I am writing about the catastrophic situation in Syria's Eastern Ghouta where more than 400,000 people have been suffering under [*sic*] Syrian Government's tightened siege since November 2017.
>
> They have been enduring hunger, malnutrition, lack of medication and escalated bombardment that has been targeting civilians, homes, hospitals and markets. In the past 30 days, hundreds of people have been killed and thousands have been injured.
>
> Mr. Putin and Mr. Assad: you have the power to end this tragedy. I am calling on you to ensure that the Syrian Government immediately ends all attacks on civilians and civilian structures and lifts the siege to allow humanitarian aid into Eastern Ghouta.[35]

AI employs (at least) two appeal letter strategies. The one I focus on in this work is the least onerous for the members receiving the email containing the appeal: they need only click SEND. The second, like the first, includes an appeal and encourages members to personalize it. To personalize an appeal, the member must cut and paste it into an email which they then electronically SEND to Message Recipients, though they may use other modes of delivery. The second strategy is specific to members who signed up for AI's Urgent Action Network (UAN), a version of which seems now to be applied to all appeals.[36] I presume that this is in response to indications from Message Recipients and others that the words of individual writers are more likely to be effective than the mere sending of already crafted appeals. The UAN format requires more, but not much more, effort on the part of the appeal sender than the earlier format. In purporting that the letter was written, or at least personalized to some degree, by the sender lends a degree of autonomy, sincerity, and authenticity, and thus authority and legitimacy, to it.[37]

The Email to AI Volunteers/Members

These emails, with their embedded appeals, are sent, often several in a day, to volunteers or members who have signed up to receive them. They provide

[35] This letter is in addition to those included in the corpora in Appendixes 2 and 3.
[36] www.amnestyusa.org/take-action/urgent-action-network/ (accessed July 31, 2025).
[37] For a critical review of these concepts, see Varga and Guignon (2020).

URGENT: We can't have another Aleppo — it's time for action

Margaret Huang for Amnesty International USA <alerts@takeaction.amnestyusa.org>

Dear Gerald,
I wish I didn't have to write this email, but the escalating attacks on the people of Eastern Ghouta in Syria can't go unanswered.

Help the People Under Attack in Eastern Ghouta

Sign the Petition ›

The Syrian government, backed by Russia, is intensifying the bombing of its own people. Hundreds have been killed and thousands have been injured in the past month.

We can't allow bombs to fall on starving people in their homes. Tell the Syrian and Russian governments to lift the siege on Eastern Ghouta immediately.

The residents of Eastern Ghouta have been trapped in a siege for nearly six years. They are being attacked daily — killed and maimed by their government. Children and elderly people are dying of malnutrition and lack of medication.

Will you speak up now? Tell the Syrian and Russian governments to end the attacks on Eastern Ghouta immediately.

I can't describe the situation better than the people on the ground, who are in contact with Amnesty's crisis team. One medical center director tells us that:

> *"The situation in besieged Eastern Ghouta is a tragedy. As for doctors, may God help them. They are doing their best, but there is a severe lack of equipment and supplies, and hospitals in Eastern Ghouta are being heavily targeted for bombardment....even nursing mothers aren't able to nurse their babies because of malnutrition."*

The attacks must stop immediately. Humanitarian aid must be allowed into Eastern Ghouta and civilians must be evacuated out of the region.

I can't do it without the voices of people like you — please take action today because the people of Syria can't wait.

TAKE ACTION

Margaret Huang

Margaret Huang
Executive Director
Amnesty International USA

Figure 2.1 URGENT: We can't have another Aleppo
TOPSHOT – A Syrian paramedic carries an injured child following reported bombardment by Syrian and Russian forces in the rebel-held town of Hamouria, in the Eastern Ghouta, on January 6, 2018. Regime and Russian air strikes on a rebel-held enclave near the Syrian capital killed at least 17 civilians, a war monitor said. (Photo by ABDULMONAM EASSA/AFP via Getty Images)

a photo and a précis of information presented in the report on the situation and are addressed to the individual member/volunteer – for example, "Dear Gerald" (see Figure 2.1).[38]

Occasionally I get emails from AI with target SEND numbers, for example, 50,000, and tallies of how many SENDs had already occurred. I assume that these target numbers and the invitation to help meet them are assumed by AI to be an effective inducement to volunteers to click SEND. This suggests (strongly) that AI tallies SENDs and sends those tallies in addition to the masses of email appeals to their Message Recipients, thus indicating the depth and breadth of concern about the exigent situation described in the email. This is in keeping with my claim that the appeals are designed to persuade their Message Recipients, to engage and retain members, and to identify likely donors. Recall that immediately after sending an appeal, the sender receives an email request for a donation.

The AI Webpage

The AI webpage, like the email, contains a brief description of the situation that is more fully described in the report. It too contains a still photo, which given its context – juxtaposed with the text – will be assumed to represent a scene from that situation, an assumption that can be accounted for by appeal to Grice's Cooperative Principle and Maxims, especially the maxim of Relation; to neo-Gricean theories such as Horn's Quantity and Relation and Levinson's Quantity and Informativeness principles; and to post-Gricean theories such as Relevance Theory (RT). The page also contains multiple links that direct readers to TAKE ACTION to redress the situation. Clicking on one of these links takes the clicker to a page giving a related description of the situation and embedding the AI appeal letter. Readers are asked to SEND this appeal, ostensibly to its named Message Recipients and tallied by AI and the tally used in AI's efforts to persuade the powerful to redress the exigent situation.[39] In the early days of AI, members wrote their appeals and sent them by snail mail to various functionaries. Neier (2012: 189–190) quotes a 1975 letter to AI from Julio de Peña Valdez, a trade union leader imprisoned in the Dominican Republic, describing the effects of the numerous letters received by his jailers on their treatment of him:

[38] A differently cropped version of this photo is reproduced in the associated AI webpage, and yet another at https://tinyurl.com/mpzdazfa (accessed July 31, 2025).

[39] An email from AI on September 24, 2019 celebrating the release of seventeen Prisoners of Conscience acknowledges that "[g]ood news like this is only possible because of you and thousands of others who swiftly take action and donate to help Amnesty make a tremendous impact around the world."

TAKE ACTION FOR HUMAN RIGHTS

HELP THE PEOPLE UNDER ATTACK IN EASTERN GHOUTA

The Syrian Government, backed by Russia, is bombing its own people in Eastern Ghouta. Hundreds of people have been killed and thousands have been injured in the past month.

Civilians in Eastern Ghouta have been trapped in a cruel siege for nearly six years; they are now being attacked daily, killed and maimed by their government. Children and elderly people are dying of malnutrition and lack of medication.

We succeeded in creating pressure and noise around the world for Aleppo – and we can succeed in helping the people under attack in Eastern Ghouta. The attacks in Eastern Ghouta must be stopped and humanitarian aid must be allowed into the region.

Tell the Syrian and Russian Governments to end the attacks and lift the siege on Eastern Ghouta immediately.

Figure 2.2 Help the people under attack in Eastern Ghouta[40, 41]
TOPSHOT – A Syrian paramedic carries an injured child following reported bombardment by Syrian and Russian forces in the rebel-held town of Hamouria, in the Eastern Ghouta, on January 6, 2018. Regime and Russian air strikes on a rebel-held enclave near the Syrian capital killed at least 17 civilians, a war monitor said. (Photo by ABDULMONAM EASSA/AFP via Getty Images)

40 The photos in the email and webpage are differently cropped versions of the original. A third version can be found on Abdulmonam Eassa's website tearsheets over the caption, "Abdulmonam Eassa, AFP | A Syrian paramedic carries an injured child following reported bombardment by Syrian and Russian forces in the rebel-held town of Hamouria in eastern Ghouta on January 6, 2018." (www.abdulmonameassa.com/) (accessed April 16, 2026)

41 Delahunty (2023) and below analyses the contributions of text and photo to the arguments made in the appeal and webpage.

When the first two hundred letters came the guards gave me back my clothes. Then the next two hundred letters came and the prison director came to see me. When the next pile of letters arrived, the director got in touch with his superior. The letters kept coming and coming: three thousand of them. The President [of the Dominican Republic] was informed. The letters still kept arriving and the President called the prison and told them to let me go.

After I was released the President called me to his office for a man to man talk. He said: How is it that a trade union leader like you has so many friends all over the world? He showed me an enormous box full of letters he had received and when we parted, he gave them to me. I still have them.[42]

Amnesty "Thank You" Email

Thank you, Gerald

Dear Gerald,

Over the last week, Syria's Eastern Ghouta has become hell on earth. Children have been killed in the streets. Homes, schools, and streets have been bombed.

At this truly exceptional time of need for Syrian children and families, we have relied on your generous, monthly donation to continue our work.

I'm on Amnesty's supporter care team, and I'm reaching out to personally say thank you for your monthly support — and for your compassion.

Our crisis team has been working in Syria for more than a decade, and this is the worst we've seen. With your generous support, we will continue to document the horrific abuses and to demand that the governments stop the bloodshed.

Thank you for standing with Amnesty — today, and always.

Andrea Kost
Supporter Care Team
Amnesty International USA

Figure 2.3 Amnesty "Thank you" email

[42] This is also quoted in Power (2001: 134).

The "Thank you" Email

Immediately upon SENDing the appeal letter, the SENDer receives an email thanking them for doing so and typically asking them to donate and to distribute the appeal more widely by emailing it to friends or posting it on Facebook and other social media (see Figure 2.3).

The Donation Request Email

The more typical follow-up to sending an appeal is an email thanking the sender and asking for a donation (see Figure 2.4).

"Thank you" and "Donate and support Amnesty's efforts" email

DONATE

Dear Gerald,

Thank you for taking action at this urgent time.

Will you take the next step? **Donate and support Amnesty's efforts.**

In order to stay independent and carry out our critical work, Amnesty does not take money from governments for our research or campaigning. That would compromise our principles.

We rely entirely on support from members like you. Thank you.

The Amnesty International USA team

Figure 2.4 "Thank you" and "Donate and support Amnesty's efforts" email

The AI Report

In many cases, the information in the webpages, emails, and appeals is based on AI reports, with consequent intertextual resonances. The information regarding Eastern Ghouta is presented in great detail in AI's report (2015).[43] It is one of many AI reports on the Syrian civil war,[44] which are a fraction of the very many reports AI has prepared on countries around the world.[45]

[43] www.amnesty.org/en/documents/mde24/2079/2015/en/ (accessed July 31, 2025).
[44] www.amnesty.org/en/location/middle-east-and-north-africa/middle-east/syria/ (accessed July 31, 2025).
[45] www.amnesty.org/en/countries/ (accessed July 31, 2025).

These documents are all intertextually related to the UN UDHR and, to a lesser extent, the Hague and Geneva and various other conventions.[46] I briefly describe the Eastern Ghouta report and some intertextual traces among the documents.[47]

The front page of the report consists of the title "'LEFT TO DIE UNDER SIEGE' WAR CRIMES AND HUMAN RIGHTS ABUSES IN EASTERN GHOUTA" and the AI logo set against AI's signature yellow background; a photo of a multi-story building severely damaged by an air strike by Assad-allied forces; and men searching for survivors among the debris.

The front inside cover page consists of AI's vision statement set against AI's yellow background and the report's publication information, the photo credit, and a description of the photo's contents. The following two pages consist of the report's table of contents.

Our genre knowledge tells us that reports may be mere descriptions of, typically, problematic situations, for example, news reports, but they may also include recommendations for solutions to those problems and recommendations to various types of recipients to adopt the proposed solution or to help bring it about. The relevant definitions of "report" range from the most general and perhaps most frequently used "account of some event" to a "formal account of the proceedings or transactions of a group, for example, a company" (adapted from the *American Heritage Dictionary*, 5th edition), to the more legalistic, "formal and sometimes official statement giving the conclusions and recommendations of a person (as a master) or a group (as a legislative committee) authorized or delegated to consider a matter or proposal" (adapted from Merriam-Webster's *Dictionary of Law*, 2011). If we combine elements of these definitions, we get "an authorized official formal account of some event or events giving conclusions and recommendations". While this definition characterizes the AI reports, we should wonder how they might be "official" and by whom they might be "authorized". We should expect AI reports to include descriptions of situations and events, evaluations of those situations/events according to AI's human rights framework, suggested responses to the evaluation, and indexes of the efforts made by their curators to establish their authority. AI reports include these descriptions, evaluations, suggested responses, and indexes of their curators' efforts to establish their authority and credibility.

AI's report is a richly intertextual, multimodal document. No authors are listed, but the copyright belongs to AI. Presumably it was written by AI staffers skilled in curating such reports. Curating "is always ideological, always rhetorical and often political" (Snyder 2015: 209) because it always

[46] https://ihl-databases.icrc.org/en/ihl-treaties/treaties-and-states-parties (accessed July 31, 2025).
[47] The following material is based on Delahunty (2021).

"involves human filtering and organizing" (213). The report is highly edited (unlike some of the appeal letters, which show occasional signs of hasty drafting or incomplete command of Standard English), with many footnotes identifying the sources of the information and the legal instruments represented. It comprises the following main sections:

The ***Executive Summary*** is a 2.5-page, footnote-free, text-only précis of the report findings on the situation, its history, its legal status (e.g., crimes against humanity, contravention of UN resolutions), AI sources of information, and calls to actors to meet their commitments under international law. It corresponds to such summaries in, for example, company annual reports, which may be in the form of a letter from the CEO.

The ***Methodology*** is a 1.25-page, footnote-free, text-only summary of the sources AI used in the compilation of the report: interviews with witnesses, email correspondence, other human rights organizations, satellite imagery, statements from the Syrian government, and expressions of gratitude to those who contributed information.

The ***Background*** provides a 6.25-page, text-only summary of the chronology of events that led up to the current exigent situation; it is heavily footnoted with references to sources of information: YouTube videos, Agence France-Presse, emails and Skype interviews with reporters and witnesses in the area, etc.

Attacks on civilians and civilian objects and the use of explosive weapons in populated areas is a thirty-page section providing information on Syrian government airstrikes on cities in Eastern Ghouta, attacks with missiles and other projectiles, retaliatory attacks by non-state armed groups, humanitarian conditions, and restrictions on access to those under siege. It includes various voices in several modes: translated quotes from witnesses, information from other NGOs such as Human Rights Watch, footnoted links to original sources, photos from various sources, including annotated aerial photos, and satellite imagery (from Digital Globe).

Under siege in Eastern Ghouta: Humanitarian conditions and access is a seventeen-page section that provides a heavily footnoted overview of the situation, including descriptions of conditions in which the civilians currently live, with a single photo, and ending with a highlighted page on "The Impact on Women."

The ***Methodology***, ***Background***, ***Attacks***, and ***Under Siege*** sections are all heavily footnoted to identify the sources of the information and links to many of those sources, presumably with the goals of establishing the report as credible and licensing the assumption that the curators and their information are trustworthy, that is, establishing its rhetorical ethos and from a Gricean (1975, 1989) point of view, supporting the maxim of Quality implicature that the information is truthful and well-evidenced.

Disregard for international law is a five-page, text-only legal brief with extensive footnoting of the various declarations, covenants, and institutions referenced: UDHR; ICCPR; ICESCR; Convention on the Rights of the Child; and institutions related to these, notably the ICJ and the UN Human Rights Committee. The footnoting supports the inference that the writers are experts in international law and that their legal analyses are reliable.

Conclusions and recommendations is a four-page, footnote-free, text-only précis of the current situation, its history, and its legal status. It includes bulleted lists of recommendations for the redress of the situation addressed to the Syrian authorities, armed groups engaged in the Syrian conflict, the UN Security Council, and the "International Community."

The last page is a statement of AI's goals and activities, the proclamation I WANT TO HELP, presented against AI's signature yellow background and juxtaposed to a pair of forms for personal information headed by the statements "I am interested in receiving further information on becoming a member of Amnesty International" and "I wish to make a donation to Amnesty International."

While the report is seventy-seven pages long, the webpage and email are designed to fit on a single screen, with links to other pages, though notably not to the report. The appeal letter is quite different. It has neither photos nor links to other pages and is less than a page of text. Clearly, all the information in the report cannot fit into any of these other documents, so just as clearly the producers of these documents must adapt the ideological, rhetorical, genre, and linguistic choices of the report to reframe them for new purposes and audiences.

We can view these documents as variants of problem/solution genres (Hoey 2001), re-contextualized and re-genrefied for their various rhetorical purposes. And overall, as the report is presented as an authoritative and accurate source for the other documents, it licenses a range of inferences, particularly related to their trustworthiness and to the legitimacy of their recommendations, anticipating their prospective readers' "epistemic vigilance" (Sperber et al. 2010).

Intertextuality

The concept of intertextuality derives from the work of Bakhtin, whose publications were translated and developed by Julia Kristeva (1986). It has been much debated and developed by literary scholars (e.g., Miola 2004) and communications scholars (e.g., Ott and Walter 2000), as well as discourse analysts (see Hodges 2018 for a recent thorough discussion).

For the purposes of this work, I think of intertextuality as the inescapable phenomenon whereby discourse elements – linguistic, visual, auditory, etc. – that are deployed in one context are reconstituted in other contexts, where they are hybridized by being re-framed and re-genrefied, typically so as to anticipate – "pre-contextualize" (Johnstone 2018) – audience reactions. This reconstitution re-ascribes participant roles and ideologically repositions participants.

Intertextual Traces in the Documents

The official UDHR and Geneva Convention documents are text-only (though illustrated versions are available). The AI documents, except the appeals, incorporate both text and photographs, and so the indices of intertextuality among them involve both modes. The Eastern Ghouta webpage and email show versions of the same photograph of a man carrying a boy by a burning car across a debris field with a destroyed building in the background. The report contains photos of boys and young men on debris fields with destroyed buildings in the background. It also contains photos of destroyed buildings and their associated debris fields and a photo of a destroyed car on a debris field in front of destroyed buildings. While the photos in the webpage and email are almost identical: the one in the webpage is rectangular and spread across the page; the one in the email is smaller, approximately square, and aligned with the right margin. While this photo could have been included in the report, it was not. Nonetheless, it re-constitutes visual themes from the report photos in ways that are more appropriate for the webpage and email genres. That is, the report is designed to be factual and authoritative in order to convince its intended recipients by visual and linguistic argument of the truth of its findings and to persuade them to act as the report recommends. In contrast, the webpage and email are designed to persuade their recipients to act by appeal to facts and empathy. The photo of a man carrying a boy past a burning car accomplishes both. I address the multimodality of these documents later in this chapter.

The visual and linguistic resonances among the documents reflect their re-framing and re-genrefication as they are adapted to their various contexts. Notably, the extensive footnoting in the report contrasts with its complete absence in the other documents, reflecting differences among the genres and the relations among participants. Notable, too, is the almost complete absence in the appeal letters of mention of reports they are based on. Only two letters reference their originating reports: (#21 Crime Task Force), USA, refers to AI's

2015 report "Deadly Force: Police Use of Lethal Force in the United States"[48] and (#40 Cobalt, Apple Corp) refers to its 2016 report "'This Is What We Die for': Human Rights Abuses in the Democratic Republic of the Congo Power the Global Trade in Cobalt."[49] It is not clear to me why (only) these two letters refer to their background reports. While not all the letters or emails are based on reports, others besides the two mentioned are, including the appeal to Putin and Assad quoted above.

Nor is it clear to me why some appeals are based on reports while others are not. The Message Recipients do not seem to be the differentiating factor as there is one other appeal addressed to Putin and sixteen more addressed to US officials that do not refer to reports. Perhaps the exigence of the situation precludes the time-consuming process of gathering all the necessary information and curating a report.

Linguistic resonances include the report's explicit characterization of the "siege" by the Syrian government and non-state armed groups as violating "international humanitarian and human rights law" (7) by depriving the residents of Eastern Ghouta of food and other necessities. "Siege" is repeated in the webpage, the email, and the appeal. The report explicitly characterizes the Syrian government's denial of "adequate food and housing" as a "breach" of international human rights law, and specifically the ICCPR and the ICESCR. The webpage and the email both describe "children and elderly people … dying of malnutrition and lack of medication," which the appeal echoes, saying that the people of Eastern Ghouta "have been enduring hunger, malnutrition, lack of medication and escalated bombardment that has targeted civilians, homes, hospitals and markets."

As we would expect, all the AI documents, except the "Thank you/Please donate" email, include expressions representing human/humanitarian rights and characterizing a situation as problematic from a human/humanitarian rights point of view; unsurprisingly, "violation" occurs frequently across the genres. So do unmitigated statements of fact: "Civilians in/the residents of Eastern Ghouta have been trapped in a cruel siege for nearly six years" (Webpage/Email), and "Nearly half a million civilians live in areas under siege across Syria …" (Report). As do directives to act: "Tell the Syrian and Russian governments to end the attacks …" (Webpage and Email), and "I am calling on you to … end all attacks on civilians …" (Appeal).

The lexical differences across the genres are also significant. The report characterizes its directives to the parties involved as "recommendations," whereas the emails to members may urge them to *demand* that authorities act to redress the violations. The webpages direct their readers using imperatives

[48] https://tinyurl.com/8p9n8y97 (accessed July 31, 2025).
[49] www.amnesty.org/en/documents/afr62/3183/2016/en/ (accessed July 31, 2025).

such as *demand*, *urge*, *tell*, and *ask*, though the appeal letters never *demand* that their addressees act, they are content to *urge*, *call on*, or merely *ask* that the Message Recipients redress the situation. This mitigation in speech act force is surely related to the "rekeying" (Goffman 1974: ch. 3) of the tenor of the relationships between AI and the various audiences for which the genres are intended: the Eastern Ghouta report's "recommendations" are addressed to powerful entities. As AI has no control over these, it cannot demand anything from them, and so the directives must be mitigated, which seems characteristic of the report genre generally. The audiences for the webpage may be assumed to be sympathetic to human rights causes and so may be baldly directed by imperatives to *tell* the Message Recipients to act to redress the problematic situation. We may also view these linguistic differences as manifestations of their authors' estimates of the degree of face threat in each context based on the social distance and power relations among interlocutors and the size of the imposition (Brown and Levinson 1987; Culpeper 2011; Culpeper et al. 2017).

The emails to AI members are addressed to "Dear (First Name)." Near the bottom of the page, beneath a directive to a link labeled TAKE ACTION, is the electronic signature of the executive director of AI at the time, Margaret Huang, or of some other AI official, such as a specialist in specific areas of the world or in specific causes. Notably, while the addressee is addressed by their first name, the AI signer is identified by first and last name and underneath this by their organizational title. This is an intriguing contrast, as the email recipients' first and last names are in AI's records and the AI functionary could have signed just her first name, with her first and last names and title typed beneath. I assume that the executive director of AI does not compose these emails and that other individuals are authorized to electronically insert her signature, name, and title; that is, I do not know the "production format" (Goffman 1981) of the letters. This asymmetry in naming may be chosen to construct a somewhat personalized version of a form letter, but without relinquishing the authority suggested by first and last name, AI affiliation, and institutional rank. This seems to be typical of philanthropic appeal letters (Delahunty 2018b; Mann and Thompson 1992).[50]

The familiarity of the first name in the address line is supported by first-person singular pronouns referring to the signer and inclusive first-person plural pronouns, presumably referring not just to the addressee and signer, but to the addressee and all AI members, and perhaps various overhearers and eavesdroppers, as articulated in Goffman's (1981) "participation framework."

And so, by AI's discursive practices, email recipients are positioned as people who can be addressed by their first name, as a familiar, as a co-member of an organization, and as one who is, in Goffman's terms, at least a

[50] The "Thank you/Please Donate" email is similar, though without its ostensible sender's signature.

principal, "someone whose position is established by the words that are spoken" (Goffman 1981: 144–145), and as someone who can be persuaded to adopt the emotional, factual, and moral stances indexed in the webpage, email, and appeal letter, as evidenced by the frequency of appeals to these factors in the genres, and to take the actions urged upon them.

The Message Recipients of the appeal, "Presidents Putin and Assad," are characterized as people who "have the power to end [the] tragedy" caused by Syria's "siege" of Eastern Ghouta. They are called on to end the "attacks on civilians and civilian structures." By mentioning civilians, the appeal indirectly invokes the Fourth Geneva Convention which is designed to protect civilians in time of war. Putin and Assad are thus positioned as people who may be persuaded by the appeal to human and humanitarian rights and international norms. However, like all such positioning, it is "not necessarily indefeasible" (Davies and Harré 1990: 48) and the appeals' "invitation to conform" (51) to the norms of human rights may be defeated by the Message Recipients or their surrogates deploying an alternative discourse that legitimizes their re-contextualization and re-evaluation of the problematic situation. Such alternative discourses occasionally surface explicitly as concessions in the appeal letters, but they are, as I've noted, always rebutted by the appeals' invocation of international human rights to "trump" (Dworkin 1984) legitimations based on local exigencies or laws. I discuss Goffman's "production format" and Harré and van Langenhove's (1999) "positioning theory" in greater detail in Chapter 4.

Discourse analysts, who might consider themselves "outside" the interplay of these genres and thus ideologically neutral and objective, have also positioned themselves and the selves indexed in the texts, and may in fact have a range of ideological commitments, stretching from activist to activist/analyst professionally interested in the discourses in which they are engaged. Other discourse analysts may have no commitments to the human rights agenda, but may have commitments to "objective" scientific analyses, while others may have broader liberationist commitments, for example, to Critical Discourse Analysis/Studies (CDA) (Catalano and Waugh 2020), for which every analysis is irremediably ideological. Because the current work invokes the guidelines presented in Verschueren (2012), it aims to present an empirical study of a discourse that I show, rather than assume, to be ideological. See Verschueren's (2012) remarks on CDA (4, fn. 5).

Words and Pictures

"A picture is worth a thousand words."

Davidson (2013) asks: "How many facts or propositions are conveyed by a photograph? None, an infinity, or one great unstatable fact? Bad question.

A picture is not worth a thousand words, or any other number. Words are the wrong currency to exchange for a picture" (465).[51] It is generally claimed that only propositions may function in arguments, so if Davidson is correct, pictures should not be able to. However, there are voices claiming that modalities other than language can contribute to arguments. Bateman (2018) proposes an abductive framework for theorizing how non-linguistic modes may be "an ingredient in an argument" (302).[52] Other voices,[53] especially from the RT wing of pragmatics, claim that visuals may express propositions. Sperber and Wilson (2015) characterize the information made manifest to an addressee as "an array **I** of propositions" regardless of whether the ostensive stimulus is verbal or not (141; emphasis in original).

The issue of whether modalities other than language may express propositions is important because argument has generally been regarded as a relationship among truth-bearing entities such that the truth of some licenses the inference that others may or must also be true. It has generally been supposed that propositions are the only truth-bearing entities and that therefore arguments can only be constructed from propositions. It is also generally assumed, especially by rhetoricians, that the goal of argument is persuasion.

As noted above, the AI reports, webpages, and emails synthesize text with photographs and other visuals, while the appeals do not. In the next section, I discuss how these multimodal documents may be interpreted as integrated communicative actions by focusing on the webpage as an example. What I say about the webpage can be extended to an analysis of the two other multimodal documents. I begin by briefly discussing the "three essential elements" identified by Bateman: a relevant community of practice, media, and genres.

Community of Practice

The concept of a community of practice derives from the work of Lave and Wenger (1991) on social learning. Such a community shares concerns, communicative media, ways of deploying elements of those media, and ways of interpreting those deployments. Communities of practice subsume speech communities, which Morgan (2014: 1) defines as "groups that share values and attitudes about language use, varieties and practices." Membership in

[51] The discussion in this section is derived from Delahunty (2023).

[52] Abduction is reasoning to the best explanation (Douven 2025). Hobbs (2004/06) explicitly compares abductive reasoning in discourse interpretation with Relevance Theory, saying that what can be done in one framework can also be done in the other, but that his abductive approach "has a more compelling justification," though "the two frameworks are almost entirely compatible" (739–740).

[53] Unsworth and Cléirigh (2014) provide a model of text/image interaction based on systemic-functional approaches to discourse. For other approaches, see Jewitt (2014).

such communities need not be fixed nor require that all members share the discourse and other practices to the same degree or with the same authority. AI can be viewed as a community of practice: its members share a concern for human and humanitarian rights and the redress of their violations; AI staff members enact a variety of roles, from director to occasional sender of an appeal; AI members engage in activist human rights discourses to varying degrees and in various genres and modalities.

Semiotic Modes

A community of practice must choose its communicative media and decide how these media are to be deployed and interpreted. The AI emails and webpages integrate photos with written English text decorated in a variety of colors, fonts, and font sizes. AI reports add other visuals such as maps.

Genre

Genres are traditionally regarded as categories of texts, especially of literary texts. More recent scholarship regards them as "socially established communicative activities which employ conventionalized strategies … to achieve their effects" (Bateman 2018: 299–300). They invoke "schemata or frames, embodying presuppositions associated with ideologies and principles of communicative conduct that bracket the talk, and that thereby affect the way in which we assess or interpret what transpires in the course of an encounter" (Gumperz 2018: 313). AI's documents are mass-communication genres developed over the course of AI's history in response to reactions to them and to the affordances of new communication technologies, as well as, I presume, to the innovations created by other media users. These genres articulate AI's arguments for persuading governments, diplomats, and members and volunteers to act for the redress of human rights violations.

Genres are devices specific to cultures at various levels of organization and, therefore, from a Relevance Theory perspective, mentally represented as encyclopedic information. They contribute contextual assumptions to the inferential phase of utterance interpretation by influencing the audience's expectations about the format of the discourse, about the sequencing of the discourse elements, about the kinds of cognitive effects to be licensed, and about how strongly those effects will be communicated (Unger 2006).[54]

[54] See Solin (2011) for a brief reprise of the history of the term *genre* and the concepts it has denoted, particularly "as [malleable GD] forms of semiotic practice [that] are socially based" (119; footnote omitted). See Swales (1990) for rhetorical move and step approaches to the analysis of genres.

Forceville (2014), "ChF" in the text quoted below, proposes that "the very first thing a would-be addressee of a mass-communicative message does is assess the genre to which the message belongs. He [*sic*] then activates, from his cognitive environment, knowledge of the genre conventions that allow him to derive pertinent explicatures and implicatures" (68). Additionally,

> [g]*enre is an element of context whose importance cannot be overstated.* Genre-attribution moreover occurs mostly subconsciously and in milliseconds and is in my view the single most important element in the addressee's cognitive environment steering his strategy of interpretation of any pictorial or multimodal message [reference omitted]. Whereas context is endless, and ever-changing, genre-attribution is quite stable and reliable. Indeed, I submit that "genre" more than any other contextual factor helps constrain what the relevance theorist Robyn Carston calls "free pragmatic processes: [...] pragmatic processes that contribute to what a speaker [or picture maker, ChF] is taken to have explicitly communicated but which are not triggered or required by any linguistic [visual, ChF] property or feature of the utterance [picture, ChF]." (Carston 2010: 265).
>
> (Forceville 2014: 63–64; emphasis in original)

The AI documents are all instances of genres that enact directive speech acts whose perlocutionary intent is to persuade their addressees to solve problems. Problems and their solutions entail evaluation. A situation deemed problematic must be shown to be so; that is, it must be evaluated as such by appeal to relevant criteria. Complementarily, the solution must be evaluated by the same criteria. Evaluation requires justification (Forst 2012), that is, argument that the evaluated problem and its related solution meet relevant criteria. Arguments are designed to persuade their audiences to act in specific ways and may be based on fact and reasoning (logos) and/or emotions (pathos), and/or the audience's assumption that the arguer is reliable (ethos) (Cooren 2015: 102, 119).

The Webpage

In what follows, I analyze the argument made by the text and photo in the Siege of Eastern Ghouta webpage above. The photo is spread across the page beneath text in large bold capitals exhorting readers to help the people of Eastern Ghouta. It is above further text in much smaller font providing information about the situation in Eastern Ghouta and exhorting readers to act. Beneath this in a separate pane is the text of the appeal.

Relevance Theory: Ostension

As I recognize the AI webpage genre, I assume that it was produced and disseminated with the intention of informing its readers of the exigency of the situation in Eastern Ghouta and of its producers' desire that readers act for its redress. Simultaneously, webpage readers assume that the producers intend to inform them of this intention. That is, the webpage fulfills the informative and communicative intentions articulated in Sperber and Wilson (1995) and is therefore an instance of "ostensive communication,"[55] RT's revision of Grice's (1971 [1957]) meaning$_{nn}$.

Just the Photo

As a preliminary to the analysis, imagine that you are out for your daily walk and find a photo on your path. What information can and can't you glean from the photo? If the photo were the one in the Eastern Ghouta webpage (see footnote 38) and you were asked to describe it to someone who cannot see it, you would probably say that it is a photo of (a) a man holding a boy (b) in front of a burning car (c) which is on what appears to be debris (d) from damaged buildings in the background. There are a great many other things you might say, such as that while the boy is looking directly at the viewer of the picture, the man is facing toward the left of the picture and seems to be moving in that direction, possibly to take the boy out of danger. While you might include many such observations in your description, if you omitted items (a)–(d) then you would have seriously misrepresented the photo.

What you would not be able to say is where the photo was taken, who the man and boy were, what caused the car fire or the damage to the buildings, or why and whither the man was carrying the boy. You might surmise that the photo is of a scene in the aftermath of an earthquake. You would not be able to say how the photo came to be on the path. Perhaps it was accidentally dropped? Perhaps it was deliberately placed there so that social scientists hidden in the bushes could observe your reactions to it? You cannot tell these things because the picture has no text in or around it and its location on the path provides no information that would allow you to contextualize it for a fuller interpretation. You would not be able to construct a discourse meaning for it (Bateman 2018: 303). One thing you could not assume is that the photo represents "one great unstatable fact": at the very least, you would have no way of knowing whether the photo represented a fact or a fiction. More on this below.

The Photo in Context

Now consider the photo back in the context of the webpage. We recognize the webpage as an instance of a genre, specifically one that seeks to persuade us to do something. The AI logo at the top left allows us to more specifically

[55] For recent synopses of RT relevant to the issues discussed here, see Forceville (2014); Forceville and Clark (2014); Rohan et al. (2018).

identify the genre as asking us to act to redress a situation violating human or humanitarian rights. We assume that the text and photo were deliberately combined and deliberately disseminated and displayed with the goal of influencing its viewers' minds and actions in the ways I've just mentioned. We assume that the text provides relevant context for the interpretation of the photo, rather than, say, that the photo is an advertisement interpolated into the webpage for a particularly shocking form of extreme tourism. The context provided by the text and other genre elements allow us to hypothesize a discourse meaning for the photo. We also assume that the photo provides context relevant to the interpretation of the text.

Photo and Text

We infer, when we contextualize the photo with information from the text, that the photo iconically (Atkin 2023) and faithfully resembles[56] (Sperber and Wilson 1995) and thereby "shows" (Forceville and Clark 2014; Sperber and Wilson 2015; Wharton 2009) a scene in Eastern Ghouta, not, for example, a scene from a movie or TV news program. That is, we take the photo to be veridical. We also infer that the fire in the car and the damage and debris were caused by Syrian and Russian bombing, not by earthquake. We might also infer, because the man appears to be wearing a jacket that might be part of a fireman's uniform, that he is an emergency responder carrying a child to safety. And we might infer that the child is one of the injured thousands mentioned in the text and the man is carrying him – perhaps because he is unable to walk – to a hospital or first aid station – or to whatever kind of medical facility has survived the bombing. More abstractly, and in RT terms, more "weakly," we might infer that the photo represents a future time when men like the one in the photo may be able to carry the children like the one in the photo to the humanitarian aid that the webpage demands be allowed into the region. We infer all this (and more) based not just on the textual context, but also on our trust in AI's veracity and reliability.

Text and Photo

And what information can we infer when we contextualize the text with the photo? What does the photo add to the text in the creation of the overall interpretation of the webpage? How does it function in the argument that the situation in Eastern Ghouta is "catastrophic" due to Syrian and Russian daily bombing attacks and their denial of humanitarian aid?

[56] Jeff Kaplan, (p.c.) suggests that Grice's maxim of Quality might be broadened to apply to visual representations.

Photo, Salience, Ground, and Strength of Communication

The photo takes up approximately half of the webpage and, except for the yellow background of the AI logo, is the only element of the page with color; consequently, it is highly salient and therefore an important element of the document. It foregrounds and thus draws the viewer's immediate attention to the man and boy. However, they are positioned slightly to the right of center, thus allowing the burning car to be foregrounded as well. The foregrounded elements are particularly salient, though the burning car may be more so than the man and boy. Because of their salience, the foregrounded elements are strongly communicated. That is, if a viewer were to overlook them in interpreting the photo, they would have missed the most important aspects of what the producer intended the photo to communicate. The backgrounded elements are considerably less salient than the foregrounded ones; they are, for example, in varying shades of gray, with which the flames from the burning car contrast intensely. The background elements communicate less strongly (Wilson and Sperber 2004: 620)[57] what they represent, in this case, circumstantial information about the state of the buildings and debris on the ground, which is important, though perhaps not essential, to the interpretation of the photo.

Deictics: Temporal and Spatial

Like any utterance, the photo indexes temporal and spatial deictic information; that is, the photographic icon is anchored (Bateman 2018: 303) in a specific time and place. Because it is not time and date stamped, the photo communicates its temporal information implicitly. As is usual in discussions of temporal deixis, I distinguish between the webpage's utterance time and time of reference, neither of which can be uniquely identified. The utterance time may be inferred to be the time at which the photo was published on the AI website or the time at which a reader accesses that site; the reference time is the time interpreters assume that the producer wants them to attribute to the scene in the photo. This is to be inferred from the contextualization of the photo with information from the associated text. It is something along the lines of *this is the kind of thing that happened (frequently) during the siege and bombing of Eastern Ghouta at the time at which the AI report was produced, August 2015.*

[57] "A proposition may be more or less strongly implicated by an utterance. It is STRONGLY IMPLICATED (or is a STRONG IMPLICATURE) if its recovery is essential in order to arrive at an interpretation that satisfies the addressee's expectations of relevance. It is WEAKLY IMPLICATED if its recovery helps with the construction of strong implicatures but is not itself essential because the utterance suggests a range of similar possible implicatures, any one of which would do" (Wilson and Sperber 2004: 620; capitalization in original).

We can make a similar distinction between the utterance and reference places. The utterance place is just the place where the photo was published or where it was accessed; the reference place is inferred from the interaction between the photo and the text and is something along the lines of *this is the kind of scene that can be seen in many places in Eastern Ghouta.*

The Photo in the Argument

How does the photo contribute to this argument? The text describes, "tells" (Sperber and Wilson 2015), the situation in general terms. The photo is a synecdochic representation of the situation in Eastern Ghouta and, we infer, a specific instance of the situation more generally described by the text. It is to be interpreted as ostensively "showing" (Sperber and Wilson 2015) what it represents, and by virtue of showing by photo, we infer that we are seeing a specific man, carrying a specific boy past a specific burning car, across a specific debris field, with specific damaged buildings in the background. It is thus a case of "determinate showing" (Sperber and Wilson 2015: 124). Nonetheless, we don't know the identities of the man or boy, or exactly where they were when the photo was taken. And we do not know exactly when it was taken. However, we must assume that the photo was not integrated into the webpage merely to represent[58] unknown people, places, and times.

Enrichment: Ad Hoc Concepts

One way to theorize our further interpretation of the photo is to analyze it in its context in the way that RT proposes that word meanings in context are to be analyzed (Carston 2002; Wilson and Carston 2007). A word's meaning may be inferentially narrowed or broadened (or both) as its interpreter hypothesizes the meaning intended by its producer. For example, the rather broad lexical meaning of *hot* is inferentially narrowed in context to something like *hot enough to burn the drinker's mouth* in *That coffee is hot* issued as a warning. That is, the interpreter will enrich the lexical meaning of *hot* to the *ad hoc* concept *hot** with the relevant, contextualized meaning. We can treat the individuals in the photo like words: the individuals in the photo, while pictorially specific, are otherwise unknown. However, in the context of the AI webpage genre, and especially of the text, the man is narrowed to a man in Eastern Ghouta; similar contextual narrowing applies to the boy, the burning car, and the damaged buildings. The context provides information

[58] "Represent" is glossed in Sperber and Wilson (2015) as to be "broadly understood as meaning *fulfill the function of making some information available for processing*" (137; emphasis in original).

interpreters can use, indeed are expected to use, to further narrow our interpretation of the photo: the buildings were damaged by Russian and Syrian bombing; the car was set alight by that bombing; the man is carrying the boy to whatever safety and medical attention might be available. We can readily imagine other such inferences an interpreter might derive from the contextualization of the photo by the webpage genre and text.

Just as word meanings can be broadened in context, for example, for metaphorical interpretation (Sperber and Wilson 2015), the meaning of the photo can also be broadened. It is a photo of a scene in bombed and besieged Eastern Ghouta, but it may be interpreted as a synecdoche for all the scenes of devastation and desperation in Eastern Ghouta, and perhaps in all wars. Interpreters will infer at least that the photo represents a scene in Eastern Ghouta and is representative of all such scenes in Eastern Ghouta; if they failed to do that, they would have failed to construct an adequate hypothesis about the producer's communicative intention. However, they may derive any number of further inferences, but they do this on their own dime, so to speak.

Enrichment: Explicatures

Explicatures are the logical forms of "explicitly communicated assumption[s]," that is, logical forms (Sperber and Wilson 1995: 182), which must be contextually enriched. I take the explicatures of the photo to be versions of the items (a)–(d) in the "Just the Photo" section above. These are inferentially enriched with information from the webpage as its viewer searches for an optimally relevant interpretation. I suggest that the contextually enriched explicatures of the photo are, at a minimum:

A specific man is carrying (note the present tense and progressive aspect) a specific boy past a specific burning car which is situated on specific building debris in front of specific severely damaged buildings in Eastern Ghouta.

The Syrian and Russian bombing caused the damage to the buildings and the car-fire.

The man is a rescue worker; the boy has been injured, perhaps by the bombing, perhaps by falling masonry (note the dirt on his face) caused by the bombing.

The man, boy, car, buildings, and their relationships are specific, but representative instances of the effects of the Syrian and Russian siege and bombing of Eastern Ghouta.

If photos license explicatures, then they must also license implicatures. The following are some implicatures that might be derived from the photo and its context:

Because the car is burning, the bombing that caused it must have occurred shortly before the photo was taken.
The bombing may be continuing.
If the bombing is continuing, then the situation must be very dangerous.
The man and boy, and other people in Eastern Ghouta, are in continuing danger.
Many people may be being injured or killed by the bombing and siege.
Dangerous situations should be made safe.
To make this dangerous situation safe, the siege and bombing must be stopped.

In fact, the webpage text explicitly articulates the consequences of the siege and bombing on the people of Eastern Ghouta: "they are now being attacked daily, killed and maimed by their government. Children and elderly people are dying of malnutrition and lack of medication." The AI webpage genre thus integrates explicatures and implicatures of the photo with explicatures and implicatures of the text into a coherent argument, designed to persuade webpage readers to act to redress the situation. The webpage is also explicit about how its readers should act. They should "**Tell the Syrian and Russian Governments to end the attacks and lift the siege on Eastern Ghouta immediately**" (emphasis in original).

But Wait, There's More!

Although verbalizing the elements of the photo as explicatures and implicatures allows us to articulate its individual and contextualized contributions to the document, there remains a strong feeling that the photo contributes much more and much differently than is verbalizable. Bateman (2018: 303–304) says that "semiotic modes may deliver material that does more than just contributing to dicents," that is, to more than just Peircean modality-independent propositions. Sperber and Wilson (2015) suggest the inclusion of "impressions" into the theoretical apparatus of Relevance Theory. "[A]n impression is a change in the manifestness of an array of propositions which all bear on our understanding of the same phenomenon, answering the same question, or deciding the same issue" (138). "However fleetingly" impressions may become "manifest or more manifest they become more likely to be attended to, and more likely to be taken as true [and] therefore more likely to influence" the decisions of their audiences (137). An impression's array of propositions results from "changes in patterns of activation, none of which would properly speaking amount to the fixation of a distinct credal representation, but the totality of which would correspond to the formation of an impression" (137). So, an impression "does not simply pick out a weak credal attitude; it picks out a certain type of vague information basic for such an attitude" (138). Its communicated meaning "cannot be paraphrased without loss" (Sperber and Wilson 2015: 122).

Sperber and Wilson's descriptions of "impression" suggest a way to characterize the residue of information communicated by a contextualized photo beyond its explicatures and implicatures. It allows us to have our analytic cake and to eat it: pictures can be cashed in for words, *pace* Davidson, but they always also communicate an excess of information that is not and perhaps cannot be verbalized, and on which Sperber and Wilson's notion of "impression" gives us some analytic purchase. This residue is indeterminately shown because its "intended import cannot be rendered as a proposition at all" (Sperber and Wilson 2015: 124), though presumably the photo above may communicate a range of rhetorical appeals, particularly combining ethos and pathos. It contributes to ethos – a credal attitude – because we take it to be a genuine icon of an Eastern Ghouta situation or event; it contributes to pathos by virtue of the deaths, injuries, and damage it evokes.

To wrap up: The webpage document provides evidence for two sets of assumptions, one derived from the text, the other from the photo. Each set is enriched by its contextualization by the other. Some of the assumptions are explicatures, both basic and higher level. The latter are evaluations of the situations described and speech acts exhorting audiences to behave in particular ways. The document, and especially the photo, also provides evidence for a range of "impressions" that support the "credal attitude" the AI producers of the webpage hope will be adopted by its audiences.

Why Study AI Appeal Letters?

I chose to study AI appeal letters for a variety of reasons that vary in importance. Least importantly, though still usefully, I study them because, as far as I know, no one has done it before, so, their study, especially from multiple perspectives, adds to our knowledge of genres. Second, they are functionally similar to philanthropic fundraising (PF) appeals, which have been studied from multiple perspectives (see references in Delahunty 2018b), though not, as far as I know, from an ideological one. They are also functionally and linguistically similar to placards displayed in protests: the imperative mood occurs in both the protest placard text FREE PUSSY RIOT and in the appeal Subject line *Free Nadezhda Tolokonnikova and Maria Alekhina* (#11 Pussy Riot, Russia). Both genres demand actions relevant to various causes. Third, unlike PF appeals but like some protests, the AI appeals call for action to redress situations of extreme exigence, for example, impending floggings or executions. Fourth, because of the extreme power differential between the letter writers and SENDers (AI staffers and ordinary citizens) and their addressees (powerful individuals such as heads of state), the letters require delicate linguistic management of that relationship if they are to be effective. The letters enact politeness in interaction in situations of extreme power asymmetry and regarding situations with the potential to threaten both the positive and negative face of their addressees and to worsen the plight of their subjects. Thus, the letters represent one organization's solutions to the challenges of managing stance and engagement in dangerous interactions (Delahunty 2013). Fifth, the study of the rhetorical moves and steps (Biber et al. 2007; Upton and Cohen 2009) that constitute the letters (Delahunty 2018b) provides a basis for responding to several of Verschueren's guidelines and an opportunity to examine the motivations underlying the characteristic linguistic choices of the genre by identifying and accounting for the choices that enact moves and steps, which previous analysts have been content to merely list and quantify. Sixth, because the letters represent the re-entextualization, re-contextualization, and re-genrefication of information in documents and discourses such as interviews with individuals affected by a situation into AI reports, webpages, emails to volunteers, and appeal letters, they provide a focus for the study of the intertextual processes that relate these mutually relevant texts; for example, as I mentioned above, the embedding emails frequently exhort the AI volunteers to *demand* action by the letter addressees, whereas the letters themselves never use such a strong directive, and merely *ask*, *call on*, or *urge* their addressees to redress an egregious wrong (Delahunty 2021). Seventh, these letters have several related but distinguishable functions: they address a specific situation that is problematic from AI's point of view and propose a solution to that problem; they engage, unify, and motivate AI members; they are intended to persuade their Message Recipients to adopt AI's solution to the problem; and they feature in AI's fundraising efforts. I provide evidence in support of these and other functions in the chapters that follow.

Why Study the AI Appeal Letters from an Ideological Point of View?

Despite early claims to the contrary (e.g., Bell 1988 [1960]), ideology is not dead. In fact, ideologies are alive and kicking. And even though human and humanitarian rights are not generally characterized as ideological constructs or formations, and AI's Letter Writing Guide implicates that its activities are not ideological, the discourses of human rights are most certainly ideological and when they are brought into conflict with competing ideologies, especially in situations of extreme power differentials, the ways in which the interlocutors' positions and conflicts are managed is of considerable importance, and has not, so far as I am aware, been studied from the perspectives of linguistic pragmatics and discourse analysis.

Conclusion

This chapter briefly introduced the important concepts of rights, then focused specifically on human rights. It provided a short overview of Amnesty International and an analysis of several of its primary document genres, paying particular attention to the linguistic and visual resonances occasioned by their contextualizations. It proposed a Relevance Theory explanation for the intimate relations between the documents' linguistic and visual modes, an approach broadly applicable to multimodal genres. It ended with a rationale for the ideological study of AI documents, particularly of the appeal letters.

3 Ideology

Ideologies, as I've noted, are alive and kicking, though opinions differ considerably on just what constitutes an ideology. One criterion dividing commentators is whether ideologies are necessarily pejorative. Most current careful commentators take the view that ideologies need not be pejorative and point to positive ideologies underlying liberationist thought and activity, like those of human rights organizations such as AI and Human Rights Watch. Nonetheless, vernacular uses of the term tend to view it as pejorative, either denotationally or connotationally: of the first 100 instances returned by a search for "ideology" in the Corpus of Contemporary American English (COCA; accessed July 9, 2018), 66 percent suggested that ideologies are pejorative. AI also seems to take this view, as its International Letter Writing Guide (rule 5) directs its letter writers/SENDers to "never give the impression that you are ideologically or politically opposed to the government in question," implicating that its activities are neither ideological nor political (Appendix 1). Though human and humanitarian rights are not generally characterized as ideological constructs, they most certainly are, as I demonstrate below, and when they are brought into conflict with competing ideologies, especially in situations of extreme power differential, how these commitments and conflicts are managed is of considerable importance, and has not, so far as I am aware, been studied from the perspectives of linguistic pragmatics and discourse analysis.

Any study of ideological discourse must address the conceptions of ideology it invokes, which in turn requires a general discussion of ideology. So before setting out my analysis of my corpus of AI appeals, I set out some thoughts about ideology and ideologies.

General surveys of ideology typically include a discussion, often brief, of the origins of the modern understanding of ideology in the Enlightenment, typically mentioning Antoine Destutt de Tracy's proposed science of ideas, which he named "ideology" (Eagleton 2007: 66 ff; Hawkes 1996: 54 ff; McLellan 1995: 5 ff; van Dijk 1998: 1 ff; Verschueren 2012: 7, fn. 1). These surveys also typically trace the (mis)fortunes of the conceptions of ideology as they careened through the tumults and conflicts of the nineteeth and twentieth centuries. In spite of being declared dead in the 1960s (Bell 1988 [1960]), ideology was revivified and killed off yet again, "exploded" (as Algernon describes Bunbury's fate in Wilde's (1982) *The Importance of Being Earnest*: Act 3) by postmodernists (Hawkes 1996: 4), but has come through into the twenty-first century, still serviceable, but stretched and strained by its collisions with Marxism, Neo-Marxism, Post-Marxism, empiricism, idealism, hermeneutics, psychoanalysis, and Critical Discourse Analysis, to name but a few. So, in this section, I review some discussions of ideology from a selection of publications on the topic, ending with the characterization of ideology that will inform my analysis of the AI appeal letters.

Power

No discussion of ideology can omit a discussion of power. However, as the Western discussion of the nature of power spans the almost 2,500 years between Plato and Foucault, I can do no more here than pick a very few notions that seem most relevant to my purposes.

Power is the capacity to act, and most relevant to our current concerns, the capacity to act to get someone to do something. Power may be exercised by force – recall Mao's dictum, "political power grows out of the barrel of a gun," and Machiavelli's precept that it is better for a ruler to be feared than loved. Power may also be exercised by persuasion, and as persuasion may be less costly from many points of view, powerful people can influence the thoughts, decisions, and actions of the less powerful so as to benefit themselves by their disproportionate influence over a community's discourses. "Power is the most fundamental process in society, since society is defined around values and institutions, and what is valued and institutionalized is defined by power relationships" (Castells 2013: 10).

As the actions of organizations like AI demonstrate, power may also be exercised by less powerful actors who can mobilize large numbers of people in support of particular values, as is typical of the exercise of counterpower, the "capacity to challenge dominant ideologies" (Featherman 2015: 6). The "archaeologies" carried out by AI and similar organizations reveal to their many members, supporters, and authoritative audiences in organizations like the UN the transgressions characterized in the AI documents, and by revealing, attempt to control them, typically via a Foucauldian "naming and shaming." The AI appeals clearly are not supported by force or even its possibility, rather, they depend upon the discursive construction of ideological justifications (Forst 2012, 2015, 2016) derived from universal legal instruments and the mobilization of media, public opinion, overtures to governments and international bodies, and large numbers of letter writers/SENDers espousing those justifications. As Hannah Arendt argued, power may derive from the human capacity to persuade by concerted action (Allen 2022; Tömmel and d'Entreves 2025) even those who all too often resort to force.

Ideology

The following discussion of ideology derives from a number of sources, primarily from Verschueren (2012) and Eagleton (2007), but also from Hawkes (1996), Hodge and Kress (1993), McLellan (1995), Menz (1989), Morris (2010), Sypnowich (2024), van Dijk (1998), and Wodak (1989).

To set the stage for my discussion of ideology, I briefly consider the characteristics identified in Verschueren (Chapter 1) and discuss them more fully below after I have reviewed several other conceptions of the notion.

Verschueren argues that ideologies are discursively constituted, social, cultural, and cognitive phenomena. They are taken-for-granted, commonsensical, normative ideas, beliefs, and opinions expressed for rhetorical purposes and representing underlying patterns of meaning, frames of interpretation, world views, or forms of everyday thinking, evaluation, and explanation that balance description and prescription of social realities. Ideologies serve as the bases for struggles over meaning and norms in order to establish and maintain relations of power. Ideologies are typically represented more or less consistently across related genres, for example, across AI reports, webpages, emails, and appeals, and are often expressed implicitly rather than explicitly in discourse. However, as we will see, AI and racist discourses, especially when addressed to like-minded audiences, can be quite explicit, as can feminist, anti-colonial, and LGBTQIA+ ideologies. These elements and others will figure in the discussion below of several conceptions of ideology.

I begin with the following synoptic definition of "ideology" from the Routledge *Encyclopedia of Philosophy*:[1]

> An ideology is a set of ideas, beliefs and attitudes, consciously or unconsciously held, which reflects or shapes understandings or misconceptions of the social and political world. It serves to recommend, justify or endorse collective action aimed at preserving or changing political practices and institutions. The concept of ideology is split almost irreconcilably between two major senses. The first is pejorative, denoting particular, historically distorted (political) thought which reinforces certain relationships of domination and in respect of which ideology functions as a critical unmasking concept. The second is a non-pejorative assertion about the different families of cultural symbols and ideas human beings employ in perceiving, comprehending and evaluating social and political realities in general, often within a systemic framework. Those families perform significant mapping and integrating functions.

The distinction between the pejorative and non-pejorative senses of "ideology" is significant for the purposes of this book and will surface and resurface in the discussion below, as will their role in "comprehending and evaluating … realities."

[1] www.rep.routledge.com/articles/thematic/ideology/v-1 (accessed August 1, 2025).

McLellan (1995: 82–83) sums up his discussion of ideology, saying that

> [t]he science/ideology and the vulgar Marxist view share at least one redeeming feature in that they both attempt, however unsuccessfully, to link ideology to domination. For successful accounts of ideology must combine two attributes. The first … is a hermeneutic subtlety which sees both that it is necessary to understand ideology before criticizing it and also adopts a self-reflexive attitude towards its own premises. The second … is to preserve the concept's critical potential by linking it with analyses of control and domination, thereby extricating it from the labyrinth of relativism associated with the hermeneutic circle. Ideology may be "an irretrievably fallen word" [footnote omitted] – but then we live in a fallen society and, until we mend it, we will continue to be implicated in ideology. It follows that, although in principle there could be an end to ideology, it is certainly nowhere in sight – not even on the horizon. This is because ideology is best viewed not as a separate system of signs and symbols that could be contrasted with – and eventually replaced by – another, e.g., science of some sort. Ideology is rather an aspect of every system of signs and symbols in so far as they are implicated in an asymmetric distribution of power and resources. And of which system is this not the case?

The goal of the current enterprise is to understand the discourse properties of the AI documents and the ideologies they enact. Though we might jib at the religious undertow of "fallen," we can agree that our world is in need of mending, and that the AI appeals are elements of a discourse "implicated in an asymmetric distribution of power and resources," though the power relations they enact are the reverse of those typically studied in ideology research. The AI documents position AI and its members and volunteers as the less powerful actors in their discourse contexts, and their intended addressees as the locally and often internationally more powerful ones in the appeal situation. Certainly, if all groups and institutions always acted in accordance with human and humanitarian rights, then it is possible to imagine an end to the need for the kinds of ideological activities in which AI and other such organizations are engaged. However, this would not allow the end of human rights ideology, for it would remain as the basis for the evaluation of situations in which asymmetrical power is wielded and as the motivation for the resumption of redressive activities, given the possibility, if not the probability, of a reversion to bad old habits. And until human rights violations cease, there will be the necessity for protests and the activities and documents to enact them.

Hawkes (1996) is an exercise in literary critical theory whose aim is to argue for "the historical primacy, philosophical validity, and continued postmodern relevance" of the understanding of ideology as "a false consciousness resulting from the belief in the autonomy and determining power of representation" and its historical relations with market capitalism (Preface). Hawkes traces the history of the concept of false consciousness from ancient Greek and Hebrew traditions through the works of writers he classifies as empiricists, idealists, Marxists, post-Marxists, and postmodernists. He defends the current relevance of the pejorative interpretation of ideology, though he does not, so far as I can tell, accept that ideologies may be neutral or positive.

Ideologies, like any system of representations, ideas, beliefs, or knowledge, are partial in both of that word's senses. First, they are necessarily incomplete: despite physicists' claims to the contrary, there can be no theory of everything and thus all systems of representation are vulnerable to critiques on the basis of information or perspectives they exclude. Second, at least because of their incompleteness, ideologies are unlikely to be disinterested because of the interests and commitments of the people who select the elements that constitute them.

The essential incompleteness of systems of representation is fundamental to the most important theories of linguistic pragmatics: Gricean, Neo-Gricean, and Post-Gricean. All agree, at least tacitly, that human cognition is limited and thus cannot attend to all the inputs it receives and is therefore necessarily selective. In response, Relevance Theory (RT) proposes that human cognition tends toward the maximization of "positive cognitive effects," which contribute to a "genuine improvement in knowledge" for the individual deriving these effects (Wilson and Sperber 2012a: 341, fn. 4). Improvements in knowledge consist of the addition of new information, and the epistemic strengthening, weakening, or abandoning of existing assumptions (Sperber and Wilson 1995), in short, "any effect 'which contributes positively to the fulfillment of cognitive functions or goals'" (Clark 2013: 103). Notably, RT does not reduce positive cognitive effects to truthfulness (Wilson and Sperber 2012b). True assumptions may indeed contribute to the fulfillment of cognitive goals; however, so may false assumptions, given our tendency to forget or reject true or well-evidenced assumptions that contradict strongly held beliefs, regardless of how well or poorly those beliefs are evidenced. Our tendency to confirm our biases may have positive social consequences such as the construction of identities and acceptance into desirable communities.

It follows from these assumptions about human cognition that the AI appeals, and more generally, the edifice of human and humanitarian rights, are partial in both senses. They selectively elide information and other points of view, which may then be used as the bases of critiques of those rights. It follows from this partiality that the discourses of rights are likely to be ideological, and as I demonstrate, actually are ideological, and whether this ideology is pejorative or not depends upon the critic's point of view. For example, a government, such as that of China or Singapore, may consider the stability of the country or social harmony to outweigh the rights of individuals, and thus regard the discourse of rights as potentially disruptive. Of course, the ideology of social stability or harmony may be critiqued in its turn as a self-serving justification for the entrenchment of the rule of a single party or of a tiny elite. Human rights claims have also been criticized as being incomplete in that they set very limited goals rather than broader claims to justice and are biased, thinly disguised attempts at Western neocolonialism, claims which have been rebutted in their turn, in a seemingly infinite regression. As AI's discourses are elements of human rights discourses, they are vulnerable to such critiques, and may be regarded as positive, neutral, or negative as determined by the evaluator's point of view. So, it would be mistaken to assume that ideologies are autonomous or that representations are determinative.

Hodge and Kress (**1993**: 157) define an "ideological complex" as a "set of versions of reality whose contradictions are intrinsic to their function." Such contradictions derive from "two components."

> One component represents the world in a way that blurs differences, antagonism, conflicts of interest. We will call this the *solidarity* function, or the S-form. The other expresses the interests of the group against its others, so that it exacerbates difference, hostility, superiority. We will call this the *power* function, or P-form. The two mingle with complex promiscuity in most rhetorical performances, but the distinction between the two is useful as an aid to tracking the process of fusion that is typical of ideology in use.
>
> (emphasis in original)

These two functions do indeed mingle promiscuously in human rights discourses and consequently in the AI documents. For example, AI's reports on situations in which rights are violated typically include sections on the methodology used to collect evidence, the recent historical background to the situation, descriptions of the violations, and conclusions and recommendations addressed to individuals and agencies deemed to share AI's human rights perspective, or at least to be obligated by international treaties to honor their human rights commitments, thus invoking Hodge and Kress' S-form. The other AI documents also invoke the S-form by presenting their evaluations of situations as common to webpage readers, email recipients, letter writers, appeal SENDers, and Message Recipients, and by justifying their appeals by reference to universal values purported to be shared.

The letters invoke the P-form by characterizing actions by their addressees as violations of authoritative universal values. On the basis of those values, AI letters rebut their occasional concessions to the contingencies faced by the Message Recipients, for example, the need to punish those guilty of major crimes. The letters also invoke the P-form by mobilizing large numbers of people, often in the tens of thousands, in protest against the rights violations, though I would not characterize the letters as exacerbating hostility, quite the opposite in fact. They are notably polite, due most likely to the power differential between AI and the typical addressees of the letters. Nonetheless, they have on occasion been met with anger and resistance.[2,3]

[2] Russian consular officials are reported to have refused to accept boxes of signed petitions from AI representatives in 2012. See https://tinyurl.com/4dkak24s (accessed August 1, 2025).

[3] Jeff Kaplan, (p.c.), suggests that AI's rhetoric is entirely S-form, in contrast with, e.g., (Neo-) Nazi, South African Apartheid, Zionist, Al-Quaeda, and US Christian groups demanding that the US Constitution declare the US a Christian country.

Morris (2010: 184) defines ideology as "[a] belief set socializing individuals with a group identity promoting social cohesion and praxis aimed at common survival, dealienation and satisfaction of fundamental human needs and associated desires." This characterization of ideology emphasizes solidarity and thus Hodge and Kress' S-form and overlaps considerably with the characteristics proposed by Eagleton that I discuss below. We might suppose that these characteristics are derived from what Chen (2015: 251–2) identifies as the strong desire for the satisfaction of the human needs for respect, power, enlightenment, well-being, wealth, skill, affection, and rectitude. The letters – and human rights in general – reflect the desire that human beings be treated in ways that meet these needs, which are often summarized as human dignity (Habermas 2010; Moka-Mubelo 2017; Muders 2018). To this desire, Eagleton (2007: xxiii) adds people's capacity to struggle for emancipation. Human rights ideals and laws, as well as the activities of organizations like AI, are devices crafted for that struggle.

Sypnowich (2024) is a discussion of the relations between law and ideology, which is pertinent to our topic in that it entails the intersection of the ideology of human/humanitarian rights and their codification in international law. In her discussion of liberal concepts of ideology, she claims that

> [i]deologies are ideas whose purpose is not epistemic, but political. Thus an ideology exists to confirm a certain political viewpoint, serve the interests of certain people, or to perform a functional role in relation to social, economic, political and legal institutions … its role is not to render reality transparent, but to motivate people to do or not to do certain things. Such a role may involve a process of justification that requires the obfuscation of reality. Nonetheless … liberal sociologists do not assume any particular relation between ideology and the status quo; some ideologies serve the status quo, others call for its reform or overthrow. (2)

As human rights laws and treaties are crafted by authoritative international organizations such as the UN by diplomats appointed by their governments, they are irredeemably political. Nonetheless, they aim to serve the interests of, and provide the grounding for justifications to, less powerful people as they advance critiques and reform of coercive institutions. In so far as the relevant legal documents are readily available for review, the realities they address are clear, though some of the processes by which these legal instruments were arrived at may indeed have been veiled.

Nonetheless, Sypnowich concludes that

> [t]he idea that law is ideological is an important contribution to legal scholarship [as it] enables a more critical view of the law and its role, and thereby demystifies a set of vital social institutions … [and] points to the importance of sociological and political factors in our understanding of the law … Properly understood, the concept of ideology offers a nuanced and illuminating approach to legality that gives a precise rendering

of the relation between law and politics that need not be nihilist or reductionist … A conception of law as having a moral source, or a source in a system's institutions, can be independent of a realistic appraisal of law's ideological function, or the ideological process in which laws are made. Indeed, radical critics of the "war on terror"[4] waged by western governments have pointed to the value of liberal legal ideals such as human rights and the rule of law at the same time as they have noted the ideological purposes to which such ideals are put. (6–7; footnote added)

As AI and similar organizations attempt to influence the minds and actions of individuals and the institutions that they represent or that represent them, they are engaged in politics, and are thus ideologically committed, though their purposes are emancipatory and redressive though claimed to be non-political and non-ideological, as the AI Letter Writing Guide implicates. An ideological analysis of AI's important discursive devices should illuminate its relationships with human rights law and the politics of human rights activism.

Van Dijk (1998) argues, from a critical discourse point of view, that the disciplines contributing to the study of ideology are cognitive science, the study of social beliefs, and the study of discourse. He also argues that the "commonsense usage [of 'ideology'] is generally pejorative" (1), an understanding supported by the brief COCA survey mentioned above, though recent understandings of ideology tend to be "more inclusive and less pejorative" (3). Nonetheless, conceptions of ideology, even when shorn of their negative and dominance dimensions, are not deprived of the "critical edge" (11) of more typical conceptions of ideology. They may be used to critically analyze both "good" and "bad" ideologies, including ideologies of resistance, even as these change to ideologies of domination (11). According to his 2013 paper,

[c]ontrary to the biased conception of ideology as an instrument of domination, we propose a *general theory of ideology and its reproduction by discourse* – of which ideologies of domination, as is the case for racism, sexism, classism, or neoliberalism, are special examples. Indeed, anti-racism, feminism, socialism, pacifism, or environmentalism, among many others, are no less ideologies by our definition, but not with the function to found and legitimate domination, but precisely to provide the sociocognitive basis for the struggle against it. (175; emphasis in original)

Nonetheless, he continues the general trajectory of ideological discourse studies by analyzing in this paper an anti-immigrant speech by a member of the British House of Commons, an example of "bad" ideology. I view his analysis as an exercise in "epistemic vigilance" (Sperber et al. 2010) or in the "hermeneutics of suspicion" (Felski 2015, cited in Cave and Wilson 2018: 16, 42; Ricoeur 2008).

[4] See Boyle (2008); Reese and Lewis (2009).

For van Dijk (1998), ideologies form the "*basis of the social representations shared by members of a group*" (8; emphasis in original), "social constructs" (9) that "allow people, as group members, to organize the multitude of social beliefs about what is the case, good or bad, right or wrong, *for them*, and to act accordingly" (8; emphasis in original). Ideologies also "determine what is accepted as true or false, especially when such beliefs are found to be relevant for the group" (8). The relationships between the cognitive and the social can be explained only by detailed analyses of the language and discourse practices of group members (10).

Van Dijk (2013) foregrounds an aspect of ideology recognized by many scholars: the othering of ideological opponents, typically characterized as the adversarial positioning of social groups as "us vs. them." His paper is an analysis of segments of the House of Commons speech against a loosening of limitations on immigration into the UK primarily on the basis of claims that many asylum seekers are economic migrants who become a burden on the UK taxpayer and violate UK laws. The following quote from that speech represents several of these characterizations of migrants and implicitly contrasts them with legitimate immigrants and law-abiding British taxpayers:

> The Daily Mail today reports the case of a woman from Russia who has managed to stay in Britain for five years. According to the magistrate's court yesterday, she has cost the British taxpayer £40 000. She was arrested, of course, for stealing. I do not know how many people who are not bona fide asylum seekers and whose applications have been rejected time and time again manage to remain in this country for so long at the expense of the British public, but the system clearly needs tightening up. (183, footnote omitted)

The AI letters likewise represent an adversarial relationship between the letter SENDers and the Message Recipients – between the proponents of human and other rights and their purported violators. However, as I've noted, the letters occasionally concede that the violations might be based on local contingencies suggesting that the Message Recipients may be persuaded to redress the violations, implying that "we" and "they" may be less antagonistic than might be assumed.

For a complete list of the conclusions van Dijk draws from his discussion of ideology and its study, see van Dijk 1998: 313–318, and see Blommaert 2005: 161–162 for remarks on van Dijk's conceptions of ideology.

The analysis of the discourse of human rights as represented in the AI documents demonstrates that it enacts beliefs shared by the organization's membership, evaluates situations and events according to those beliefs, and seeks to persuade powerful individuals in authoritative institutions to bring about redress by conforming to the relevant human rights, ideally, I assume, to establish the global dominance of human rights.

Wodak (1989) characterizes ideologies as "myths,"[5] which are "systems of ideas which constitute and pilot the large powerblocks of our society" (140), thus rejecting the "negative connotation" typically assigned to the word. "Ideologies create and propagate a secondary reality which one either has to believe[6] in (totalitarian systems) or may believe in (democratic systems) … This new reality appears to be logically consistent and self-contained; and it is manifest in its very own language.[7] The indicators are to be found on all linguistic levels" (140). I will return below to Wodak's characterization of the language that manifests ideology, but first I examine her synonymizing "ideology" and "myth." Intuitively, "the ideology of human rights" seems semantically consistent, even if it might be objected to by people, such as AI staffers. In contrast, "the myth of human rights" does seem contradictory, perhaps because it seems to cast doubt on the existence of human rights, or at least to locate them in a realm quite far, far away from that of the "real world."

If we accept that "myth" and "ideology" are synonymous, then we must examine what "myth" brings to our understanding of the two. Frog (2018) examines the trajectory of "myth" and its meanings from classical Greek times to the present. "The very word *myth*," he writes, "is so deeply encoded with ideological and evaluative stances that these remain subliminal" (2; emphasis in original), noting specifically "the implicit 'othering' that has historically been built into the use of the word 'myth' and that continues to structure our thinking today" (2). However, "more nuanced approaches see modern myths as, for example, distinctively compelling narrative paradigms in relation to which people reflect on and construct their own identities and experiences" (3), which may also manifest as "image, location, entity, conception, or something else" (4). And "[m]ore or less all uses [of the word] hold that *myths are or were linked to socially established convictions*. Something is not usually called a myth unless it is connected to convictions about the world, how it works, or the agents and forces inhabiting it, whether in the present or in the past" (5; emphasis in original, footnote omitted).

Moreover, "*myths are never universal but always myths-of–* myths of a culture, religion, society, or group: *myths are always myths of some people as opposed to others*" (5; emphasis in original). "Myth" implicates an ideology of "us" versus "others": we possess true knowledge and understanding in contrast to others who have myths (5–6), and our knowledge, most especially scientific knowledge, is clear, while myths are "obscure" (7).

[5] In his discussion of French syndicalist calls for a general strike, Merriman (1996: 925–926), echoing George Sorel, similarly uses "myth" to characterize "a widely accepted belief capable of motivating action."

[6] Or at least act as if one believed.

[7] "Language" here is too broad; "register" seems more appropriate.

The "othering" indexing a mythic "us" vs. "them" applies most aptly to sectarian ideologies/myths, for example, the American National Socialist Party (ANSP) 25 Points distinguishes those who are of "pure White blood" from those who are not, most especially Jews. Human rights, in contrast, apply universally, to every human being, not just to those of groups definable in ways that demarcate them from the rest of humanity.

The "obscurity" associated with myth is also better applied to negative ideologies than to positive ones. The criterion for membership in the "nation" of American National Socialists is possession of "pure White blood," which, from the non-mythic perspective of modern science, is impossible to apply. "Pure White blood" defines the "race," which is also characterized as "Aryan" and "Nordic" (in the American Nazi Party document "What we stand for"), all of which are infamously "obscure" notions.

While we might reasonably consider beliefs in such obscure notions as "pure White blood" to be irrational, Hood (2009) argues that "[i]rrationality makes our beliefs rational because these beliefs hold society together," or at least hold groups such as the American National Socialists together. He adds that "[w]e see ourselves as part of a group, to be distinguished from other groups. This belief is cemented by our sense that our own group has hidden properties that are essentially different from the invisible properties of other groups" (253). Indeed, (professed) beliefs in irrational, unprovable, undisprovable propositions may be to be taken on faith as requirements for membership in certain types of groups – religious and political.[8] Because such beliefs are undecidable, they are subject to competing interpretations, which may be vehemently and violently held, leading to schisms in which each group regards the others as holding heretical beliefs, and often as less than fully human, as suggested by the US Nazi document's demand "that steps be taken to halt the spread of hereditary defects and racially impure blood within the gene pool of the racial community," and its characterization of certain others as "parasites."[9,10]

Beliefs, heretical or otherwise, are truth claims, and as Forst (2012) argues, we owe and are owed justifications for claims we make or are made against us.[11] However, Wason (1968), cited in Mercier and Sperber (2017: 211–218), proposed that we are biased toward evidence that supports our own positions,

8 See Márquez (2020) for discussion of the expression of unbelievable propositions in cult production.

9 See the following website for a brief recent history of American Neo-Nazi organizations: https://tinyurl.com/bpapjac7 (accessed August 1, 2025).

10 On various occasions, Donald Trump has characterized illegal immigrants to the US as "animals" (see https://tinyurl.com/mcswy55c [accessed August 1, 2025]) and "vermin" who are "poisoning the blood of our country" (see https://tinyurl.com/3pxrkv3w [accessed August 1, 2025]).

11 This echoes Spinoza's dictum (quoted in Pinker 2019: vii, 410): "Those who are governed by reason desire nothing for themselves which they do not also desire for the rest of humankind."

a "confirmation bias."[12] Mercier and Sperber argue for a "myside bias," by which they mean that we work systematically "to find reasons for our ideas and against reasons we oppose" (218). Moreover, our reasoning is "biased and lazy" in the production of arguments supporting our own positions, but "demanding and objective" in evaluating the arguments supporting others' positions (332). We should expect then that documents such as the AI appeals and ANSP 25 Points would provide justifications for their epistemic, deontic, and conative claims, and that the rigor of these justifications would correlate with the documents' intended audiences. As we have seen, the AI appeals frequently include evidential indicators and characteristically base their evaluations and directives on international laws, thus meeting Forst's requirement that claims be justified. However, as the appeals are designed to engage AI volunteers in continuing their AI activities and are elements in AI's efforts to garner funding, we should expect to find the AI positions to be minimally elaborated in the webpages and appeals and thus to depend upon their uncritical ("lazy"?) acceptance by AI members. This is in stark contrast with related AI reports, which are abundantly footnoted with information about their information sources, as we saw in Chapter 2. This contrast is due to the different purposes and audiences of the documents and so we should temper Mercier and Sperber's characterization of the production of myside arguments by noting that when circumstances demand it, we can adduce abundant and effective arguments in support of our positions. As I've noted, a few letters contain concessions to the positions of their Message Recipients. We might view the ease with which these are rebutted as a reflection of Mercier and Sperber's characterization of evaluations of others' arguments as "demanding and objective," though we might also wonder why AI, or anyone, would construct arguments supporting their opponents' positions unless they can be readily rebutted.

I return now to Wodak's discussion of the linguistic manifestation of ideology. She characterizes ideological language as "jargon," which she defines as "group languages with specific functions … of establishing group identity, of consolidating the group vis-à-vis the external world, of designating the group to outsiders, and, naturally, of communicating specific contents as well" (141). She enumerates some characteristics of ideological "jargons," a term that she wishes to use without its usual negative connotations. Jargons exhibit new lexical coinages, meaning extensions, euphemisms, syntactic "condensing and abbreviation," abbreviations, and characteristic argument strategies. These devices are designed to confer respect and authority upon their users, though the expressions may also become "slogans and catchwords" without "specific and precise content" (142). As examples of lexical jargon in a broadcast "Club-2" discussion (137), she cites

[12] On confirmation bias and related phenomena, see Gorman and Gorman (2021) and Kolbert (2017).

Daniel Cohn-Bendit's use of "fascistoid," and "ego-identity." She characterizes "need" as "such a vast concept that the listener will wonder what is really meant" in the context. And "projected" "effectively add[s] prestige" (157).

As later chapters of this book present an analysis of the language of AI appeal letters, I will deal fully with that language there. Here, I will merely say that some of the discourse characteristics Wodak ascribes to the political speech analyzed in her paper have resonances in the language of the AI documents, though others do not. Briefly, the documents, by invoking directly or indirectly the authority of international human rights laws, serve to confer group identity and authority on their writers and senders and to distinguish AI from groups associated with the Message Recipients. While it is not clear what criteria Wodak uses to determine when an expression has become a mere slogan or catchword and how specific and precise she expects a word's meaning to be, we might, giving her the benefit of our doubt, regard the frequently occurring generic expressions "human rights" and "violation of human rights" and their local variants as non-specific and imprecise, though their interpretation in context may be quite clear and specific, and many such expressions are more precise and contentful, for example, "the fundamental freedom of expression." It is perhaps noteworthy that the appeals use the full form, "Amnesty International," rather than the abbreviation, "AI." The reports and news releases abbreviate the official name to "Amnesty."

Menz (1989), following Wodak, conflates ideology and myth as "structures of faith" (234). These structures "guide a society or a group and, combined with political symbols … describe and justify their claims" (234). In the creation of new myths, language "becomes emotionally charged and patterns of identification are offered which replace common-sense and rational thinking" (234). To ideological language, Menz attributes strategies that include "*antithetic pronouns* (we/the others)," "*haziness* of central concepts," "*labelling* of polarized groups" (234; emphasis in original), "mythical groups" that serve to *legitimate* the ideologist's position, and the "emotionalization of facts" by "metaphors, clichés, stereotyping and especially the creation of handy *trivial myths* which serve as a frame for the emotionalization." The "trivial myths" include nature, mystic Christmas, and a new human being (237; emphasis in original).

We might consider the expression "human rights" and its variants to be political symbols; certainly, these expressions are deployed with political intent, and they invoke the power of authoritative international organizations to justify evaluations of actions and events and their redress. The AI documents also frequently deploy descriptions designed to appeal to the emotions of their readers; for example, in an appeal to the Salvadoran authorities to allow the abortion of an anencephalic fetus, we find, "Beatriz wants to live. She wants to see her one-year-old son grow up … she doesn't know if she will live or die …

she is suffering mental and physical anguish amounting to cruel and inhuman treatment" (#8 Beatriz, El Salvador).[13]

The AI documents also display "antithetical" pronouns, though these are not the first-person vs. third-person pronouns typically referenced by ideology scholars. In the appeal letters, the antagonists are first and second persons, "I" and "you," referring to the letter's SENDer and its Message Recipients, for example, "I am writing to you ..." The webpages and emails do use the typical antithetical *we/they*. I discussed the "haziness of the central concepts" above in my discussion of Wodak's claim that ideological expression may lack specificity and precision. However, while the concepts of human and humanitarian rights are typically invoked generically in the AI webpages, emails, and letters, they are specified in legally binding language in the universal laws and treaties and legal proceedings and decisions derived from them. Nonetheless, as with all language use, these documents are subject to varying interpretations, and thus to accusations of haziness.

While it is conceivable that some commentators critical of the concepts of human rights might regard them as "trivial myths," most commentators, regardless of their attitudes, would deem them and the groups that define and propagate them as substantial and important. Nor are the facts of appeal cases emotionalized by "metaphors, clichés, [and] stereotyping." Rather, the facts of cases tend to be characterized straightforwardly, for example, "[Beatriz] has been denied life savings [*sic*] treatment by doctors despite several requests to terminate her pregnancy in order to save her life. Three scans have confirmed that the fetus is anencephalic. Almost all babies with anencephaly die before birth or within a few hours or days after birth" (#8 Beatriz, El Salvador).

Eagleton (2007), in agreement with the scholars mentioned above and many others, argues that

> [i]deology is a matter of "discourse" rather than of "language" – of certain concrete discursive effects, rather than of signification as such. It represents the points where power impacts upon certain utterances and inscribes itself tacitly within them. But it is not therefore to be equated with just any form of discursive partisanship, "interested" speech or rhetorical bias; rather the concept of ideology aims to disclose something of the relation between an utterance and its material conditions of possibility, when those conditions of possibility are viewed in the light of certain power-struggles central to the reproduction (or also, for some theories, contestation) of a whole form of social life.[14] (223)

[13] The Inter-American Court of Human Rights ruled that El Salvador had violated Beatriz's human rights when it denied her an abortion. See https://tinyurl.com/4nkmfhwp (accessed August 1, 2025).

[14] Similarly, Blommaert (2005: 163) argues that "[i]deas operate alongside and inside material conditions and institutions; it is the conjunction of both dimensions which lifts particular sets of ideas to the level of ideology," and that "[i]deas themselves do not define ideologies; they need to be inserted in material practices of modulation and reproduction" (164).

While none of the words, syntactic constructions, semantic meanings, or pragmatic implications is unique to the AI documents, or indeed to human rights discourse in general, their uses in the letters are "inscribed" by power and by the desire and contestation for power. The primary "material conditions" that make the AI documents possible are those identified as "participants" in "the global process of authoritative decision": nation-states (e.g., El Salvador); international governmental organizations (e.g., the United Nations); non-governmental organizations (e.g., Amnesty International and Human Rights Watch); and individual human beings (Chen 2015: 23–97). To these we can add states and provinces within nation-states (e.g., the US state of Louisiana); unions of states (e.g., the European Union); governments and government functionaries (e.g., Presidents, Governors, Attorneys General, Prosecutors General, etc.); inter-government agreements (e.g., UN Universal Declaration of Human Rights; the Geneva and Hague Conventions); individual members of NGOs (e.g., AI volunteers); news media; social media; and (electronic) mail.

Eagleton argues that "[t]he force of the term ideology lies in its capacity to discriminate between those power struggles which are somehow central to a whole form of social life, and those which are not" (8). One might argue, for example, that slowing, stopping, and reversing the existential threat of global warming is "more central to a whole form of life" than working to redress injustices. However one ranks such challenges, one might well argue that redressing human rights violations is worthy of the struggle it requires. The struggles represented by the AI documents are those between a non-governmental organization representing individuals and classes of individuals whose human and/or humanitarian rights have been violated and governments and government officials deemed by AI to be responsible for those violations and with the power to redress the injuries. By invoking universal values, AI positions human rights as central to its conception of social and political life and contrasts them with local, though widespread and persistent, deviations that it aims to bring into compliance with those values.

Additionally, Eagleton (16) argues that "[t]o say that the statement is ideological is then to claim that it is powered by an ulterior motive bound up with the legitimation of certain interests in a power struggle." The "motive" powering AI and similar organizations that are engaged in a struggle with powerful government agents is the desire to persuade those agents and the governments and institutions they represent to accept and abide by the norms codified in the UN UHDR and various other human/humanitarian rights treaties and conventions, that is, to accept that these treaties apply universally and supersede local laws that conflict with them. Human rights proponents might be expected to reject the negative connotations associated with "ulterior," while critics might suggest more trenchant attributes.

Because neither AI nor its volunteers can "coerce" their document addressees to comply, they must rely on "the construction of meaning," whose main element is the invocation of universal norms to evaluate the violative situation and legitimate the appeals for redress, while indicating (by the numbers of appeals sent by volunteers and webpage readers) that the evaluation and appeal represent a large group of people, a "cyber community" (Featherman 2015: 37), but also an international discourse community that can be mobilized on behalf of human rights, while also engaging and unifying community members.

In the AI documents, the power of this ideological community licenses the use of strong conative and deontic expressions, for example, *must (not)*, *should (not)*, *it is essential*, while the asymmetry of power between the producers and recipients of these documents encourages the use of mitigated directive speech act verbs, for example, *ask*, *call on*, *urge*, rather than, for example, *demand*, which can be prescribed by the AI email writers to their volunteer addressees. This difference is particularly noticeable when the appeal letters are contrasted with the emails they are embedded in.

Eagleton addresses three important themes in discussions of ideology relevant to human rights discourses and specifically to AI's discourses. First, the "false consciousness" hypothesis: ideologies are misleading ideas deployed by powerful interests to co-opt less powerful sectors of their societies by disguising their exploitation. Second is the related hypothesis that ideologies are designed to "legitimate a dominant political power" (Eagleton 2007: 1). Third is the claim that ideology is dead (Bell 1988 [1960]).

Eagleton (2007: 14–27) offers several arguments against equating ideology with false consciousness. First, "ideology is no baseless illusion but a solid reality, an active material force which must have at least enough cognitive content to help organize the practical lives of human beings" (26). Second, while some ideological propositions may be false, "[i]t is quite possible for a ruling order to make pronouncements which are ideological in the sense of buttressing its own power, but which are in no sense false. And if we extend the term ideology to include oppositional political movements, the radicals at least would want to uphold that many of their utterances, while ideological in the sense of promoting their power-interests, are nonetheless true" (26). Third, not all "commitment[s] to the dominant social order" are delusional. It is possible to live "by false values but [be] ironically aware of doing so," without being "mystified in the traditional sense of the term" (27). Fourth, "[i]deological statements may be true to society as at present constituted, but false in so far as they thereby serve to block off the possibility of a transformed state of affairs" (27). He adds that

> [i]f ideology is sometimes falsifying, then, it is for what are on the whole rather hopeful reasons: the fact that most people react strongly to being unjustly treated, and that most people would like to believe that they live in reasonably just social conditions …

> If, then, ideology sometimes involves distortion and mystification, it is less because of something inherent in ideological language than because of something inherent in the social structure to which that language belongs. There are certain kinds of interests which can secure their sway only by practicing duplicity; but this is not to claim … that *all* of the statements used to promote those interests will be duplicitous. (27–28; emphasis in original)

He concludes that "[i]deology … is not inherently constituted by distortion, especially if we take the broader view of the concept as denoting any fairly central conjunction between discourse and power. In an entirely just society, there would be no need for ideology in the pejorative sense since there would be nothing to explain away" (28). While it is certainly false that the ideals represented by the UDHR and related documents reflect the world as it currently is, it is just as certainly true that those ideals express strongly desired states, as reflected in the choice of emphatic directive expressions. However, as I argued above, and *contra* Eagleton here, it is not at all clear that an entirely just society is possible, but it is absolutely clear that societies that are just during one period in their history may re-establish or re-invent injustices during another. So, while ideologies of human rights may be granted occasional sabbaticals, they must always be available for re-deployment when the needs arise.

And given that human and humanitarian rights are enacted and coded by authoritative international institutions, one might reasonably ask whether they can form the basis of an oppositional ideology rather than that of a "dominant political power." One element of the answer is that because these rights are invoked by AI (and many other similar organizations) in situations in which AI and its members are not the more powerful actors, they undergird a counterpower that invokes universal rights in opposition to whatever other ideologies or interests underlie the actions of the locally powerful that result in the situation the letters typically characterize as "violations" of those rights.

Even if we accept Eagleton's (and many others') rejection of the "false consciousness" conception of ideology, we must still demonstrate that the discourses of human/humanitarian rights are ideological, and, specifically, that the AI appeals are ideological, especially as the AI Letter Writing Guide implicates that they are not. We are licensed to consider these discourses as ideological because they exhibit the characteristics of ideologies identified in Eagleton (2007), which summarizes the characteristics of ideologies identified by him and other scholars: "[i]deologies are often thought … to be *unifying*, *action-oriented*, *rationalizing*, *legitimating*, *universalizing* and *naturalizing*" (45; emphasis in original), though he also asserts that "it is doubtful that one can ascribe to ideology any *invariable* characteristics at all" (222; emphasis in original).

Moreover, because an influential current in Western thought claims that ideology is dead, and AI appears not to regard human or humanitarian rights or the legal frameworks that codify them as ideological, it is necessary for me to demonstrate that AI does in fact operate from an ideological position. My demonstration is based on the characteristics and functions of ideologies presented in Eagleton (2007), richer and more finely articulated conceptualizations of ideology than Verschueren's (though quite consistent with them), and those that I will have occasion to refer to below. Eagleton (2007: ch. 2) lists the following ideological functions.

Promoting the Interests of a Group

AI explicitly claims to "campaign for a world where human rights are enjoyed by all"[15] on behalf of Prisoners of Conscience (PoCs), but more generally on behalf of all people everywhere, as long as they do not advocate hatred or violence. In an ideal world, human rights would be observed everywhere and there would be no need for organizations like AI or for their activities. However, though we might wish otherwise, there are now, and there probably will be forever, groups whose interests lead them to violate the rights of others, in contravention of universal statutes and of the interests of the groups represented by AI.

Unifying

"Ideologies are often thought to lend coherence to the groups or classes which hold them, welding them into a unitary, if internally differentiated identity, and perhaps thereby allowing them to impose a certain unity upon society as a whole … How unified ideologies actually are, however, is a matter of debate"[16] (Eagleton 2007: 45) and "oppositional ideologies often seek to unify a diverse array of political forces" (61).

AI's websites claim that it is a movement of over 10 million people who campaign to end human rights abuses. This implicates that these people are unified by virtue of their collective campaign to end human rights abuses. While it would be overly optimistic to assume that all 10 million actively campaign or that they all understand human rights in the same way – remember Hodge and Kress' S-form – AI offers coherent and consistent[17] positions on human rights that are at least tacitly agreed to by its membership. The AI documents enact a unified and unifying stance on *human* and *humanitarian rights*, manifested in frequent mentions of those rights, as well as notions such as

[15] www.amnesty.org/en/ (accessed August 1, 2025).

[16] Van Dijk (2013) argues that while ideologies are shared by social groups and are thus sociocognitive representational systems, they allow for group and personal variability.

[17] AI's consistency has been called into question on occasion, e.g., for its decision not to designate Julian Assange a PoC. For a critical view, see https://tinyurl.com/yc2ttahm (accessed August 1, 2025). For AI's position, see https://tinyurl.com/4t5bw3md (accessed August 1, 2025).

international standards of judicial proceedings derived from them. The first-person pronouns of the appeal letters refer to all the people who SEND them, or even just receive them from AI, thus creating a community brought together by a commitment to AI's actions on behalf of human rights.

Action-Orienting

"However abstrusely metaphysical the ideas in question may be, they must be translatable by the ideological discourse into a 'practical' state, capable of furnishing their adherents with goals, motivations, prescriptions, imperatives and so on" (Eagleton 2007: 47) and "oppositional ideologies … are geared to effective action" (61). Sypnowich (2024: 2), discussing liberal concepts of ideology, echoes Daniel Bell's characterization of ideology as "an action-oriented system of beliefs." De Gaay Fortman (2011: 1) characterizes human rights as "highly action oriented in general."

AI is certainly action-oriented and we may view its staffers and volunteers as a community of practice (Wenger 1998). Its website proclaims that "We campaign for a world where human rights are enjoyed by all." And "We work to protect people wherever justice, truth, freedom, and dignity is denied."[18] Note the action-denoting words "campaign," "movement," "fighting," and "promoting." The documents perform at least four actions: (1) motivating (and unifying) volunteers; (2) maintaining volunteers' commitment; (3) persuading addressees to act as the letters prescribe; and (4) participating in AI's fundraising campaigns prompted by the automatically emailed requests for donations described in Chapter 2.

Consistent with AI's proclamations of action, the AI genres – appeals, emails, webpages, and reports – are produced to persuade their addressees by appeal and protest to redress (potential) violations of human/humanitarian rights. These appeals and protests are enacted in the appeal letters by directive expressions and by imperatives in Subject lines: *Release Prisoners of Conscience* (#26 PoCs, Vietnam).

Rationalizing

"[I]deologies can be seen as more or less systematic attempts to provide plausible explanations and justifications for social behavior which might otherwise be the object of criticism" (Eagleton 2007: 52). AI genres rationalize their evaluations and directives by arguing from the legal premises articulated in universal declarations and covenants. Though Eagleton notes that *rationalizing*

[18] www.amnestyusa.org (accessed August 1, 2025).

connotes attempts "to defend the indefensible," he acknowledges that "[n]ot all ideological discourse need be of this kind" (51).

The AI letters provide "explanations and justifications" for their appeals. These are typically criticisms of the actions of governments or of individual government functionaries that are derived from international laws and their associated procedural norms. For example, "I am deeply concerned that [*sic*] US government's so-called 'targeted killing' program allows for the use of lethal force, including with drones, that violates the right to life under international law" (#1 Targeted Killings, USA). Complementarily, the AI letters prescribe actions that are claimed to be consistent with international laws and procedures, for example:

> I write to urge the United States Government to support and champion the highest possible human rights standards within a new Arms Trade Treaty, including ensuring that arms transfers shall not be permitted where there is a substantial risk the arms are likely to be used to commit or facilitate serious violations of international human rights law or international humanitarian law, and ensuring that a broad scope of weapons, all types of arms transfers as well as ammunition are included in the scope of the treaty.
>
> (#2 Arms Trade, USA)

Legitimating

"Legitimation can simply mean establishing one's interests as broadly acceptable" and "rationalization is closely allied to … *legitimation*" (Eagleton 2007: 54; emphasis in original).

We can approach legitimating as deriving from institutional or from more general discourse processes. Van Dijk (1998: 256, cited in Mackay 2013: 352–353) limits legitimation to "institutional language," and distinguishes legitimation from "everyday informal talk," which he characterizes as "justifications, explanations, or accounts." While the AI genres typically invoke universal legal instruments to legitimate their evaluations, they also include appeals to pathos and therefore present a broader basis for their positions. Carston (2002: 241) argues that the quest for a cause, for a reason why, plays "a fundamental role in our mental lives." This very general cognitive bias may be understood to underlie what Forst (2016) calls "the right to justification," on which he bases his "constructivist" theory of morality. The right to justification is reciprocal and general. "*Reciprocity* means that no one may make demands that he or she denies to others and no one may impose his or her non-generalizable views, interests or values on others. *Generality* means that all those for whom norms claim to be valid have to be equally involved" (14; emphasis in original).

In addition to its invocations of legal instruments and court decisions, AI legitimates its actions more broadly by appeal to values assumed to be generally accepted, including fairness and empathy, as attested by the frequent occurrence of *(un)fair(ness)* and their colligation and collocation with *trial(s)*, and by such appeals to pathos as petitions for medical attention for prisoners and ubiquitous expressions of *concern*.

Eagleton (2007: 5–6) briefly discusses several other legitimating activities that (dominant) groups may engage in. They may promote beliefs and values congenial to themselves: AI explicitly claims to be "demanding human rights," for everyone, including its own activists, who are not infrequently targets of oppression.[19] Groups may obscure social realities and AI has been criticized for ignoring the negotiating realities that preceded the ratification of the UN UDHR, and its characterization as a Western imperialist and neo-colonial enterprise (e.g., Bartholomew and Breakspear 2004; Devlin 2012; Mutua 1996). However, AI does not obscure the social realities that it evaluates as violations of human rights, though occasionally its evaluations may be mistaken. Groups may also mask social conflicts, though while AI may mask the conflicts involved in its own internal divisions and in the development, ratification, and promulgation of human and humanitarian rights, it certainly does not mask the conflicts generated by its evaluations of situations as violating those rights. Groups may also denigrate ideas that challenge them and may exclude alternative ideas and ideologies. Generally, AI reports, webpages, emails, and appeals do not debate alternatives to human rights, though the appeals occasionally make rhetorical concessions, immediately rebutted, to the authorities in appeal situations by attributing to them alternative evaluations of those situations.

Universalizing

"Values and interests which are in fact specific to a certain place and time are projected as the values and interests of all humanity" (Eagleton 2007: 56). AI invokes rights that are deemed universal; they are "enshrined" (AI's word, remarkable for its religious connotations) in the *Universal* Declaration of Human Rights. AI is explicitly committed to universalizing the values undergirding human and humanitarian rights: "Amnesty *International* is a *global* movement of more than 10 million people"[20] (emphasis added). However, the fact that AI and many similar organizations exist and are kept intensely active demonstrates that universal observation of these rights has yet to be achieved.

Naturalizing

"Successful ideologies are often thought to render their beliefs natural and self-evident – to identify them with the 'common sense' of a society so that nobody

19 www.amnestyusa.org/about-us (accessed August 1, 2025).
20 https://tinyurl.com/ykvzyskk (accessed August 1, 2025).

could imagine how they might ever be different" (Eagleton 2007: 58). Echoing this, Verschueren (2012: 10) characterizes ideology as "felt to be commonsensical." AI genres naturalize their stances and directives by presenting human and humanitarian rights as uncontroversial and by presenting cases and rebuttals of positions attributed to opponents as decided and irrefutable.

Propositions or assumptions can be naturalized by presenting them as uncontroversial and accepted by both authors and audiences. For example, AI's assertion that it campaigns for the release of PoCs presents as taken-for-granted that people who meet the definition should not be jailed:

> Amnesty International defines a prisoner of conscience as someone who is imprisoned or otherwise physically restricted (like house arrest) solely because of their political, religious or other conscientiously held beliefs, ethnic origin, sex, color, language, national or social origin, economic status, birth, sexual orientation or other status –who has not used violence or advocated violence or hatred in the circumstances leading to their imprisonment, Amnesty calls for the immediate and unconditional release of all prisoners of conscience.[21]

This definition presents AI's campaigns for the release of PoCs as if no justification for their release were required.

AI letters take for granted that characterizing an action or situation as a violation of human rights is sufficient warrant for its evaluation and redress: "I call on you to quash Raif Badawi's flogging sentence immediately, as it is a flagrant violation of the prohibition on torture or other cruel, inhuman or degrading treatment under international law" (#18 Badawi, Saudi Arabia). Here, too, the bold, indeed boosted, assertion that Badawi's, and presumably anyone's, flogging violates international law is presented without supporting justification, thus presenting the claim as "commonsensical."

AI appeal letters typically invoke "human rights," or "international standards," or "the prohibition against torture" as if there were no controversies about them. Even when they make concessions to the addressees' situations, the letters rebut those concessions by again invoking "human rights" and related concepts and instruments in ways that imply that the rebuttal is natural, irrefutable, and closed. AI always wins the arguments in their letters by presenting as natural that international laws and court rulings "trump" national ones. The letter excerpt below represents the Inter-American Court of Human Rights as ordering the Salvadoran government without any hedging that might suggest that this directive might be open to argument.

> Beatriz wants to live. … Please grant her immediate access to the life-saving medical treatment she needs and wants, and which the Salvadoran government has been ordered to provide her with by the Inter-American Court of Human Rights.
>
> (#8 Beatriz, El Salvador)

[21] www.amnestyusa.org/issues/individuals-at-risk/ (accessed August 1, 2025).

Various linguistic devices serve to naturalize, notably presuppositions, which I discuss in greater detail later in this work.

However, the very fact that AI's documents present justificatory arguments for the redress they call for indicates that people can very readily "imagine how [things] might ever be different" (Eagleton 2007: 58) and implies that human rights is not (yet) a dominant ideology.

Normative

"Human rights are norms that aspire to protect all people everywhere from severe political, legal, and social abuses" (Nickel and Etinson 2024). AI appeals are typically based on legal instruments, which I take to be at least aspirationally normative (Atiq et al. 2025), as are the language of rights, their legal bases, and their violations.

The functions of ideologies discussed above demonstrate that AI, its staffers, volunteers, and like-minded people who access its websites are engaged in an ideological enterprise. We can therefore accept that the discourse genres created by AI are ideological instruments in that enterprise.

Verschueren (2012: ch. 2) Language Use and Ideology

I have elected to organize this book according to Verschueren's "[t]heses, rules, guidelines, procedures, and caveats" synopsized in his Appendix 1: 200–204. He devotes his chapter 2, "Language use and ideology," to a discussion of ideology. He articulates his conception of the study of ideological discourses in a set of theses, which are generally consistent with the major themes of the authors discussed above. His first thesis provides his general understanding of ideology and subsequent ones develop its individual themes.

> ***Thesis 1: We can define as ideological any basic pattern of meaning or frame of interpretation bearing on or involved in (an) aspect(s) of social "reality" (in particular in the realm of social relations in the public sphere), felt to be commonsensical, and often functioning in a normative way.***[22] ***(Verschueren 2012: 10)***

I take the "frame of interpretation" relevant to the AI letters as the discourse of human/humanitarian rights, their violations, and appeals and protests against those violations. The relevant human and humanitarian rights have been codified in conventions and declarations, for example, The Hague and

[22] Verschueren's definition of ideology is very general, intended, I presume, to accommodate a broad range of discourse ideological manifestations. It is not specific enough for the analysis of the AI data and must be augmented by more specific conceptions, such as those developed in Eagleton (2007) to account most especially for the multi-functionality of the appeal letters.

Geneva Conventions,[23] the Universal Declaration of Human Rights, and the International Covenant on Civil and Political Rights,[24] enacted by various international bodies (e.g., the United Nations), and signed on to by most nations of the world, thus creating a "social 'reality'" and defining "social relations in a public sphere." Because these conventions have the force of law, they are by definition "normative." Hence, rights and their violations are also normatively interpreted. The AI documents treat these rights as universal, uncontroversial, and commonsensical.

Verschueren presents several more theses and subtheses that expand upon his basic definition of ideology. Thesis 1.1 expands on the commonsensical and normative aspects of ideology.

> ***Thesis 1.1: The common-sense (basic/normative) nature of ideological meaning is manifested in the fact that it is rarely questioned, in a given society or community, in discourse related to the "reality" in question, possibly across various discourse genres. (Verschueren 2012: 12)***

The AI letters treat human and humanitarian rights as unquestioned, and there is no indication of questioning these rights in the emails in which the letters are embedded. Nor am I aware of any discourse critical of human/humanitarian rights per se by the leaders of AI. However, the major rights documents are the products of many years of development, discussion, and negotiation among the states represented in the UN and other fora, and there certainly are critics of the concept of universal human rights, for example, Devlin (2012) and Mutua (1996), as well as defenders, for example, Chen (2015), Forst (2012), Neier (2012), Pinker (2019), and Sikkink (2017), to mention just a very few.

Though the AI genres generally present human rights and the evaluations based on them as commonsensical, nonetheless, as I have mentioned, the AI letters do occasionally include (apparent) concessions to the addressees:

> I understand that your government has as an obligation to bring those responsible for serious crimes to justice, and that Iraq must confront violence by armed group [*sic*].
>
> (#4 Al-Qahtani, Iraq)

The letter in which this paragraph occurs is an appeal to the Iraqi authorities to reverse the death sentences on two men. This paragraph and the one that precedes it concede that the authorities have legitimate interests in the case, but these concessions are rebutted by appeal to universal values and standards of legal procedure. None of the concessions mooted and rebutted in the AI letters calls for a re-examination of the human rights ideology.

[23] http://avalon.law.yale.edu/subject_menus/lawwar.asp (accessed August 1, 2025).

[24] https://treaties.un.org/doc/treaties/1976/03/19760323%2006-17%20am/ch_iv_04.pdf (accessed August 1, 2025).

Thesis 1.1.1 addresses the issue of whether ideologies are hegemonic. Verschueren argues that ideologies may but need not be hegemonic, and that the idea of hegemony is relevant more to how ideologies get established in societies and their effects rather than to the ideas themselves. However, hegemony affects how ideological ideas get expressed (13).

> ***Thesis 1.1.1: The wider the society or community, and the wider the range of discourse genres in which a given pattern of meaning or frame of interpretation escapes questioning, the more "hegemonic" it may be*. (Verschueren 2012: 13)**

The society or community relevant to the issue at hand is a global one, consisting of countries/states, multi-state organizations, and non-governmental organizations, as well as large numbers of individual people.

The "range of [relevant] discourse genres" includes the appeal letters, the emails in which they come embedded, AI webpages, AI press releases, and the reports that AI publishes about particular cases, for example, *USA: 100 Years in Solitary: The "Angola 3" and their Fight for Justice*,[25, 26] as well as the human and humanitarian rights treaties, conventions, and protocols. These documents, though for different audiences and purposes, are consistent in not questioning the ideology of human rights.

However, to claim that human rights are "hegemonic" on Verschueren's interpretation, "the internalization of the authority one may be subjected to" (12), would be to accord it far more power than it actually has. Human rights are always in competition with other ideologies, for example, religion-derived prohibitions on abortion, as in the case of Beatriz (#8 Beatriz, El Salvador) mentioned above. Institutions tasked with policing human rights violations (e.g., the International Criminal Court), though growing stronger and more effective, have very limited power to enforce these rights. Consequently, organizations like AI attempt to influence governments by the weight of public opinion, indicated by the number of appeal letters sent by volunteers. Nonetheless, as I mentioned above, within AI, and certainly in the appeal letters, there is little if any questioning of the human rights ideology, though AI personnel argue about how the organization's International Statute and human rights documents should be interpreted in specific (classes of) cases.

Thesis 1.2 characterizes how ideological meanings are typically expressed.

> ***Thesis 1.2: Its not being questioned means that the meaning concerned is often (though not always and not exclusively) carried along implicitly rather than being formulated explicitly*. (Verschueren 2012: 13)**

[25] www.amnesty.org/en/documents/amr51/041/2011/en/ (accessed August 1, 2025).

[26] AI reports are available at www.amnestyusa.org/tools-and-reports/reports/ (accessed August 1, 2025).

While human and humanitarian rights are extensively codified in laws, covenants, and treaties, references to these rights in AI letters tend to be generic rather than explicit, expressed by common noun phrases (NPs) (e.g., "human rights"), which are often definite (e.g., "the right to life"), rather than by proper NPs (e.g., "The United Nations Declaration of Human Rights, Article 23"). While this pattern may reflect the assumption that these rights are "commonsensical" and so can be referred to generically, it seems also to reflect the group-unifying and action-orienting roles of the webpages, emails, and appeal letters, for which the allusive references are sufficient, whereas more specific references might elicit, among the AI volunteers, disagreement with specific articles or a sense of alienation from a legalistic AI staff and culture. The letters, after all, are not legal briefs. I will have more to say about these linguistic patterns later in this work.

Thesis 2 claims that because ideological ideas tend to be implicitly expressed, they tend also to be unquestioned even in the face of contradictory evidence.

> ***Thesis 2: Ideology, because of its normative and common-sense nature, may be highly immune to experience and observation. (Verschueren 2012: 14)***

Perhaps within AI, and probably within the larger community of human rights supporters and especially among human rights activists, the human rights ideology might be "highly immune to experience and observation." Nonetheless, while AI staffers and volunteers are unlikely to regard AI's discourses of human rights as ideological, they would certainly regard human rights as legally, if broadly, defined and thus normative and commonsensical, but also as readily available for observation, discussion, and argument, as histories of AI demonstrate.

The categorical, normative, evaluative language of "rights" and their "violations" and the directive language, *urge*, *call on*, *must*, etc., suggests that human rights are accepted by members of the human rights community, their default assumption being that these rights should be but are not everywhere observed. Current arguments against universal human rights (e.g., Devlin 2012; Mutua 1996) are not, so far as I can tell, generally engaged within that community. However, having said that, "[s]ome NGOs such as Amnesty International, are able to successfully employ a dual strategy, working directly with the U.N. system while maintaining an independence that allows public criticism of U.N. shortcomings and failures" (Chen 2015: 83, footnote omitted). AI and other NGOs "exert influence on the whole range of decision functions (intelligence, promoting, prescribing, invoking, applying, terminating, and appraising)" (Chen 2015: 80). At this level of discussion and decision making, it must be assumed that AI representatives cannot avoid engaging with fundamental as well as specific critiques of human rights as universal values, which are therefore not "immune to experience and observation." Recall my discussion in Chapter 2 of some conceptions of rights and human rights and how they came to be.

The linguistic representations of human rights in the AI webpages, emails, and letters suggest that the human rights perspective is generally taken for granted, though, as I mentioned, occasionally the letters appear to concede the importance of other social goods such as combating armed violence within a state. Other arguments such as the necessity of political stability, self-defense, and such essentials as food and water might also be proposed as reasons for setting aside human rights. Verschueren (2012: 14) points out the stark contradiction between the claimed pacific and civilizing intentions of colonization and the violence with which it is achieved and maintained in the history textbooks he examines, a contradiction apparently unobserved by the books' authors.[27] I have not found any contradictions in the appeal letters between their overtly stated values and goals and negative effects deriving from their realization.

Thesis 2.1 addresses the possibility of contradictions between what is implicitly rather than explicitly communicated in ideological discourses.

> ***Thesis 2.1: Just as there may be a discrepancy between ideology and direct experience, there may be discrepancies between the level of implicit meaning and what one would be willing to say explicitly. (Verschueren 2012: 16)***

The ideologies of human rights are explicitly stated in various legal and widely circulated documents and are criticized and defended in academic and other publications, but they are taken for granted by AI staffers, who typically refer generically to "human rights," and who use references to these rights as the basis for evaluating situations, events, and policies, as well as to counter ideological, legal, and pragmatic positions attributed in the genres to powerful government and other officials, as in the Al-Qahtani letter (#4 Al-Qahtani, Iraq) quoted above. It is notable, however, that responsibility for the appeal situation is rarely directly or explicitly attributed to the individuals to whom the appeals are addressed. As I discuss later, this reticence may be due to a desire to be polite and thus to avoid threats to the addressees' positive face (Brown and Levinson 1987) and to avoid giving the addressees yet another reason for rejecting the appeals – AI's Letter Writing Guide directs letter writers to be

[27] While Verschueren's authors may not have acknowledged conflicting views on colonialism in their textbooks, they cannot have been oblivious to contemporary competing discourses on colonialism (see Kohn and Reddy 2024). Current ideological conflict over textbook content thrives, as Agarwal (2019) shows in a report on social studies textbook revisions by the Texas Board of Education, and as demonstrated by almost daily reports of book bans in US libraries and schools as reported in https://pen.org/book-bans/ (accessed August 1, 2025).

polite, noting that "[g]overnments don't respond to abusive or condemnatory letters (however well deserved)."[28] It would appear, therefore, that whether ideological ideas and evaluations are expressed implicitly or explicitly depends on who is expressing what, to whom, and in what circumstances.

Thesis 3 asserts that the fundamental assumption in modern ideological studies is that ideologies are matters of language use rather than of language per se.

> ***Thesis 3: (One of) the most visible manifestation(s) of ideology is LANGUAGE USE or DISCOURSE, which may reflect, construct, and/or maintain ideological patterns. (Verschueren 2012: 17; capitalization in original)***

None of the linguistic elements in the AI genres is unique in themselves or to those genres. These elements do, however, display distinctive patterns of use in the genres, which is, as Thesis 3 asserts, a matter of discourse. These genres are elements in the oppositional legal and political discourse of human and humanitarian rights. By invoking the human/humanitarian rights frames of interpretation and evaluation, they reflect the ideology of human rights, which has been under construction over at least two centuries, and which they maintain by unifying AI members, motivating them to action, and legitimating their stances. Because states have considerable power over the media within their jurisdictions and thus over the means of persuasion, organizations like AI are forced to adopt collective oppositional practices, with the result that AI webpages, emails, and appeal letters often share linguistic characteristics with such quintessentially oppositional practices as street protests. The subject line of the letters is frequently expressed as an imperative, for example, "Stop US Government's Targeted Killings" (#1 Targeted Killings, USA), as are protest signs such as "Bring the Troops Home Now," and "Stop Job Discrimination."

Thesis 4 articulates the functions of ideological discourse in terms very similar to Eagleton's, perhaps unsurprisingly given Verschueren's multiple references to Eagleton's books.

> ***Thesis 4: Discursively reflected, constructed, and/or supported ideological meanings may serve the purposes of framing, validating, explaining, or legitimating attitudes, states of affairs, and actions in the domains to which they are applicable. (Verschueren 2012: 19)***

The AI genres frame the states of affairs with which they deal as violations of human or humanitarian rights. They validate, explain, and legitimate their evaluations of those states of affairs by reference to those rights, for example, "Raif Badawi's flogging sentence … is a flagrant violation of the prohibition on torture or other cruel, inhuman or degrading treatment under international law"

[28] https://aiusaoc.org/common/letter_writing_guide.html (accessed August 1, 2025).

(#18 Badawi, Saudi Arabia). They also frame and legitimate the redressive actions they propose by reference to human rights, on occasion by reference to specific rights, for example, "I call on you to stop arresting, charging, prosecuting and sentencing activists for simply exercising their rights to freedom of expression, association and assembly" (#18 Badawi, Saudi Arabia). Note, though, that the source of these rights is not mentioned, as is generally, though not always, the case in the letters.

Given the trajectory of the understandings of ideology outlined above – from the assumption that they are necessarily injurious to the conclusion that they may also be neutral or beneficial – it is surprising that the critical discourse studies of ideologies still take as their objects of study discourses that their authors find objectionable, including Verschueren's (2012) analysis of colonialist discourse in British and French history textbooks, and others that I mention in Chapter 1.

However, the study of a subset of discourses chosen for critical analysis cannot in principle allow us to derive universal characteristics of ideological discourse. For example, not all ideological discourses seek to hide their participants' racist, colonialist, sexist, anti-Semitic, or Islamophobic beliefs. Some such discourses are overt and explicit in articulating their ideologies, as can be seen, for example, on such current white supremacist websites as that of the American National Socialist Movement.[29]

Verschueren (2012: 21) remarks that "[i]n actual research practice, most discourse-based studies of ideological processes start from *basic intuitions* that are not unrelated to the researcher's *involvement*."[30] This book is the result of the convergence of two of my interests – in pragmatics/discourse analysis and human rights activism. These two interests have led me to believe that ideological discourses are not necessarily nefarious, as is often claimed. I believe that a world in which human and humanitarian rights are observed is better than one in which they are abused. Consequently, I believe that human rights activism and the ideologies that motivate it are essential oppositional elements in reducing the abusive behavior of state and non-state actors. However, I do not believe that all oppositional ideologies have positive effects, as the current racist and white-supremacist activities of alt-right groups demonstrate.

To his remarks about researchers' involvements, Verschueren adds their "sense that 'something is wrong.'" While I did not feel that something was wrong with the letters, or with AI's other genres, I was puzzled initially by the close relationship between sending the appeal and the immediate receipt of a

[29] www.nsm88.org/ (accessed September 7, 2025).

[30] Emphasis in original. The Epilogue in Blommaert and Verschueren (1998) also addresses issues related to authors' involvement in scientific research.

donation request, and later by being unable to discover where my appeal went after I had clicked SEND, despite several phone calls to AI USA.

More generally, it behooves all of us to examine critically those local and global political and ideological discourses in which we are involved, regardless of our political preferences or activism, so that we may contribute to "*an ecology of the public sphere*" (Verschueren 2012: 197; emphasis in original).

Conclusion

This chapter reviewed several influential understandings of ideology and concluded with discussion of Verschueren's Theses 1–4, which articulate his characterization of ideology, its manifestation in discourse, and its roles in discourse. These theses, along with the attributes identified in Eagleton (2007), provide the bases for the arguments that the AI appeals and related documents are indeed ideologically suffused.

4 Pragmatic Guidelines and Procedures

Data, Context, and Lines of Vision

In his chapter 3, "Pragmatic guidelines and procedures," Verschueren (2012: 51–193) lays out his "theses," "rules," and "methods" for the study of ideology in discourse. The goal of these "general 'guidelines' and practical 'procedures'" and "caveats" is "*a package of methods grounded in a clear methodological perspective inspired by a general theory of linguistic pragmatics, viewed as the interdisciplinary science of language use*" (51; emphasis in original), which will "*provide sufficient grounds for interpretation*" (51; emphasis in original). These methods provide "the building blocks of an overall act of interpretation" (51).

Verschueren leads off with "[a] brief summary of the core elements of the theory of pragmatics that underlies [his] approach" to the study of discourse and refers readers to his 1999 book for additional information. Very briefly: language use generates meaning; language use consists of making linguistic and contextual choices that are relevant to both production and interpretation, which may be more or less automatic and more or less marked; choices always contrastively evoke their alternatives and always involve the metapragmatic and monitoring functions of human cognition; choices are negotiated adaptably on the basis of "highly flexible principles and strategies" from an unstable range of linguistic and contextual variables.

These assumptions imply "four research angles": "[c]ontextual correlates of adaptability have to be identified; processes have to be situated with reference to different structural objects of adaptability; the dynamics of adaptability must be accounted for; and we must keep in mind the salience of the adaptation processes, that is, their status in relation to a human cognitive apparatus" (51–52). These abstract desiderata are rendered practicable by the caveats, guidelines, and procedures presented in the remainder of this chapter.

Verschueren prefaces his guidelines and procedures with the following two "Preliminary Caveats":

> ***Preliminary Caveat 1: The following guidelines and procedures may be followed step-by-step. However, actual research will develop cyclically rather than linearly. Some steps cannot be completed without going on***

> ***to further steps, while sometimes a new step will force you to go back to earlier ones. Therefore: Get to know the entire set of guidelines and procedures before beginning to apply them.*** ***(Verschueren 2012: 53)***

The core of this Caveat is that data analysis relevant to one guideline often requires data analysis relevant to others, and hence my reading and re-reading of Verschueren's text while constantly referring to my data. Verschueren gathers all of his methodological precepts into an easily consulted list in his Appendix 1 (200–204).

> ***Preliminary Caveat 2: The following guidelines and procedures only serve the purpose of analyzing collected language use data in view of their relationship with ideological patterns and processes. A complete research project may have to involve other, in particular ethnographic, stages preceding or coinciding with the analysis stage.*** ***(Verschueren 2012: 53)***

I discussed in Chapter 3 various understandings of ideology from which I derived the ones I use in this project (Eagleton 2007; Featherman 2015; Hodge and Kress 1993; McLellan 1995; Menz 1989; Morris 2010; van Dijk 1998; Verschueren 2012; Wodak 1989). I also briefly discussed human and humanitarian rights (Forst 2012), the history of the development of treaties, declarations, and covenants on human and humanitarian rights (Donnelly and Whelan 2017; Neier 2012; Sikkink 2017); as well as international law (Chen 2015). An ethnographic study would require interviews with the staffers at AI who are responsible for individual AI projects. Unfortunately, this has not been feasible, and is a limitation of this study, which is partly made up for by the overview of an AI report in Chapter 2, paying particular attention to its sources of information, though see Hopgood (2006) for an ethnographic study of AI's International Secretariat.

> ***Guideline 1: Get to know your data thoroughly.*** ***(Verschueren 2012: 54)***

In tandem with this investigation of the ideologies manifested in my AI corpus, I prepared conference presentations and publications on a variety of aspects of the appeal letters: genre, speech acts, and (im)politeness (Delahunty 2013); stancetaking (Delahunty 2014); a comparison of the moves and steps in the AI and philanthropic fundraising letters (Delahunty 2018b); the linguistic and discursive management of ideological conflict (Delahunty 2015); the ideological positioning of writers, senders, and recipients (Delahunty 2017); ideological positioning of persons mentioned in AI appeal letters (Delahunty 2018a); the ideological positioning of participants and the intertextual relations among the AI letters, their embedding emails and webpages and AI reports (Delahunty 2021); and a Relevance Theory analysis of the multi-modal argument made by

AI's Eastern Ghouta webpage discussed in Chapter 2 and in Delahunty (2023). These all entailed multiple re-analyses of the data.

> ***Procedure 1.1: In the case of audio-video-recorded data: Listen to/ watch several times; transcribe all the data that you want to subject to closer investigation. (Verschueren 2012: 55)***

As all the appeal letters are written, this procedure is irrelevant to the current research, though the multi-modality of other AI documents is not. I have not come across relevant audio(-visual) documents, though some AI reports use such data as evidence.

> ***Procedure 1.2: In the case of written text: Read and re-read until you are fully familiar with the materials. (Verschueren 2012: 55)***

Verschueren distinguishes the text from reading the text, saying that texts *per se* do not "mean": reading the texts is the sense-making activity. As the letters came to me embedded in emails from AI and/or I accessed them on AI webpages, I carefully read each email and webpage, and then each letter. The research for this project and for the papers and presentations mentioned above necessitated my reading and re-reading them and related AI documents "cyclically," as each became relevant again and again in the analysis and discussion. I encourage my readers to review the corpora of appeal letters in Appendixes 2 and 3.

> ***Guideline 2: Get to know the context of your data. Ask yourself what it is you need to know in order to interpret the data, i.e., about the linguistic context, the immediate context of situation, and the wider context (social, political, historical, geographical, etc.). (Verschueren 2012: 56)***

Verschueren, like most pragmaticists and discourse analysts, argues that linguistic data such as the AI texts is always contextually embedded, and that (political) discourse is constrained by (political) institutions embedded in (political) power structures. Consequently, analysts must take care not to overlook relevant aspects of context by introducing "a gap" (57) between texts and their contexts and must maintain an analytic balance between the textual (linguistic) data and the contextual, both linguistic and otherwise.

The letters and other documents constituting the corpus come from AI, which, as discussed in Chapter 2, is one of many non-governmental organizations which work with, as well as independently of, governmental institutions such as the United Nations to promote human rights (Baehr 2009; Donnelly and Whelan 2017; Neier 2012; Sikkink 2017). It publishes reports on situations of significant rights abuses, as well as reports regarding how well or poorly countries observe their human and humanitarian rights obligations, and particularly on violations of those rights, such as the report discussed in Chapter 2.

The immediate linguistic context of the AI appeal letters consists of the emails I receive from AI – the embedding emails – and the AI websites that contain the letters. Both provide further information on the appeal situation, as well as exhortations to act. The embedding emails and webpages typically contain still photos, often of the individual whose rights are claimed to have been violated. The more remote linguistic context is the AI report on the violative situation. Yet more remotely related are the documents upon which the AI reports are based, and the documents upon which they are based, and so on.

The immediate context of situation is the AI member's initial reading of the embedding emails or webpages and of the embedded letters and their deciding whether to SEND the letters. The situational specifics of each case, as described in the embedding emails and webpages, constitute the next wider context of situation. These specifics are substantially expanded in the yet wider context of the AI report on the situation, which, among other factors, describes the political and juridical processes that determine the legal definitions of the rights, laws, treaties, declarations, and covenants referenced in the letters.

The still wider context of situation includes all the efforts by individuals, organizations, and institutions to promote human and humanitarian rights and to ensure that governments and other powerful bodies observe these rights in their dealings with individuals and classes of individuals. These efforts include appeals and protests to governments and government functionaries on behalf of individuals whose rights have been infringed, and more generally in support of the various classes of rights. The philosophical, legal, political, and sociological discourses around AI and human rights provide further relevant context.

Characterizing the widening linguistic and situational contexts as I have suggests that they form concentric circles. However, conceptualizing them in this way risks overlooking the rich linguistic and contextual "spokes" intersecting these circles.

A major historical element of the context of situation of several AI documents is the G. W. Bush administration's "global war on terror," a "political phrase, not a legal term of art."[1] While violations of human rights and efforts to redress and eliminate them predate (and have continued after) the G. W. Bush administration, the international and civil wars that that administration's policies and actions provoked provide the historical backdrop for several situations addressed in the documents (e.g., #1 Targeted Killings, USA; #6 Guantanamo, USA; #7 Aamer, USA; #10 Drone Wars, USA; #19

[1] International Humanitarian Law, https://cglj.org/human-rights-law/international-humanitarian-law/ (accessed April 21, 2026).

Torture Report, USA; #39 al-Hawsawi, USA). Additionally, that administration's attempts to legitimize torture as an interrogation technique by providing an appearance of legality that the US and other governments, many of whom were and continue to be serial and serious violators of their citizens' civil and human rights, could appeal to is the subject of a number of documents (e.g., #4 al-Qahtani, Iraq).

While the letters' broader geographic context of situation is the entire world and all the nations and states that constitute it,[2] only a small number of countries are represented in the documents, though some of these are the subject of several documents. The following lists the countries, states, and corporations, along with the numbers of appeals made to them:

Algeria (1)
Apple Corporation (1)
Burkina Faso (2)
California, USA (1)
Dominican Republic (1)
Egypt (2)
El Salvador (1)
Indonesia (2)
Iraq (1)
Louisiana, USA (3)
Malawi (1)
Myanmar (1)
People's Republic of China (1)
Russian Federation (3)
Saudi Arabia (1)
South Africa (1)
Sudan (1)
Turkey (1)
United States of America (13) (not including California and Louisiana)
Uzbekistan (1)
Vietnam (1)

The documents raise a variety of issues of concern, as the following from an AI webpage suggests:

Amnesty Evolves

Over the years, human rights have moved from the fringes to centre stage in world affairs. Amnesty has grown from seeking the release of political prisoners to upholding

[2] There are 195 countries in the world, 193 of which belong to the UN. See www.un.org/en/about-us/growth-in-un-membership (accessed July 2, 2025).

> the whole spectrum of human rights. Our work protects and empowers people – from abolishing the death penalty to protecting sexual and reproductive rights, from combating discrimination to defending refugees and migrants' rights. We speak out for anyone whose freedom and dignity are under threat. After more than 50 years of groundbreaking achievements, Amnesty has been through a major transformation, adapting to dramatic changes in the world.[3]

These issues appear to correlate with the political status and structure of the countries involved. Thus, seventeen letters – almost half – were sent to government functionaries of the US. Three of these were sent to authorities in Louisiana (#12 Wallace; #16 Woodfox; #20 Woodfox, Louisiana, USA) regarding the long-term solitary confinement of two men whose convictions and continuing incarceration were of dubious legality. In this respect, Louisiana is similar to countries in which individuals are sentenced and punished in circumstances that AI alleges violate procedural due process, for example, Iraq (#4 al-Qahtani, Iraq).

The remainder of the letters take the US authorities to task for "targeted killing" (#1 Targeted Killings, USA), drone strikes (#10 Drone Wars, USA), mass surveillance (#23 Mass Surveillance, USA), the Guantanamo Bay detention facility (#6 Guantanamo, USA), and torture (#19 Torture Report, USA), and seek to persuade those authorities to support an arms trade treaty (#2 Arms Trade, USA), restrict arms sales (#34 Arms Sales, USA), support women's human rights (#32 Violence Against Women, USA), and support the Creation of a National Crime and Justice Task Force (#21 Crime Task Force, USA).

It is conceivable, perhaps even arguable, that so many of the appeals are addressed to US functionaries because AI staffers believe, or perhaps just hope, that these are more likely to respond positively to the appeals than representatives of other countries, many of which are autocracies whose leaders are less influenced by public opinion. This optimism should be tempered by the recalcitrance of the Louisiana authorities in the cases of Herman Wallace (#12 Wallace, Louisiana, USA) and Albert Woodfox (#16 Woodfox, Louisiana, USA).

The situations of concern represented in the other letters include the right to abortion (#8 Beatriz, El Salvador), suppression of free speech (#3 Satire as Crime, Egypt; #14 Restrictive Legislation, Russia), danger to members of the LBGTQI community (#5 LGBTQI, South Africa), imprisonment of human rights activists (#15 Vitishko, Russia; #25 Missing, China), violation of women's rights (#13 Women Protesters, Egypt; #24 Indecent Dress, Sudan), arbitrary deportation (#22 Haitians, Dominican Republic), excessive use of force by police (#9 Police Action, Turkey), freedom from torture (#18 Badawai, Saudi Arabia), freedom from the death penalty (#4 al-Qahtani, Iraq), and freedom for Prisoners of Conscience (#11 Pussy Riot, Russia; #26 PoCs,

[3] https://tinyurl.com/33cnrzbr (accessed August 2, 2025); links removed.

Vietnam). The letters appeal for the redress of these violative situations, the cessation of related actions, and general compliance with international law and human rights.

> ***Caveat 2.1: Context is not a stable "outside" reality, nor is it finite in any sense. Hence it cannot be described exhaustively. Those aspects of context may be most relevant – without radically excluding others – which are actualized in the discourse (hence the dictum that discourse constructs context) and which may thus become recoverable in the analysis. (Verschueren 2012: 58)***

Caveat 2.1 emphasizes the potential infinitude of the physical, socio-historical, mental, and linguistic elements of context, as well as the inescapable mutual and generative, though mutable, interaction between context and document. Interpreters of documents "carve out lines of vision," that is, they attend to those aspects of context indexed as relevant to their interpretation by textual cues (recall Gumperz's 1982 "contextualization cues"[4]).

References to various rights occur in almost all of the appeal letters, and some of these references are, explicitly or implicitly, to treaties, covenants, and declarations, documents that are subject to revision and re-interpretation, but which constitute the unstable contextual frame of reference against which certain actions and situations are evaluated as "violations" and others proposed as redress of those violations.

As I discussed in Chapter 2, the descriptions of situations and events in the letters are related to their descriptions in the embedding emails or webpage, largely repeating those descriptions and re-entextualizing, re-contextualizing, and re-genrefying them for the appeal letter audiences. In turn, the email and webpage descriptions are derived from information sources available to AI, which are generally not identified in the emails or the letters, but which may be accessible online as AI reports. Some of the evidentiary sources of these reports are available via the extensive footnotes in the reports.

Occasionally, the letters do identify specific sources of information about situations, for example, "images showing police actions against demonstrators in Istanbul and other Turkish cities" (#9 Police Action, Turkey), and court decisions, for example, "The Inter-American Court of Human Rights ruled on May 29 that the Salvadoran government is obligated under international law to ensure Beatriz's life and health" (#8 Beatriz, El Salvador).

[4] "I use the terms *contextualization cue* to refer to any verbal sign which, when processed in co-occurrence with symbolic grammatical and lexical signs, serves to construct the contextual ground for situated interpretation and thereby affects how constituent messages are understood" (Gumperz 2018: 315; emphasis in original).

In most cases, however, the references to rights and their violations are generic, for example, "human rights," "forced confessions," and so are "underspecified" and with "*suggestive vagueness*" (Verschueren 2012: 59, emphasis in original), thus implicating the existence of those rights and their violations, as well as the existence of legal instruments that define the rights relevant to a specific situation and the implications of their violations. I assume that (at least some) AI staffers are knowledgeable enough to be able to identify the specific rights violated in each case and could, without (much) extra effort, include that information in the letters. I also assume that the fact that they rarely do this is significant. The more generic formulations are certainly less burdensome for both writers and readers of the letters, and so to be preferred over more specific formulations (Clark 2013; Grice 1975, 1989; Sperber and Wilson 1995). For example, the expression "human rights" in an email, webpage, or appeal is sufficiently informative for an AI member or volunteer and more easily processed – and perhaps less question-begging – than "The United Nations Universal Declaration of Human Rights". I argued in Chapter 2 that the choice of the generic formulations is an element in AI's efforts to engage, motivate, and mobilize the volunteers to whom the letters are emailed.

> ***Procedure 2.1: Investigate the wider (social, political, historical, geographical, etc.) context, to the extent that it is accessible. (Verschueren 2012: 63)***

> ***AD 2.1, IN GENERAL: Investigate the wider (social, political, historical, geographical, etc.) context, to the extent that it is accessible. (Verschueren 2012: 63)***

The wider context of the investigated discourse is essentially the current status of civil, human, and humanitarian rights across the globe. These situations range from torture by US interrogators in the name of the "global war on terror," through public floggings in Saudi Arabia as an application of Sharia law, to continued detentions and the denial of medically necessitated abortions because of religiously based laws and in spite of legal rulings, and to support for nuclear and other arms reduction treaties. The letters are elements in AI's ongoing activity in support of human rights and associated issues. In this respect, they are akin to the activities of a great many governmental and non-governmental organizations in support of an international order in which respect for international law and its related standards, especially human rights, is the expected norm.

Since the fall of communism in the USSR in the 1980s and 1990s, many states have experienced "vicious internal conflicts" driven by "nationalistic and ethnic tensions," leading to "egregious human rights violations" (Chen 2015: 10).

These tensions have been exacerbated by people fleeing severe economic and/or climatic distress and/or violence in their countries of origin and exploited by resurgent far-right individuals, organizations, and governments in Europe and the USA.

Other conflicts and rivalries implicated in human rights violations include the destruction of civil society, military, and governmental institutions in Iraq following the US invasion in 2003; unrest in many Middle Eastern and North African countries in response to US President G. W. Bush's cynical call for the spread of democracy across the Middle East; the civil war in Syria exacerbated by Russian engagement and its rivalry with the US; the overthrow of a democratically elected – if flawed – government in Egypt by military coup; the civil war in Yemen, exacerbated by rivalries among Islamic sects, represented by Saudi Arabia and Iran; "ethnic cleansing" of Rohingya and incarceration of human rights activists in Myanmar; and Russia's 2020 invasion of Ukraine, along with a great many others.

Nationalist and xenophobic impulses have created centrifugal forces in the European Union, as evidenced by the British vote to leave the EU in 2020 and Hungarian flouting of EU standards of academic, judicial, and media independence. Similar forces in the US have led to street violence, including an attack on the US capitol on January 6, 2021, and the entrenchment of rigid rightwing ideologies in many US courts and in the US Republican party, which is argued to have elicited corresponding entrenchments on the left (Applebaum 2020). Relatedly, and of considerable importance, is the growth of anti-democratic movements and governments in Australia, Austria, France, Germany, Guatemala, Hungary, Ireland, the US, Venezuela, and many others.

International laws and the institutions created to enforce them, for example, the International Court of Justice and the International Criminal Court, are unable to command the political or financial support needed to adjudicate conflicts or bring more than a very few human rights violators to justice. Chen (2015: 70) sums up his discussion of international organizations and their roles in international law, saying that

> [t]hough the proliferation of international governmental organizations has been impressive, the aggregate contribution of such organizations to global decision making has been less so. The resources, independent of state control, made available to such organizations have been far from adequate. The structures of the organizations remain somewhat primitive, lacking proper regional or functional balance. Their technical procedures are largely unsystematized and uneconomical. Too often particular national elites still view such organizations as instruments of their own national policy rather than as instruments to clarify and protect genuine common interests.

Nonetheless, despite these concerns, Chen (2015: 538) also paints a rather more positive picture of the status of international law, at least up to 2015 when his book was published:

While many of the preceding pages have documented examples of deviations from the dictates of international law, it is worth remembering that such deviations are the exception. In fact, compliance with international law is overwhelmingly the norm.

Similar optimistic notes are struck by Sikkink (2017) and Pinker (2019).

AD 2.1.1: How does the context of the investigation relate to the context of the investigated discourse? (Verschueren 2012: 63)

Relevant elements of the context of this investigation are, first, that I am a member of AI who reads and SENDs many of the appeal letters that arrive in my email box or that I find on the AI webpages, and second, that I am a linguist with research interests in pragmatics and discourse analysis. I began this research because I felt that the letters, their embedding emails, and related texts would repay investigation as they represent a genre developed over many years by AI in the discourse of political counterpower, which, as far as I am aware, has not been investigated before, though Featherman (2015) comes close. He takes a critical discourse analytic approach to protesters' uses of media, especially Twitter and Flikr, following the controversial 2009 election in Iran. More generally, as I've noted, the discourses of "positive" ideologies, those supporting human dignity, have been far less studied than the discourses of "negative" ideologies.

Verschueren remarks (2012: 64) that "the best test for the validity of the proposed set of methods … would be to use them for the analysis of data one can feel aligned with and then come up with unexpected findings." While I feel "aligned with" the values of AI and the purposes of the letters, I am nonetheless aware of the tensions in the letters between the desire to redress violations of human and other rights and the need to seek funding to continue that work, typically in competition with other human rights and eleemosynary organizations; the tensions between the ideals of universal rights and the exigencies of governing in violent circumstances; as well as the tensions between appealing to authority figures and persuading and motivating AI volunteers. These tensions arise in a world in which power is distributed unevenly and ideologies compete while individuals and groups seek to assert their power and legitimize their actions, for good or ill. And, as I've noted, human rights, like the ideology of colonialism in its own time, have not gone "uncontested." They have been criticized as thinly disguised devices for Western neo-colonialism, as anti-Israeli propaganda, and as representing values legitimized by flawed and Western-dominated institutions such as the UN. (Recall Chen's remarks just above on the constraints on international courts.)

AD 2.1.2: How does the context of the investigated discourse relate to the social, cultural, political, historical context in which the discourse is (presenting itself as being) "about"? (Verschueren 2012: 65)

The primary letter corpus for this study, collected in Appendix 2, dates from March 2013 through June 2016, though I discuss occasional examples from outside this range. During this time, Barack Obama was President of the US and Vladimir Putin was the President of Russia. Europe saw the emergence of right-wing political parties and leaders. Some of these won general elections and established governments, most notably in Hungary and Poland (and later in Austria). Others became important opposition parties, for example, in France and Holland. In Britain, a referendum supported withdrawal from the EU, largely in reaction to perceptions of uncontrolled migration portrayed by right-wing nationalist groups and to concerns about the limitations on UK "sovereignty" entailed by membership in a multi-state organization like the EU. Elsewhere, Xi Jinping became General Secretary of the Communist Party of China and initiated significant reductions in personal freedom for Chinese citizens, greater central control of economic functions, repression of religious minorities, especially of the Muslim Uighurs (aka Uyghurs), and massive surveillance even of ordinary daily activities throughout the country. In the Philippines, Rodrigo Duterte became President in 2016 largely because of his encouragement of a policy of extra-judicial killings of people suspected of drug use or sale. In late 2016, Donald Trump, a right-wing authoritarian, won the presidential election in the US, and inaugurated a nationalistic, anti-immigrant – especially anti-Muslim – regime. So, the brief historical period contextualizing the letters was one of resurgent nationalism and authoritarianism, marked by increases in violations of civil, human, and humanitarian rights.

In this context, the AI letters function as a genre of oppositional, activist discourse, arguing and agitating for governments to abide by their legal commitments to human and humanitarian rights. The letters occasionally acknowledge local conditions which the governments might characterize as necessitating abrogations or re-interpretations of those rights to allow them greater latitude in how they treat and, particularly, interrogate prisoners, especially political prisoners (#19 Torture Report, USA), silence human rights activists (#25 Missing, China), and suppress dissent (#11 Pussy Riot, Russia; #14 Restrictive Legislation, Russia; #15 Vitishko, Russia).

Though they may not index them, some letters are written in the context of power struggles within countries, for example, within the US between President Obama and Congress, especially the Republican majority at the time in both the US Senate and House of Representatives, over the closing of the "detention center" at the US naval station at Guantanamo Bay, Cuba, and bringing the remaining prisoners to the US (#7 Aamer, USA).

AD 2.1.3: How does the investigated discourse carve out lines of vision in the "world" it refers to? (Verschueren 2012: 66)

"Lines of vision" are

> those aspects of context that language users orient to (as well as aspects that might be carefully or carelessly left out) that are the most relevant for interpretation. More often than not, such orientations leave traces in the discourse itself, which makes it possible to subject them to investigation. In other words, the way in which discourse itself "constructs" or "generates" its own context by choosing to select focal points from a vast continuum enables the researcher to find out what the relevant aspects of context are.
> (Verschueren 2012: 58)

In response to AD 2.1.3, Verschueren discusses the causes of the Indian Mutiny and its sequence of events as presented in his chosen texts. He lists the causes of the mutiny and then in Table 2 (69) displays a cross-tabulation of authors and causes. In his Table 3 (78), he lists the sequence of events that constitute the mutiny mentioned in his texts, and in Table 4 (79–80), he provides a cross-tabulation of authors and the events they mention. From this examination of events and their causes, he derives several observations. First, he notes the importance of the ways in which the causes of the mutiny are presented in the texts. Cultural conflict is presented as a significant cause deriving from conflicting perceptions of national characteristics, for example, Indian "backwardness" and English "lack of consideration" and impatience to modernize.[5] It is worth noting here the similarity between these notions and the now discredited "scientific" national character studies carried out by American anthropologists and social psychologists during and after World War II (e.g., Benedict 1946). Second, he notes the ways in which putative causes of the mutiny are dismissed or downplayed by epistemically hedging them as reports or rumors (73).

Verschueren ends his discussion of AD 2.1.3 by noting how the different ways in which his authors presented their discussions of the mutiny and how these differences affect the "'lines of vision' which the discourse carves out in the 'world,'" reflecting different rhetorical goals (82).

The aspects of context most relevant to the interpretation and ideological analysis of the AI letters are civil, human, and humanitarian rights and their violations, and the social, cultural, political, and historical situations in which the contested situations occur and to which the letters refer directly and indirectly. Other aspects of context to which the letters refer are more specific rights, especially women's, children's, and LGBTQIA+ rights and the legal documents that encode and legitimize them.

The motivations for the letters include political engagement and activism, for example, urging President Mutharika to stop the killing of people with Albinism in Malawi (#38 Albinism, Malawi); attempts to effect social changes, for example, encouraging South Africa to better train its police officers in their

[5] And that the value of modernizing mitigates any impatience and lack of consideration in its pursuit.

treatment of LGBTQIA+ people and to more thoroughly investigate crimes against LGBTQIA+ individuals (#5 LGBTQI, South Africa); and the desire to reverse the religiously based denial of human rights, for example, requesting the removal of the prohibition on abortion in El Salvador (#8 Beatriz, El Salvador).

More generally, the letters represent one of AI's (and other such organizations') efforts to create a global culture in which universal, secular concepts of rights trump local, traditional, nationalistic, and religious assumptions, for example, a world in which torture and the death penalty do not exist and in which all human and humanitarian rights are respected. As I've noted, none of the letters in my corpus explicitly identifies the religions or religious doctrines that legitimize flogging or deny access to abortion or family planning.

Notably, also, the letters do not address economic issues, which, arguably, provide motivating context for at least some of the activities that evoked the violative reaction from a government. Though several letters might well have done so, none addresses economic anxiety and competition for work, factors that, for example, contributed to the expulsion of Haitians from the Dominican Republic (#22 Haitians, Dominican Republic). Occasional references seem to invoke the right to education asserted in UDHR Article 26: (#27 Syrian Refugees, USA) notes that Syrian children in refugee camps are "out of school," though this is a minor item in the letter's appeal to the US to accept more refugees.

AI is well-respected for the quality, accuracy, and reliability of its investigations and it has consultancy status with the various units within the UN. It is an important contributor to what Chen (2015: ch. 20) calls "the intelligence function," that is, the "gathering, processing, and disseminating [of] information essential to making decisions" (403). AI claims that

> [b]efore any statement or report is issued, its text is approved within the IS [International Secretariat GD] to ensure it is accurate, politically impartial and falls within AI's mandate. AI is often dealing with allegations rather than undisputed facts. It makes this plain and usually calls for an investigation of the allegations. If AI makes a mistake, it issues a correction.
>
> AI's research is recognized as reliable and is widely consulted by governments, **intergovernmental organizations**, journalists, scholars and other human rights organizations and campaigning groups (46; emphasis in original).[6]

The reliability justified by these procedures is indexed in the letters by the occasional hedge such as the modal emphasized in "[t]here are also serious concerns that the men *might* not have received a fair trial, in line with international standards" (#4 Al-Qahtani, Iraq), but mainly by the general absence

[6] www.amnesty.org/en/wp-content/uploads/2021/06/org200012002en.pdf (accessed August 3, 2025).

of epistemological hedging about the facts of cases or about the evaluation of events or situations as violations of rights, for example, "I urge you to release Dahmane Kerami and his six co-defendants immediately and unconditionally, as they are prisoners of conscience, jailed solely for the peaceful exercise of their rights to freedom of expression and assembly" (#37 PoCs, Algeria).

> ***Procedure/AD 2.2: Investigate the immediate context of situation that presents itself, i.e., the way in which the discourse carves out lines of vision into its own physical, social, mental world. (Verschueren 2012: 82)***

Verschueren paraphrases this guideline as "How do the 'actors' involved in the discourse (in the case of our sample data, mainly the author, but with clear assumptions about the targeted readers as well) position themselves and their discourse?" (83).

The "actors," as noted earlier and discussed further below, are problematic constructs in the context of these letters. Nonetheless, we can say that the letters ideologically position their Message Recipients as persuadable by appeal to human rights and as capable of effecting the requested changes, while ideologically positioning the letter SENDers as committed to those rights – by rationalizing, universalizing, naturalizing, and legitimizing their human rights commitments, thereby attempting to unify them as a group and motivating them to act in support of those commitments.

We can characterize the physical, social, and mental aspects of the world that the letters' lines of vision carve out. The relevant physical world is, literally, the world: AI concerns itself with the rights of people everywhere in the world. Individual letters typically address issues in specific countries, which may be explicitly named in the Message Recipients line, for example, "Bobby Jindal – Governor of Louisiana" (#12 Wallace, Louisiana, USA) or in the body of a letter, for example, "in South Africa" (#5 LGBTQI, South Africa). Occasionally, specific physical and temporal locations are identified, for example, "in front of al-Jafali mosque after Friday prayers" (#18 Badawi, Saudi Arabia), and sometimes the letters express concern that an individual's "whereabouts and final destination are still unknown" (#15 Vitishko, Russia).

We can also interpret "physical" to include the physical condition of the individuals who are the subjects of the letters. The letters include references to individuals having been flogged (#18 Badawi, Saudi Arabia), imprisoned (#15 Vitishko, Russia; #11 Pussy Riot, Russia), in solitary confinement (#12 Wallace, Louisiana, USA; #20 Woodfox, Louisiana, USA), in danger of death because of untreated illness (#8 Beatriz, El Salvador) or genetic condition (#38 Albinism, Malawi), in danger of deportation (#22 Haitians, Dominican Republic), or in danger of execution (#4 Al-Qahtani, Iraq).

This social world is populated by national and state governments, their administrative and legal institutions, and their representatives and functionaries. It includes authoritative international institutions established by these governments, their declarations and covenants, and the courts authorized to enforce their laws. It is a world of governmental power and activist counterpower; of government action and citizen protest; of religious precepts and values and secular, universal, and legal conceptions of human rights; of the development, maintenance, and activation of constituencies motivated by competing ideologies, for example, government actions characterized as necessary and legitimized because a polity is presented as under threat by outsiders, often in league with insiders,[7] and the (re-)actions of individuals, organizations, and institutions characterized as necessitated by the actions of governments that violate human rights.

The letters may provide particulars of the local, legal, political, social, and historical background to the appealed situation and of which rights have been infringed and how, and of how the situation physically and mentally affects the individuals involved:

> I urge you to stop the persecution of civil society activists, including members of Environmental Watch for North Caucasus. Yevgeniy Vitishko and his fellow environmental activists have been actively involved in protests regarding the deforestation and illegal construction in Krasnodar Region of Russia in and around the city of Sochi, and have been met with repeated arrests and detentions, personal searches, police questioning and unofficial warnings from police and security officials. It is essential that the Russian authorities respect the human rights of free expression and assembly of Yevgeniy Vitishko and all others who raise their voices in peaceful protest. Amnesty International considers Yevgeniy Vitishko a Prisoner of Conscience, persecuted for speaking out against environmental damage in Krasnodar region. Please see that he is immediately released and the charges against him dropped.
>
> (#15 Vitishko, Russia)

This letter also expresses concern "that Yevgeniy Vitishko's whereabouts and final destination are still unknown," and calls on the Message Recipients "to inform his family and lawyer of his whereabouts without delay" and to "please also inform them of the state of his health, as there is serious concern about his condition following a recent hunger strike and ensure that he receives all necessary medical support."

The mental world of the letters mirrors the social world of competing ideologies. However, if we allow "mental" to include emotions as well as cognitions, the letters express concern and desire. They typically begin with an expression of the writer's concern about a particular situation or event that affects an individual or class of individuals by infringing one or other of their rights. They then typically express the writer's desire that the infringement be

[7] https://tinyurl.com/5fhh2dt9 (accessed August 3, 2025).

redressed by urging the addressees to do so. They may also express how the individual subjects of the letter are mentally affected, for example:

> Beatriz wants to live. She wants to see her one-year-old son grow up but as the court has yet to make a ruling, she doesn't know if she will live or die. Every additional day the government is debating the merits of her case, she is suffering mental and physical anguish amounting to cruel and inhuman treatment.
>
> (#8 Beatriz, El Salvador)

Sub-procedures 2.2.1–2.2.3 and their sub-sub-procedures add further specifics to Procedure 2.2.

Procedure 2.2.1: Who are the utterers and interpreters in the discourse?

In particular:

2.2.1.1: What system of person deixis is used? (Verschueren 2012: 84–88; see also Verschueren 1999: 20, 77–78)

First Person

"Who am I?"

(Mühlhäusler and Harré 1990: 98ff)

"*I* am certainly I."

(Reboul 1992: 200; emphasis in original)

"I am not I; thou art not he or she; they are not they."

(Waugh 1945: *Author's Note*)

"I don't have the feeling that I write my books, I have the feeling that my books get written through me … I never had, and still do not have, the perception of feeling my personal identity. I appear to myself as the place where something is going on, but there is no 'I,' no 'me.'"

(Levi-Strauss 1978: 3–4)

"***I*** refers straightforwardly to the speaker, ***you*** to the addressee: no further commentary is needed."

(Huddleston and Pullum 2002: 1465; emphasis in original).

Well, perhaps a little more commentary. To begin with, expressions do not refer: utterers refer and use expressions to guide interpreters to their intended referents. Interpreters use the information represented by the expressions and whatever context is indexed to try to identify the intended referents and the characteristics the expressions attribute to them. And while interpreters are typically successful, they also often fail.

In the prefaces to his history textbooks, Verschueren identifies the usual deictic suspects. For the utterer, he finds first-person singular and plural pronouns, the latter in both nominative and genitive cases. The first-person plural pronouns include both the "royal" and inclusive *we*, which includes both author and readers

Email regarding imprisonment of the Philippines Senator de Lima

Dear Gerald,

In the Philippines, President Duterte's national police and unknown armed persons have killed thousands of people suspected of using or selling drugs. These killings appear to be systematic — those that are killed are overwhelmingly from poor, urban neighborhoods. In many cases, police have tried to cover up unlawful killings by planting evidence at crime scenes and falsifying incident reports.

One voice has been strongly vocal and critical against Duterte's policies: Senator Leila de Lima. The Senator voiced her concerns against Duterte's "war on drugs" and has been imprisoned on politically motivated charges since February 24, 2017.

Take action now: Ask the Secretary of Justice to immediately release Senator Leila de Lima and drop all charges against her.

Shortly after President Duterte took office on June 30, 2016, Senator de Lima voiced her concern regarding the increasing number of extrajudicial killings of suspected drug offenders. Following this, the President and other state officials began a campaign of harassment and intimidation against her.

As Chair of the Senate Committee on Justice and Human Rights, Senator De Lima opened a Senate Inquiry into unlawful killings committed in the context of the "war on drugs" and called in key witnesses to testify before the Senate in September 2016. Shortly after, allies of President Duterte brought 10 people, 7 of them prison inmates, to testify before Congress that drug money was paid to de Lima's driver to help fund her campaign to the Senate. It was later revealed that, following their testimony, prison inmates received benefits in jail.

Senator Leila de Lima has been imprisoned since February 24, 2017. Amnesty International believes that the charges against the Senator are politically motivated, and calls on the authorities to immediately and unconditionally release the Senator and drop all charges against her.

Join me in calling on the government of the Philippines to drop all charges against Senator Leila de Lima.

From her prison cell Senator de Lima has continued to issue daily handwritten dispatches, commenting and responding to current social and political issues in the Philippines, and continued to call for attention to human rights violations in the country.

While neither the use nor sale of drugs is confined to poor neighborhoods, police operations have overwhelmingly targeted those living in poverty, making the so-called 'war on drugs' a war on the poor. Drug-related killings have created a pervasive climate of fear in poor communities, with families of victims unable to seek justice, and many forced into hiding due to fear of further attacks.

Senator Leila de Lima is still in prison for protecting low income communities against systematic attacks by the police. She is a champion of human rights in her country. Take action now and demand her immediate release.

TAKE ACTION

Sincerely,

Margaret Huang

Margaret Huang
Executive Director
Amnesty International USA

Figure 4.1 Email regarding imprisonment of the Philippines Senator de Lima[8, 9]

8 A *Guardian* article on Senator de Lima's freedom can be read at https://tinyurl.com/359ve8xw (accessed August 3, 2025).

9 Just to the right of the first paragraph was a photo of Senator de Lima. It can be found in the article at https://www.hrw.org/news/2017/02/24/philippines-arrest-duterte-critic-widens-drug-war. (Accessed February 10, 2026).

and on occasion others. The authors are also referred to by third-person descriptions, for example, "the author" and indexed by impersonal expressions of the authors' stances, for example, "it is hoped/felt/believed …" Interpreter references are by second-person pronouns, imperatives, and indirectly by third-person noun phrases (NPs), for example, "busy people," "the children of today," "our children."

We might view the embedding emails as akin to the history textbook prefaces in that they introduce the appeal issue to their addressees. The email in Figure 4.1, which I received on February 12, 2019, is a typical example of the genre.

The addressee and addressor of this email are both identified by name, the addressee by first name and the addressor by first and last name, in both cursive (presumably an auto-signed version of her signature) and print, along with her position in AI.

The addressee is not explicitly referred to again in the email, but presumably is to be invoked by the deleted subjects in imperatives, for example, *Take action now and demand her immediate release*. It might appear that the identity of the addressee is unproblematic, after all, I am addressed by name. However, presumably that name is derived from an electronic list of the names and email addresses of AI members and donors (and, no doubt, other information) and that neither the ostensible addressor nor the writer of the email see each email or have any but the most indirect relationship with the addressee. Presumably the email writer – along with other AI staffers – crafts the email in an electronic template or artificial intelligence system that allows their computers to insert the first name of each intended recipient, essentially assigning a series of values to a variable. These values are letter sequences which, in most cases, are identifiable as names, which, in most cases, refer to individuals, though just which sequences are actual names and which actually refer depends on how frequently and carefully AI culls its electronic lists. The sign-off at the end is presumably similarly inserted, thus allowing for other AI officials to be named as addressors.

The email contains four references to the ostensible addressor: the cursive and print versions of her name in the sign-off; *me*[10] in the second directive; her title, "Executive Director"; and arguably the metonymic *Amnesty International*. As with the addressee expressions, these raise interesting problems of interpretation. While the references to Verschueren's textbook authors are presumably to be taken straightforwardly as the books' actual authors, the addressor references in the emails can only be interpreted as intended by the email writer to be taken by the addressee to refer to Margaret Huang. The email is to be read by the addressee as if it were written by the ostensible addressor, and thus any first-person references are to be taken to refer to her. Presumably, all involved understand how these aspects of this genre are constructed.

[10] The referent of this *me* is identified cataphorically as Margaret Huang at the end of the email, thus indicating that first-person pronouns may be anaphoric, in the general sense of that word, just as third-person pronouns can be.

Because neither the ostensible addressor nor the email writer can intend the addressee expressions to actually refer to any specific individual and because some recipients of the emails may ignore them or consign them to JUNK or TRASH, while others may read and perhaps act as they direct, the addressee expressions must be taken as invitations to the addressees to reverse the usual reference assignment – speaker assigns reference to second-person addressee expressions – and to assign themselves as referents to those expressions.

Revisions of Althusser's (2001 [1971]) concept of "interpellation" – the individual's process of internalizing a society's ideologies – are useful here. According to Althusser, "Ideological State Apparatuses" (ISAs) "call out" to people and thereby ideologically constitute them. ISAs are institutions such as families, schools, religions, and media, and for our purposes here, non-state organizations such as AI. Later scholars (see Ryder 2015–16) criticized Althusser's minimization of subjects' agency, and it is clear that reading an email ostensibly addressed to one by one's first name, and more tellingly, by clicking to SEND the appeal to its ostensible Message Recipients, are actions undertaken by the AI members or volunteers, who thereby interpellate themselves into the ideological positions prepared for them by AI, and more broadly by the human rights communities, and more broadly still into global conflicts that involve not just Althusser's ISAs, but also his RSAs (Repressive State Apparatuses). In my more homely terms, when I SEND the appeal, I inhabit[11] the *I*; when I read the email addressed to "Gerald," I inhabit that, too. That is, I deliberately and consciously (contra Fairclough 1989: 105) install myself as the referent of those expressions and thus position (Harré and Moghaddam 2003) myself ideologically, even though I am fully aware of how this "synthetic personalization" (Fairclough 1989: 62) is electronically and otherwise ginned up.[12,13]

[11] We find a similar use of "inhabit" in the voiceover by Julie Christie in the movie *The Bookshop*: "She told me once, when we read a story, we inhabit it. The covers of a book are like a roof and four walls – a house." See https://tinyurl.com/2s3nm252 (accessed August 3, 2025).

[12] The pattern of "Dear Firstname, … Sincerely, Firstname Lastname (in cursive), Firstname Lastname (typed), Official Title" is far from specific to AI. I have philanthropic appeals with the same synthetic personalization from the American Association of Retired Persons. However, variations on the pattern appear, too: Dear Firstname Lastname (Project Hope; Rocky Mountain PBS); Dear Friend (International Rescue Mission; Public Citizen; March of Dimes [which spelled my Lastname incorrectly]); Dear Friend of [Organization Name] (CARE); Dear Title and Lastname (ACLU; Médicins Sans Frontières; Human Rights Watch; Southern Poverty Law Center); Dear Neighbor (Meals on Wheels); no letter and no salutation, just inserts (Salvation Army). Investigating which types of organizations are likely to use which pattern would be intriguing, but would take us too far afield from here.

[13] On August 5, 2024, I received an email from AI USA consisting of an introductory note to "Gerald," ostensibly from "—Kate," who, upon a web-search, appears to be Kate Hixon, Advocacy Director, Africa Government Relations & Advocacy for AI USA. The note is followed by a typical email regarding the civil war in Sudan and asking me to "Please, add your name to our letter and help us reach our goal of delivering at least 10,000 more signatures to the UN Security Council and the African Union." The email was from, but not signed by, Flavia Mwangovya, Deputy Regional Director – Campaigns, East and Southern Africa

Generalizing, we can say that any AI member or volunteer – or anyone receiving the email or accessing the webpage – who SENDs the appeal thus positions themselves ideologically. They are not positioned or co-opted by malign powers presenting a distorted version of reality to benefit themselves. This is not to say that everyone who SENDs an appeal is fully knowledgeable about human rights or about AI's values and methods, or indeed that everyone who SENDs an appeal is committed to those rights and values. There are always insincere participants (Searle 1969: 62).

The issue of insincerity raises questions about the speech act involved in SENDing an appeal. Searle (1969: 62–71) identifies four classes of "rules," his reduction of Austin's felicity conditions (Austin 1962: Lecture III), that together constitute speech acts: the propositional content, preparatory, sincerity, and essential conditions. Research on speech acts, especially in legal contexts, has demonstrated that sincerity is not a necessary condition for at least certain kinds of speech acts, contracts most particularly (Schane 2012; Kaplan 2020). That is, a contract freely agreed to is legally binding regardless of whether one or both parties were insincere. Apologies, likewise, do not require sincerity to be felicitous. Ideally, parties to contracts, issuers of apologies, and SENDers of AI appeals are sincere in their actions. Certainly, neither AI nor the Message Recipients can distinguish the sincere from the insincere. Neither can they discern the motives of any appeal SENDer. Sincerity and motive seem irrelevant to the system AI has set up. Like the party to a contract, once I have sent an appeal, absent evidence to the contrary, I will be taken to have positioned myself in alignment with AI and its human rights agendas, and specifically to AI's evaluation of the appeal situation and its proposed amelioration.

The person deictics used in the appeals include the case, gender, and number forms of the first-, second-, and third-person English pronouns. After I briefly discuss Verschueren's textbook findings, I will list the forms that occur in the corpus and their frequencies and describe and illustrate their grammatical and semantic roles in the letters.

Verschueren (2012: 84–88) finds that expressions used to refer to utterers, interpreters, authors, and readers are sharply different in the prefaces and main bodies of the textbooks. The textbook genre, at least in the late nineteeth and early twentieth centuries, expected "the backgrounding of both the utterer and the interpreter," leading authors to shun the use of *I* in the main text. Prefaces allowed authors to come out of the shadows and refer to themselves directly and "to position the author in relation to his own communicative act" and "its subject matter" (85). In the textbooks, "[d]irect first-person reference in the singular is exceptional" (84). In the appeals, in contrast, it is the norm, alternating only, and only occasionally, with *we*.

Regional Office, Amnesty International USA, a noteworthy mix of the professional and synthetic personal.

Verschueren finds that *we* occurs "slightly more" frequently than *I* in his corpus. It functions as the "royal *we*," apparently referring only to the author; Huddleston and Pullum (2002) remark that "this usage is no longer current" (1467). Verschueren notes the inclusive use of *we* to embrace writers, readers, and others with whom they may be identified (85). Huddleston and Pullum's "authorial" *we* is widely recognized, particularly in academic writings, as a means of avoiding the use of *I*, which "may make the text appear inappropriately personal and subjective," but retaining "some suggestion that the reader is being invited to engage in a joint enterprise" (1467). Mühlhäusler and Harré (1990: 175) quote Wales' (1980: 28 ff) observation that this usage is "predominantly egocentric, but implicating the involvement of an audience/reader … [and] particularly common in utterances that hint that the argument, thesis, experiment, etc. is not only being followed by the audience, but also being worked out together by demonstration or ratiocination." They characterize this use of *we* as a marked one which may be used for "diffusing responsibility" (102), though the "speaker [does] integrate with his or her audience, but his or her responsibility for what is known, suspected and so forth is diminished" (175).

In the appeals, while the first-person pronouns are typically singular, plural *we* is also found. In contrast to Verschueren's corpus, *I* occurs approximately six times more frequently than *we* (118 vs. 20). *We* may alternate with *I* as the ostensible agent of a speech event, as in:

> ***I*** am writing you on behalf of satirist Bassem Youssef, comedian Ali Qandil, blogger Ahmed Anwar and at least 30 other Egyptians who have been put under investigation in the past three months and are now facing charges and trial for their free expression of speech [*sic*] … The fundamental right to freedom of expression must be guaranteed to all Egyptians. ***We*** urge you to drop the criminal defamation charge against Ahmed Anwar and any other person charged with insulting public officials or religion …
>
> (#3 Satire as Crime, Egypt; emphasis added)

There is no antecedent in the text of this appeal to motivate the shift from *I* to *we*, though we must assume that this *we* subsumes its text-mate *I*, though exactly who co-habits the *we* besides the *I* is left unclear, as the group indexed by *we* is unspecified, though presumably it includes AI members and staffers. However, *you* referring to the Message Recipients occurs just after *we*, thus clearly indicating that they must be excluded from the *we* group. This *we* is therefore exclusive of the ostensible addressee of the letter.

Mühlhäusler and Harré (1990: 177 ff) remark on the "general flexibility and multifunctionality of English *we*," and identify "its use to signal group indexicality," its inclusive reading, as one of its "most prominent features." In choosing inclusive *we* rather than another pronoun, "a speaker introduces a bond with his/her interlocutors" and thus brings "other persons" "into an obligation pattern and the responsibility of the speaker is accordingly reduced," though the "speaker speaks as a representative of an (unspecified) group rather than as a self," this "self remains the centre of the group." The most likely group indexed by *we* in the letters is the AI organization and at least the members to whom the email embedding the appeal is sent, a claim substantiated by the fact that in one other instance the context suggests that *we* is intended to include both AI and the volunteer: "Amnesty International believes this must change, ***we*** urge you to condemn sexual violence and take steps to end it" (#13 Women Protesters, Egypt, emphasis added). In another instance, *we* indexes the citizenry of the US and includes the Message Recipients: "Your Congressional Representative."

> I am writing to express my concern about the global refugee crisis and to urge you to help ***the United States*** lead the global community in effectively addressing the crisis … ***We*** are a country of immigrants and refugees.
>
> (#36 Refugees, USA; emphasis added)

Verschueren identifies "indirect first-person reference" (86–87): third-person descriptions such as "the author/writer," references to "our book/aim" and "the/this (little) book," and expletive *it* constructions "positioning the author personally in relation to his own communicative act" – "it is hoped/ believed … or in relation to the subject matter" – "Our own times may … be regarded as …" None of these distancing devices occurs in the appeals; all first-person references in the appeals are direct, either *I* or *we*.

The list just below distinguishes the various semantic roles assumed by the *I*s of the letters. The numbers in brackets indicate the number of times the associated item occurs in the corpus.

First person

I nominative [123]

- Agent of directive: [61]
  - urge you to (31)
  - call on (12)
  - ask (12)
  - appeal (4)
  - request (2)
- Experiencer: [27]
  - concerned (11)
  - encouraged (2)
  - worried (1)
  - disturbed (2)
  - disappointed (1)
  - shocked (1)
  - fear (1)
  - welcome (1)
  - have sympathy (1)
  - hope to hear back (1)

look forward to hearing (4)
want to (1)

Agent of meta-speech-event verb: [18]
write/am writing (18)

Experiencer of epistemic stance: [9]
believe (5)
doubt (1)
recognize (1)
know (1)
understand (1)

Agent of expressive: [7]
thank (1)
express (6)

Other agentive [1]
send (1)

Assuming that the letters are ideological instruments, and that ideologies are action-oriented and action-orienting, it is not surprising that almost 50 percent of the occurrences of *I* are the agents of directive predicates attempting to get the addressees to take action. Nor should it be surprising, given the evaluative functions of ideology, that the *I*s of the second largest set of *I* occurrences represent the experiencers of predicates that characterize the typically negative feelings attributed to the referents of the *I*s as emotional responses to actions, events, and situations described in the letters and evaluated as violations of various important human rights. Nor should we be surprised that the number of epistemic predicates are relatively few in comparison with directive and feeling predicates, given Sypnowich's (2014: 2) claim, that "[i]deologies are ideas whose purpose is not epistemic, but political," and whose "role is not to render reality transparent, but to motivate people to do or not do certain things."

The meta-speech-event predicates function in several ways. They may introduce the spatial, temporal, and other context of an appeal, for example, "I am writing to you today with regard to the major prisoner amnesty that has been announced to mark Vietnam's National Day on 2 September 2015" (#26 PoCs, Vietnam). They can introduce the reason for the writing. This may introduce a directive, for example, "I am writing to ask you to immediately and unconditionally release environmental activist Yevgeniy Vitishko" (#15 Vitishko, Russia). Most frequently, they introduce an expression of concern about the subject of the appeal, for example, "I am writing to express my deep concern for Dahmane Kerami, and his six co-defendants …" (#37 PoCs, Algeria). Jeff Kaplan, (p.c.) suggests that the structure of the appeal openings may lessen the face threat posed by a bald-on-record directive, for example, "Release Dahmane Kerami ..." This is consistent with the typical choice of mitigated directives such as *ask*, rather than more face-threatening ones such as *demand*.

Notably rare in the appeals are closing elements: "Sincerely," or "Yours sincerely" (#11 Pussy Riot, Russia; #37 PoCs, Algeria; #39 Al-Hawsawi, USA). "Thank you" with variants such as "Thank you for your attention" occur in only ten (25 percent) of the letters. These salutations allow the SENDer to include their name or perhaps signature. I suggest that we can account for these apparent rarities by considering an important purpose of the letters – to motivate the AI volunteers – and by regarding the appeals as genre hybrids. They have characteristics of letters (some begin with a direct address: "Dear ..."). They are also akin to protest placards, which often display imperatives, for example, "Stop police brutality," just as the appeal subject lines most often do, for example, "Free Muhammad Bekzhanov" (#29 Bekzhanov, Uzbekistan). Protest placards seem to frequently display assertions, for example, "Black Lives Matter," while the AI appeal Subject lines only very occasionally do, for example, "The US Must Open its Doors to Syrian Refugee Resettlement"(#27 Syrian Refugees, USA). While the AI appeals and philanthropic appeals both petition for the redress of exigent situations, the latter typically open with an assertion, for example, "Children belong in school and at home, not in prison camps" (American Friends Service Committee). The appeals also share characteristics of memoranda – they are embedded beneath a Message Recipients line and a Subject line, for example:

> **Message Recipients**: Dr. Karen S. Guice, Acting Assistant Secretary of Defense for Health Affairs
> **Subject**: Medical Treatment of Mustafa al-Hawsawi, Detainee at Guantánamo
>
> (#39 Al-Hawsawi, USA)

Compare this format with that of a standard memo with TO, FROM, SUBJECT, and DATE lines:

> TO: President Joe Biden
> FR: Gerald Delahunty
> RE: US Violation of Rights of Asylum Seekers
> DATE: June 24, 2023

The relevant senses of *memorandum* in the *American Heritage Dictionary* (5th ed.: 1098) are:

2. A written record or communication, as in a business office. **3**. **b**. A writing submitted to a court by a party arguing an aspect of a case; a brief. **5**. A brief, unsigned diplomatic communication.

In addition to information on formatting a memo, websites on how to write them typically provide guidance regarding their contents and tenor. The following is from one such site, which distinguishes five types of memo, one of which is the "directive."

The directive is not a piece of general information but, as its title makes clear, directions that direct readers to follow a particular procedure or policy.

Unlike the general information memo, a directive generally starts with the rationale behind the directive so that people feel that it is a reasonable request, and also to help people remember it. It then ends by stating the policy or procedure that readers are directed to follow. For example, let's say that for security reasons, the janitorial staff will no longer be allowed access to employee offices. Instead, employees will put their trash cans outside their offices on Mondays, Wednesdays, and Fridays for the janitorial staff to empty. Employees will then put their trash cans back in their offices the following morning. This is a new practice, so you want to issue a directive.

First, you explain the situation. You don't want to give too many details because you don't want to encourage similar incidents, and you don't want to cast suspicion on any particular employees, but you do want to provide enough details so that employees understand the rationale behind this policy. You might write that in the past two weeks, a few employees have entered their offices in the mornings to find their computers on. A forensic investigation confirms that the computers were tampered with. As an extra precaution, the janitorial staff will no longer have access to the employee offices. This step is taken to help narrow down who might be responsible for these incidents. At this point, it is not clear if any sensitive information was stolen, but you will let the employees know as soon as any information becomes available. You might also ask everyone to change his or her passwords now for extra security and remember not to leave passwords written down and lying around their computers.

You end with the directive: effective immediately, employees are directed to place their trash bins outside their office doors on Mondays, Wednesdays, and Fridays at 5pm. The bins are to be put back in the offices on the following business morning. The janitorial staff will no longer enter your offices to empty your trash.

So that's it. A directive is different from a general information memo in that it involves a policy or procedure, and it generally starts by providing an explanation and ending with the new policy or procedure that is being implemented.

Typically, memos do not include a sign-off at the end, though they may express a wish for a response or further communication. This website remarks that:

Paper memos NEVER have a closing and signature. Instead, the writer indicates that he or she really wrote the memo by initialing by his or her name in the paper heading using blue or black ink.[14]

The appeals, therefore, are hybrid genres, incorporating formal (the Message Recipient and Subject lines) and functional (directive) elements of the memo with functional characteristics of protest placards (directives), and interpersonal

[14] This text is from Kennesaw State University Department of Technical Communication and Interactive Design. Unfortunately, it is no longer online.

characteristics of philanthropic appeals (direct personal appeals to redress an exigent situation).[15]

The other case forms of the first-person singular pronoun manifest similar semantic roles, though primarily experiencer rather than agentive ones.

me objective [(2)]
Experiencer: the sounds as their bodies hit the pavement far below, will remain with me … (1)
Stance taker: It is important to me … (1)
my genitive [(11)]
Experiencer: my deep concern … (5)
Owner/Possessor: my smartphone, my products (2)
Agent: my service, my support (2)
Agent/Instrument: **Subject**: No Refugee-Bashing in My Name (1)
Miscellaneous: for the rest of my life (1)

I have considerably more to say about the interpretation of genitive forms in context in my discussion of *your* below.

Like the roles of the nominative case forms, the roles of these other case forms are supportive of the core ideological impetuses – evaluation and action. The experiencer roles are typically expressions of evaluation and the agentive and instrumental roles are action-oriented.

Mühlhäusler and Harré (1990) propose that *I*[16] in "normal use" indexes a person occupying a "double location" as "an embodied being located in a spatio-temporal structure of things and events, so having a point of view." *I* also indexes "an active being located in a structure of rights and obligations, so having a sense of moral obligations" (88).[17] These rights and obligations "tend to vary in different cultural and social settings, but not absolutely" (93). The concept of a double location indexed by an *I* provides a basis for investigating the ideological positioning of the referents of the *I*s of the letters, while those *I*s provide us with a basis for a critique of the concept.

Indexing the double location of the referent of an *I* is "normally" simultaneous with the utterance of the *I*. Though they discuss some abnormal usages of *I*, it is this "normal" case that Mühlhäusler and Harré's double location seeks to model. However, in the case of the appeal letters, this simultaneity is disrupted and the *I*s are produced before they index an utterer. This raises two (at least) questions: First, if the recipient of the embedding email fails to click

15 Philanthropic appeals often come with a survey or a petition, ostensibly designed to imply to the recipients that their opinions can effectuate change. The AI appeals likewise imply that the sender may positively influence the Message Recipients.
16 And other case forms of the singular first-person pronoun.
17 This aspect has been developed by Harré and his colleagues within the framework of positioning theory; see Harré and Moghaddam (2003).

SEND to dispatch the appeal, does the *I* of that appeal index anyone at all? In this case, the email recipient does not "inhabit" the *I*, does not locate him-/herself as the embodied referent or the being active in a network of culturally defined rights and obligations. This failure to SEND may signal a rejection of the specific case, of AI, of human rights, or of the ideologies they represent. Or it may simply be due to email overload, CLICK fatigue, or mere mishap.

Second, if the email recipient does SEND the appeal, what are the inferential steps by which they inhabit those locations? These steps are clearly not identical to the inferencing required to identify the referent of an *I* in a personal face-to-face conversation, though surely they are related. We might reasonably assume that the embedding email is an exhortation to its addressee to SEND the appeal, that is, both the embedding email and the appeal belong to Longacre's (1992) "hortative" discourses. The appeal may then be assumed by its Message Recipients to have been sent by someone indexed by *I* – who might not have identified him-/herself by name – who is embodied and active in representing him-/herself as an agent in a particular nexus of rights and obligations, even if the recipient cannot uniquely identify the *I* referent. If sent appeals do not go to their named Message Recipients, but are merely tabulated by AI, the double location thesis still allows us to infer the embodied existence of a sender indexed by *I*.

The second clause of the double location premise allows the inference that the embodied individual is located and active in a specific network of rights and obligations. In the case of the letters, this is readily identifiable as those of human rights and responsibilities. As I have argued that the discourse of human rights constitutes an ideology and is therefore action-oriented, the second clause implicates the *I* as active in a variety of roles in that discourse. This activity is legitimized by the letters' invocations of the UDHR, whose Preamble charges that "every individual … shall strive by teaching and education to promote respect for [the] rights and freedoms" established by the Declaration and its enabling legislation. Article 29.1 of the Declaration decrees that "[e]veryone has duties to the community in which alone the free and full development of his [*sic*] personality is possible." One of those duties must be assumed to be to strive to promote the rights identified in the Declaration, and thus to be active in a network of human rights and obligations.

Second Person

Who are you?
Black Sabbath (1970)
Ozzy Osbourne
© T.R.O. Inc.

Who are you?
The Who (1978)
Peter Townshend
© Spirit Music Group[18]

More prosaically, perhaps, who is the *you* in the appeals? Verschueren (87–88) distinguishes four usages indexing the textbook readers: direct second-person pronouns "interpretable as referring to 'anyone' and not just as 'you, the reader'"; imperatives; indirect third-person forms, for example, "the reader"; and more personalized third-person references, for example, "our children."

Verschueren notes particularly (88) switches of footing (Goffman 1981) within the main text of Lavisse (1902) indicated by "apparent breaches of expected or discovered patterns" in the author's shift from the third-person narrative expected of a history textbook to the use of direct, second-person address to the readers in the main body of the text. This "breach" is apparently motivated by the author's explanation for France's loss of North American and Indian colonies to their British competitors during "le triste règne de Louis XV" and to engage the young readers in imagining a country – late nineteenth-century France – in which human rights are denied (and this without a trace of irony). I begin with third-person forms as they are the least frequent in the corpus and then discuss the more frequent second-person alternatives.

Indirect third-person forms typically name an institution with which the Message Recipients are associated. I have bolded the referentially interdependent expressions in the following examples:

> **Message Recipients: President Barak[19] Obama**
>
> **Subject**: Secure a strong arms control treaty
>
> I am writing in support of the establishment of a robust Arms Trade Treaty that will help stop irresponsible and illegal arms transfers around the world …
>
> I write to urge **the United States Government** to … (#2 Arms Trade, USA)
>
> **Message Recipients: Recep Tayyip Erdogan – Prime Minister, Ayhan Sefer Üstün – Parliamentary Commission on Human Rights Chair**
>
> **Subject**: End Abusive Police Action and Reveal Extent of injuries

[18] Rashkin et al. (2017) report on research showing "that first-person and second-person pronouns are used more in less reliable or deceptive news types," perhaps because "trustworthy" news sources seek to appear more "rigorous" and eschew the more "personal" expressions.

[19] President Obama's personal name is misspelled as Barak seven times in the letters and once correctly as Barack, suggesting rapid drafting and editing. The AI letter writers are not alone in using "Barak"; the *Economic Times of India* did too: https://tinyurl.com/mu2z9fts (accessed August 4, 2025).

Dear (recipient name),

I have been shocked by images showing police actions against demonstrators in Istanbul and other Turkish cities and call upon **the Turkish government** to immediately end the excessive use of force against peaceful demonstrators. **Turkish authorities** must ensure the right to freedom of expression and assembly, rights that are essential for any truly democratic state.

(#9 Police Action, Turkey)

Second-person pronoun direct address is the most frequent choice. These pronouns almost exclusively refer to the Message Recipients:

Message Recipients: Charles Timothy Hagel (Republican), Barack Obama (Democrat) – President

Subject: Transfer Shaker Aamer from Guantanamo

Dear (recipient name),
I urge **you** to …

(#7 Aamer, USA)

The appeal letter template allows the sender to insert the name(s) of the Message Recipient(s) after *Dear*, so the *you* highlighted in the first sentence of the appeal text is anaphorically linked to **Message Recipients**: Charles … and thus coreferential with it. In formats akin to "**Message Recipients**: Your Congressional Representative" (#36 Refugee-Bashing, USA), *your* refers to the hoped-for SENDer of the appeal, who might or might not enter their congressional representative's name. We can view the choice of *your* in this context as an index of AI's attempts to personalize communication with its members and volunteers, so as to engage them in its activities and to position them as in alignment with AI and the human rights ideology, as well as to personalize and position the congressional representative.

Imperatives are also very frequent, particularly in the Subject lines, for example, "**Subject**: Stop California from jumpstarting executions!" (#35 Executions, California, USA).[20] They also occur in the body of the appeals where they are frequently mitigated with *please*; the corpus contains fifteen examples like "Please make the choice to give them a choice" (#33 Contraception, Burkina Faso). As the default subject of imperatives is *you*, which in this instance and

[20] Of the forty subject lines, thirty-one are bald imperatives, while one is mitigated by "please" and five are non-imperative directives, e.g., "Rape Survivor Must Not be Caned" (#17 Caning, Indonesia), "No More Mass Surveillance" (#23 Mass Surveillance, USA), "No Refugee-Bashing in My Name" (#36 Refugees, USA), and "Where are the missing" (#25 Missing, China). The remaining subject lines announce the topic of the appeal, e.g., "Drone Wars" (#10 Drone Wars, USA).

in general in Subject lines refers to the Message Recipients, who are thus positioned as bearing some responsibility for "jumpstarting executions" and with the power to prevent it. As thirty-two of the forty Subject lines (80 percent) are imperatives, AI must assume that this is an effective choice, both in addressing the Message Recipients with unmitigated directives and in implicating that the AI members have the power to make demands in this way.

Occasional footing switches occur, in the following, from the second- to first-person pronoun, as emphasized:

> [AI's report[21]] exposes how the cobalt mined by adults and children working in these conditions ends up in the lithium-ion batteries that power **your** smartphone …
>
> I'm very concerned that DRC cobalt mined by children or by adults working in hazardous conditions is in the lithium-ion battery used in **my** smartphone.
>
> (#40 Cobalt, Apple Corp.)

The Message Recipients of this appeal are "Apple, Supplier Responsibility Team," though it is unclear whether this refers to just one recipient or two. *Your* presumably applies to Apple Corporation and its Supplier Responsibility Team, while *my* refers to the ostensible SENDer of the appeal. These two are in a conversive antonymic relationship, positioned in almost identical sentences that underscore the reciprocal relationship of producer/seller and buyer of smartphones. The parallel lexical and grammatical positioning of *your* and *my* also differentially evaluates the corporation and its ostensible customer with respect to the cobalt mining and thus positions them as potentially in ideological opposition. The letter, of course, appeals to Apple to remedy this violative situation and thus to bring it and the letter SENDer into ideological convergence.

In the list below, I distinguish the various semantic roles assumed by the *you*s of the letters, and discuss them in parallel with my discussion of the semantic roles of *I* above.

you [[(90)]]
- Addressee of speech act/Agent of directed action (24):
  - I urge you to …
  - I am urging you to …
  - I ask (that) you …
  - I (respectfully) call on you to …
- Addressee of meta-speech-event: I am writing to you …
- Experiencer: You will know …
- Source: You have another opportunity to …
- Agent: You have failed to …
- Recipient: Thank you.

The letters are written in Standard English (SE) and in that variety *you* does not differentiate singular from plural. Nor does SE *you* index any of the

[21] www.amnesty.org/en/documents/afr62/3183/2016/en/ (accessed August 4, 2025).

social relations of "respect and condescension, of contempt, adulation and patronage" that are associated with second-person pronouns in other languages (Mühlhäusler and Harré 1990: ch. 6). However, we cannot assume with Huddleston and Pullum (2002) that "***you*** [refers straightforwardly] to the addressee."[22] At the very least, we must take issue with the singularity of Huddleston and Pullum's "the addressee": *you* may refer to multiple referents. Additionally, the definite article in "the addressee" implicates that the referent(s) of *you* – or in the case of Relevance and other pragmatic theories, mental representations of those referents – are readily identifiable in context (Lyons 1999: 198, 273). However, given that identifying such referents depends on context, the process requires inferencing that need not be either correct or complete. That is, interpreters may associate referents with NPs that are not intended by utterers or may give up the search for referents for various reasons, such as processing costs.

Indexicals, and referential expressions generally, are items in search of referents. In the embedding emails, the referents of *you* and *I* are, at one level, "straightforwardly" identifiable as the named addressee and the ostensible signer of the email, respectively, for example, "Dear Gerald … Margaret Huang." At another level, however, the utterer/writer and addressee of the email are problematic constructs. The email writer is most likely an AI staffer rather than its apparent signer. So the referent of the *I* of the emails is vague, probably to the point of being indeterminable to the addressee, though in this and analogous contexts this may not matter. What does matter is that the email has been sent by some representative of AI, and AI is responsible for its content and its distribution, though the idea that an organization can be responsible for anything is conceptually, ideologically, and legally fraught. It is worth remembering in this context that the US supreme court has decreed that corporations are "persons":

> [T]he decision in *Citizens United v. Federal Election Commission* conferred new dignity on corporate "persons," treating them – under the First Amendment free-speech clause – as the equal of human beings.
>
> At least in politics, the Court majority indicated, corporations have a voice, and they have worthy political ideas. Here is the way Justice Anthony M. Kennedy put it (partially quoting from an earlier ruling): "Corporations and other associations, like individuals, contribute to the 'discussion, debate, and the dissemination of information and ideas' that the First Amendment seeks to foster."
>
> (Lyle Denniston SCOTUSblog, January 21, 2010)[23]

[22] Nor with the Relevance Theory claim that first and second pronouns procedurally identify the producer and addressee of utterances: *I* refers to "the producer of this utterance" and *you* refers to "the addressee of the utterance"; Reboul (1992: 178–181).

[23] www.scotusblog.com/2010/01/analysis-the-personhood-of-corporations/ (accessed August 4, 2025).

Cooren and Matte (2010) and Cooren (2015: 11) argue that an organization's discourse "constitutes" the organization and that without the organization's "official statements, directives, memos, newsletters, annual reports, organizational charts, and so on" the organization would not exist.[24] To this list we might add AI's research reports, annual reports on international human rights, press releases, webpages, emails to members, and appeal letters.

The Washington Post provides a useful, if pre-theoretic, characterization of the roles of the individual – human – members of its editorial board in creating its editorial policy and writing its editorials that is consistent with Cooren's constitutive position.

About the Post's View

Editorials represent the views of The Post as an institution, as determined through discussion among members of the Editorial Board, based in the Opinions section and separate from the newsroom.[25]

And

[t]he board highlights issues it thinks are important and responds to news events, mindful of stands it has taken in previous editorials and principles that have animated Post editorial boards over time. Articles in the news pages sometimes prompt ideas for editorials, but every editorial is based on original reporting. News reporters and editors never contribute to editorial board discussions, and editorial board members don't have any role in news coverage.

These excerpts provide a clear articulation of the roles of individuals, as members of the board of an institution, for determining the "views" presented as those of the institution. The members of the various groups governing Amnesty International – International Secretariat, International Board, the Secretary General's Global council – are similarly responsible for the organization's policies, practices, and values.[26]

Your [(37)] Much of the research on genitive constructions has focused on their various forms – inflections such as the English *-'s* and phrases such as the English *of* genitives and their respective interpretations, for example, alienable vs. inalienable possession, and has typically represented these meanings by simple paraphrases. Huddleston and Pullum (2002) (H&P) is an important representative of this approach. H&P, while acknowledging that the range

[24] Jeff Kaplan, (p.c.) considers this formulation to be too restrictive. We should include discourses in modes other than the written and in registers other than the legal. For example, a group of neighbors might verbally agree to address their city council as a group on some issue of collective concern.

[25] www.washingtonpost.com/opinions/the-posts-view/?page=19 (accessed August 4, 2025).

[26] www.amnesty.org/en/about-us/our-leadership/ (accessed August 4, 2025).

of possible meaning relations between the genitive and its complement is "vast," nonetheless identify twenty-three separate semantic relations, typically expressed as clausal templates. For example (474):

i. *Mary's green eyes* *Mary has green eyes* [d has body part h]
vii. *Mary's debut* *Mary performs her debut* [d is performer of h]

In these templates, "d" stands for the genitive NP and "h" for the NP head modified by "d," variables whose values must be identified from context. In addition to identifying the values of the "d" and "h," interpreters must infer a meaning relation between the genitive expression and the expression it modifies. Some of the *your* phrases in the appeals seem to be paraphrasable by one or other of H&P's templates, for example, "your wisdom and compassion" (#22 Haitians, Dominican Republic) may be paraphrased as *You have wisdom and compassion* and viewed as an instance of H&P's xi. [d has human property h].

Many genitive phrases may have more than one paraphrase. *Your government* occurs seven times in the corpus. *Your* in three of these (#4 Al-Qahtani, Iraq; #30 Forced Marriages, Burkina Faso; #37 PoCs, Algeria) refers to government ministers and may be represented by H&P vii. [d is a member of h]. *Your* in the remaining four refers to ambassadors from China (#25 Missing, China) and Vietnam (#26 PoCs Vietnam; twice). None of H&P's templates fits these, though one might add a template to H&P's list: [d represents h]. For others, no such template seems possible, for example, "your utmost" (#21 Crime Task Force, USA) and "your excellency" (#4 Al-Qahtani, Iraq).

In some instances, a series of conjoined *your* phrases occurs, each with a different meaning relationship between *your* and its complement, for example, "Your constitution, your policies, your own citizens" (#22 Haitians, Dominican Republic). In this phrase, "your" refers to President Medina of the Dominican Republic. "Your constitution" is *the constitution of the Dominican Republic that you Medina are president of.* "Your policies" are *the policies that you, Medina, and your government are responsible for.* "Your own citizens" are *the citizens of the Dominican Republic of which you, Medina, are President.*

"Your own citizens" merits a fuller analysis than that just given. It occurs in the sentence, "Immediately stop violating the rights of your own citizens." The Dominican government at the time of the appeal distinguished between "Dominicans of Haitian descent" and Dominicans of other descent. The latter were deemed legally entitled to Dominican citizenship; the former, regardless of the fact that many claimed descent from Haitians who had entered the Republic 100 years earlier, were deemed ineligible for citizenship and were being forced to "return" to Haiti. So, the legal referents of "your own citizens" must have been Dominicans not of Haitian descent, though the interpretation intended in the appeal must refer to those of Haitian descent whose rights were being violated and thus implied that they too are Dominican citizens and thus to have the same rights as other Dominican citizens.

In addition to claiming that the range of meanings of genitive expressions is "vast," Huddleston and Pullum (2002) also say that "the semantic relation that holds between subject determiner and head nominal is not predetermined. Rather the interpretation is dependent on what semantic relation the context allows" (474). At the very least, the referents of "d" and "h" must be identified, and this crucially depends on context. In the case of "your government" (#30 Forced Marriages, Burkina Faso), "your" refers to the Message Recipient, the Minister of Justice and Human Rights, and "government" refers to that of Burkina Faso. In thirty-four of the thirty-seven instances of *your* constructions, *your* refers to one or more Message Recipients; in the remaining three, it refers to the AI member considering whether to SEND the appeal, for example, in "Your Congressional Representative" (#36 Refugees, USA).

Typically, of course, the interpretations are considerably more elaborate than merely finding values for the variables "d" and "h." For example, consider "your authority" in (#23 Mass Surveillance, USA). The Message Recipient is President Obama, and so the phrase might be paraphrased as *President Obama, you have the authority* or *the authority that you President Obama have*. However, having authority implies having authority over some things (and not others) by virtue of holding some authoritative office in an institution capable of conferring that authority. So, a more contextually complete paraphrase might be, *President Obama, you have the authority "to end indiscriminate mass surveillance practices that are jeopardizing the privacy of millions of Americans and people around the world" because you are the president of the United States.*

More intriguing is the contextual interpretation of "your desk," also in (#23 Mass Surveillance, USA). The phrase occurs in the sentence "You do not need to wait for legislation to reach your desk." Here, again, "your" refers to President Obama and the phrase suggests Huddleston and Pullum's (2002) paraphrase x. [d owns h]. Most recent US presidents have signed legislation on the desk in the Oval Office called the Resolute Desk. So, if Obama were to sign legislation in the Oval Office, "your desk" might well refer to the Resolute Desk – which he does not own. However, it could refer to any desk on which Obama might sign legislation, or indeed to any surface on which he might do so, regardless of who owns it or where it resides. Indeed, it need not refer to any desk at all. It can be – and should be in its context – taken metonymically to refer to legislation presented to the President for his signature.

While reductive paraphrases like Huddleston and Pullum's (2002) may be appropriate for certain analytic or expository contexts, they are inadequate for analyses of genitive expressions in context. Kolkmann (2016), from a Relevance Theory perspective, argues, convincingly I believe, that the meanings of genitive expressions are "better characterized in fully pragmatic terms" (237), that is, constructed by inferential pragmatic enrichment in context "on the basis of addressee-dependent considerations of relevance" (239), thus obviating "the need for taxonomies of possessive relations" (239). Crucially, it is only by such enrichment that the ideological implications of the expressions can be identified, for example, the legitimating character of "your country's laws" (#30 Forced Marriages, Burkina Faso) and "your constitution's provisions" (#22 Haitians, Dominican Republic); the unifying function of "your wisdom and compassion" (#22 Haitians, Dominican Republic); or the action-orienting function of "Your immediate action is urgently required" (#40 Cobalt, Apple Corp.).

While the interpretations I've identified above are possible, they are this analyst's constructions, not those that either the AI volunteers who send the appeals or their Message Recipients (or their surrogates) might construct. Their interpretations will only be as rich as their interpretative interests require. That is, actual interpreters will enrich the meanings of the *your* expressions only to the degree that they deem relevant in context, typically perhaps, minimally, though on occasion, perhaps, as richly as those identified above, and everything in between.[27, 28]

Third Person

The third-person pronouns typically refer anaphorically to the individuals or groups who are the subjects of the appeals:

[S]tudies have shown that ***at least one third of girls in Burkina Faso*** are married before the age of 18, with far-reaching consequences for ***their*** health, safety and human rights. (#30 Forced Marriages, Burkina Faso; emphasis added)

I am writing to express my deep concern about the situation of **Mustafa al-Hawsawi**, a detainee held in Department of Defense custody at the US naval station at Guantánamo Bay in Cuba since September 2006. According to **his** lawyers, **he** is in chronic extreme physical pain, and has injuries sustained during torture and other ill-treatment **he** endured while in the custody of the Central Intelligence Agency (CIA) between 2003 and 2006. **He** is reported to be suffering chronic and potentially life-threatening illness, and **he** requires appropriate and ongoing medical assessment and treatment. (#39 Al-Hawsawi, USA; emphasis added)

Though they may also refer to the addressees of the appeals:

Amnesty International is calling on **companies** to investigate **their** cobalt supply chain and prove **they** are addressing human rights abuses. (#40 Cobalt, Apple Corp.; emphasis added)

[27] This referential dependency indicates that second-person pronouns may be anaphoric as well as deictic.

[28] *Your* also occurs in conventional greetings to institutional office holders, e.g., Your Excellency (e.g., #4 Al-Qahtani, Iraq).

This use of third-person pronouns is akin to Verschueren's "indirect third-person" "interpreter-reference" (87), as it seems to share with his examples an ambiguity between actual third-person reference, that is, that the sentence above merely reports AI's appeals to the companies (named earlier in the appeal), and an indirect address to Apple because Apple is a named Message Recipient and listed among the companies AI is calling on.

The referents of these first-, second-, and third-person expressions are all positioned in the ideological formations activated by the letters and their associated documents, as individuals associated with AI appeals, as individuals or institutions that AI and the letter senders deem (potential) human rights violators, and as people or classes of people whose human rights have been violated.

Intimately associated with the pronominals in the letters are the "voices" they represent, to which we now turn.

AD 2.2.1.2: What types of voices are involved on the utterer's side? (Verschueren 2012: 89–91)

Verschueren (2012) notes that, in his history textbooks, "a chain of communicative acts underlies what ends up as an historical narrative" (89). As I demonstrate in Chapter 2, a similar chain of communicative acts underlies the embedding emails and the appeal letters, stretching from those who directly observe and report the relevant events, through those who curate this information as AI reports, to those who craft the webpages, emails, and appeals, and to those who receive and choose to SEND the appeals. It is this polyphonic chain of evidence that is designed to warrant the veracity of the claims made in AI's downstream documents, though the information itself is re-contextualized, re-entextualized, and re-genrecized.

In this context, Verschueren introduces his concept of "virtual utterer." A virtual utterer is one whose voice[29] is represented in the text and may be "real or imagined" (89, fn. 30). In the appeals, these voices may be those of the real individuals whose plight is the object of the appeal, often invoked to elicit sympathy, as Beatriz's voice is invoked in:

> Beatriz wants to live. She wants to see her one-year-old son grow up but as the government has yet to act, she doesn't know if she will live or die.
>
> (#8 Beatriz, El Salvador)

Occasionally, the voices of the Message Recipients are invoked, ostensibly to counter AI's claims, as in:

> I understand that your government has as an obligation to bring to [*sic*] those responsible for serious crimes to justice, and that Iraq must confront violence by armed group.
>
> (#4 Al-Qahtani, Iraq)

[29] "Voice" is "a cover term to distinguish different sources of the context of an utterance" (Verschueren 2012: 89, fn. 30).

While the main voices manifested in Verschueren's history textbooks are those of the authors, carefully modulated for their specific pedagogical and ideological purposes, the main voices of the appeal letters are rather more problematic. The letters are written by AI staffers, who may or may not be the same people who embed the letters in AI webpages and covering emails and then forward them to volunteers, who may then SEND them to their Message Recipients. We might reasonably consider the resulting emails and appeals to represent AI's corporate voice: communications crafted by AI staffers to represent AI's messages about situations of concern to it and addressed to classes of individuals identified by AI as at least potentially concerned about such situations. Consequently, as we have seen, the first-person pronoun of the letters poses interesting challenges of interpretation and analysis, especially in the context of a discussion of the ideological issues raised by the letters.

Linguists have generally distinguished between speakers/writers and hearers/readers, often without differentiating the various roles subsumed by these terms: the speaker/writer is the person who creates and articulates the utterance and the hearer/reader is the one who perceives and interprets it. However, such a simple analysis is inadequate for the appeal letters – and discourse in general – and researchers have proposed several schemas that allow us to assign more precise roles to the various entities involved. Verschueren (1999: 77–87) distinguishes utterers and interpreters and distinguishes utterers' many voices and interpreters' many roles. Goffman (1981) likewise identifies several speaker and hearer roles and I discuss his proposals below because they constitute perhaps the most influential such schema.

Verschueren (1999: 78 ff) distinguishes sources of information from the utterers of the information represented in a text. The utterer(s) who physically produce(s) a text may differ from sources of the utterer's information, for example, a witness describing an event vs. the journalist who re-casts the witness' testimony for a media report. Different sources may determine different elements of the "content" of an utterance. Utterers give voice to the information provided by sources and, of course, may be sources themselves. In the case of the AI appeals, we might view their writers as their "physical utterers" (78), though these writers are far from the ultimate source of the information they represent, and the notion of an ultimate source may make one a tad queasy. Behind some of the appeals and perhaps before they are written, AI documents the appeal situation, often in a report, for example, AI's 2020 report "'We Dried Our Tears': Addressing the toll on children of Northeast Nigeria's Conflict."[30] The information in these reports is curated ideologically and rhetorically (Snyder 2015: 209) from a great many sources, including UN Security Council resolutions, interviews with observers in the affected

[30] https://tinyurl.com/mr245cc6 (accessed August 5, 2025).

area, news media reports, which may be based on prior sources, indefinitely. Verschueren (1999) represents this schematically as: "source^1 … source^n," which are aligned with various utterer roles representing the voices comprehended within a text (78–82), and invoking the Bakhtinian notion of "polyphony" (Roulet 2003).

Verschueren (1999) also distinguishes utterers from virtual utterers (80) to conceptualize situations in which utterers appear to be, or present themselves as, quoting what someone, including the current utterer, has or might have said. This distinction is similar to Relevance Theory's notion of "echoic use" and would seem to allow Verschueren to account for irony, though he does not make this move.[31] We do, of course, find instances of virtual utterances in the letters. Some of these are quite explicit as indicated by "so-called" and the quote marks in:

> I am deeply concerned that the US government's so-called "targeted killing" program allows for the use of lethal force.
>
> (#1 Targeted Killing, USA)

"So-called" explicitly marks an expression as echoic and to be interpreted as ironic, thus indicating the speaker's critical stance toward the use of that expression, in this case implying doubt about the accuracy of the targeting implied by the wording. The virtual utterer is explicitly identified as the "US government."

Somewhat more complex is the use of "criticizing" in "He's on trial for 'criticizing' the Interior Ministry" (#3 Satire as Crime, Egypt). Here, the AI staffer is ostensibly quoting the Egyptian authorities who seem to be quoting Egyptian law which proscribes criticizing those authorities. *Criticize* is a "verb of judging" that licenses the implication that the agent of the verb presupposes that the criticized action is to be disapproved of (Levinson 1983: 182). However, without excavating the original utterance of "criticizing," we cannot determine from the letter who to attribute the disapproval to. Nor should we ignore the ironic interpretation prompted by the single quotes around "criticizing."

As AI emails and appeals are frequently based on AI reports, these may then be cited explicitly:

> On January 19, Amnesty International launched the report "'This is what we die for': Human Rights Abuses in the Democratic Republic of the Congo (DRC) Power the

[31] Somewhat surprisingly, Verschueren adopts a very traditional conception of irony, as implicating "the opposite of what is said literally" (34–35), a conception convincingly rebutted in Sperber and Wilson (1986: 240–242) and replaced by their concept of echoic use. An utterance is echoic if it expresses an idea that someone (including the speaker) expressed or has or had in mind. The utterance is ironic if it conveys the speaker's dissociative attitude toward that idea (Cave and Wilson 2018: 195–198; Clark 2013: 280–294; Wilson and Sperber 2012: 94–96, 123–145).

Global Trade in Cobalt,"[32] which found that major electronics brands, including Apple, Samsung, and Sony, are failing to do basic checks to ensure that cobalt mined by child labourers has not been used in their products.

(#40 Cobalt, Apple Corp.)

The relative clause beginning with "which" summarizes the relevant elements of the report and forms the basis for the remainder of the appeal. The report, of course, is based upon information from a variety of sources, which may be dependent upon earlier sources, and so on indefinitely (Delahunty 2021; Verschueren 1999: 80–82).

Even more complex is the disassociating stance indicated by "confession" in:

Abdullah al-Qahtani testified that his "confession" was obtained through torture and other ill-treatment including severe beatings and partial asphyxiation.

(#4 Al-Qahtani, Iraq)

Presumably what al-Qahtani said under torture was characterized as a confession by his torturers, then by the Iraqi authorities, but this characterization of Al-Qahtani's utterances is called into question by AI on the basis that these utterances were coerced by torture, a violation of Article 15 of the UN UDHR. We have at least eight layers of voices: (1) Al-Qahtani's utterances, (2) reported by his interrogators to their various levels of superiors, (3) someone (at least) of whom characterized these utterances as a confession, (4) a characterization criticized by AI appeal writers, (5) endorsed by the appeal SENDers as a violation of Al-Qahtani's human rights, but (6) probably to be rejected by the Iraqi Message Recipients or their surrogates, (7) interrogated by me, and (8) by you, my dear reader.

So, various utterers are represented in the appeals: *I* (the SENDer of an appeal), the AI staffers who crafted that appeal, the AI staffers who crafted the embedding emails, the AI staffers who curated the information upon which the AI report was based, the layers of sources of that information, and the Message Recipients or their surrogates whose voices may be represented in various ways in the appeal. All of these utterers perform various ideological roles in the processes of (re-)entextualizing, (re-)contextualizing, and (re-)genrecizing the "original" information.

An alternative, very influential, sociologically oriented, but *sui generis* approach to the study of verbal interaction is that of Goffman (1981: 124–157). I present, somewhat reductively, the relevant elements of his "participation framework" (137).[33] He distinguishes three "participation statuses," subsumed by speaker/writer:

[32] www.amnesty.org/en/documents/afr62/3183/2016/en/ (accessed August 5, 2025).

[33] Levinson (1988: 169, Note) characterizes Goffman's term "participation framework" as misleading and substitutes "participation roles." He substantially elaborates Goffman's schema in that publication.

a. Animator (An): "the sounding box"; "the individual active in the role of utterance production"
b. Author (Au): "someone who has selected the sentiments that are expressed and the words in which they are encoded"
c. Principal (Pr): "someone whose position is established by the words that are spoken, someone whose beliefs have been told, someone who is committed to what the words say"

(Goffman 1981: 144)

The AI staffers who write the appeal letters must be their Animators and most probably also their Authors and Principals. But because the letters are ostensibly sent on to their Message Recipients by the volunteers to whom AI sends them, those volunteers must be their Principals, as they, by virtue of being AI volunteers and by SENDing the letters to their addressees, are presumably "committed to what the words say." The volunteers may, at their discretion, revise the letters, thereby becoming at least partially the letters' Animators and Authors, as well as their Principals. That is, the SENDers of the letters, while relying on the AI staffers' research, assume responsibility for the truth, accuracy, and stances of the letters; like actors inhabiting a role, the SENDers "inhabit" the *I* of the letters and the ideological stances and alignments that this implies. See my discussion of *I* above regarding Procedure 2.2.1.

AI's decision to frame the letters as first-person appeals must be seen as an element in AI's engagement of its volunteers. By SENDing a letter and thus "inhabiting" the *I* and acceding to their inclusion in *we*, the volunteer appeal SENDer adopts the identity of an AI member and, in concert with corporate AI, performs the speech acts that constitute the letter – expressing concern about a situation, declaring that the situation violates certain rights, urging the addressees to redress the situation by bringing it into conformity with those rights, and by inviting the addressees to respond – the volunteer enacts their commitment to, and engagement with, AI's values. This enactment positions the volunteer as someone committed to human and humanitarian rights and identifies him/her as a member of a group committed to supporting and acting on behalf of those rights.

The letters are enactments of speech acts and so we must consider the felicity conditions that constitute these acts. Earlier speech act analyses, well represented in Levinson (1983: ch. 5), proposed that speech acts must meet sincerity conditions. Thus, an expression of concern implicates that the utterer feels that concern; an assertive implicates that the assertor believes their assertion; a directive implicates that the utterer desires what the direction demands. On this view, we are, on the basis of these implicatures, licensed to assume that the AI volunteer who SENDs a letter sincerely feels the concern it expresses, believes what it asserts, and desires the redress it asks for.

However, as noted earlier, the sincerity requirement has been controversial, at least for promises, since at least Searle (1969: 62). Solan and Tiersma (2005:

182–183) make the broad claim that "[l]inguists and philosophers of language generally agree that sincerity is not required to perform a speech act successfully … making an insincere promise is a wrongful act, but it is a promise nonetheless," and counts as such in legal contexts. Applying this logic to the letters implies that the act of SENDing a letter counts as an expression of concern, as an endorsement of the truth of the assertions made, and as an attempt to get the Message Recipients to redress the situation. That is, SENDing a letter implies that the SENDer meets the conditions for the felicity of the speech acts involved, though not necessarily sincerely or committedly, a disassociation summarized in "clicktivism" or "slacktivism," which we might compare with Bonhoeffer's (1995) concept of "cheap grace." (See Blommaert 2005: section 4.2 on a "theory of voice.")

The *I*s of the letters may be understood also by appeal to Foucault's (1995) notion of "subjectivization," as represented in Tarver (2017: 26–27).

> Subjectivizing practices are means by which individuals both subordinate themselves to a discipline and, by virtue of it, achieve a sense of their own identities. So, for example, a religious practitioner creates and obtains new forms of self-knowledge by participating in confession, prayer, and the observance of lent, just as a student creates and obtains new forms of self-knowledge by subjecting herself to the rigors of the comprehensive examination process of her graduate program in philosophy. The individual "receives as his status his own individuality" (Foucault 1995: 192) in and through these disciplines. The disciplines through which individuals gain such self-knowledge call to mind, for Foucault, the dual meaning of the word "subject." One may be "subject" to a law, state, or moral order, in the sense of being governed by or obligated to it. One may also be a "subject" in the philosophical sense of being an "I" – the first-person subject of a life. Foucault argues in *Discipline and Punish* (1995) that one of the distinguishing features of the modern era is the extent to which the latter sense of "subject" is dependent on the former. It is by being subjected to particular rules, disciplines, and power relations that we come to understand ourselves as particular kinds of subjects.[34]

By SENDing the letters and thus inhabiting their *I*s, AI volunteers subject themselves to the legal and "moral order" of universal human and humanitarian rights and the obligations they entail. They adopt the ideological positions espoused by the letters and thereby enact a particular identity and engage in specific power relations and come to understand themselves as defenders of human rights.

Nonetheless, the *I*s of the letters remain problematic. Inhabiting one implies that I, Gerald Delahunty, wrote the letter, which I did not. The letter attributes words to me that I did not utter. Nonetheless, I am the *I* of the letters. I forward

[34] Reboul (1992: 174–175, fn. 4) remarks on disagreements about the concept of subjectivity and suggests, perhaps too comprehensively, that it comprises "the set of all the spatio-temporal coordinates" that an individual occupies during their existence, as well as "consciousness (or even self-consciousness) and memory of past events."

them and thereby may be assumed to endorse their messages. Additionally, the original letter may have been written by more than one AI staffer, and it is written within the specifications for such letters laid down in AI policy. All these raise issues of "voice," "dialogism," and "polyphony" (Dendale 2006; Verschueren 2012: 89, fn. 30) that I do not develop here.

AD 2.2.1.3: What types of interpreter roles are involved? (Verschueren 2012: 91–93)

> "Pompeo Denounces Hezbollah in Lebanon, With an Israeli Audience in Mind"[35]

The research literature provides a range of theoretical typologies of interpreter roles in communicative events. I begin by briefly discussing the proposals in Verschueren (2012: 91–93). Verschueren's main distinctions are between primary and secondary audiences and between addressees and side participants (Table 5, 92). The primary audience for the main texts of the history textbooks are "those the author wants to inform or teach about the narrated events: students, other scholars, or members of a general readership outside schools or academia." Because these are the interpreter types that the writers designed the textbooks for, they are the books' addressees. The secondary audience for the main texts are readers with interests other than being informed about the narrated events. These are side participants that the writers might reasonably have taken into account – colleagues, parents, and school authorities. The primary audience of the textbook prefaces may be their addressees – scholars, students, and general readers, who may or may not be directly addressed. The primary audience may also include side participants who must therefore be taken into account, for example, students who may read the prefaces. The secondary audience for the prefaces – colleagues, parents, school, supervisors, etc. – are their addressees.

Verschueren (1999: 82–87) provides a more elaborated conception of interpreter roles, characterizing them as a subcategory of "**presences**, i.e., the totality of persons who are 'present' at or in the vicinity of the speech event or … in a position that would enable them to become engaged in the event" (82; emphasis in original). Once engaged in the event, by listening or reading, presences become "**interpreters**" (emphasis in original). Presences who are not engaged – though they might become so – are "**non-interpreters**" (emphasis in original). Interpreters may be participants or non-participants. Participants may be addressees – those to whom the communication is directed – or side participants – those who attend to the communication and whose attention is taken into account by the addressers, but who are not directly engaged.

[35] https://tinyurl.com/2p9c7mpn (accessed August 5, 2025).

Non-participants may be bystanders or overhearers, and if the latter, may be listeners-in or eavesdroppers (Verschueren 1999: 85, figure 3.4). Utterances may be adapted to the possibility that they will be engaged by "presences" other than their ostensible addressees.

Clearly, the AI volunteers who access the appeals on the AI website or who receive them by email are presences who can generally be expected to read the appeals before SENDing them, otherwise AI could omit the letters and just ask volunteers to click on a labeled link, such as, "Take action now and ask Finland to change the law to support transgender rights" (AI email, January 8, 2018). Verschueren's presences do not allow for such clicktivists, though they are among that "totality of persons who are 'present' at or in the vicinity of the speech event … in a position that would enable them to become engaged in the event." But for Verschueren being engaged requires reading the appeals, which clicktivists, by definition, do not. They are not engaged, in Verschueren's sense, in the speech event of SENDing the appeals. They seem also not to be overhearers, who must be listeners-in or eavesdroppers, implying a degree of intentional active engagement in the event. They share characteristics of Verschueren's "non-interpreters," but non-interpreters who act, minimally, by merely clicking SEND.[36]

Verschueren's roles are illustrated and broadly defined, but leave considerable room for interpretation. The named Message Recipients of the appeals are the intended primary audience – the addressees of the appeals. They are constructed, positioned, and identified as people with the power to accede to the request(s) made in the appeals and as potentially persuadable by arguments based on human/humanitarian rights. They are also persons to whom potential concessions may be attributed. However, it is most likely that the intended Message Recipients do not read (any or all of) the letters; this is done, if at all, by lower level functionaries, who may or may not report on the appeals to their superiors, though they may record the numbers of letters they receive regarding a particular situation.[37] These functionaries may be considered side participants, though they might also be considered non-participants. Nothing in the letters seems chosen specifically to index them, probably because they are unknown, perhaps unidentifiable, but most likely because to do so might imply that they, not the Message Recipients, are the more important participants, perhaps even the decision-makers.

The AI volunteers who receive and perhaps read and perhaps SEND the appeals present significant analytic challenges to Verschueren's schema. They

[36] On various kinds of clicktivism and their effects on activism, go to https://tinyurl.com/vp5ceumj (accessed August 5, 2025).

[37] As I discuss in Chapter 2, in the early history of AI, hand-written appeals from AI volunteers did get to their Message Recipients, as Power (2001) and Neier (2012) demonstrate.

might be regarded as side participants or non-participants who "listen in." As neither option seems adequate to characterize their interpreter roles and ideological positioning, I look to alternative analytic frameworks. Here, I synoptically lay out Goffman's (1981) proposal, as articulated in McCawley (1999: 596) and Levinson (1988: 169, Table 7.1). Beneath that, I briefly review Allan Bell's (1984) audience design framework.

Ratified (official) participants:

a. Addressed recipient (AR): person(s) to whom the utterance is addressed:
"the one to whom the speaker addresses his visual attention and to whom, incidentally, he expects to turn over the speaking role" (Levinson 1988: 169);
b. Unaddressed recipient (UR): has official status in the encounter, but to whom the utterance is not directed.

Unratified (non-official) participants:

a. Overhearers: unintentional, inadvertent listeners;
b. Eavesdroppers: listeners who have purposely engineered their participation.

Others:

a. Intended recipient (IR): those whom the "speaker" intends to hear/read and understand the utterance (can take in eavesdroppers or bystanders);
b. Recipient in general (R): those who hear/read the utterance, irrespective of what the "speaker" intends or is even aware of.

While the Goffman/McCawley/Levinson Addressee(s) are the named Message Recipients of the AI letters, the lower-level government staffers with responsibility for dealing with matters such as these appeals seem to be best categorized as ratified recipients.[38] The AI volunteers, who if they read the appeals before deciding whether to SEND them, may be viewed as ratified unaddressed recipients and intended recipients. The volunteers have an "official" role in the encounter – the appeals are sent in emails addressed to them and if they merely SEND the appeal, they will have fulfilled that function. However, it is a central argument of this work that the appeals have two primary functions – to persuade their Message Recipients to act as they direct and to ideologically

[38] "AI had 100,000 signatures and took them to the Russian Embassy in Washington, DC, and were physically removed from the building. They had a scheduled meeting and presented them with the names, and the Russian officials immediately asked them to leave. They said they were leaving the petitions behind and the Russian officials refused to accept them and physically escorted them from the building and threw the petitions on the curb" (PunkNews.org quoting *Rolling Stone*, August 29, 2012).

engage the AI volunteers to whom they are emailed, specifically by enabling them to perform an ideological action by SENDing the appeal, and thus to be and perhaps feel personally engaged in AI's work on behalf of victims of human rights violations. That is, they are designed to motivate AI volunteers, just like the other parts of the emails and of the webpages in which they are embedded.[39]

Bell's audience design framework (1984) also distinguishes between several audience types based on three criteria from the perspective of the speaker: known (whether an addressee is known to be part of a speech context); ratified (the speaker acknowledges the listener's presence in the speech context); or addressed (the listener is directly spoken to). Bell defined the following audience types:

a. Addressee – listeners who are known, ratified, and addressed
b. Auditors – listeners who are not directly addressed, but are known and ratified
c. Overhearers – non-ratified listeners of whom the speaker is aware, but does not address
d. Eavesdroppers – non-ratified listeners of whom the speaker is unaware (Bell 1984:158–160)

In addition to distinguishing these audience types, Bell also claims that the impact of audience members on the speaker's style-shifting is proportional to the degree to which the speaker recognizes and ratifies them. The letters present indications that they are designed for audiences other than their named Message Recipients, in particular, for the AI volunteers and potential letter SENDers, though they are not overtly acknowledged in the letters as audience members. These indications are stylistic and can be best appreciated by contrasting the register of the appeals with that of the report and by the similarities between the email and webpage language and that of the appeals. The AI volunteers would then be categorized as at least overhearers if not auditors in Bell's schema.

While these role differentiations make problematic the attribution of responsibility for evaluating situations as violations of norms, it is clear from the letters that the Author/Principal purports to engage the Intended Recipient/Addressee in a dialogic exchange, as my discussion of *I know* and *I understand* below will make clear. As Du Bois (2007: 173) puts it, the Authors/Principals take responsibility for their acts of evaluation, "with potentially profound consequences for the relationships of stance takers with their dialogically co-responsible partners and with their expanding networks of social relations

[39] And as the response email discussed in Chapter 2 demonstrates, to motivate them to make financial donations to AI.

along wider horizons of time and space." In the case of AI appeals, these expanding social networks must include the AI staffers, all the volunteers who receive and SEND the appeals, the various hearers/readers, the news media who amplify the opposing stances, the international diplomatic networks that from time to time become involved in negotiations for the release of prisoners, and the foreign ministers and heads of state who "raise the issue" of human rights at summit meetings and other venues. That is, a broad range of "presences" with many different positions and levels of engagement. Activating these takes time and effort – and money – distributed across the globe.

"Stance," according to Du Bois (2007), "always invokes, explicitly or implicitly, presupposed systems of sociocultural value, while at the same time contributing to the enactment and reproduction of those systems" (173). The AI appeals invoke, as we have seen, explicitly and implicitly, a variety of international and universal legal frameworks such as the UDHR, which explicitly characterize those rights. The appeals may also address the sociocultural value systems that legitimized the sentencing of the people who are the objects of the appeals, and may, to one degree or another, attribute those values to the Addressees and other presences and participants. The appeals urge the Message Recipients to adopt the writer's values or to (at least) act accordingly. The letters explicitly urge the Message Recipients to adopt values characterized as "international standards," for example, the abolition of the death penalty. This may be in addition to more urgent appeals such as a stay of execution based on the principle that "[t]he death penalty violates the right to life" guaranteed by the UN Declaration, or because "a miscarriage of capital punishment cannot be undone" (#4 Al-Qahtani, Iraq) which seems to invoke not just some specifically legal framework of values, but a general sense of fairness that all might agree on, thus enacting and reproducing values endorsed by AI.[40]

The letters appear to be designed, as I have been claiming, for at least two types of audience, the Message Recipients and the AI volunteer letter-SENDers. The letters are clearly designed for the Message Recipients: they are directly addressed in many of the letters, for example, "Dear Prosecutor General" (#11 Pussy Riot, Russia), "Dear Mr. Hagel, Mr. Kerry, Mr. Obama" (#10 Drone Wars, USA). It is harder to make the case for the other audience, but the use of *I* does double duty: it proposes an engagement between the volunteer and the Message Recipients, and it proposes an engagement between AI and the letter SENDers who thereby adopt for themselves the claims and evaluations enacted in the letters written by AI staffers on behalf of that organization. Other elements that seem to be selected for both audiences (though perhaps just for the volunteers) are the occasional appeals to pathos in the

40 Evaluation in texts is also discussed as *appraisal*: see White (2011).

letters, for example, "both mothers in their twenties" (#11 Pussy Riot, Russia) and "Beatriz wants to live. She wants to see her one-year-old son grow up but as the government has yet to act, she doesn't know if she will live or die" (#8 Beatriz, El Salvador).[41]

AD 2.2.2: What mental states are expressed or appealed to? (Verschueren 2012: 93–95)

Verschueren (2012: 93) remarks that "the history textbooks ... are full of expressions that reveal beliefs, goals, aspirations, intentions, etc., and topics ... often clearly anchored into concerns that are 'personal' for the author, at least in his/her capacity as a citizen of the nation he/she represents." Likewise, the letters include expressions of the *I*'s feelings about the situation or event; for example, "I am deeply concerned that ..." (#1 Targeted Killings, USA), "I'm deeply worried about ..." (#25 Missing, China), "I am profoundly disturbed that ..." (#18 Badawi, Saudi Arabia), "I am encouraged by ..." (#8 Beatriz, El Salvador), and "I am disappointed to learn ..." (#21 Crime Task Force, USA). The letters also contain expressions of the *I*'s sense of exigency of the situation, for example, "I am writing with an urgent request ..." (#4 Al-Qahtani, Iraq), "I urge you to ..." (#7 Aamer, USA), and many others. These feelings are "anchored into" the *I*'s "capacity" as a member of AI and as a human rights activist.

In addition to expressing the *I*'s emotions, the letters also express the *I*'s epistemological stances. While the main expression of epistemological stance is the indicative mood, more explicit epistemic expressions also occur, for example, "I know ..." "I understand ..." (#4 Al-Qahtani, Iraq), and "Accurate information regarding ..." (#9 Police Action, Turkey). Besides indicating the epistemological stances of the *I*, the letters also attribute such stances to others, including AI, for example, "AI considers ..." (#15 Vitishko, Russia), and especially the Addressees, for example, "US authorities have no intention of ..." (#7 Aamer, USA), "End claims that ..." (#1 Targeted Killings, USA), though others less central to the appeal may also have stances attributed to them, for example, "Teenie Rogers, the widow of Brent Miller, doesn't believe that ... she believes that ..." (#16 Woodfox, Louisiana, USA). On occasion, who the stances are attributed to is left obscure in truncated passives, for example, "Herman Wallace and Albert Woodfox are believed to ..." (#12 Wallace, Louisiana, USA).

[41] These appeals to pathos, and specifically to motherhood and characteristics assumed to be associated with it, raise the issue of the gender of the writers of the appeals. They are appeals to empathy and there is an abundant literature claiming that women are more empathetic than men, or at least that they act as if they are. (See, e.g., Christov-Moore et al. 2014.) These appeals suggest, but merely suggest, that (some of) the appeals may be written by women, which is consistent with the fact that the emails are typically signed by women.

As the letters typically make a (quasi-)legal argument on behalf of individuals or causes, the Authors appear to (act as if they) assume that the Message Recipients are potentially persuadable by such arguments, though the size of the protest may be more persuasive in many cases. Nonetheless, the letters are typically organized as enthymematic arguments, that is, arguments in which a premise or the conclusion is unexpressed. The letters' invocation of human rights and governmental obligations is typically implicit.

We should ask why the appeals include arguments at all. At an abstract level, an argument may be deductive, inductive, or abductive. At a pragmatic level, arguments are discourses intended to provide reasons for participants to believe the conclusions, and in the case of the appeal letters, to act on the basis of those conclusions. In the appeals, the premises invoke (or better, evoke) various rights documents and the conclusions purport to be consistent with those documents, and thus with the ideologies of human and humanitarian rights.

Also from a discourse perspective, we can view these appeals as threats to the addressees' face, both positive and negative (Brown and Levinson 1987) and, mixing approaches and stretching a bit here, thus dispreferred in the Conversation Analysis sense. Dispreferred turns are typically "more elaborated" than preferred ones, and "[s]pecifically … are commonly accompanied by (among others) accounts …" (Schegloff 2007: 65). These accounts provide reasons for why the dispreferred turn has been chosen, in the case of the appeals, why the Message Recipients are being imposed upon and at least potentially made to seem and, perhaps, feel responsible for the rights violations.

The arguments presented in the letters are also likely to be intended to persuade AI volunteers. Indeed, if we assume that AI assumes that the individual letters will not be read by their Message Recipients, and that AI relies, at least partially, for its effectiveness in motivating many thousands of volunteers to TAKE ACTION and click SEND when they receive AI requests to do so, and that it is the numbers of SENDs that are effective in "persuading" Message Recipients to redress rights violations, then we might conclude that the primary audiences for the letters are AI volunteers, not the named addressees, and thus that the letters' arguments are designed for them.

According to rhetoricians (e.g., Williams and Colomb 2001: 5–9), arguments "make us rational," "sustain a civil community," "define academic and professional communities," and "enable democracy." An argument involving true premises and valid inferences is a display of the arguer's rationality and it implies an expectation of rationality in return from the addressee, and thus implicates the possibility of a rational resolution of whatever the argument is about, for example, the return to adherence to norms of human respect and dignity. Mere demands, as often seen on signs in protests, imply only that the addressees should capitulate and grant the demand. Demands are based on assumed power; they imply that one side will win and the other lose. Rational arguments suggest reciprocity and equality; both sides may gain.

Within the framework he characterizes as "informal logic" (Walton 1989), Walton (2009: 2) defines what he calls a "minimal" argument:

An argument is a set of statements (propositions), made up of three parts, a conclusion, a set of premises, and an inference from the premises to the conclusion. An argument can be supported by other arguments, or it can be attacked by other arguments, and by raising critical questions about it.

He goes on to contrast monological with dialogical or dialectical arguments:

dialogical (or dialectical) [argumentation] … looks at two sides of an argument, the pro and the contra. According to this approach, the method of evaluation is to examine how the strongest arguments for and against a particular proposition at issue interact with each other, and in particular how each argument is subject to probing critical questioning that reveals doubts about it. By this dialog process of pitting one argument against the other, the weaknesses in each argument are revealed, and it is shown which of the two arguments is the stronger. (4–5; footnote omitted)

This understanding of argument is consistent with that proposed in Mercier and Sperber (2011: 57), which approaches the understanding of argument from an evolutionary point of view and claims that "the function of reasoning is argumentative. It is to devise and evaluate arguments intended to persuade" (57). Mercier and Sperber contrast this essentially dialogical understanding of argument with the "majority view" of scholars studying reasoning which "seems to be that the main function of reasoning is to enhance individual cognition" (59).

The typical appeal letter sets out an argument, which we can view as minimal and monological from Walton's point of view. That is, it presents a conclusion derived from premises. The premises derive from various international declarations and legal instruments and facts specific to the appeal. The conclusion is that the facts of the appeal situation violate clauses of the legal instruments.

Of course, the letters (or, more accurately, their Authors) seek to do more than merely derive the conclusion that some situation is in violation of a law; they seek to persuade their addressees to redress the violation, that is, to "make better decisions," as Mercier and Sperber put it.

Forst (2012: 1; emphasis in original) argues that human beings are

justificatory beings. They not only have the ability to justify or take responsibility for their beliefs and actions by giving reasons to others, but in certain contexts they see this as a duty and expect that others will do the same. If we want to understand human practices, we must conceive of them as practices bound up with justifications; no matter what we think or do, we place upon ourselves (and others) the demand for reasons, whether they are made explicit or remain implicit (at least initially). From this perspective, we can call a social context "political" when human beings find themselves in an "order of justification," which consists of norms and institutions that are to govern their lives together – in cooperation as well as conflict – in a justified or justifiable way. The most important normative concept that applies to this order is that of *justice*.

If the AI letters are about anything, they are about justice – the word occurs thirty-seven times in the forty letters – and so we should expect the letters to present justifications to the Message Recipients and the AI volunteers for the evaluations they present and for the remedies they urge.

Forst (2012: 214–215; emphasis in original) elaborates on his claim, saying that

> [c]onnected to the cognitive insight into the principle of justification (and the criteria of reciprocity and generality) is the normative insight that moral persons have a duty not to withhold the basic right to justification from anyone. These two dimensions of practical reason are linked insofar as the cognition of the correctness of the principle of justification must be a *practical* cognition: individuals must understand both themselves and others as subjects of this principle, as members of a moral community in which one is inevitably the author and addressee of validity claims for actions or norms that concern others (or oneself) and therefore must be justified in specific ways.

If we adopt Forst's position, then we have a way of understanding two elements of the letters. First, occasionally (and only very occasionally) the letters include concessions to the addressees, most elaborately in (#4 Al-Qahtani, Iraq), which includes the following two concessions:

> I know that all six convictions have been upheld by the court of cassation, and that four of the defendants, Manaf 'Abdulrahim 'Abdulhamid 'Issa al-Rawi, Mohammad Nouri Matar Yassin, Ibrahim 'Abdulqader 'Ali 'Antik, and Mohammad Jaber Tawfiq 'Obaid, have already been executed.
>
> I understand that your government has as an obligation to bring to [*sic*] those responsible for serious crimes to justice, and that Iraq must confront violence by armed group.

And in letter (#1 Targeted Killings, USA):

> I fully recognize the US government's duty to take robust action to protect the life and physical integrity of people within its jurisdiction, and to bring to justice perpetrators of crimes under international law.
>
> Those responsible for the attacks in the USA on September 11, 2001, attacks that deliberately targeted civilians and were a crime against humanity, should be brought to justice through fair criminal trials without recourse to the death penalty, as should anyone responsible for planning further such attacks.

Each concession is immediately followed by a rebuttal justified by appeal to the rights of accused, to international standards of judicial procedure, to international law, and to "fair criminal trials without recourse to the death penalty" (#1 Targeted Killings, USA).

Second is the marginally more frequent invitation from the Authors to the Message Recipients to respond, "I look forward to hearing from you regarding this matter" (#17 Caning, Indonesia). Both of these rhetorical moves can be seen as instantiations of Forst's (2012: 215) claim that individuals are "inevitably the author[s] and addressee[s] of validity claims for actions or norms that concern others (or oneself) and therefore must be justified in specific ways." In the first case, AI presents a justification on the Message Recipients' behalf; in the second, it invites the Message Recipients to provide their own justifications for their actions.

AD 2.2.3: What (aspects of) social settings or institutions are involved/invoked? (Verschueren 2012: 95–97)

In this section, Verschueren focuses on the "processes of institutional identity construction" that "position the texts in a world of discourse and of real-world social relations" (96). He notes particularly references in the titles and prefaces of his history textbooks to the educational institutions and practices in which the textbooks are to be taken to be embedded. He notes also the personal opinions of the authors regarding the "educational role of history teaching" (96) in the personal, political, and ideological lives of the readers. Such explicit personal opinions are "almost completely absent from the main body of the texts," nonetheless the texts reflect "struggles for *authority* and authorization" (97; emphasis in original) which derive from their institutional contexts:

> The discursive reflection of authority is the right to speak on behalf of the institution, a group. In an educational or academic context, this combines with an assumption that the institution itself stands for objective knowledge. As a result, authority is established – or attempts at establishing authority are made – by distancing, the avoidance of personal positioning. In other words, educational or academic face is established by being faceless. (97)

As the AI appeals are physically contained within their embedding emails, which are signed by high-ranking AI officials whose role within the organization is indicated, thus establishing a chain of authorization from the organization itself through these officials to the volunteer who receives and ideally SENDs the appeal, ostensibly to its Message Recipients. In stark contrast to the facelessness attributed by Verschueren to his textbooks and to academic writing in general – an attribution belied by Verschueren's own academic writing – the appeals are designedly personal, from an *I* to a *you* about matters that the *I* is personally invested in and who urges the *you* to become personally invested in.

Because the letters are elements of AI's exercises in counterpower, they are designed to motivate AI volunteers and persuade government officials to act in accordance with human rights. By invoking various legal instruments, the letters also invoke the institutions responsible for those instruments, for example, by invoking the UDHR, AI invokes the United Nations; by invoking a decision by the Inter-American Court of Human Rights, AI invokes the Organization of American States. And by invoking these institutions, AI invokes their power. Citing Bourdieu (1991), Verschueren (97) says that "individual language users may derive authority from the way in which they fit into an institutional context, which always involves relations of power," aspects of their *habitus*.[42] Though AI staffers write the letters and volunteers SEND them, the volunteers thus play two roles: they adopt unto themselves the authoritative language and authority of AI and the instruments and institutions invoked in the letters, and, by their numbers confer authority and power upon AI and the individual appeals, and, arguably, back upon the institutions from which the authority and authoritative language derive.

Other social settings and institutions invoked by the letters include the Geneva and Hague Conventions and elements of national legal systems such as the Iraqi Court of Cassation (#4 Al-Qahtani, Iraq) and local police and prison systems. By acting to redress contraventions of human and humanitarian rights, typically in political and social systems under internal and/or external stress, AI augments a large number of such organizations which derive their authority from these declarations and conventions. Chen (2015: 80 ff) characterizes these as "organizations concerned with rectitude," and this concern confers additional authority, which is irremediably ideological.

Ad 2.2.4: How is the discourse anchored temporally and spatially?

In particular:

Ad 2.2.4.1: How do event time, time of utterance, and reference time relate to each other? (Verschueren 2012: 97–99)

Many linguists adopt the Reichenbachian temporal distinctions deployed by Verschueren. In an idealized and highly simplified scenario, the time of utterance is the time at which the utterer produces the (spoken) utterance – the temporal deictic center; the event time is the time at which the events spoken about occur; and the reference time is the time with reference to which the event time is identified. The times of utterance and reference may coincide; for instance, if I were to say to my wife, *I let the cat out*, the time of utterance is the time at which I said this; the event time is prior to the utterance time, though how long prior is not indicated; and the reference time coincides with the utterance time. If I were to say to my wife, *I will be back by 5 p.m. this evening*, then the

[42] Habitus is "a subjective but not individual system of internalized structures, schemes of perception, conception, and action common to all members of the same group or class" (Bourdieu 1977: 86; cited in Gillespie 2019).

reference and utterance times no longer coincide as the reference time is 5 p.m. on the evening of the day on which I uttered the sentence and the utterance time is when I spoke, clearly earlier than 5 p.m. on that day.

The temporal deictic center of Verschueren's textbooks is problematic, as it generally is with published materials. In a conversation or other synchronous communicative event, the time of speaking or writing is the utterance time. However, for "utterances" such as published materials that require considerable time to produce, we might take their times of publication as their utterance times.

History textbooks typically narrate events that occurred prior to the time of utterance, and so typically are represented in the past tense. They represent many events and thus many event times. In the simplest case, these events may be presented in their chronological order, indicated by temporal adverbials, though Verschueren notes some more complex organizations.

In the simplest case also, event and reference time coincide, though in the history texts, they frequently diverge, as one past event is presented as prior to some other past event, often indicated by their occurrence dates.

Verschueren notes the deployment of various tense forms – to indicate how a past event is relevant to the time of utterance or to represent general truths or authors' evaluative commentary.

The appeal letters entail considerable complications of these three times. Each letter refers to at least two situations: the situation that precipitated the appeal and the situation that redresses it. The letters therefore entail two event times, the first of which necessarily precedes the other. The first event begins prior to the time and date on which AI emailed the letter to its volunteers, and, assuming that a volunteer SENDs the letter as soon as it arrives in his/her mailbox, it continues until the second event, the requested redress, occurs (if it does), and therefore for an unpredictable length of time after the letter is sent. When a violation is not redressed shortly after the time when the embedding email is sent to AI members and volunteers, AI continues to press for its redress for a considerable time.

The time of utterance presents complexities not unlike those presented by the letters' Authors and Message Recipients, that is, the *I*s and *you*s of the letters. We must distinguish the times at which the various Goffman speaker roles – Animator, Author, and Principal – were enacted, and thus apportion utterance time by these roles. I assume that the AI staffers are Authors, Animators, and Principals and that the volunteer who SENDs the letter, but who also asserts "I am writing …" (though, of course, they aren't), is a Principal. It is probable that the AI Authors, Animators, and Principals are distinct, and, if so, the AI Author's utterance time would precede that of the Animator, and that both of these would precede the Principal's, though it is impossible to be certain about any such sequence without investigating AI's procedures.

As there are at least two event times, there must be at least two reference times, one for each event time. The reference time for the event time of the appeal situation coincides with that event time; the reference time for the event time of the redress event reflects the exigency of the need for redress, frequently characterized as "urgent," and so letters typically urge "immediate" action (#22 Haitians, Dominican Republic), or that a prisoner be released "immediately" (#7 Aamer, USA; #8 Beatriz, El Salvador) or "today" (#12 Wallace, Louisiana), or that charges be dropped "expeditiously" (#24 Indecent Dress, Sudan), or that death penalties be overturned "before it is too late" (#4 Al-Qahtani. Iraq).[43]

AD 2.2.4.2: What aspects of temporal ordering are involved? (Verschueren 2012: 99–100)

Verschueren notes the "iconicity" of representing historical events in the sequence in which they occurred in history books. This iconicity is pithily captured in Grice's (1989) sub-maxim of Manner: Be orderly. Verschueren also notes the occurrence of alternative "episodic" modes of coherence when "temporal ordering … becomes impossible" or when "expansions into circumstances … causes and consequences" are required (100).

As I noted in response to AD 2.2.4.1, the letters typically involve three times or periods: (1) the times of the situations or events about which the letters are written, which necessarily precede (2) the times at which the letters are written, emailed to volunteers, and sent to the Message Recipients, which logically (if not necessarily actually) precede (3) the times of the asked-for redress. For example, one letter ends, "I ask you to stop arresting, prosecuting, and imprisoning those exercising their rights to freedom of expression and peaceful assembly" (#37 PoCs, Algeria). The aspectual verb *stop* – which occurs twenty-one times in the corpus, primarily in SUBJECT lines – presupposes that whatever is stopped must have occurred prior to its stopping; thus, the Algerian authorities must have been "arresting, prosecuting, and imprisoning" activists before, up to, and after the time the letter was written and sent.

As we should expect, the different time-frames in the letters are indexed by different tense and aspect combinations. In a simplest, idealized instance of an appeal, we might expect the opening expressions of concern to be in present tense forms, the narrative of the events leading up to the current situation to be in past tense forms, the appeal for redress to index the future, and invitations to respond to be in the present tense. What we actually find is a pattern of variations on this.

Fourteen of the letters open with the present progressive form "I am writing …," which introduces either an expression of concern and/or a

[43] Recall my discussion of deictics in multi-modal discourse in Chapter 2.

directive. Verschueren's (1999: 152) distinction between speech activities and speech events provides us with some analytic purchase on the use of the present progressive in these openings. Speech events are conventional "sequentially organized stretches of speech," whereas speech activities are "the creative involvement of the participants in constructing the activity." The present progressive emphasizes the activity of creating the text and thus contributes to the sense of urgency of the appeals.

The present progressive is also used occasionally to direct addressees, for example, "I am calling upon your government to …" (#26 PoCs, Vietnam), though this is more typically done using the simple present of a speech act verb complemented by an infinitive, for example, "I urge you to …" The present progressive is also used in the representation of ongoing effects of the appeal situation on individual(s) affected by it, for example, "She is suffering …" (#8 Beatriz, El Salvador), though the appeal situations are more typically presented in the simple present, for example, "current state laws on the use of lethal force by law enforcement officers do not comply with international human rights law and standards and … the United States does not even keep track of how many lives are lost every year" (#21 Crime Task Force, USA). The simple present plus infinitive also occurs on those rare occasions in which the letter invites the addressee to respond, for example, "I hope to hear …" (#8 Beatriz, El Salvador). The present tense in all of these forms indicates that the writing and the concern or directive are immediately relevant, thus emphasizing the urgency of the appeal situation. The progressive emphasizes the situation's ongoing exigency.

As the appeal situation precedes the writing, we should expect to find the narrative simple past, for example, "The two men were …" (#4 Al-Qahtani, Iraq), or the present perfect, indicating a period of time up to the time of utterance, for example, "Shaker Aamer has been held … for over 11 years" (#7 Aamer, USA).

These tense and aspect choices have ideological positioning implications. The simplest of these is the past tense, which positions the *I* of the letters as committed to the truth of the narrated events and their ideological framing. The present perfect likewise commits the *I* to the truth and ideological implications of the characterization of a situation that obtained from some time in the past up to the ostensible time of utterance. The simple present and present progressive with *I* subjects represents attempts to get the Message Recipients to engage with the *I* in ideological argument designed to (try to) persuade the Message Recipients to act as the appeals specify, thus positioning both participants with respect to the appeal situation and the human rights agenda.

AD 2.2.4.3: What spatial orientations are involved/invoked? (Verschueren 2012:100–101)

Verschueren summarizes his discussion of spatial orientation saying that "two types of spatial concepts" permeate the presentation of events in the histories: "points in space (that can be approached or moved away from) and contained spaces (that one can move into or out of). Both support the overall strategic-military approach" to the discussion of events. Place-names locate events, for example, "at Delhi," geographical relations, for example, Cawnpore is "a short distance from Lucknow," and movement, for example, "then [Havelock] marched toward Delhi."

While AI takes as its remit the entire globe and all the countries on it, the letters in my corpus are sent to representatives of just twenty countries and US states, which are listed earlier in this chapter.

In addition to the countries and states listed, one appeal is to Apple Corporation's "Supplier Responsibility Team" concerning the use of child labor in the mining of cobalt in the Democratic Republic of Congo (DRC), part of the "Global Trade in Cobalt" (#40 Cobalt, Apple Corp.). The letter asks Apple to disclose on its website the work conditions for people in its cobalt supply chain. The letter identifies conditions only in the DRC.

Given the small size of the corpus, no statistical significance should be assigned to these numbers. However, the relatively large number of letters addressed to US officials is worthy of note, as it suggests that the US is seventeen times more likely to commit human rights violations than, say, Turkey or the People's Republic of China. Given the multiplicity, complexity, and global distribution of US activities, we should expect that it would receive more appeals than other countries, though we might hope otherwise. We might infer also that AI believes that the US government and governments of other democratic countries might be more persuadable than autocratic ones by the arguments in the appeals, an inference belied by the number of appeals to authorities in Louisiana, USA, on behalf of Herman Wallace and Albert Woodfox, as discussed earlier in this chapter.[44]

Some letters identify specific spaces, for instance, Guantanamo, though this word names both a place and a "facility." The UK is mentioned as the place to which one Guantanamo prisoner should be released (#7 Aamer, USA). Sometimes mention is made of specific prisons, for example, "Angola 3"

[44] The letters to US officials deal with targeted killings by drone strikes (#1 Targeted Killings, USA); a prisoner held in the Guantanamo Bay detention facility (#7 Aamer, USA); human rights violations by the CIA (#19 Torture Report, USA); the establishment of a national crime and justice taskforce on the use of lethal force by police (#21 Crime Task Force, USA); mass surveillance (#23 Mass Surveillance, USA); settlement of Syrian refugees in the US (#27 Syrian Refugees, USA); violence against women (#32 Violence Against Women, USA); arms sales to Saudi Arabia (#34 Arms Sales, USA); the global refugee crisis (#36 Refugees, USA); and medical treatment for injuries caused by torture to a Guantanamo prisoner (#39 Al-Hawsawi, USA).

(#16 Woodfox, Louisiana, USA) refers to the Louisiana State Penitentiary in Louisiana, USA, and the infirmary at Hunt Correctional Center in Louisiana, USA (#12 Wallace, Louisiana, USA).

In addition to the countries whose officials are addressed in the letters, several additional countries are mentioned, but do not have letters addressed specifically to them: Australia, Canada, Cuba, Democratic Republic of Congo, Haiti, New Zealand, and the UK.

The cities mentioned are Beijing, Ferguson (Missouri), Khartoum, Los Angeles, Moscow, New York, Sochi, St. Louis (Missouri), Washington, DC, and Istanbul and "other Turkish cities."

Two regions are mentioned: North Caucasus and Krasnodar in Russia, and a route: "in transit on his way to the (penal) colony" (#15 Vitishko, Russia).

Several specific buildings and spaces are mentioned: Christ the Savior Cathedral in Moscow; in front of al-Jafali mosque (Saudi Arabia); Thanh Minh Zen monastery (Vietnam); and Tahrir Square (Cairo, Egypt).

The letters contain a considerable number of non-specific spatial references: "whereabouts"; "foreign agents"; "global" (war on terror; trade in small arms; theory of war; surveillance; refugee crisis; community; trade in cobalt), "international" (law; human rights; human rights law; humanitarian law; standards; [legal] obligations; organizations; prohibition; community; human rights treaties; human rights consequences). The eighty-seven mentions of "international" provide a clear indication of the letters' ideological universalizing and AI's scope of activity.

Other spatial expressions have to do with the positions, conditions, and movements of prisoners: confined in "a cell the size of a parking space"; "in isolation," "prison colony," "his whereabouts unknown," "transferred from Afghanistan to the US Naval Base at Guantanamo Bay in Cuba," "returned to the UK."

Even though the letters in my corpus are addressed to just eighteen countries, the AI webpage characterizes the organization as "a global movement of more than 10 million people in over 150 countries and territories who campaign to end abuses of human rights."[45]

Ad 2.2.4.4: Are there any temporal and/or spatial constraints on the construction of the discourse itself? (Verschueren 2012: 101–103)

The temporal and spatial constraints on the production of Verschueren's history books include the time available to the authors to write them; their length as determined by their authors for their specific audiences; and the effects of these constraints on the choices and density of the information presented. In spite of these constraints, the main focus of each book is the colonial "power

[45] https://tinyurl.com/mr3yf4ea (accessed August 6, 2025).

relations" and the "military and strategic nature of the events" that established and maintained them.

The AI webpages and emails embedding the appeals are a single screen or a little more in length and present a brief description of exigent events interspersed with an underlined hyperlink set against AI's signature yellow background requests "urgent action today" for its redress:

You must take a moment to read this. I know you care. We need your urgent action today. (3/8/19)

The letters are temporally constrained in that they enact appeals for the redress of highly exigent situations and so should be sent as soon as the volunteer receives them from AI. However, letters sent substantially later than their arrival in a volunteer's email box receive the same response from AI – a "Thank you" note embedded in an appeal for donations.

The spatial constraint on the letters is interactional or psychological rather than physical. While the email system would allow for letters of indefinite length, they are in fact generally short, often just a single screen or between about a third and one-and-a-half hard-copy pages. The AI Letter Writing Guide advises writers to keep letters short as longer letters are less likely to be read. Their characteristic brevity is consistent with their relationship to protest signs and placards, which are also characteristically short and to their point. Their brevity is also consistent with my assumption that the numbers of letters may matter more than the development of their content. The letters typically omit, for example, information about the sources AI staffers used to develop the case and craft the webpages and embedding emails. And they are restricted to the immediately relevant details of the appeal situation and directives for its redress.

AD 2.2.4.5: Are there any "material" conditions that constrain/orient the discourse production or interpretation? (Verschueren 2012: 103)

Verschueren's history texts are physical objects produced by commercial publishers who expect to turn a profit on them. Verschueren characterizes these conditions as "relatively simple when compared to what is happening [in 2012] with newer media," adding that "[i]deology research based on discourse in the new media will have to address most of the issues reviewed in this book, but will have to take into account the specificities produced by the highly different material conditions" that have emerged and developed since the early twentieth century. Verschueren notes also the historians' typical "lack of direct access" to the events they discuss, and the "remarkably" sparse references to sources in the textbooks, with consequences for any analysis of their intertextuality.

The appeals are elements of the "new media"; they exist and are delivered electronically, embedded in other multi-media documents, though the appeals themselves are text-only. As the pane they are displayed in is small, readers must sometimes scroll to be able to read the entire appeal. However, the electronic appeals are direct descendants of AI's earlier, hard-copy appeals and are categorizable as personal letters and are so categorized by AI in its letter-writing guides. Thus the "flow" (Chafe 2018: 391–405) of information in the electronic version of the appeal is the same as it would be if it had been crafted in hard-copy.

The letters often show signs of constraints on their production, most notably minor typographical and editing errors that suggest time constraints on the AI staffers who write them, some of whom may not be native English speakers. This is consistent with the extreme exigency of many of the situations the letters address. Of course, volunteers may revise the letters before sending them on, though I typically do not, and I do not know (if AI knows) how many volunteers do revise the letters and in what ways. If my assumption that the letters are as much protest as appeal and unlikely to be read carefully anyway, then there is little reason for AI staffers to be concerned with minor editing errors or for volunteers to correct them, and if the volunteers merely SEND them, then the errors are irrelevant to them.

While the letter writers do not have direct access to the events and situations they write about, they are much closer to those events than Verschueren's historians, and their sources of information are much more reliable. As I've noted, AI has an excellent reputation for careful investigation and provides substantial reports copiously footnoted with source information. I do not know what demographic information AI keeps about its members and volunteers; however, for them to function they must have access to the internet, which suggests that they may be from the educated middle class. Klandermans (2011: 225) describes typical Dutch AI members as

> highly educated, above average female breadwinner, biographically available, which is to say from one- or two-person households, without full-time employment, often retired or student [footnote omitted]. Their income is above average. Furthermore, they are socially and politically engaged, culturally educated, read newspapers and weekly magazines; watch the news, documentaries and educative programs. This characterises the AI participants as the typical new social movement crowd: highly educated, young, professionals, cosmopolitan, and adhering to so-called "post material values." In particular, active members – that is to say members of local groups or voluntary workers – are displaying these features.

AI members and volunteers may be familiar with the appeal situations from other sources of information.

Identifying constraints on the interpretation of the letters raises again the issues discussed above regarding the multiple roles of Addressees. I do not know where the sent messages go. Do they return to AI or do they go to the Message Recipients' email addresses? Do the Message Recipients even have (identifiable) email addresses? Or snail-mail ones? (AI's Urgent Action mailing instructions used to include only snail-mail addresses, but now include these, fax and phone numbers, Facebook, Twitter, Instagram and other social media electronic addresses.) Are there intermediaries who filter messages for the addressees? Does anyone actually read them once they are sent? As I noted in a footnote earlier in this chapter, in August 2012, a Russian embassy official dumped on a New York sidewalk an AI petition with 100,000 signatures on behalf of the incarcerated members of Pussy Riot, thus supporting my claim that the letters may be viewed as protests and thus as an annoyance or an impertinence and thus a threat to their addressees' positive and negative face.

As I've noted, a small number of letters include concessions to the Message Recipients. These concessions are, of course, constructed by AI staffers and so there is no way to know how accurately these concessions reflect the frames of interpretation that the Message Recipients would adopt if they read the letters.

Ad 2.2.5: ... In the case of written data: What graphic features (typography, pictorial representation) are used? (Verschueren 2012: 104–105)

There are no pictorial representations in the letters, though photographs do occur in the embedding emails and other relevant AI documents. The letters all employ the same font, and except for the headings **Message Recipients** and **Subject**, there is no bolding, italicizing, or underlining. Some letters include numbered, bulleted, asterisked, or hyphenated lists (or some combination of these), usually of directives. The following letter (#10 Drone Wars, USA) uses a mix of numbering and bullets:

> **Message Recipients**: Mr Hagel – Secretary of Defense, Mr.[46] Kerry – Secretary of State, President Obama
>
> **Subject**: Drone Wars
>
> I urge you to help prevent extrajudicial executions by adopting the recommendations in Amnesty International's 5 Point Plan for reform:
>
> 1) Reject the "global war" theory
> - End claims that the U.S. government is authorized by international law to use lethal force anywhere in the world under the theory that it is involved in a "global war" against al Qa'ida and other armed groups and individuals.
> - Repeal the 2001 Authorization for Use of Military Force.

[46] The inconsistency in placing a period/full stop after Mr/Mr. suggests either hurried copy-editing or confusion between British (omit full stop) and American (add period) usage. Thanks to Jeff Kaplan, (p.c.) for bringing my attention to this.

Recognize the application of international human rights law to all US counterterrorism operations, wherever they occur.

2) Follow the law

Bring policies and practices relating to the use of lethal force in line with the USA's obligations under international human rights law and, in the exceptional circumstances where it applies, international humanitarian law (the law of armed conflict), particularly by:

- Ensuring that lethal force outside of specific recognized zones of armed conflict is used only when it is strictly unavoidable to prevent a truly imminent threat to life.
- Ensuring that any use of lethal force within a specific recognized zone of armed conflict complies fully with the USA's obligations under international human rights and humanitarian law. If there is doubt as to whether a person is a civilian, the person is to be considered a civilian.
- Ensuring independent and impartial investigations in all cases of alleged extrajudicial executions or other unlawful killings; respect for the rights of family members of those killed; and effective redress and remedy where killings are found to have been unlawful.

3) Release more information

- Disclose further legal and factual details about US policy and practices for so-called targeted killings, signature strikes, and Terrorist Attack Disruption Strikes, including any secret Department of Justice legal memorandums, and specific information about who has been killed.

4) Uphold the rights of all people, not only US citizens

- International human rights law explicitly prohibits discrimination on grounds of national origin when it comes to respect for human rights. The US government is not allowed to treat the right to life of a non-US citizen as less worthy of protection than the right to life of a US citizen, just because the person is a foreign national.

5) Ensure justice and security with human rights

- The U.S. government should ensure that those responsible for the attacks of September 11, 2001, or other crimes under international law are brought to justice in fair and public trials without recourse to the death penalty.

While most of the appeals consist of simple paragraphing, typically separated by a space with first line left-justified, a number of the appeals, like the one above, employ many levels of organization, suggesting that they are designed to be carefully read as arguments deployed to persuade their readers, in the case above, by multiple references to US obligations under international laws. Just which exigencies are or are not deemed deserving of such detailed discussion as above is unclear to me.

Language and Linguistic Context

Procedure 2.3: Investigate the linguistic context.

AD 2.3, IN GENERAL: [Investigate the linguistic context] (Verschueren 2012: 106–117)

Verschueren is here concerned about text preceding and following the linguistic elements in analytic focus, as they index what has come before them and what they anticipate, that is, what they "precontexutualize" (Johnstone 2018: 185).

AD 2.3.1: What linguistic channel(s) is/are involved? (Verschueren 2012: 106–107)

Like Verschueren's textbook corpus, the AI letters are written documents. They are intended to (appear to) be dialogic, as evidenced by such salutations as "Dear Mr. Hagel, Mr. Obama," (#7 Aamer, USA), complimentary closes like, "Yours sincerely," (#11 Pussy Riot, Russia), expressions of gratitude, "Thank you for your time and consideration of this important matter" (#13 Women Protesters, Egypt), and hopes for responses from Recipients, "I look forward to hearing from you regarding this matter" (#17 Caning, Indonesia).

Unlike Verschueren's textbooks, the letters, with one exception, do not incorporate such genre constituents as prefaces or comprehension checks. The single exception is the inclusion of the Foreword to the US Senate Intelligence Committee's report on the use of torture and various other human rights abuses by the CIA (#19 Torture Report, USA). This is included in the appeal because the US Justice Department had "failed to commit to reading and reviewing the document."

AD 2.3.2: What intertextual links are required and how are they appealed to? (Verschueren 2012: 107–113)

"The first type of intertextuality concerns *the positioning of parts of a text in relation to each other*" (Verschueren 2012: 107; emphasis in original). Moves are parts of texts that perform specific communicative functions (Biber et al. 2007: 23). Steps are thematic elements that constitute moves (Upton and Cohen 2009). Following Biber et al. (2007), I distinguish the genre's "structural elements" [STRL] from its moves and steps:[47]

A. Message Recipients list (e.g., **Message Recipients**: James Caldwell – Attorney General …)
B. Subject line (e.g., **Subject**: Grant Albert Woodfox his freedom)
C. To line (e.g., **To**: President Obama) or Salutation
D. Announcement of imminent closing (e.g., In closing,)
E. Complimentary close (e.g., Yours sincerely,)

[47] This analysis is based on that in Delahunty (2018b).

And the moves and steps that constitute the appeals:

Move 1 Describe the exigent situation and the basis for its undesirability (Obligatory)
- Step 1 Announce the reason for the communication (express concern)
- Step 2 Describe the situation motivating the communication
- Step 3 Characterize the situation in M1S2 as undesirable
- Step 4 Identify the normative basis for M1S3
- Step 5 Express the exigency of the situation characterized in M1S3

Move 2 Direct addressee(s) to redress the situation characterized in M1 in accordance with norms identified in M1S4 (Obligatory)
- Step 1 Describe desired change(s) to situation characterized in M1S3
- Step 2 Direct addressee(s) to bring about situation described in M2S1
- Step 3 Identify normative basis for M2S2 (same as or closely related to M1S4)
- Step 4 Express exigency of bringing about the changes described in M2S1

Move 3 Make concession(s) to addressee(s) (Optional)
- Step 1 Make the concession(s)
- Step 2 Note limitation(s) on concession(s)
- Step 3 Rebut concessions, typically by reference to normative basis in M1S4/M2S3
- Step 4 Solicit action(s) on basis of rebuttal
- Step 5 Express the exigency of the situation characterized in M3S4

Move 4 State related concerns and solicit related actions (Optional)
- Step 1 Describe related situation (related to M1S2)
- Step 2 Characterize the situation in M4S1 as undesirable
- Step 3 Solicit specific actions in response to M4S2
- Step 4 Identify normative basis for M4S2 (same as/closely related to M1S4/M2S3)
- Step 5 Express the exigency of the situation characterized in M4S2

Move 5 (Re-)state situation(s) requiring redress and solicit redressive action(s) (Optional)
- Step 1 (Re-)state situation(s) of concern (typically related to M1S3)
- Step 2 (Re-)characterize the situation in M5S1 as undesirable
- Step 3 (Re-)state action(s) to redress situation(s) in M5S1

Step 4 (Re-)state normative basis for action(s) solicited in M5S2 (same as/closely related to M1S4/M2S3)
Step 5 (Re-)state exigency of situations characterized in M5S1

Move 6 Engage addressee(s) (Optional)
Step 1 Express gratitude
Step 2 Express hope for response from addressee[48]

The analysis is illustrated by its application in the following letter (#11 Pussy Riot, Russia):

> [STRL A] **Message Recipients**: Yuri Yakovlevich Chaika – Prosecutor General
>
> [STRL B] **Subject**: Free Nadezhda Tolokonnikova and Maria Alekhina
>
> [STRL C] Dear Prosecutor General,
>
> [M1S1] I am writing to express my deep concern about Nadezhda Tolokonnikova and Maria Alekhina, [M1S2] who were sentenced to two years in a penal colony for their participation in a February 2012 protest action by the feminist punk-rock group Pussy Riot at the Christ the Savior Cathedral in Moscow. [M1S3] These two women, both mothers in their twenties, were detained solely for their peaceful expression of their beliefs. [M1S4] They are Prisoners of Conscience.
>
> [M2S2] I call on you [M2S1] to ensure that Maria Alekhina and Nadezhda Tolokonnikova are immediately and unconditionally released. [M4S1] While they remain incarcerated, [M4S3] the two women must not be ill-treated by prison staff or inmates, and they must be allowed regular contact with their families and legal teams.
>
> [STRL D] In closing, [M3S1] I welcome the news of Ekaterina Samutsevich's freedom, [M3S2] but remain concerned about the conditional status of the release. [M3S3] The three Pussy Riot members should not have been prosecuted in the first place. [M3S4] I call on you and all authorities to respect and uphold the right to freedom of expression in the Russian Federation, and to remedy the unjust treatment of these young women [M3S5] immediately.
>
> [M6S1] I thank you for your attention.
>
> [STRL E] Yours sincerely,

Verschueren's second type of intertextuality pertains to the texts' "*positioning in relation to a wider body of literature*" (108; emphasis in original). As I

[48] My thanks to Nora Gordon for her help with this analysis.

have demonstrated, the texts are designed to (appear to) be dialogic. More systematically, however, the letters contain frequent references to various rights: human, humanitarian, to life, etc. This is most frequently done by generic reference to, for example, "human rights," and occasionally by direct reference to specific legal texts such as the UDHR, to local laws, legal proceedings, and rulings, for example, a US Federal Court (#12 Wallace, Louisiana, USA); the Iranian Court of Cassation (#4 Al-Qahtani, Iran); the Inter-American Court of Human Rights (#8 Beatriz, El Salvador); and the Executive Summary and Foreword to Senate Select Committee on Intelligence Study on the CIA's Detention and Interrogation Program "Torture Report" (#19 Torture Report, USA). These documents are invoked in the characterization of situations as violations of rights articulated in them.

The letters are also a re-entextualization,[49] re-contextualization, and re-genrefication of information in the AI webpages and embedding emails, which in turn are re-entextualizations, etc., of information in AI's files, in AI's occasional reports, and in reports in various media. (See Chapter 2; Delahunty 2021.)

Verschueren's third type of intertextuality is "*reported speech* or *direct quotations*" (109; emphasis in original). With few exceptions, direct quotations do not occur in the letters; indirect quotations introduced by speech act, epistemic, and evaluative expressions occur moderately frequently: for example, courts may "overturn" convictions or "deny" appeals; states may "appeal" legal decisions; authorities may "repeat" claims; which individuals may or may not "believe"; and UN Special Rapporteurs may "condemn" certain practices as torture (#16 Woodfox, Louisiana, USA). These might be conceptualized as Verschueren's "embedded utterers."

Verschueren's fourth aspect of intertextuality is the occurrence of "*common 'master narratives'*" (112; emphasis in original). The letters and their related documents are similar, and often linguistically identical, in presenting situations as exigent violations of various rights and directives to redress those violations. More generally, the AI letters are a sub-genre of the large class of fundraising appeals (Mann and Thompson 1992; Delahunty 2018b), which belong to Longacre's (1992) hortatory discourse, which are a sub-class of the very broad genre of situation/problem/solution/evaluation texts (Hoey 1994 and references therein; Winter 1994).

Verschueren's fifth class of intertextual "links … take the shape of *identical or near-identical phrasings* for the same actors, actions, and events" (112–113; emphasis in original). To appreciate how similar the "phrasings" of the embedding emails and the letters can be, compare the following two texts

[49] Entextualization is "the process by which circulable texts are produced by extracting discourse from its original context" (Park and Bucholz 2009: 486).

regarding Herman Wallace. The first is the embedding email, the second is the appeal letter. Both documents are based on a much larger document, "USA: 100 YEARS IN SOLITARY: THE 'ANGOLA 3' AND THEIR FIGHT FOR JUSTICE."[50, 51]

The email:

> Dear Gerald,
>
> Herman Wallace shouldn't have to die behind bars.
>
> Herman is 71 years old and has advanced liver cancer. He and fellow prisoner Albert Woodfox have been held in solitary confinement longer than anyone else in modern US history. The men have spent the past 41 years of their lives alone in tiny cells for 23 hours a day, deprived of any meaningful human interaction.
>
> No human being deserves to live like this. Herman Wallace should not die alone.
>
> Urge Louisiana Governor Bobby Jindal to release Herman Wallace.
>
> **Why wouldn't Louisiana officials simply release an elderly prisoner with advanced cancer on humanitarian grounds?** Evidence suggests that it is in part because Herman dared to organize and speak out against inhumane treatment and racial segregation inside one of United States' most brutal prisons.
>
> Herman Wallace and Albert Woodfox are the two imprisoned members of the "Angola 3," **three young black men who were thrown in solitary confinement after working against continued segregation, systematic corruption, and grave abuses** in the infamous Angola prison. Originally imprisoned for unrelated cases of armed robbery, Herman and Albert were later convicted for the murder of a prison guard in 1972. However, no physical evidence links either man to the murder.
>
> In the decades since Herman and Albert's conviction, numerous legal concerns have risen to the surface from the racially charged underbelly of the U.S. prison system. These are just a few glaring flaws we documented in our report "100 Years in Solitary: The 'Angola 3' and their Fight for Justice":

[50] A report on the "Angola 3" is available at www.amnesty.org/en/documents/amr51/041/2011/en/ (accessed August 6, 2025).

[51] I have deleted a photograph of Herman Wallace, text in large font against a red background exhorting the reader to "Help free Herman Wallace before it's too late," and links to TAKE ACTION.

- DNA evidence that might have established the men's innocence was somehow "lost"
- Outcomes were based on questionable inmate testimony
- Prison officials bribed the main eyewitness
- One witness later retracted his testimony

Prison authorities have broken their own policies to justify Herman's continued incarceration in harsh and inhumane conditions. After decades in these conditions, a highly **questionable conviction** that continues to be challenged by the courts and the now a [*sic*] **tragic prognosis of terminal cancer**, the next step seems all too clear: **Herman Wallace should be released**.

Help begin to correct more than 40 years of injustice right now – call on Louisiana's Governor Bobby Jindal to release Herman Wallace immediately.

In Solidarity,

Jasmine Heiss

Amnesty International USA

P.S. Please join us in reminding the two men that we are standing with them, even if the state of Louisiana tries to keep them in isolation. <u>Send your letter of support directly to Herman and Albert – show them you care</u>. (emphasis in original)

The appeal letter (#12 Wallace, Louisiana, USA): 7/11/13

Message Recipients: Bobby Jindal – Governor of Louisiana, Paul Rainwater – Chief of Staff, Emily Riser – Executive Assistant, Tammy Woods – Assistant Chief of Staff

Subject: Free Herman Wallace

As I write you, 71-year-old Herman Wallace is being held in isolation in the infirmary in Hunt Correctional Center. After spending more than four decades held in cruel and unusual solitary confinement, he has been diagnosed with terminal liver cancer. The time to act is now. I ask you to release Herman to his family on humanitarian grounds, so that they can care for him during his last months on earth.

Both Herman Wallace and fellow "Angola 3" prisoner Albert Woodfox have spent most of the past 41 years of their lives alone in a tiny cell for 23 hours a day. Such conditions are cruel, inhuman and degrading. Prior to Wallace's cancer diagnosis, these conditions had already negatively impacted both men's physical and psychological health. In fact, in 2007,

> a US federal judge ruled that the conditions constituted a deprivation of a basic human need and that prison officials should have been aware of the potential for serious harm to physical and mental health.
>
> Contrary to requirements under both international human rights law and the US Constitution, Herman has had no meaningful review of his continued isolation. Herman's prison records do not demonstrate that he is a threat to the security of the institution, himself or others. Furthermore, there are substantial concerns about the fairness of the legal process that resulted in Herman's conviction; a conviction that is still being challenged before the courts today. Evidence suggests that the decision to keep him in solitary is based at least in part on his political activism and association with the Black Panther party.
>
> Herman Wallace and Albert Woodfox are believed to have spent more time in solitary confinement than virtually any other US prisoner in recent history. Now, after surviving 41 years of a nightmare, Herman doesn't have much time left. Please release Herman to his family today.

The following list demonstrates just how similar the two documents are. Both documents:

1. mention Wallace's age, "71 year(s) old";
2. mention that Wallace suffers from cancer, though the email characterizes it as "advanced liver cancer" and "terminal cancer," while the appeal integrates these as "terminal liver cancer";
3. mention that Wallace and Woodfox have spent forty-one years in prison, mostly in solitary confinement, and that they may have been held in solitary for longer than any other prisoner in modern US penal history;
4. mention Wallace's political activism as a possible reason for his continuing solitary confinement;
5. express concerns about the fairness of the legal proceedings that convicted Wallace;
6. appeal for Wallace's release on humanitarian grounds: the email, so that he does not die alone; and the appeal, so that he can be with his family.

Nonetheless, there are also differences between these two documents:

1. The embedding email includes a photograph of Herman Wallace; the appeal does not.
2. The email includes large font headlines on a colored background; the appeal does not.
3. The email includes highlighted links to other online documents; the appeal does not.

4. The email lists several of the flaws in the prosecution's case against Wallace; the appeal does not.
5. The email includes bolded expressions; the appeal does not.

The documents are similar because they pertain to the same appeal situation. They differ because they perform different roles in that situation. The email is designed to persuade its viewers to click on one of its links and thereby act on behalf of Herman Wallace. While the letter is ostensibly designed to persuade the Louisiana authorities to release Wallace, given those authorities' recalcitrance over many years, its primary purpose may be to more deeply engage AI members and volunteers in the organization's activities and to identify with its goals and ideology, and identifying likely donors to AI's coffers.

Ad 2.3.3: Is sequencing an issue? (Verschueren 2012: 113–115)

Verschueren notes the inescapable linearity of language and contributions of conversation analysis to our understanding of the sequencing of utterances in interaction. We can view an appeal as the first turn in a sequence projecting a second turn in which the Message Recipients respond to whatever action is requested in the first. In two instances, the projected second turn is a verbal response to the appeal – "I look forward to hearing from you regarding this matter" (#17 Caning, Indonesia). This latter sequence is rare, most likely because the ostensible goal of the appeal is to get the Message Recipients to redress an abuse, not enter into discussion about it. Five appeals end with variations on "Thank you for your time and consideration of this important matter" (#3 Satire as Crime, Egypt), which taken alone would seem to retreat from the most important goal of the appeal, to get the addressees to redress the violation. However, these closings typically occur after a directive enjoining the abuse. The corpus includes one segment that combines all three turn types:

> Thank you for your urgent attention to [*sic*] matter and I hope to hear back from you regarding the steps that you are taking to provide Beatriz with the medical care she has requested and is entitled to receive.
>
> (#8 Beatriz, El Salvador)

As the move and step analysis laid out above makes clear, the typical topical trajectory in the appeals is an expression of concern about a situation, a characterization of that situation as a violation of various classes of rights, and then a directive to the addressees to redress the situation by bringing it into compliance with the relevant rights. This organization is quite flexible. Some elements are optional, notably the concessions and their rebuttals, and also the attempts to engage the addressees. Elements may also be expanded, in particular, elements of the appeal situation may be listed, in bulleted or similarly enumerated lists. While the message and its constituents have ideological import, their order seems constrained by other, coherence, factors.

AD 2.3.4: What kinds of contextual cohesion are established, and how? (Think of conjunctions, anaphora, co-reference, self-reference, exemplification, explanation, ellipsis, enumeration, highlighting, contrasting, comparison, repetition, substitution, etc.) (Verschueren 2012: 115–117)

Verschueren says that "all instances" of the items on this list "may give rise to implicit meanings," of which he provides several examples from his corpus. I will comment on any ideologically significant implicit meanings as I discuss occurrences of Verschueren's list of cohesive devices in my AI letters corpus.

Conjunctions: The conjunction *and* (450 occurrences in the corpus) is used to conjoin NPs: "international human rights and humanitarian law" (#1 Targeted Killings, USA); participles: "a disturbing and increasing pattern" (#13 Women Protesters, Egypt); adjectives: "long and unnecessary delays" (#8 Beatriz, El Salvador); manner adverbs: "to immediately and unconditionally release" (#15 Vitishko, Russia); and chained conative expressions: "[W]e urge you to condemn sexual violence and take steps to end it" (#13 Women Protesters, Egypt). Except for the last of these, the order of conjuncts seems immaterial and could be reversed. The last one cannot be reversed as it implicates a specific order of elements and a causal relation between them; recall Grice's submaxim of Manner: Be orderly.

Many of these conjoined expressions may be more or less fixed (Wray 2002), invoking multiple legal instruments: "international human rights and humanitarian law" (#1 Targeted Killings USA), and the wording of legal documents: "Such conditions are cruel, inhuman, and degrading" (#12 Wallace, Louisiana, USA). Many of the conjoined expressions list multiple items, as in the Wallace list. The rhetorical strategy appears to be to maximize the number of situationally and ideologically relevant items included in a single expression.

The complementizer *that* is used to introduce a clausal complement to a speech act or epistemic expression related to judicial procedures and evidential status, for example, "ruled that," "demonstrate that," and "suggests that." *That* is also used to introduce relative clauses, for example, "a conviction that is still being challenged before the courts today" (#12 Wallace, Louisiana, USA). In this example, the head noun is qualified in such a way as to cast doubt on its legal status. Occasionally, *that* occurs several times with different roles in a single sentence:

> I am deeply concerned *that* US government's so-called "targeted killing" program allows for the use of lethal force, including with drones, *that* violates the right to life under international law.
>
> (#1 Targeted Killings, USA; emphasis added)

The first *that* above introduces the clausal complement of "concerned," which includes reference to "lethal force," which is then modified by a relative clause introduced by a second *that* which evaluates "lethal force" as a violation of international law, which invokes the normative element of ideology.

The conjunction *but* is used with its usual effect of introducing a denial of an inference derivable from prior text or context (Blakemore 1989, 2002). For example:

> Recently, the Senate Select Committee on Intelligence released to the public a summary of its 6,700 page report on these matters, known as the "Senate torture report." It contains information about potential violations of federal and international law.
>
> *But* shockingly, the Justice Department has failed to commit to reading and reviewing the full report.
>
> (#19 Torture Report, USA; emphasis added)

Blakemore (2002), working within Relevance Theory (Sperber and Wilson 1995; Wilson 2017), says that "*but* encodes a procedure which can be defined in terms of the cognitive effect of contradiction and elimination" (103). Reasonable people might reasonably expect that the US Justice Department might at least commit to reading a US Senate report on such an important human rights matter as the torture of prisoners in US custody, for at least the reason that its executive summary had already been made public, but, "shockingly" the Department failed to do so. *But* thus contradicts and eliminates the reasonable inference that at least because the Torture Report's executive summary had been published, the Justice Department would commit to reading the whole report.

The problem motivating this appeal is that "for years, those who ordered and committed torture, enforced disappearance and other human rights violations in the CIA's secret detention program have enjoyed impunity." The solution proposed is that the Department of justice must take "the first step" of reading the report and then

> must also re-open and expand its investigations into all CIA interrogations, detentions and renditions. It must bring to justice in fair trials all the persons, regardless of their level of office or former level of office, suspected of being involved in the commission of crimes under international law, such as torture and enforced disappearance.
>
> (#19 Torture Report, USA)

The implication is that the Department of Justice did not commit to reading the report because it would have to "bring to justice" all members of the CIA, regardless of their rank, who are suspected of violations of international law.

The semi-fixed correlative *not only ... but also* occurs in two letters (#5 LGBTQ, South Africa; #17 Caning, Indonesia), for example, "I urge you *not only* to ensure that this woman is not caned, *but also* to end the use of caning as a form of punishment" (#17 Caning, Indonesia; emphasis added). This construction incorporates two structures in parallel. The fact that the propositions are expressed in a parallel construction allows a structural reduction – "I urge you to" need not be repeated – thus reducing the hearer's processing effort (Sperber and

Wilson 1995: 222). The parallelism also "indicates to the hearer that the search for parallel contexts and implications will be successful" (Sperber and Wilson 1995: 223). *Not only* denies the singularity of the proposition it introduces and *but also* makes that denial even more salient by contradicting and eliminating the potential assumption that only one proposition is contextually relevant. The construction thus makes particularly salient the relevance of the combined propositions in the context, as well as their intimate connection. In this instance, the appealer urges the government not to cane the woman accused of adultery and to generalize this restraint by abandoning the use of caning because it "violates the international prohibition on torture and other cruel, inhuman and degrading punishment," thus providing a universal justification for both elements of the appeal.

According to Blakemore (2003), *however* indicates that the hearer

> is expected to follow an inferential route which results in the contradiction and elimination of an accessible assumption *p* AND that apart from *p*, the context includes at least one other assumption which carries a guarantee of relevance accepted by the speaker. (emphasis in original)

For example:

> The two men were sentenced to death with four others on March 6, 2011. Abdullah 'Azzam Saleh Musfer al-Qahtani, Manaf 'Abdulrahim 'Abdulhamid 'Issa al-Rawi, Mohammad Nouri Matar Yassin, Ibrahim 'Abdulqader 'Ali 'Antik, Safa Ahmad 'Abul'aziz 'Abdullah and Mohammad Jaber Tawfiq 'Obaid were convicted of being members of al-Qa'ida and participating in the 2009 robbery of a goldsmith shop that left the owner dead. *However*, Abdullah al-Qahtani testified that his "confession" was obtained through torture and other ill-treatment including severe beatings and partial asphyxiation.
>
> (#4 Al-Qahtani, Iraq; emphasis added)

In this instance, "however" initiates the rebuttal of the apparent concession expressed in the first two sentences of the paragraph and directs the reader to reject the inference readily accessible from those two sentences that al-Qahtani's conviction and death sentence were legitimate. The rebuttal is justified by the inadmissibility under international humanitarian law of confessions obtained under torture. According to Chen (2015: 435),

> in the arena of international humanitarian law, officials and non-officials look to the Geneva Conventions as representing customary expectations of conduct during times of war. The treaties' authoritative effect is evidenced by the degree to which they have been invoked by states as legitimate expressions of basic rights by both signatory and non-signatory nations. Provisions outlawing practices, most notably torture, have attained status as *jus cogens*[52] as the result of their widespread adoption and over the decades since the conventions' ratification.

[52] *Jus cogens* is a principle of international law that is based on values taken to be fundamental to the international community and that cannot be set aside (as by treaty) (Merriam-Webster's *Dictionary of Law* (2011): 273).

As I have noted and as the discussion of *but* and *however* has shown, the letters occasionally include apparent concessions to local exigencies that might be presented to justify the rights violations that are the subject of the letters. These concessions are always rebutted by appeal to universal values of human rights and standards of judicial procedure, such that when "[i]nternational law and national law sometimes conflict … in general it is international law that should prevail. States (and the individuals who compose the state) ought to be held to international standards. This is the essence of the supremacy of international law that is so indispensable to maintaining world order" (Chen 2015: 4).

Co-reference is accomplished in a broad range of ways. The most straightforward way is the initial use of personal names followed by an appropriate personal or *wh*-pronoun, for example, "*Beatriz, who* is now five months into *her* pregnancy, suffers from health problems that put *her* life at risk" (#8 Beatriz, El Salvador; emphasis added). In other cases, we find chains of anaphorically related common noun phrases with varying degrees of detail and overlapping lexis and semantics, as we find in the following appeal.

> **Message Recipients**: Mohamed El Baradei (Constitution Party), Younes Makhioun (Nour Party), Amre Moussa, Hamdeen Sabahi
>
> **Subject**: End the harassment of Egyptian women protesters
>
> At this important moment in Egyptian history, women are being denied their full political rights by a disturbing and increasing pattern of sexual violence during public and peaceful demonstrations. To date, political authorities are standing idle in face of these attacks. Amnesty International believes this must change, we urge you to condemn sexual violence and take steps to end it.
>
> On June 30, as Egyptians met in Tahrir Square to peacefully demonstrate for their rights, Amnesty International received documented reports of at least 47 incidents of women being violently sexually assaulted during the protests. Tens if not hundreds of men surround their victims, tearing-off their clothes and veils, unzipping trousers, groping breasts and backsides. Sticks, blades and other weapons are frequently used in such attacks. Activists who sought to intervene to prevent the attacks were attacked with blades and other weapons.
>
> The attacks continued during the following night of protests. On July 1, we received 17 further cases of sexual assaults, including elderly women and girls as young as seven. And on July 3, we received another 25 reports of attempted sexual harassment or assaults.
>
> Unfortunately, these events follow a long-established pattern of violence against women in Egypt and a culture of impunity that protects those who

attack women. Amnesty International has recently documented abuses by both the military and police and security forces against Egyptians. The Egyptian government to date has failed to provide justice to victims of this violence and to hold the perpetrators accountable.

Egypt's political parties have been part of their failure. Their silence on this issue has helped to entrench discriminatory practices and attitudes. We call upon you to end this silence and combat the sexual violence and discrimination that prevents women from claiming their rights.

...

Thank you for your time and consideration of this important matter.

(#13 Women Protesters, Egypt)

The pattern in the first body paragraph is typical; the first relevant NP, "a disturbing and increasing pattern of sexual violence during public and peaceful demonstrations," is quite detailed and the co-referential NP, "these attacks," though less detailed, adds the characterization of the events as "attacks." A similar pattern can be observed in the second body paragraph, while the third paragraph reverses the pattern by beginning with the minimal NP, "the attacks," and then going on to characterize them as "cases of sexual assaults" and "25 reports of attempted sexual harassment or assaults," noting the nature of the evidence in support of the characterizations of the events. Each successive NP either repeats a previous one or adds legally and ideologically relevant information.

(Self-)reference: Earlier in this chapter, I discussed the complications arising from the use of first-person pronouns as well as analogous complications arising from the interpretations of second-person pronouns. These latter pronouns indicate direct address and (apparently, hoped for) dialogic engagement between writer and addressee(s). Third-person pronouns typically refer to the subjects of the appeals, which may be either individuals, for example, "*Mustafa al-Hawsawi* has been diagnosed with rectal prolapse, anal fissure (torn rectum) and chronic hemorrhoids. These ailments are so severe that *he* is forced to ..." (#39 Al-Hawsawi, USA; emphasis added), or abusive situations, for example, "*Funding for refugee resettlement programs is inadequate and resettlement programs in many countries takes* [*sic*] *too long, leaving refugees at grave risk.* The U.S. resettlement program is a sad example of *this*" (#36 Refugees, USA; emphasis added).

Exemplification: Many letters begin with an expression of concern about an individual and then generalize to expressions of concern or directives to redress violations of rights that apply to a class of individuals exemplified by the initial individual, for example, "I am writing to ask you to immediately and unconditionally release environmental activist Yevgeniy Vitishko ... In closing, I urge you to stop the persecution of civil society activists, including members of Environmental Watch for North Caucasus" (#15 Vitishko, Russia).

Explanation: The typical explanation given in the appeals for AI's evaluation of a situation as abusive and in need of redress is the situation's violation of local and/or international law and universal rights.

> [Dominican Republic] Law 169-14 and the threat of mass deportation violate international law. Article 13 of the International Covenant on Civil and Political Rights (ICCPR) and Article 22 of the American Convention on Human Rights guarantee every person the right to protection against arbitrary or collective deportation. In particular, Article 22.5 of the American Convention forbids expelling nationals. Though the Dominican Republic has the right to control migration and deportation in its own borders, it must do so in compliance with international law and it cannot expel nationals.
>
> (#22 Haitians, Dominican Republic)

Ellipsis: Verschueren's (2012: 116) very brief illustration of ellipsis in his corpus consists of the elision of co-referential subjects in a sequence of conjoined clauses. We find similar examples in the AI letters ([*e*] represents the site of an elided subject):

> I urge your Government [*e*] to disclose the whereabouts and legal status of all those detained and [*e*] guarantee unrestricted access to their families and lawyers, as well as [*e*] ensure those detained are not at risk of torture and other ill-treatment.
>
> (#25 Missing, China)

Critical Discourse analysts often regard ellipses as indicating attempts to hide the agents of questionable activities; however, I see no ideological significance to such grammatically and stylistically determined ellipses in the example above. It is clear that each [*e*] is to be interpreted as "your Government."

We also find elisions of agent phrases in nominalizations and passive clauses, though the referents are usually readily inferable from context. I have highlighted examples in the following excerpt.

> I wish to express my deep concern about the nationwide *crackdown* on human rights lawyers and activists in China, which started on July 9 with the *disappearance* of prominent human rights lawyer Wang Yu. Wang Yu worked at the Fengrui Law Firm in Beijing; the director, financial director and other staff members of this law firm have also *been detained*. Lawyers across the country have *been targeted*, including Zhou Shifeng, Sui Muqing and Li Heping. Many of those *detained* were part of a group of over 100 lawyers and human rights activists who signed a public statement condemning Wang Yu's *disappearance*.
>
> (#25 Missing, China; emphasis added)

The obvious invited inference here is that it is the Chinese authorities who are responsible for the disappearances, detentions, and targetings, and thus ideologically positioned as violators of international laws.

However, as noted, a very few letters include concessions and their rebuttals, so we might consider the non-occurrence of such pairings in the majority of letters as an elision. If we do, then this may be an elision of considerable ideological importance. I can only speculate here, but it is conceivable that if the letters did typically include concessions to the addressees, then AI volunteers might come to consider human rights to be contingent rather than universal, thus undercutting AI's unifying and action-orienting goals. Additionally, such arguments may be construed by the Message Recipients as indicating that the writer is ideologically or politically opposed to the government in question, rather than committed to upholding human rights and the principles of international law.

Enumeration: Several letters use one or more of the listing devices of numbering, bullets, and/or dashes, or a combination, as in:

> The US government must:
>
> 1. Disclose further legal and factual details about US policy and practices for so-called targeted killings, signature strikes, and Terrorist Attack Disruption Strikes;
> 2. End claims that the USA is authorized by international law to use lethal force anywhere in the world under the theory that it is involved in a "global war" against al-Qa'ida and other armed groups and individuals;
> 3. Recognize the application of international human rights law to all US counterterrorism operations including those outside US territory;
> 4. Bring US policies and practices in line with the USA's obligations under international law, particularly, by:
>   - Ensuring that any use of lethal force outside of specific recognized zones of armed conflict complies fully with the USA's obligations under international human rights law, including by limiting the use of force in accordance with law enforcement standards.
>   - Ensuring that any use of lethal force within specific recognized zones of armed conflict complies fully with the USA's obligations under international human rights and humanitarian law, including by recognizing and respecting the rule that if there is doubt as to whether a person is a civilian, the person is to be considered a civilian.
>   - Ensuring independent and impartial investigations in all cases of alleged extrajudicial executions or other unlawful killings, respect for the rights of family members of those killed, and effective redress and remedy where killings are found to have been unlawful.
>
> (#1 Targeted Killings, USA)

The modal in "The US government must" expresses a directive and the four action verbs that complement it express the action orientation of ideological formations, while the nominalizations heading the bulleted list complementing the preposition *by* at the end of item 4 enumerate the internationally legitimated ways in which those directives are to be carried out.

One letter organizes a sequence of events by dates and enumerates "incidents" that occurred on each date:

On June 30 … Amnesty International received documented reports of at least 47 incidents of women being violently sexually assaulted … Amnesty International has recently documented abuses by both the military and police and security forces against Egyptians.

(#13 Women Protesters, Egypt)

"Documented" as a factive predicate implicates the reliability of AI's evaluation of the incidents enumerated, thus legitimizing its stance. The reliability of AI's claims and evaluations legitimize its directives to the Egyptian authorities:

* Condemn all forms of sexual and gender-based violence and harassment, without reservation.

* Order full, impartial and independent investigations into sexual and gender-based violence and ensure the perpetrators are brought to justice in fair trials.

* Implement a comprehensive plan to eradicate sexual violence and harassment against women.

* End discrimination against women in law and practice, and introduce new legislation to tackle gender-based violence, including domestic violence, marital rape and sexual harassment.

(#13 Women Protesters, Egypt)

Highlighting: Besides the enumeration devices, the letters consist of plaintext with no highlighting, except bolding outside the letter proper of **Message Recipients** and **Subject**. The embedding webpages and emails and related AI reports use a variety of highlighting devices.

Comparison and contrast: At their most elemental, the appeals and webpages are comparison/contrast documents: they compare and contrast a current human rights violation with a future in which that violation is redressed. We can also view the concessions and their rebuttals as comparisons and contrasts between undesirable actual situations or events and desired redresses of those situations. We also occasionally find explicit comparisons/contrasts as in, "Herman Wallace and Albert Woodfox are believed to have spent *more* time in solitary confinement *than* virtually any other US prisoner in recent history" (#12 Wallace, Louisiana, USA; emphasis added), thus indicating the egregiousness of the violation of their human rights. We also find implicit comparisons/contrasts such as that between "indecent dress" and "skirts and trousers" in:

I write to urge Sudanese authorities to immediately and unconditionally drop the charges against the 10 female Christian students who were arrested 25 June 2015 in Khartoum and charged with "indecent dress" under Article 152 of Sudan's 1991 Criminal Act. The students were wearing skirts and trousers and were subjected to degrading treatment and humiliating verbal abuse during their detention.

(#24 Indecent Dress, Sudan)

The implication here, of course, is that deeming "skirts and trousers" to be "indecent" under Article 152 licenses the arrest and abuse to which the women were subjected.

The context invites us to ask what dress would be deemed decent for women in Sudan, and the categorization of the arrested students as "Christian" implies a contrast with Muslim women, whose dressing conventions would presumably be decent and would thereby, hopefully, protect them from similar abuse.

That the arrest and abuse of the female students is licensed by Article 152 of Sudan's 1991 Criminal Act invites evaluation of those acts and the appeal urges "the Sudanese government to repeal Article 152 of the 1991 Criminal Act" because it "is vague and discriminatory and fails to adhere to Sudan's international human rights obligations. The public order law is imposed against women in particular and violates women's human rights" (#24 Indecent Dress, Sudan).

It is noteworthy that this appeal makes no mention of the religious basis for the Article, perhaps to lessen the likelihood of its being rejected as anti-Islamic, and more generally of implicating that AI might be anti-religious.

Repetition: We find a considerable amount of repetition in the letters, usually in a sequence of directives, typically in the imperative mood and using various speech act verbs. I've highlighted the directive expressions in the following letter.

> ***Subject**: Stop the horrific public flogging of blogger, Raif Badawi*
>
> I am profoundly disturbed that Saudi blogger Raif Badawi was publicly flogged in front of al-Jafali mosque after Friday prayers. I call on you to *quash* Raif Badawi's flogging sentence immediately, as it is a flagrant violation of the prohibition on torture or other cruel, inhuman or degrading treatment under international law. Please *ensure* that he is not flogged again in the coming months.
>
> I believe that Raif Badawi is a Prisoner of Conscience, held solely for peacefully exercising his right to freedom of expression. Please *drop* all charges against Badawi and *ensure* that he is unconditionally released without further delay.
>
> I am also deeply concerned about the number of activists in Saudi Arabia who, like Raif Badawi, are persecuted for openly expressing their views online. I call on you to *stop* arresting, charging, prosecuting and sentencing activists for simply exercising their rights to freedom of expression, association and assembly.
>
> (#18 Badawi, Saudi Arabia; emphasis added)

Letters frequently repeat directives for very closely related actions pertaining to the initial subject of the letter, for example, the letter just above directs the addressees to quash Badawi's conviction, to stop flogging him, to drop charges against him, and to unconditionally release him. In accord with Grice's submaxim of Manner: Be orderly, this sequence of directives mirrors the sequence of legal events that would lead to Badawi's freedom. Letters also frequently repeat expressions of concern, also illustrated by the Badawi letter above.

Occasionally two or more appeals will address the same or a closely related exigency under different Subject titles and use very similar or identical wording as the quotations above from (#1 Targeted Killings, USA) and (#10 Drone Wars, USA) illustrate.

Substitution: Rather than refer to the subject(s) of the appeal by the same expression throughout a letter, writers substitute co-referential expressions. For example, in (#11 Pussy Riot, Russia), the two subjects of the appeal are twice referred to by their names, Nadezhda Tolokonnikova and Maria Alekhina, and also by "These two women, both mothers in their twenties," "the two women," as well as the pronoun "they" and its case forms. This letter also refers to them as members of "the feminist punk-rock group Pussy Riot." Varying the expressions in these ways allows the letter writers to highlight multiple aspects of the (classes of) individuals that might be pertinent to the appeal, in the case of "mothers in their twenties," an appeal to pathos. Appeals to pathos are somewhat unusual in the letters, presumably because the letters' primary argument is that the appeal situation violates international law and universal rights, though one can also see them as designed for the AI volunteer audience, thus making appeals to pathos more acceptable.

Juxtaposition: Verschueren includes this category in his discussion even though he omits it from his list in AD 2.3.4. I address this category as it is an important basis for inferring the meaning relations between an initial and immediately following utterance. For example, we interpret the first of the following two sentences as the evidential basis for the categorization in the second sentence of the two women as Prisoners of Conscience: "These two women … were detained solely for their peaceful expression of their beliefs. They are Prisoners of Conscience" (#11 Pussy Riot, Russia).

Conclusion

This chapter investigated the ideological relevancies of the appeals' social, political, historical, and geographical contexts; their immediate context of situation; and their linguistic contexts, guided by Verschueren's preliminary caveats, his Guidelines 1 and 2, and their associated procedures regarding the data to be analyzed. This investigation required that Verschueren's broad guidelines be implemented by a broad range of discourse analytic theoretical apparatuses: deixis; speech act theory; Gricean and post-Gricean pragmatics; contextualization cues; various theories of participant roles; positioning theory; theories of argumentation; move and step analysis; epistemic vigilance; and discussion of a large number of specifically linguistic devices.

5 Language, Social Structures, Processes, Relations, and Meaning

This chapter discusses the AI appeals from the perspectives articulated in Verschueren's Guideline 3 and its associated Caveats, Procedures, and ADs. These inform the investigation of the interactions of language with contextual factors beyond those of the immediate situation discussed in Chapter 4.

> ***Guideline 3: The core task consists in tracing the dynamics of meaning generation in relation to issues pertaining to social structures, processes, and relations. (Verschueren 2012: 117–191)***

As a preliminary to the Procedures that more precisely define Guideline 3, Verschueren interposes three Caveats.

> ***Caveat 3.1: There are hardly any fixed form-function relationships. Hence there are no interpretation rules that can be applied mechanically. (Verschueren 2012: 117–118)***

As is generally accepted, no linguistic element is ideological per se, though its context may make it so. To illustrate Caveat 3.1, Verschueren briefly discusses two forms whose interpretations depend crucially on context – quotation marks and passive voice. Quotation marks can be interpreted in two contradictory ways, as indicators of direct quotes, thus "strengthen[ing] a claim by invoking someone's authority," or by indicating ironic distancing (Sperber and Wilson 1995: 237 ff) to weaken a claim. As I mentioned earlier, the letters contain examples of both uses of quote marks: "indecent dress" (#24 Indecent Dress, Sudan) appears to quote the relevant section of the Sudanese law purportedly violated by the women who were the subjects of the appeal, and "confession" in (#4 Al-Qahtani, Iraq) to cast doubt on the legal admissibility of the appeal subject's confession, which is implied to have been forced.

The passive voice as a linguistic form is routinely accused of being "passive" as the phrase in its subject position is typically associated with a patient role. Subjects, it is claimed, largely for ideological reasons, should represent an "active" agent. The passive is also accused of perfidy when its *by*-phrase is omitted, as it typically is. Examples of the "Mistakes were made" type are claimed to obscure responsibility for nefarious deeds by the omission of its *by*-phrase. In response to these accusations, researchers have pointed out that there may be discourse cohesion reasons for placing a patient phrase at the beginning of a sentence; that the agent role may be recovered from context and so its expression would be redundant; that many other constructions allow for the elision of information without exciting commentary that reveals nothing more than the commentators' ignorance of discourse analysis; and that the information included in a text indexes its context, audience, and purpose.

The letters include lots of passive constructions, many of which include the agent in a *by*-phrase:

> Uzbekistan is party to numerous international human rights treaties, which prohibit torture and the use of torture-tainted evidence in court. In spite of this, torture continues to be used *by Uzbekistani security forces* to extract confessions which are used in courts to secure convictions.
>
> (#29 Bekzhanov, Uzbekistan; emphasis added)

Others provide sufficient context to allow readers to infer at least the institution or class of individuals responsible for the situation. The following is addressed to the Algerian Minister for Justice, so we may infer that it is personnel in the Algerian justice system who are responsible for sentencing and jailing the subjects of the appeal, though more specific allocations of responsibility cannot be inferred:

> I am writing to express my deep concern for Dahmane Kerami, and his six co-defendants who were recently sentenced to one year in prison for taking part in a peaceful protest outside the Tamanrasset governorate headquarters in December 2015 about a real estate dispute.
>
> I urge you to release Dahmane Kerami and his six co-defendants immediately and unconditionally, as they are prisoners of conscience, jailed solely for the peaceful exercise of their rights to freedom of expression and assembly.
>
> (#37 PoCs, Algeria)

The following invites the inference that the 1965–66 Indonesian massacre survivors "remain threatened and marginalized" by members of their own communities, but it leaves the other threateners no more precisely identifiable than "those who terrorized and killed their relatives."

> More than 50 years after the massacres of 1965–66, survivors of that time and their families remain threatened, marginalized and sometimes living in the same communities as those who terrorized and killed their relatives.
>
> (#31 Massacre Survivors, Indonesia)

It is not clear from the following who discriminates against women and girls and denies them their rights: government personnel perhaps, though possibly (also) others in positions of power, for example, medical personnel and perhaps others with religious objections to contraceptives and the power to deny them:

> Under the Universal Declaration of Human Rights, and Burkina Faso's Constitution, women and girls are entitled to the same human rights as men and boys. But in practice, they are discriminated against and denied their rights.
>
> (#33 Contraception, Burkina Faso)

However, the appeal is directly addressed to the president of the country, who is thereby positioned as one with the power to redress the violation, but is also positioned as someone who may be responsible for that violation.

Similarly, it is impossible to infer from the following who is responsible for abducting, killing, and selling the body parts of people with albinism, though here again, the letter is addressed to the president of the country, who is assumed to have the power to stop these horrors and so may be held (at least partially) responsible for them:

> It is profoundly troubling that thousands of people with albinism in your country live in fear of being abducted or killed, and that their body parts are being sold for use in rituals.
>
> (#38 Albinism, Malawi)

From the following, we may infer that Bekzhanov was sentenced by some court, though who tortured him into confessing is unknowable. But we can infer that it is the government of Uzbekistan that failed in its responsibility to conduct a "proper investigation" and must therefore bear responsibility for Bekzhanov's torture:

> Muhammad Bekzhanov, a respected journalist, has spent the last 16 years in prison following an unfair trial in which he was sentenced on the basis of a confession he gave after being beaten, suffocated and given electric shocks. No proper investigation into his torture has ever been conducted and repeated calls for a fair retrial have been ignored.
>
> (#29 Bekzhanov, Uzbekistan)

Note that it is also impossible to identify those who made the "repeated calls for a fair retrial," because nominalizations, like passives and many other constructions, allow the omission of information that would be obligatory in their full active, declarative counterparts.

Relatively few of the passive constructions may be said to completely obscure the agents of actions. Presumably this is because the appeals are typically addressed to high-ranking individuals who head institutions – governments, ministries of justice – whose lower-ranking members may have carried out tortures and killings, probably in accord with policies set by the institutional leaders. While these ministers are typically not portrayed as (personally) responsible for the abuses, they are positioned in the letters as powerful enough to bring about their redress and as legally responsible for that redress.

Less benignly omitted, perhaps, are expressions that might identify the agents of actions that the letters evaluate as violations of various rights, for example,

> I am writing you on behalf of satirist Bassem Youssef, comedian Ali Qandil, blogger Ahmed Anwar and at least 30 other Egyptians who have been put under investigation in the past three months.
>
> (#3 Satire as Crime, Egypt)

We can only speculate about who put these individuals under investigation, though we probably wouldn't, because the ostensible goal of the appeal is to persuade its addressees (Talaat Ibrahim Abdallah – Office of the Public Prosecutor) to stop such investigations regardless of their specific agents.

Passives are typical in the characterization of the rights violations inflicted on the subjects of the appeals, for example, "I am profoundly disturbed that Saudi blogger Raif Badawi was publicly flogged in front of al-Jafali mosque after Friday prayers" (#18 Badawi, Saudi Arabia); "No other prisoner in the U.S has been held in solitary confinement longer than Albert Woodfox" (#20 Woodfox, Louisiana, USA); "the 10 female Christian students who were arrested 25 June 2015 in Khartoum and charged with 'indecent dress'" (#24 Indecent Dress, Sudan); and "the two men were sentenced to death …" (#4 Al-Qahtani, Iraq).

The passive voice is also used to express what is to be done to or for the appeal subjects, for example, "I urge you to ensure that Shaker Aamer, and all those held in Guantánamo, are released immediately unless … they are to be charged with a recognizably criminal offence and fairly tried in U.S. federal court …" (#7 Aamer, USA).

The letters are not entirely shy about identifying individuals responsible for rights violations, for example, "Were it not for the Louisiana Attorney General's attempts to pursue vengeance, Albert Woodfox would already be a free man." Attorney General, Buddy Caldwell, is named twice in the letter (#20 Woodfox, Louisiana, USA). However, in general, the Message Recipients of the appeals are government officials who may not be directly responsible for the violations being appealed, though they may very well be responsible for the policies and political tenor that enable those violations. The Message Recipients of the Woodfox appeal are the then Governor and Attorney General of Louisiana.

Even more so than passives, nominalizations allow the omission of information, about both agents and patients, though typically it is only agent phrases that are omitted from the nominalizations in the corpus that characterize what befell appeal subjects, for example, "the disappearance of prominent human rights lawyer Wang Yu," "Wang Yu's disappearance" (#25 Missing, China). The choice of the intransitive *disappear* here prevents the expression of an agent within the nominal phrase, though it could have been included elsewhere in the text.[1]

The AI Letter Writing Guide requires letter writers to be polite, and the letters accomplish this in general by not accusing addressees of (direct) responsibility for the violations being appealed, though as powerful addressees of the appeals they become (directly) responsible for acceding to or rejecting the appeals and thus for whatever situation or events ensue after the appeal.

[1] *Disappear* occurs as a transitive verb in discussions of Argentinian human rights abuses carried out by the military dictatorship there from 1974 through 1983.

One device for deflecting attributions of responsibility for undesirable situations is by attributing that responsibility to an institution rather than an individual, for example, an appeal addressed to the then US Attorney General Loretta Lynch protesting the decision of the US Justice Department not to read the US Senate report on the CIA's torture regime in Iraq attributes that decision to the Justice Department, even though Lynch presided over this department and must have endorsed the decision not to read the report: "But shockingly, the Justice Department has failed to commit to reading and reviewing the full report" (#19 Torture Report, USA).

While none of these expression types is intrinsically ideological, their use in the letters does contribute to the evocation of "social structures, processes, and relations" (Verschueren 2012: 117) that do have ideological resonances – laws, legal processes, the hierarchy among legal functionaries, individuals accused of crimes, and activist organizations such as AI and their members.

> ***Caveat 3.2: Though Caveat 3.1 does not allow jumping from observation of forms to interpretations, whatever can be detected with a reasonable degree of certainty on the basis of "formal" analysis can never be ignored. (Verschueren 2012: 118–119)***

To this caveat, Verschueren (2012) adds the rider that "*describable patterns do matter for interpretation*" (119; emphasis in original).

A number of formal patterns are salient. For example, fixed phrases or formulaic expressions (Wray 2002) such as *the right to X* (sixteen occurrences) or *the rights of X* (ten occurrences), where X can be filled with such expressions as *life* or *family members*, as well as the related *violates X* (five occurrences) and *violations of X* (five occurrences), where X can be filled by expressions such as *international human rights law*, and so can be readily interpreted as invoking the frame of human and humanitarian rights, which include, to varying degrees of specificity, such legal instruments as the United Nations Universal Declaration of Human Rights and the Geneva and Hague Conventions, though whether these referents are actually accessed by writers, AI volunteers, or readers/addressees is unknowable.

Patterns in the choice of grammatical voice are also notable. The active voice is typical in the expression of writers' actions, for example, "I am writing …"; "I urge you to …"; and writers' epistemological stances, for example, "I know …"; "I fear …"; "I understand …" (#4 Al-Qahtani, Iraq). Active subject-complement sentences are used to classify, for example, "I believe that Raif Badawi is a Prisoner of Conscience" (#18 Badawi, Saudi Arabia), or otherwise characterize appeal subjects, for example, "The Most Venerable Thich Quang Do is the head of the banned Unified Buddhist Church of Viet

Nam (UBCV) and a leading advocate of religious freedom, human rights and democracy" (#26 PoCs, Vietnam).

Infinitives are frequently used to characterize actions to be taken to redress the appeal situations or events, for example, "I urge you to ensure that the US government follows international law governing the use of lethal force …" (#1 Targeted Killings, USA); "Furthermore, we ask for you to stop investigating defamation cases as a criminal offense" (#3 Satire as Crime, Egypt); and "I call on you to uphold the right to freedom of expression, association and peaceful assembly in Russia" (#14 Restrictive Legislation, Russia). These infinitival forms allow for the inclusion of an agentive subject, typically referring to the letters' Message Recipients, thereby implicating them in the violative situation and ideologically positioning them.

Caveat 3.3: Because form-function relations are never absolute, ideology research is necessarily comparative and contrastive. (Verschueren 2012: 119–120)

Referring back to AD 2.3.4, Verschueren (2012) reiterates the importance of comparison and contrast as "a powerful tool for the interpretation of texts, as often patterns of implicit meaning are involved" (119).

In response to AD 2.3.4, I noted the ideological, and especially the evaluative, implications of explicit and implicit contrasts in several of the appeals, as well as the contrast between concessions and their rebuttals, which is revealing of the contrast between AI's ideologically approved and disapproved situations. To these, I add here a brief discussion of AI's categorization of many of the subjects of its appeals as "Prisoners of Conscience" (PoCs) (five occurrences). However we theorize it, categorization implies that the categorized object has certain qualities (cf. Wodak and Reisigl's [2018: 585] "nomination" and "predicational strategies"). It also implies contrast: if I categorize something as fish, I am implicating that it is not fowl. Thus, if someone is categorized as a PoC, then they are deemed by AI to have the qualities required for that categorization:

> Amnesty International defines a prisoner of conscience as a person imprisoned (or otherwise detained) solely because of **who they are** (ethnic origin, sex, colour, language, national or social origin, economic status, birth, sexual orientation, gender identity or expression, or other status) **or what they believe** (political, religious or other conscientiously held beliefs), who has not used violence or advocated violence or hatred in the circumstances leading to their detention.[2]

This definition is crafted as a set of necessary and sufficient conditions which are transparently derived from the UDHR. As all the conditions are necessary,

[2] www.amnesty.org/en/what-we-do/detention/ (accessed August 7, 2025); emphasis in original.

anyone who fails to meet any one of them will not be deemed a PoC by AI. Four individuals are categorized as PoCs in the letters: (#15 Vitishko, Russia; #18 Badawi, Saudi Arabia; #26 PoCs, Vietnam; #28 PoC, Myanmar). They were all held in custody because they exercised their right to freedom of speech or to the free exercise of their religion.

A controversial (June 3, 2019) case relevant to PoC designation is that of Julian Assange,[3] the creator of Wikileaks, who was accused of espionage by the US government for "obtaining and publishing secret military and diplomatic documents."[4] He was also accused of rape and sexual assault in Sweden. Citing the Swedish rape accusation, a crime of violence, AI refused to declare him a PoC:

> Rape allegations should always be treated with utmost seriousness. It is vital that the allegations against Julian Assange are properly investigated, in a way that respects the rights of both the complainant and the person under investigation.[5]

This decision has been widely criticized; for example, the World Socialist Web Site characterizes the decision as a "travesty."[6]

AI, however, does argue that Assange should not be extradited to the US:

> Amnesty International calls on the UK to refuse to extradite or send in any other manner Julian Assange to the USA where there is a very real risk that he could face human rights violations, including detention conditions that would violate the absolute prohibition of torture and other ill-treatment and an unfair trial followed by possible execution, due to his work with Wikileaks.[7]

AI is here carefully distinguishing between Assange's alleged sexual abuse, which is not protected by international human rights law, and the human rights violations he is likely to face in the US because of his Wikileaks work, from which he is legally protected.[8]

Designating a person as a PoC is ideologically and practically valuable. It is ideologically valuable because it affirms and broadcasts the legitimacy of whatever activities the PoC was engaged in and, because ideology is action-oriented, it directs AI members and others to work for the PoC's proper treatment and release.

Comparison and contrast, in addition to being intratextual, may also be intertextual, and I add, intergeneric. The appeal letter genre under study here may be compared and contrasted with:

[3] www.biography.com/activist/julian-assange (accessed August 7, 2025).
[4] www.nytimes.com/2019/05/23/us/politics/assange-indictment.html (accessed August 7, 2025).
[5] https://tinyurl.com/2zetdsdy (accessed August 7, 2025).
[6] www.wsws.org/en/articles/2019/05/23/assa-m23.html (accessed August 7, 2025).
[7] https://tinyurl.com/2w6wmufh (accessed August 7, 2025).
[8] In June 2024, Assange pleaded guilty to a US Espionage Act violation in return for a sentence of time served. See https://tinyurl.com/3drpy2y2 (accessed August 7, 2025).

1. the embedding emails and other relevant AI documents – AI webpages and reports (Chapter 2; Delahunty 2021);
2. the historical development of the AI appeal genre in relation to changes in historical, social, political, and institutional contexts, and especially in response to changes in those rights and in their legal and other interpretations to determine what if any ideological changes have occurred in that time (see Chen 2015: 147ff on "A Developing Bill of Human Rights");
3. studies of any changes in the tenor (Eggins 1994: 63–67) of the appeals over that time to reveal how AI staffers viewed the relations between themselves, their volunteers, and the letter addressees;
4. appeals by other activist rights organizations, for example, Human Rights Watch, American Civil Liberties Union, etc.;
5. historical corpus studies of expressions such as "rights," "human rights," "humanitarian rights," "violation," "Prisoner of Conscience," and their variants and collocates.

Delahunty (2018b) compares and contrasts the AI appeals with philanthropic fundraising (PF) letters (Mann and Thompson 1992). Both genres identify a problem, propose a solution to that problem, and attempt to persuade addressees to act to solve the problem. The paper also demonstrates that the moves and steps (Swales 1981, 1990) of PF and AI appeals differ in substantial ways. For example, the PF letters include moves that AI does not. The PF letters offer incentives to their addressees for responding and donating; they refer to inserts accompanying them, and typically conclude with pleasantries toward the addressees. In contrast, the AI appeals allow for the making and rebuttal of concessions whereas PF does not, perhaps because PF letter writers assume that their characterization of situations as problems is so persuasive that they do not need to engage potential counterarguments. Because AI letters base their appeals on universal laws, it may be rhetorically effective to imagine and rebut what might be the major arguments that addressees could mount against an appeal, reflective, perhaps, of argument and counterargument in legal contexts.

These differences are due to the differences in the kinds of problems and solutions addressed, the types of addressees, the power of the addressees *vis à vis* the writers, and the mode of delivery. The differences also reflect the positions the two genres occupy in their genre continua – PF letters are related to business letters, whereas AI letters are similar in certain respects to protest placards – thus reflecting fundamental differences in how their writers conceptualize their modes of persuasion – PF letters by single pathetic appeals to individuals and AI letters by demonstrating mass public disagreement with the actions of the addressees or the authorities they represent, as an AI website declared:

By telling the powerful stories of the people we work with, we mobilize millions of supporters around the world to campaign for change and to stand in defence of activists on the frontline.[9]

Biber et al. (2007) examine stance expressions (Biber and Finegan 1989; Biber et al. 1999; Englebretson 2007) in PF letters, categorizing and listing them primarily by grammatical and very general semantic characteristics, for example, Stance verb + *to*-clause: Verbs Expressing Probability (likelihood): *appear, happen, seem, tend* (of Biber et al.'s (2007) twenty-six, only eight occur in the AI letters). Biber et al. (2007) define stance expressions as signifying "personal feelings, attitudes, value judgments, or assessments" and provide a list of works that use different terms for stance (sixty-two), the most revealing one being "evaluation" (Hunston 1994, 2000; Martin 2000; Thompson and Hunston 2000). Evaluation is accomplished in discourse (Du Bois 2007; Hoey 1983) against a set of norms (Hyland 2005; Johnstone 2009). Unfortunately, Biber et al. (2007) provide no bases for the evaluations legitimating the PF stance expressions, just post hoc discussion of their linguistic findings.

In contrast, the AI letters allow us to identify both the stance expressions and the norms they invoke, for example, *punishment* occurs ten times in the corpus, along with synonyms like *penal/penalty/penalties* (eleven occurrences). In discourse, *punishment* invokes a frame (Goffman 1974; Tannen 1993) in which someone violates a norm, or most relevantly to AI letters, a law. It is what is imposed upon individuals after they have been found guilty by a court of breaking some law.

However, frames may be re-framed and laws and legal procedures subject to higher laws, so we find in the AI letters evaluation expressions invoking universal laws to evaluate local legal proceedings, for example, punishment by flogging, even when legitimate under local law, is characterized as a "flagrant violation of the prohibition on torture or other cruel, inhuman or degrading treatment under international law" (#18 Badawi, Saudi Arabia), which both evaluates flogging and identifies the norm it violates.[10]

Procedure 3.1/AD 3.1: Define the activity type or speech event type (providing a general frame of interpretation) to which the investigated. discourse belongs (Verschueren 2012: 120–126)

Verschueren's corpus is of academic writing, which he characterizes as prototypically transparently structured, expository, socially distancing,

[9] The website is no longer available.
[10] See Dagistanli et al. (2018) for a discussion of an Australian court case regarding flogging as a religious practice.

objective, explicit, and explanatory (2012: 121–122). In contrast, the AI letters purport to be expressions of the writer's concern and urgent appeals to government officials to redress situations that AI deems violations of human rights or to take actions that AI deems important or necessary to protect the rights of (groups/classes of) individuals. The appeals are generally transparently structured, as my move and step analysis above demonstrates (see also Delahunty 2018b). They also purport to be objective, explicit, explanatory expositions of the situations they address. They are not, however, socially distancing, as evidenced by their use of first- and second-person references, expressions of personal concern, and their occasional concessions to the exigencies of the addressees' situations. The linguistic style of the letters is personal, respectful, generally clear, and explicit, and aims to persuade. The letters contain indicators of personal engagement with the letters' subjects and with their addressees and occasionally purport to seek to engage their addressees in dialog regarding the subjects. The letters also include elements of protest against the violations and while the language of the letters is not neutral with respect to their subjects, it is nonetheless evidence-based, thereby legitimizing the writers' concern and appeal. While the history textbooks may seek to convince their readers of the essential benignity of British and French imperialism and to encourage them to adopt and act upon their respective values, the letters also serve to persuade AI volunteers of the righteousness of human and humanitarian rights, to act in their defense, and to donate for their support (Delahunty 2017).

AD 3.1.1: Identify the speech acts or language games of which the activity or event predominantly consists. (Verschueren 2012: 126–129)

Verschueren (2012: 126) says that "[a]ctivity or event types are always 'meaningful' in the sense that, like any form of social action, they are interpreted by the actors (in this case language users) involved [footnote omitted]. Those interpretations use 'types' as anchoring points, definable in terms of (proto) typical properties and corresponding normative expectations." The move analysis identifies the letters' prototypical speech acts.

Verschueren (2012: 127, fn. 49) distinguishes between "genre," by which he means "general discourse worlds associated with spheres of human activity (e.g., the genre of academic discourse in general)" and "activity type" or "(speech) event type" for "more specific, but still general, manifestations of a genre (e.g., the activity type of academic writing)." This distinction suggests that the appeals are an activity or (speech) event type that belongs to the genre of human and humanitarian rights discourse with specific purposes.

Procedure 3.2: Investigate the use of languages, codes, and styles. In particular:

AD 3.2.1: What language(s) is/are used? How does this relate to the wider linguistic context of the society/community in which the discourse is to be found? (Verschueren 2012: 129–132)

With a very occasional interloper from British (or British-influenced) English, the letters in my corpus are in current American English (e.g., use of *-ize* rather than *-ise*, *defense* rather than *defence*, etc.). This is hardly surprising as most were sent from the US branch of Amnesty International (AI USA). Thus, the letters are in English regardless of the language(s) of the addressees. This choice presumably reflects the status of English as a major international lingua franca, especially of diplomatic communication. It probably also reflects the assumption that the volunteers to whom the letters are emailed are Americans and speakers of English, and if my claim that the letters are to engage AI volunteers is correct, then it makes sense to write to them in English. It is noteworthy, however, that AI suggests writing Urgent Action letters in English, in the language of the addressees(s), or in the writer's own language.

AD 3.2.2: What codes are used? Is there any code switching? Is a specific communicative style involved?

AD 3.2.3: Is the style formal, informal, …? (Verschueren 2012: 130–132; ellipsis in original)

The letters are neither highly nor expertly edited. Their occasional errors are suggestive of rapid composition. They display no code switching between languages, but occasionally among registers and styles.

The letters' style is moderately formal, designed to be personal but serious, respectful, and persuasive. It is consistent across the corpus, even though the letters seem to have been written by several different AI staffers, apparently all following the prescriptions laid out in the AI Letter Writing Guide like that in Appendix 1.

The genre, in Verschueren's sense, is that of the discourse of human rights protest and engagement. It includes references to various relevant rights, typically generically, for example, "These programs are a violation of the human rights of people across the globe" (#23 Mass Surveillance, USA), but occasionally to specific rights and legal instruments, for example, "Article 13 of the International Covenant on Civil and Political Rights and Article 22 of the American Convention on Human Rights" (#22 Haitians, Dominican Republic). It also includes references to legal institutions and procedures – parliaments, courts, covenants, conventions, laws, constitution, guilt, innocence, prison, etc.

The letters appeal to universal values articulated in internationally agreed upon treaties, conventions, covenants, and laws, along with the urgency of individual situations and their normative expectations. While some of these may not be provided for by law, they are generally accepted values. For example, "Beatriz wants to live. She wants to see her one-year-old son grow up …" (#8 Beatriz, El Salvador) suggests that the denial of such treatment for a mother who wants to live to see her son grow up violates a norm, which though unexpressed, is implied to be shared by AI volunteers and Message Recipients. Similarly, the characterization of two of the imprisoned members of the Pussy Riot group as "mothers in their twenties" (#11 Pussy Riot, Russia) suggests that young mothers deserve leniency, perhaps because youthful transgressions may be regarded as remediable folly and motherhood invites ideologized connotations of gentle nurturing, especially when the mothers are responsible for young children (Williamson et al. 2023).

These "personal" values are integrated, more or less successfully into the more impersonal, universal civil, human, and humanitarian rights. Thus, the appeal for life-saving treatment for Beatriz is for an abortion to terminate a pregnancy that endangers her life and for the repeal of the Salvadoran laws that ban abortions regardless of the circumstances of the pregnancy, thereby bringing El Salvador into compliance with a ruling by the Inter-American Court of Human Rights (IACtHR).

The letters are characteristically crafted as direct person-to-person/SENDer-to-Message Recipients appeals, enacted by the choice of first- and second-person pronouns, typically *I*, occasionally *we*, and *you*, and frequently imperatives with understood second-person subjects.

As I demonstrated in Chapter 4, the referents of *I* in the letters are problematic. They could be the writers, who, as AI staffers, presumably articulate their own feelings and beliefs. They could also refer to the AI volunteers who SEND the letters on, again presumably expressing their feelings and beliefs, thus aligning themselves with AI's human rights ideology. Thus, the letters (seek to) position (Foucault 1980) the volunteers as individuals who endorse the feelings, values, and evaluations that AI endorses.

The use of *you* in the letters presumably attempts to directly and personally engage the putative addressees and is thus consistent with the hope expressed in some letters that the addressees will respond to the *I* of the letters, implying that they can be persuaded by appeals to human rights values and to respond to personal expressions of concern.

The temporal juxtaposition of appeals for donations to AI immediately upon the SENDing of a letter is a clear indication that the letter-sending system is inextricably intertwined with AI's fundraising efforts. Indeed, who are better targets of requests for donations than the people who have just acted in support of an AI cause?

While I cannot estimate how powerful or effective the letters are at either fundraising or redressing rights violations, AI continues to use them.[11] I suspect that the integration of the personal and the universal is deemed effective for the purposes of the letters.[12] Indeed, this mix of appeal on behalf of a good cause and for donations to the organization dedicated to that cause seems to be standard operating procedure in the eleemosynary industries.

Procedure 3.3: Look for overt carriers of information structure.

AD 3.3.1: How is information "chunked" prosodically (with spoken data) or in writing? (Verschueren 2012: 132–135)

Like Verschueren's history books, the AI letters are written, and so phonological prosody is irrelevant. However, Verschueren (2012) lists several written analogs to spoken prosody: "(numbered) chapters and paragraphs, punctuation, font changes, and layout" (133). We find several of these in the letters, and a few others. As the letters contain no bolding, italics, or underlining, we can put font changes aside. Punctuation is conventional, if not always consistent. It includes periods, commas, semi-colons, and colons, as well as bullets, asterisks, dashes, and numbers to introduce items in lists:

I believe that these laws are inconsistent with Russia's international obligations and the Russian Federation's own Constitution and must be repealed:

- Re-criminalization of defamation of public figures punishable by even heftier fines, which is likely to inhibit criticism of public officials and policies by the media and NGOs. (#14 Restrictive Legislation, Russia)

And so on for another four dashed paragraphs.

As the genre would lead us to expect, we do not find chapter breaks in the letters. Typically, the letters comprise multiple short paragraphs, generally of one to three sentences, clauses, or phrases. The first paragraph typically represents, implicitly or explicitly, one or more actions or situations as violating the rights of some individual(s) and a later one typically, directly or indirectly, urges the Message Recipients to redress those violations. The following is an unusually dense example:

The shooting death of Michael Brown in Ferguson, as well as other cases, including Kajieme Powell in St. Louis, Ezell Ford in Los Angeles and Eric Garner in New York

[11] Recall the discussion of AI's effectiveness in Chapter 2.

[12] An AI email received on November 8, 2021, includes the following: "Gerald, we know that writing these letters matters. They help bring international pressure to demand justice – and they remind these individuals and their families that they are not forgotten. **Over the past 20 years of Write for Rights, Amnesty supporters have taken over 34 million actions and helped free dozens of people unjustly held**." (This sentence is bolded and highlighted in red in the original.) That only "dozens of people" have been freed in spite of "over 34 million actions" invites reflection on the effectiveness of AI's actions and overall strategy.

City, all highlight the need to reform state legislation to reflect international standards on the use of lethal force.

(#21 Crime Task Force, USA)

Brown, Powell, Ford, and Garner were African-American men killed by police officers. Their cases are represented as a sequence of noun phrases (NPs) functioning as the subject of the single sentence that constitutes the paragraph. The predicate expresses the desired redress and the standards by which it and, implicitly, the deaths of the four men are to be evaluated.

In several letters, paragraphs are numbered as a list after a colon, as in (#1 Targeted Killings, USA):

I urge you to ensure that the US government follows international law governing the use of lethal force: international human rights law and, in the exceptional circumstances where it applies, international humanitarian law as well. The US government must:

1. Disclose further legal and factual details about US policy and practices for so-called "targeted killings," "signature strikes," and "Terrorist Attack Disruption Strikes" …

And so on to paragraph 4, which introduces a bulleted list:

4. Bring US policies and practices in line with the USA's obligations under international law, particularly, by:

- Ensuring that any use of lethal force outside of specific recognized zones of armed conflict complies fully with the USA's obligations under international human rights law, including by limiting the use of force in accordance with law enforcement standards

And so on for another two bullets.

Presumably to facilitate readability, the layout of the letters includes a great deal of white space. The paragraphs are separated by a space, their first lines are not indented, and they are left- but not right-justified:

The refugees cannot go home. In the refugee camps, many are barely surviving on as little as 50 cents a day. Syria's children are becoming a lost generation – traumatized and out of school, working to support their families.

It's beyond time for the US to step up and take leadership. Please publicly make a strong commitment to significantly increasing Syrian refugee resettlement in the US.

(#27 Syrian Refugees, USA)

In the move and step analysis presented in Chapter 4, I distinguished, per Biber et al. (2007), between structural elements and the rhetorical moves and steps. The structural elements are constituents of the email layout. For convenience, I re-present them here.

A. Message Recipients list (e.g., **Message Recipients**: President Obama)
B. Subject line (e.g., **Subject**: Grant Albert Woodfox his freedom)
C. *To*-line (e.g., **To**: President Obama) or Salutation (e.g., Dear President Obama,)

D. Imminent closing announcement of (e.g., In closing …)
E. Complimentary close (e.g., Yours sincerely,)

The Message Recipients and Subject lines are placed above the letter pane in the email and webpage; the *To*-, imminent closing, and complimentary close lines are optional parts of the letters themselves.

The language choices represented in these structural elements are worthy of discussion. The Message Recipients are always referred to by official name, often with official title, for example,

Message Recipients: Thein Sein, President of the Republic of the Union of Myanmar (#28 PoC, Myanmar)

The *To*-line is always either constructed as *To*: and the addressee's (title and) last name or with the traditional salutation *Dear title and last name*, which AI's Letter Writing Guide characterizes as "the proper salutation." A very few letters include what I have called an imminent closing announcement. And relatively few include a complimentary close, typically "Yours sincerely," which the Letter Writing Guide truncates to "Sincerely."

The following synoptically, with minor adjustments, illustrates the main moves of the analysis and the characteristic linguistic enactments; the full set of moves and steps are laid out in Chapter 4.

Move 1 Express concern about the exigent situation and identify the normative basis for its undesirability (Obligatory), for example, "I share Amnesty International's grave concern that the U.S. administration's policy on intentional use of lethal force appears to permit violations of the right to life" (#10 Drone Wars, USA).

Move 2 Direct addressee(s) to redress the situation characterized in M1 in accordance with norms identified in M1 (Obligatory), for example, "I urge you to help prevent extrajudicial executions by adopting the recommendations in Amnesty International's 5 Point Plan for reform" (#10 Drone Wars, USA).

Move 3 Make and rebut concession(s) to addressee(s) (Optional), for example, "I understand that your government has as an obligation to bring to [*sic*] those responsible for serious crimes to justice, and that Iraq must confront violence by armed group [*sic*]. However, I am deeply concerned about convictions that are based on forced confessions and trial proceedings that fall short of international standards" (#4 Al-Qahtani, Iraq).

Move 4 State related concerns and solicit related actions (Optional), for example, "Furthermore, we ask for you to stop investigating defamation cases as a criminal offense. If such cases are to go to court, please ensure they are dealt with under civil, not criminal, law" (#3 Satire as Crime, Egypt).

Move 5 (Re-)state situation(s) requiring redress and solicit redressive action(s) (Optional), for example, "In closing, I urge you once again to stay the executions of 'Abdullah 'Azzam Saleh Musfer al-Qahtani and Safa Ahmad 'Abul'aziz' Abdullah and overturn their convictions" (#4 Al-Qahtani, Iraq).

Move 6 Engage addressee(s) (Optional), for example, "Thank you for your urgent attention to [*sic*] matter and I hope to hear back from you regarding the steps that you are taking to provide Beatriz with the medical care she has requested and is entitled to receive" (#8 Beatriz, El Salvador).

The individual moves tend to be expressed in single, short paragraphs; occasionally numbered, bulleted, or hyphened, or combinations of these, for example,

- End intelligence sharing relationships with foreign states that subject individuals' communications to surveillance that contravenes international human rights law

(#23 Mass Surveillance, USA)

It is worth comparing the move analysis above with the Letter Writing Guidelines in the Sample Letter in Figure 5.1. It consists of the structural elements: the sender's address, the addressee's title, names, institutional affiliation, and address, a salutation using the addressee's title and last name, complimentary close with signature and printed name, and indications of copies sent. The first paragraph consists of Moves 1 and 2; the second might be regarded as consisting of Move 4, and the third of Moves 6 and 5.

A search for AI letter writing guides will return a great many but generally consistent variations. The sample letter in Figure 5.1 occurs in Amnesty International USA and the Urgent Action Network USA's Letter Writing Guide.[13] Another version is provided in Appendix 1.

The annotations surrounding the sample letter are particularly revealing, especially the one that tells writers not to "discuss political ideology or politics." Nonetheless, the sample letter expresses the concern that the letter-subject "may be at risk of torture." As torture is proscribed in UDHR Article 5, "No one shall be subjected to torture or to cruel, inhuman or degrading treatment or punishment," it is therefore an ideological issue. In fact, the very gesture of declaring issues such as the ban on torture to be non-ideological can itself be seen as an effort to naturalize and make them appear commonsensical, thus attesting to their status as ideologically based norms (Eagleton 2007: 58; Verschueren 2012: 10).

[13] https://student.uncw.edu/org/ai/library/GuideToLetterWriting.pdf (accessed August 7, 2025).

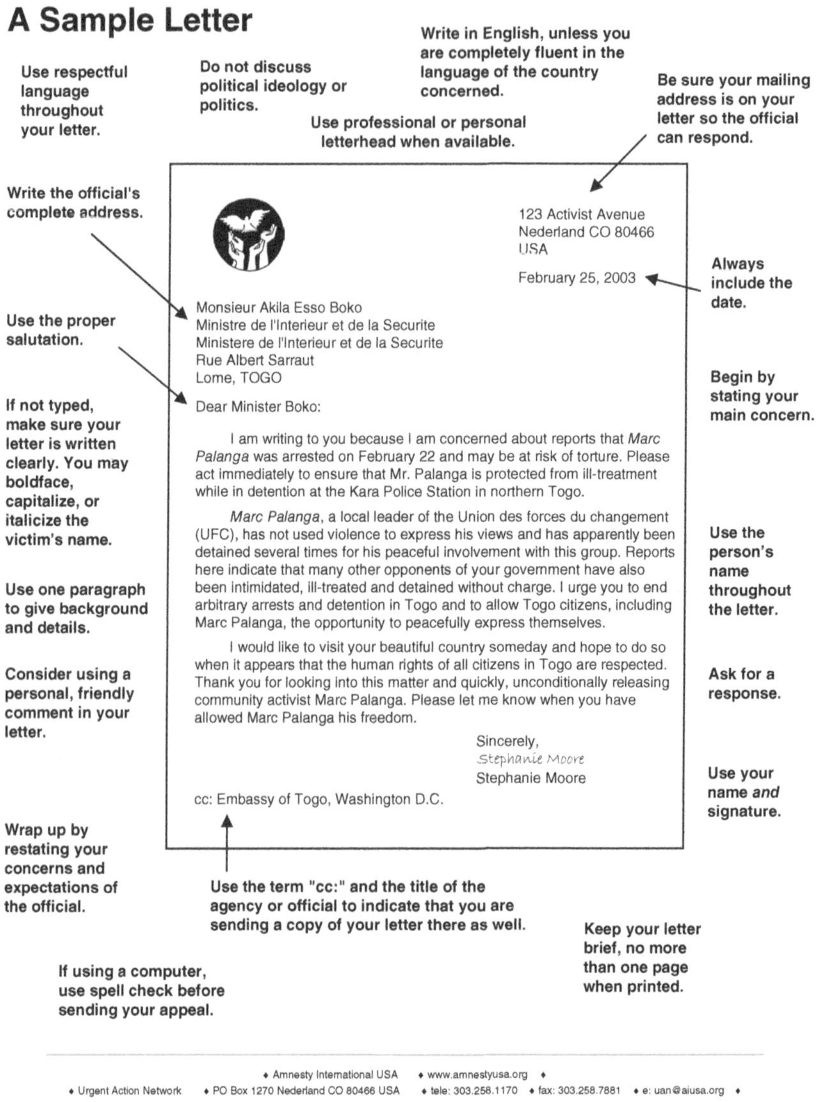

A Sample Letter

Use respectful language throughout your letter.

Do not discuss political ideology or politics.

Write in English, unless you are completely fluent in the language of the country concerned.

Use professional or personal letterhead when available.

Be sure your mailing address is on your letter so the official can respond.

Write the official's complete address.

123 Activist Avenue
Nederland CO 80466
USA

February 25, 2003

Always include the date.

Use the proper salutation.

Monsieur Akila Esso Boko
Ministre de l'Interieur et de la Securite
Ministere de l'Interieur et de la Securite
Rue Albert Sarraut
Lome, TOGO

Dear Minister Boko:

Begin by stating your main concern.

If not typed, make sure your letter is written clearly. You may boldface, capitalize, or italicize the victim's name.

I am writing to you because I am concerned about reports that *Marc Palanga* was arrested on February 22 and may be at risk of torture. Please act immediately to ensure that Mr. Palanga is protected from ill-treatment while in detention at the Kara Police Station in northern Togo.

Use one paragraph to give background and details.

Use the person's name throughout the letter.

Marc Palanga, a local leader of the Union des forces du changement (UFC), has not used violence to express his views and has apparently been detained several times for his peaceful involvement with this group. Reports here indicate that many other opponents of your government have also been intimidated, ill-treated and detained without charge. I urge you to end arbitrary arrests and detention in Togo and to allow Togo citizens, including Marc Palanga, the opportunity to peacefully express themselves.

Consider using a personal, friendly comment in your letter.

Ask for a response.

I would like to visit your beautiful country someday and hope to do so when it appears that the human rights of all citizens in Togo are respected. Thank you for looking into this matter and quickly, unconditionally releasing community activist Marc Palanga. Please let me know when you have allowed Marc Palanga his freedom.

Sincerely,
Stephanie Moore
Stephanie Moore

Use your name *and* signature.

cc: Embassy of Togo, Washington D.C.

Wrap up by restating your concerns and expectations of the official.

Use the term "cc:" and the title of the agency or official to indicate that you are sending a copy of your letter there as well.

Keep your letter brief, no more than one page when printed.

If using a computer, use spell check before sending your appeal.

♦ Amnesty International USA ♦ www.amnestyusa.org ♦
♦ Urgent Action Network ♦ PO Box 1270 Nederland CO 80466 USA ♦ tele: 303.258.1170 ♦ fax: 303.258.7881 ♦ e: uan@aiusa.org ♦

Figure 5.1 Amnesty sample appeal letter with annotations

AD 3.3.2: What patterns of word choice can be found? (Verschueren 2012: 135–138)

Verschueren notes that choosing one word rather than another evokes the "sense potential of those alternatives," especially when the chosen item is marked and evaluative rather than neutral. He notes also the evaluative uses of comparative and superlative forms and of various adjectives and adverbs as markers of "perspective" and the use of "jargon" to index readers' membership in classes of people familiar with the genre of history textbooks.

I broaden the category of "word choice" to include ideologically relevant phrases, beginning with the language of human/humanitarian rights. And as AI and the AI letters frequently mention various laws, I begin with a legal definition:

> **law 1 :** a rule of conduct or action prescribed or formally recognized as binding or enforced by a controlling authority: as **a** : a command or provision enacted by a legislature **b :** something (as a judicial decision) authoritatively accorded binding or controlling effect in the administration of justice **2 a :** a body of laws <the ~ of a state>; *broadly* : laws and justice considered as a general and established entity <the ~ looks with disfavor on restraints on alienation> **4 :** the whole body of laws and doctrines relating to one subject <contract ~> <the ~ of attractive nuisance>
>
> (Merriam-Webster's *Dictionary of Law*, 2011: 279)

And as rights are also very frequently mentioned, I provide a relevant legal definition:

> **right 2 :** something to which one has a just claim: as **a :** a power, privilege, or condition of existence to which one has a natural claim of enjoyment or possession <the ~ of liberty> <that all men are endowed by their Creator with certain unalienable ~s –*Declaration of Independence*> – see also NATURAL RIGHT **b :** a power, privilege, immunity, or capacity the enjoyment of which is secured to a person by law <one's constitutional ~s>[14]
>
> (Merriam-Webster's *Dictionary of Law*, 2011: 431)

The letters contain, unsurprisingly, many phrases denoting and referring to "right" and "rights":

"Right" expressions in the corpus:

the right to life
the right to life of a non-U.S. citizen
the right to life under international law
the right to freedom of expression
the right to freedom of expression and assembly
the right to freedom of expression, association and assembly
the right to a fair trial
the right to privacy
the right to be free from arbitrary detention
the right to protection against arbitrary or collective deportation
the right to the truth about your mass surveillance program

Note that these are all definite expressions, indicating that the existence of these rights is presented by AI as to be taken for granted in the interactional context, that is, as presupposed (Beaver and Geurts 2014; Levinson 1983: ch. 4; Lyons 1999; McCawley 1981: ch. 9).

[14] Recall the discussion in Chapter 2 of rights and human rights.

"Rights" expressions in the corpus:

rights
human rights
international human rights law
international human rights and humanitarian law
human rights protection
human rights violations
LGBTI rights
full political rights
Russian human rights defenders
Violence against women and girls is one of the world's most pervasive human rights abuses
torture, enforced disappearance and other human rights violations
human rights violations, including the crimes under international law of torture and enforced disappearance
international human rights law and standards
international human rights standards
the widespread pattern of human rights abuses within the US criminal justice system, including the alarming use of lethal force nationwide
Sudan's international human rights obligations
women's human rights
human rights lawyers
the disappearance of prominent human rights lawyer Wang Yu
a group of over 100 lawyers and human rights activists who signed a public statement condemning Wang Yu's disappearance
a leading advocate of religious freedom, human rights and democracy
his peaceful human rights activism
the rights of family members of those killed
champion the highest possible human rights standards
the rights of the remaining defendants
the rights of all people, not only US citizens
the balance between security and privacy rights
international human rights
the human rights of free expression and assembly
the rights of your own citizens
the human rights of people across the globe
their rights to freedom of expression, association, and assembly
Ayhan Sefer Üstün – Parliamentary Commission on Human Rights Chair

And the legal instruments from which the rights derive:

UN Universal Declaration of Human Rights
African Charter on Human and People's Rights
International Covenant on Civil and Political Rights, Articles 7 and 13
American Convention on Human Rights, Article 22
The Inter-American Court of Human Rights

The aspects of the human rights mentioned in the letters:

Whom they apply to:
women, LGBTQIA+ persons, citizens, non-U.S. citizens, people across the globe, family members of those killed, defendants

What they authorize:
privacy, political (activity), freedom of expression, association and assembly, freedom from torture, the truth about your mass surveillance program

What they effect:
protection [from torture, etc.], respect

Whom they involve:
lawyers, activists, advocates, Russian human rights defenders

How they are infringed:
abuses, violations, disappearances, illegal deportations

As the moves and steps of the genre are enacted by specific linguistic expressions, I identify the main linguistic expressions that enact the moves and steps, many of which are evaluative. I amalgamate the linguistic analysis of similar moves and steps under the rubric "The language of X." (Much of what follows is lightly edited from Delahunty 2018b.)

The Language of Engagement and Gratitude

I begin with the language of the least complex move, M6 *Engage addressee(s)*, which comprises two steps, S1 *Express gratitude* and S2 *Express hope for response from addressee.*[15] This move occurs in only twelve (30 percent) of the forty appeals, a somewhat surprising finding, given the generally polite tone of the letters, and the fact that it occurs in the suggestions included in the AI Letter Writing Guide.

Engagement is most obviously expressed by the use in almost all of the letters of first- and second-person pronouns, representing, problematically, the letter SENDers and Message Recipients. Engagement is also enacted by the use of imperatives, which implicate an addresser and addressee.

Overall, only nine (22.5 percent) of the forty appeals include an expression of thanks, expressed by variants of the following composite:

(I) thank you for your (time and) (urgent) consideration/attention (to this (important) matter).

It is to be expected that M6S1 would be enacted by expressive speech acts from the THANK group of speech acts, as described, for example, in Wierzbicka

[15] Structural element E: Complimentary close, *(yours) sincerely*, might be included here. It occurs three times in the corpus.

(1987: 214–215). She characterizes "*thanking* as an addressee-oriented act" and formulates its meaning as:

> I know that you have done something that is good for me
> I say: I feel something good towards you because of that
> I say this because I want to cause you to know what I feel towards you
> I assume that you would want to hear me say this to you (214; emphasis in original)

The specific "something good" done by the addressees of AI letters is characterized as giving time, consideration, and/or attention to the subject of the letter, notably not for acceding to the writer's request. Wierzbicka (1987: 214) adds the caveat that "the speaker's real intention may be different (he may simply want to be thought of as polite)," and this is consistent with the choice of *attention*, which is vague between mental effort and "[t]he act of dealing with something or someone" (*American Heritage Dictionary* [*AHD*], 5th ed.). This vagueness, reflecting the writer/addressee power differential, does not presuppose that addressee(s) will enact the solicited redress and is consistent with Brown and Levinson's (1987: 149) negative politeness dictum *Don't presume/assume*. Certainly, it imposes a significantly weaker presumption than the corresponding move in the philanthropic appeals: *Thanks for current & future financial or other support*.

Only three AI letters include M6S2 *Express hope for response from addressee*:

> I look forward to hearing from you regarding this matter.
>
> (#17 Caning, Indonesia)

We should expect that M6S2 would be enacted by speech acts that attempt to engage addressees by expressing anticipation of future action: *look forward to* is defined as "to think of (a future event) with pleasure, eager anticipation" (*AHD*, 5th ed.).

The Language of Concern

Seventeen (42.5 percent) of the forty appeals open with an expression of affect, for example, *extremely concerned*, *profoundly disturbed*. We can view this as a matter of "staging" (Grimes 1975, cited in Blommaert et al. 2007: 42) which

> describes the way a speaker or writer uses the initial element of a text or utterance as a signpost, to indicate a point of departure for what s/he wants to say. The choice of point of departure is a powerful rhetorical device. It ensures that the audience knows what is to be talked about, but it also indicates what the speaker regards as focal.

These expressions also purport to indicate the SENDer's feelings and evaluation of what is to be talked about.

The following expressions of concern occur in the appeals:

concern, deep concern, deeply concerned, extremely concerned, Amnesty International's grave concern, disturbed, profoundly disturbed, urgent request, shocked, disturbing (pattern of), disappointed, substantial concerns about the fairness of the legal process, worried

Having expressed a concern, the letters then describe its object, typically by characterizing a situation as a violation of human or humanitarian rights, having the potential to violate them, and/or in support of some measure that will reduce rights violations:

I am deeply concerned that US government's so-called "targeted killing" program allows for the use of lethal force, including with drones, that violates the right to life under international law.

I urge you to ensure that the US government follows international law governing the use of lethal force: international human rights law and, in the exceptional circumstances where it applies, international humanitarian law as well.

(#1 Targeted Killings, USA)

The Language of Exigency

Express exigency occurs in Moves 1–5 and, given the purposes of the AI letters, we should expect the language of exigency to denote extreme temporal exigency, dire consequence, the importance and/or urgency of the appeal, the urgency of the need to redress injustice, and the (legal) manner in which the requested action should be fulfilled:

TEMPORAL: *immediately; without delay; quickly; it is well past time; more than a year has passed; today, nearly 41 years after*
CONSEQUENCE/RESULT: *(a miscarriage of the death penalty) cannot be undone*
IMPORTANCE: *urge, urgent*
MANNER: *(release) unconditionally*

The Language of Directing Redressive Action

Moves 2, 3, 4, and 5 include steps requesting actions to redress HR violations. We expect these steps to be enacted by moderately forceful directive speech acts reflecting the writer/addressee power differential and writer's inability to force compliance while attempting to avoid being ignored because of impoliteness:

urge (occurs forty times)
ask (occurs seventeen times)
call on (occurs twelve times)

request (occurs four times)
remind (occurs once)

Biber et al. (2007: 71) characterize these as "Verbs Expressing Speech Act" stance. And *urge*, *ask*, *call on*, and *request* are all mitigated directive speech act verbs whose degrees of mitigation can be characterized in their felicity conditions, and which are occasionally further mitigated by *please* (fifteen occurrences) and even *respectfully* (five occurrences), for example, "I respectfully call on you to …" (#4 Al-Qahtani, Iraq). According to Wierzbicka (1987: 50), "[t]he asking person wants the addressee to do something that would be to his (the speaker's) benefit. He assumes that the addressee can do it, but he doesn't assume that the addressee will do it."

Urging, according to Wierzbicka (1987),

> is an attempt to get the addressee to do something … [I]t doesn't imply that the speaker has power over the addressee.
>
> The attitude of an *urging* person is as pressing and forceful as that of someone who *orders* or *commands*. But since he has no power over the addressee, the only kind of pressure he can exercise is psychological. In this respect, *urge* is closer to *demand* than to either *order* or *command*. However, it is far below *demand* in forcefulness. The person who *demands* feels that his utterance has an inherent force (whatever the nature of this force is). The person who *urges* would want to endow his utterance with a similar force, but he can't. All he can do is try to **infect** his addressee with his own conviction that action (of the kind indicated) is necessary. … *Urging* as a speech act is an attempt to implant in the addressee's mind the idea of another such irresistible "must."
>
> Thus, the position of the *urging* person is that of powerlessness, not of power. And yet the powerless speaker is trying to impose his will on the addressee, even though he perceives or anticipates unwillingness or lack of response on the addressee's part. He is trying to achieve this goal by trying to convey to the addressee his own sense of urgency, his own conviction that the action is imperative, and also by implying that he won't take "no" for an answer, that he will not give up easily … (in this respect *urging* is like *begging* or *nagging*); the urging person does not see himself as someone who tries to impose his will on the addressee. Rather, he sees himself as someone who tries to impose his own (superior) understanding of the situation. His attitude is not "I say: I think you should do X" but a confident "I say: you should do X."
>
> Finally, there is usually, in *urging*, a sense of urgency. The speaker wants the addressee to respond, and to respond **now**.
>
> (61–62; emphasis in original)

We might add that the speaker's "judgment" may be informed by "conviction" based on ethical, moral, legal, or ideological principles.

Call on directs an addressee to do something: "the speaker who *calls on* somebody to do something uses the weapon of public pressure to make it harder for the target person to refuse to do what is needed" (Wierzbicka 1987: 84; emphasis in original). This characterization of *call on* is consistent with my argument that AI appeals are designed to persuade by argument and by numbers. *Requesting*, on the other hand, is markedly polite; this may be partly accounted for by its indirectness … but only partly. The elaborate politeness of *request* seems to derive also from the fact that the speaker pointedly refrains from assuming that the target person has to comply with the request …

Request doesn't imply any superiority or inferiority either. But it does imply a specific sort of relationship: formal, distant and impersonal …

If the target person "doesn't have to do it," how can the speaker assume that he will do it? Presumably, because the situation is standardized, with well-defined roles, well-defined routines, well-defined rules of behaviour.

(Wierzbicka 1987: 52)

This is consistent with the polite tenor expected of AI appeals, the power difference between AI and addressees, and the expected attention to both SENDers' and Message Recipients' face wants.

Condoravdi and Lauer (2012: 45) propose that imperatives, for example, "Allow him his freedom" (#16 Woodfox, Louisiana, USA),

commit the speaker to a particular kind of preference and to be bounded by a condition that limits his active involvement in making the content true. Imperatives do not create obligations as a matter of course by linguistic convention, but give rise to obligations only indirectly when the context is right.

Imperatives are typically regarded as forms that "are characteristically used as directives," including the issuing of orders (e.g., Huddleston and Pullum 2002: 929–933). Clearly, neither AI appeal writers nor SENDers fit the social criteria required for the felicitous issuing of orders to the Message Recipients. Nonetheless, the letters do contain imperatives, and Condoravdi and Lauer's description of the functions of the form implies far less imposition on addressees than imperatives are typically assumed to prescribe. Sperber and Wilson (1995: 251) say that

[t]he hearer on recovering the propositional form *P* of an imperative utterance would integrate it into a description of the form *The speaker is telling the hearer to P*. *Telling the speaker to P* might be analysed as communicating that the thought that *P* interprets is entertained as a description of a desirable state of affairs.[16]

Who it is desirable to is determined in context: the imperatives in the corpus clearly represent states of affairs desirable to AI, to the letter writers and SENDers, and, presumably, to the subjects of the appeals. The fact that AI deems it necessary to write these appeals suggests that the Message Recipients do not regard the state of affairs proposed in the letters as desirable, though they may be brought to regard it in that way, even if not for the reasons adduced in the letters.

However, bare imperatives are "bald-on-record" directives and appropriate in circumstances "of great urgency" (Brown and Levinson 1987: 100). The

[16] See also Wilson and Sperber (1988) on non-declarative sentences.

bare imperatives in my corpus seem to be licensed in this way, though their face threat also seems to be reduced by context, for example, "Allow him his freedom" follows an imperative introduced by *please* and occurs as the last sentence in a letter as the final expression of the appeal. The verb *allow* implicates that the addressee has the power to accede to the request or not. The polite mitigation of the imperative, "Please remove Albert Woodfox from solitary confinement," is also consistent with the polite tenor of the letters and their general acknowledgement of the limits of the addressees' power in the situations. These directives are also expressed by the strongly conative impersonal construction, "It is essential that …" (#15 Vitishko, Russia) and the strongest modal, *must*, "the Guantanamo detention facility must be closed" (#7 Aamer, USA), neither of which are mitigated.

It is valuable to compare the directive expressions above with *demand*. This occurs in the embedding emails, which urge AI volunteers to *demand* redressive action by the appeal letters' addressees. "What is always implied by *demand* is the speaker's assumption that his utterance carries great force, a force which the addressee is bound to recognize. This force may be moral, but it may also be physical … Thus, the addressee is expected not only to understand the content of the utterance but also to assess its force" (Wierzbicka 1987: 40–41; emphasis in original). As we might expect, none of the AI letters uses *demand* as the directive to its addressees.

The Language of Norms of Evaluation

Moves 1 through 5 include steps that refer to norms of evaluation and as the letters typically appeal for redress of violations of human and/or humanitarian rights, we should expect that they would include reference to the various (codifications of) human/humanitarian rights upon which those evaluations are based. The following were frequently invoked:

international law/standards; international humanitarian law; human rights; right to life; prohibition on torture and other cruel, inhuman or degrading punishment; United Nations Declaration of Human Rights

Somewhat surprisingly, these expressions are almost exclusively common rather than proper NPs. My initial expectation was that the letters would explicitly reference the various declarations, bills, and covenants in which human and humanitarian rights are legally enacted by such bodies as the United Nations. While the letters present arguments, they are not technical legal briefs and so would not be expected to explicitly reference specific articles in specific legal instruments, though AI reports do, as Chapter 2 demonstrates. That the legal instruments that constitute the letters' norms of evaluation are referred to informally and generically support my claim that they play at least the dual roles of appeal and protest, while engaging AI members, the great majority of whom are not lawyers – recall Klandermans' (2011) description of Dutch AI members, quoted in Chapter 4 under AD 2.2.4.5.

The Language of Norm Violation

Of course, what these letters appeal and protest are violations of the human or other major rights of individuals or groups, so we should expect language that expresses violations of these rights, the norms violated, and the manner and degree of violation:

> flagrant violation of the prohibition on torture and other cruel, inhuman or degrading treatment under international law
> violate minimum international standards
> the death penalty violates the right to life
> trials that fall short of international standards
> miscarriage (of justice)
> unjust/unfair/flawed (trials)
> should not have been (prosecuted)
> persecuted
> forced (confessions)
> "confession"
> torture
> ill-treatment
> Prisoners of Conscience

Violate and its related forms are the most frequently occurring expressions denoting contraventions of these norms (twenty-six occurrences); its relevant definitions in the *Oxford English Dictionary* (*OED*) (online version) are:

2.2. To break, infringe, or contravene (a law, rule, etc.). Also: to fail to maintain or respect (a right or privilege).
3.3. To act in a way inconsistent with or contrary to (a moral quality or accepted standard of behaviour); to fail to conform to, betray (an ideal, principle, etc.).
4.4. To treat (a person, a person's feelings, etc.) with contempt or disrespect.

Other expressions denote generic legal failures, *miscarriage* (of justice), or more specific ones, *unjust/unfair/flawed* (trials), *forced* (confessions), or they ironize the characterization of legal proceedings by enclosing expressions in quotes, for example, "confession." Some expressions characterize these legal failures as egregious abuses of the legal system or even as extra-judicial abuses: *persecution* is defined as "punishment or harassment usu. of a severe nature on the basis of race, religion, or political opinion in one's country of origin" (Merriam-Webster's *Dictionary of Law*: 358).

Expressions associated with violation of human/humanitarian rights also include:

arbitrary detention, obligation, obligated, comply, impartial, extrajudicial, unlawful, redress, remedy, respect, protect, responsible, crime against humanity, fair criminal trial, illegal, unregulated, victimization, forcibly recruited, impunity, support, champion, permitted, serious violations, free expression of speech, crackdown, trumped-up or politically motivated criminal charges, muzzling, international standards, violations of the right to life, violence, murder, rape, bring to justice, lack of access to justice, a climate of harassment, discrimination and hate-motivated violence, hate crimes, non-discriminatory, unbiased, targeted violence, harassment and abuse, respect, protect and fulfill human rights, indefinite detention, unfair trials, decriminalize abortion in all circumstances, cruel and inhuman treatment, comply, grant, held, release, excessive use of force, peaceful demonstrators, ill-treated, authorized, discrimination, infringes, necessary, legitimate, proportionate, justify, obligations under domestic and international law, held in isolation, cruel and unusual solitary confinement, cruel, inhuman and degrading, deprivation of a basic human need, no meaningful review of his continued isolation, denied their full political rights, a disturbing and increasing pattern of sexual violence during public and peaceful demonstrations, condemn sexual violence, peacefully demonstrate for their rights, abuses by both the military and police and security forces against Egyptians, failed to provide justice to victims, condemn all forms of sexual and gender-based violence and harassment, order full, impartial and independent investigations, sexual and gender-based violence, end discrimination against women in law and practice, etc., etc.

These are remarkable for their variety, specificity, and abundance.

Related to the language of norms and norm violation is the language of legal procedures:

court, Court of Cassation, prison, detain, decriminalize, transfer, detention, penal colony, trial, interrogations, charged, convicted, execution, overturn (sentences), confession, testify, uphold (conviction), defendant, justice, death penalty, stay (an execution), investigate, investigation, arrest, prosecution, criminal prosecution, criminal offense, order, guaranteed, custody, try, evidence, case, quash

To these, we might add antonyms of rights and their violations:

life/death, freedom/imprisonment, justice/injustice, comply with (laws)/violate (rights)

The Language of Concession and Rebuttal

Several of the AI letters include M3S1 Make concession, M3S2 Note limitations on concession, and M3S3 Rebut concession. The following are examples of concession and rebuttal:

I understand that your government has as an obligation to bring to [*sic*] those responsible for serious crimes to justice, and that Iraq must confront violence by armed group [*sic*]. However, I am deeply concerned about convictions that are based on forced confessions and trial proceedings that fall short of international standards.

(#4 Al-Qahtani, Iraq)

President Obama's recent commitment to resettle 10,000 Syrian refugees deserves praise, but it is, unfortunately, far from enough.

(#27 Syrian Refugees, USA)

Understand is a factive verb and thus presupposes the truth of its complement propositions, but as such is redundant here because the truth of the complement clauses without "I understand" would be implicated by virtue of being asserted. *Understand* also implies a less certain epistemological stance than, for example, *know*. It can and in this context seems to mean *believe* (Huddleston and Pullum 2002: 1022), while suggesting tolerance or sympathy toward a proposition (*AHD*, 5th ed.: 1889). We might also view "I understand" as an attempt to engage the addressees by ostensibly reading their minds and responding to propositions the writer attributes to them. (See Kärkkäinen 2003 on *I think*.) So, "I understand" appears to indicate the writer's anticipation of the addressees' response to the writer's developing argument and projects a rebuttal to that concession, which is clearly indicated as such by "however" (see Blakemore 2002: 117–122 on *however*), in (#4 Al-Qahtani, Iraq) and "but" in (#27 Syrian Refugees, USA), above.

AD 3.3.2.1: How are people, events, relations categorized? (Verschueren 2012: 138–146)

"Categorization is a matter of perspective" (Verschueren 2012: 146) and perspective in the context of the appeals is based on the appeal writers' ideological assumptions and the goals of redressing the appeal situation and motivating the volunteer recipients of the embedding emails.

The letters distinguish three main categories of people: the appeal SENDer (the *I* of the letters), the Message Recipients/intended addressees (the *you* of the letters), and the individuals and/or classes of individuals affected by the situations or events that are the subjects of the appeals. Other individuals or classes of individuals related to the appeal subjects may also be mentioned.

As the embedding emails are sent to AI volunteers' or members' email addresses and include the volunteers' names and addresses, the *I* of the letters is known to AI. The sender's name, email address, post or zip code, and country of residence must sometimes be provided to activate the SEND button and so may be sent on to the Message Recipients. If this information is not forwarded, the Message Recipients have no way of individually identifying the volunteers, and no way of categorizing them except as members or volunteers of AI. This identification is occasionally directly indicated in the letters by expressions such as, "I join Amnesty International USA in respectfully urging the creation of a National Crime and Justice Task Force to finally address the widespread pattern of human rights abuses within the US criminal justice system, including the alarming use of lethal force nationwide" (#21 Crime Task Force, USA); "Amnesty International believes this must change, we urge you to condemn sexual violence and take steps to end it" (#13 Women Protesters, Egypt); and even more indirectly by the appeal writer's affiliation with the categorization of Badawi as a PoC in, "I believe that Raif Badawi is a Prisoner of Conscience" (#18 Badawi, Saudi Arabia).

The linguistic identification of the letter SENDers with AI, its concerns, and its stances is crucial for AI's ideological positioning of its members, volunteers, and activists. As argued above and in Delahunty (2017), the letters are important instruments in ideologically motivating its members, as well as persuading their Message Recipients and fundraising.

Addressees are categorized by their relevant institutional titles, for example, Salman bin Abdulaziz Al Saud, *King of Saudi Arabia*; Joseph Westphal, *United States Ambassador to Saudi Arabia* (#18 Badawi, Saudi Arabia); *Attorney General* Loretta Lynch (#15 Torture Report, USA); Bobby Jindal – *Governor of Louisiana*, and Buddy Caldwell *Attorney General* (#12 Wallace, Louisiana, USA). They may also be categorized by their association with authoritative institutions, for example, Talaat Ibrahim Abdallah – *Office of the Public Prosecutor* (#3 Satire as Crime, Egypt), and by their political party affiliation, for example, Charles Timothy Hagel (*Republican*), Barack Obama (*Democrat*) (#7 Aamer, USA).

The addressees may also be categorized as representatives of governments that are "obligated under international law to …" (#8 Beatriz, El Salvador), that "failed to provide justice to victims of violence" (#13 Women Protesters, Egypt), that put individuals "on trial for 'criticizing' the [Egyptian] Interior Ministry and 'misusing' the internet" (#3 Satire as Crime, Egypt), or putting people "under investigation" (#3 Satire as Crime, Egypt). They are also categorized as individuals who are able to "stop" violations (#22 Haitians, Dominican Republic), to "drop charges" against individuals (#24 Indecent Dress, Sudan), to "overturn their sentences" (#4 Al-Qahtani, Iraq), to "[p]rotect people from indiscriminate or otherwise abusive surveillance" (#23 Mass Surveillance, USA), to "stay the executions" (#4 Al-Qahtani, Iraq), to ensure "independent and impartial investigations in all cases of alleged extrajudicial executions or other unlawful killings" (#1 Targeted Killings, USA), to "allow the immediate and unconditional return to the Dominican Republic for any expelled Dominicans of Haitian descent" (#22 Haitians, Dominican Republic), to "uphold the right to freedom of expression …" (#11 Pussy Riot, Russia; #15 Vitishko, Russia), and in general to "ensure" the appealed-for outcomes. These categorizations ideologically position the Message Recipients as possibly complicit in the rights violations and as powerful enough to redress the violations enumerated in the letters.

Individual subjects of appeals may also be categorized according to AI's internal categorization scheme, for example, as a "Prisoner of Conscience" (#18 Badawi, Saudi Arabia).

Appeal subjects are typically assigned the semantic role of patient in situations or events that the letters characterize as violations or abuses of their rights:

> At this important moment in Egyptian history, women are being denied their full political rights by a disturbing and increasing pattern of sexual violence during public and peaceful demonstrations.
>
> (#13 Women Protesters, Egypt)

Or, complementarily, as the patients of appealed-for redressive actions: "Guarantee protection as well as shelter and support services for victims of early and forced marriages" (#30 Forced Marriages, Burkina Faso).

The "*relations* between (categorized) groups of actors in the described events and states of affairs" (Verschueren 2012: 144; emphasis in original) may be characterized in terms of three overlapping relations. The first relationship is among the people playing roles in the rhetorical situation – the SENDers, the Message Recipients, and the subjects of the appeal. The second relationship is between (1) the letter SENDer's ideological authority derived from their affiliation with AI and its invocation of legally binding international human and humanitarian rights, (2) the Message Recipients' authority derived from their state-based institutional positions, and (3) the SENDers' and Message Recipients' respective framings of the appeal situations or events. The third relationship consists of the letter writers' attempts to get the addressees to revise how they frame the appealed situation or event so as to bring it into alignment with the letter SENDers' framing (Du Bois 2007).

AD 3.3.3: At the sentence level: How are grammatical relations, case categories, and semantic roles handled when describing events, actions, or relations between (groups of) people? (Verschueren 2012: 146–152)

In this section, Verschueren examines the alignment of semantic and grammatical roles in active and passive clauses. He pays particular attention to agent and patient roles and how they are used to construct contrasting representations of the British and Indians in the textbook sections on the Meerut rebellion (1857–59). He introduces a discussion of the role of voice with a critique of Fairclough's (1992) Critical Discourse Analysis (CDA) take on passives and nominalizations. As discussed above, Fairclough fails to take into account the possibility that even though passives may omit reference to agents, and nominalizations may omit reference to agents and patients and other roles, these roles may be readily inferred from context. Additionally, the frequency with which the various construction types occur may be a function of the "*specific verbal activity*" in which they occur (151; emphasis in original).

Jackendoff (1990) distinguishes between Action and Thematic "tiers" of semantic roles. The Thematic tier comprises the spatial roles of theme, location, and the like. The action tier comprises what Verschueren calls the "agentivity" structure, that is, the agent/patient roles. For the study of ideology, the Action tier is more important than the Thematic one, and so I focus primarily on that.

Semantic roles[17] interact importantly with the voice systems of languages, and the most important voice distinction in the letters is between active and passive. This voice contrast allows for flexibility in the correlations between grammatical and semantic roles of the Action tier. It also allows for the omission of roles, particularly of the agent role in truncated passive sentences. I take seriously Verschueren's (2012: 150) caution that the passive must not be "mechanically handled as an analytic instrument," as early CDA analysts did.

I organize my discussion of ideologically relevant grammatical and semantic roles in the appeals according to the three-way division I used above, that is, between the letter SENDers, the *I*'s; their addressees/Message Recipients, the *you*'s; and the subjects, that is, the individuals, classes of individual, or causes that occasioned the letters.

The *I*'s of the letters are represented as the subjects and experiencers of the expression of concern clauses that characteristically begin the letters, for example, "I am deeply concerned …" The *I*'s also typically denote the agents of the letters' directive speech acts, for example, "I ask/call on/urge …"

The Message Recipients are typically represented as the objects and patients of directive speech act clauses, for example, "I urge you to …" and as the (understood) subjects and agents of the directives' complement (*to*-)clauses: "I call upon the Turkish government to immediately end the excessive use of force" (#9 Police Action, Turkey). They are thus ideologically positioned as having the power to accede to the appeal and implied to be responsible for acceding or not: "I hope to hear back from you regarding the steps that you are taking to provide Beatriz with the medical care she has requested and is entitled to receive" (#8 Beatriz, El Salvador).[18]

The individuals who are the subjects of the appeals are referred to by third-person expressions which may function as the subject and patient of clauses representing violations of human rights, for example, "[H]e's on trial" (#3 Satire as Crime, Egypt); "Since the conflict in Yemen began, thousands of civilians have been killed and injured" (#34 Arms Sales, USA). They are represented as patients of unfair trials, incarceration, solitary confinement, torture, and execution.

These individuals are also represented as the subjects of active clauses, thus typically representing them as agents of what should be legal activities, for

17 Verschueren (2012: 149, fn. 58) provides a list of "a few of the frequently distinguished semantic roles," though the lists of these roles and their definitions vary greatly from one author and theory to another. See Saeed (2016: ch. 6).

18 Only two other letters indicate an expectation of a response from the Message Recipients: "I look forward to hearing from you …" (#5 LGBTQI, South Africa; #17 Caning, Indonesia).

example, peacefully protesting, demonstrating, speaking out about various causes: "When blogger Ahmed Anwar posted a video of belly-dancing policemen on-line, he expected to get some laughs" (#3 Satire as Crime, Egypt). They may also be represented as the (understood) subject and agent of clauses representing locally illegal, but universally legalized human-rights activities, for example, "[H]e's on trial for 'criticizing' the Interior Ministry and 'misusing' the internet" (#3 Satire as Crime, Egypt; quote marks in the original).

The grammar of various construction types allows the omission of various categories of information. For instance, the stative, copular sentence, "[H]e's on trial …" does not tell us who put him on trial, though we may be sure from the co-text that it was elements of the Egyptian authorities. Similarly, the truncated passive, "These two women, both mothers in their twenties, were detained solely for their peaceful expression of their beliefs" (#11 Pussy Riot, Russia) does not tell us who detained the two women, though we may assume that it was members of some branch of the Russian security services. However, the letter does not allow us to infer who ordered and who was ultimately responsible for the women's detention. Similarly, "Accurate information regarding those injured by police violence must be released" (#9 Police Action, Turkey) does not tell us – nor can we infer from the letter – who should release this information.

The Message Recipients are rarely directly implicated in the violations, though by virtue of the genre they are implicated to have the power to redress these violations. The responsibility for the violations may be diffused upward to the institutions that the individuals represent, as in the following, addressed to Turkish Prime Minister Erdogan and the Chair of the Turkish Parliamentary Commission on Human Rights Ayhan Sefer Üstün:

> I … call upon the Turkish government to immediately end the excessive use of force against peaceful demonstrators. Turkish authorities must ensure the right to freedom of expression and assembly, rights that are essential for any truly democratic state.
>
> (#9 Police Action, Turkey)

And the following to US President Barak [*sic*] Obama:

> I am deeply concerned that [*sic*] US government's so-called "targeted killing" program allows for the use of lethal force, including with drones, that violates the right to life under international law.
>
> (#1 Targeted Killings, USA)

This diffusion of responsibility is probably not directly driven by ideological considerations, but, rather, by attention to the face-wants of the addressees, who might object to being personally accused of human rights violations, accusations that might make them even less willing to accede to the appeals than they probably already are.

These patterns are what we should expect to find in letters in which writers and SENDers appeal to addressees to perform certain actions on behalf of individuals who have been penalized for engaging in activities legitimized by universal values, covenants, laws, and treaties. The letters portray – and position – their subjects as people who by acting on behalf of various causes become the agents of counterpower whom government policies penalize and against whom the government agencies act, while portraying – and positioning – their Message Recipients as people with the power and responsibility to redress violations and abuses of human rights. The elision and diffusion of responsibility for the violations is consistent with the AI Letter Writing Guide's advice to writers to "[a]lways be polite" and to "[a]lways write on the basis that the government concerned is open to reason and discussion," and the power asymmetries in the appeal situation.

Ad 3.3.4: Still at the sentence level: How are moods, modalities, negation, and evidentiality handled? (Verschueren 2012: 152–157)

Modalities are "what utterers do with a proposition to indicate (degrees of) necessity, possibility, certainty, likelihood." These are expressed by "grammatical mood (declarative, subjunctive, imperative), modal auxiliaries, adjectives, adverbs, sentence adverbs, and particles" and various hedging expressions (Verschueren 2012: 152). I begin with grammatical moods.

The major English moods are the declarative, interrogative, and imperative. The vast majority of the sentences in the appeals are in the declarative mood, with only one interrogative, "Where are the missing?" in a Subject line (#25 Missing, China), and perhaps surprisingly few imperatives, given the directive purposes of the letters. However, if we were to assume, simplistically, that these moods correlate with statements of fact,[19] questions, and commands, we would get a distorted picture of the how the letters accomplish their goals. Many of the declaratives include directive speech act verbs, such as *ask*, *call on*, and *urge*, and therefore function as indirect directives rather than merely as assertions. I discuss these matters below under other headings.

The declarative is the typical mood in those letter sections that express the writers' feelings about the appeal situation:

> I am profoundly disturbed that Saudi blogger Raif Badawi was publicly flogged in front of al-Jafali mosque after Friday prayers.
>
> (#18 Badawi Flogging, Saudi Arabia)

The declarative is also used to announce the writers' purposes, for example, "I am writing to ask you to immediately and unconditionally release environmental activist Yevgeniy Vitishko" (#15 Vitishko, Russia). And to provide factual information about the cases:

[19] For a current refraction of the relations between declarative mood and asserting, see Jary (2020).

> More than a year has passed since Judge James Brady of the U.S. District Court overturned Albert Woodfox's conviction. Today, nearly 41 years after he was first placed in solitary confinement, Albert is still behind bars in isolation.
>
> (#16 Woodfox, Louisiana, USA)

It is also used to characterize individuals in ideologically relevant ways, for example, "They are Prisoners of Conscience" (#11 Pussy Riot, Russia). These categorizations are typically unmitigated and thus indicative of unhesitating certainty, as the examples above illustrate.

Other markers of the epistemic status of information include verbs, for example, "I believe that …" (#18 Badawi, Saudi Arabia), "I know that …" (#4 Al-Qahtani, Iraq), "I understand that …" (#4 Al-Qahtani, Iraq), "I do not believe that …" (#16 Woodfox, Louisiana, USA); nouns "I have no doubt that …" (#16 Woodfox, Louisiana, USA), "In light of …" (#16 Woodfox, Louisiana, USA), and "There is much we do not know" (#23 Mass Surveillance, USA). "I fear that …" (#4 Al-Qahtani, Iraq) combines the writer's belief and apprehension.

Verschueren (2012: 153) says that deontic[20] modality in his history textbooks is "rare." In contrast, the deontic is the major modality in the appeal letters, as is to be expected given their ostensible main purpose – to persuade their addressees to do something. The main deontic device is the imperative mood. This occurs in many of the letters' Subject lines, for example, "Grant Albert Woodfox his freedom" (#16 Woodfox, Louisiana, USA). While not all the letters have Subject lines, the majority of those that do express those subjects as imperatives, all of which are unmitigated, bald-on-record directives.

The imperatives that occur in the letter bodies are typically mitigated with *please*:

> Please ensure that he is not flogged again in the coming months. Please drop all charges against Badawi and ensure that he is unconditionally released without further delay.
>
> (#18 Badawi, Saudi Arabia)

We do occasionally find unmitigated imperatives in the letter bodies:

> Immediately stop violating the rights of your own citizens, meet international standards for deportation (including judicial oversight, individualized assessment and right to appeal the deportation decision), and do not expel Dominicans of Haitian descent!
>
> (#22 Haitians, Dominican Republic)

Note the exclamation point at the end of the quote just above. It boosts the already high exigency of the demand indicated by "immediately."

[20] Deontic modality expresses the speaker's intention that their utterance be interpreted as obligation, permission, prohibition, regulation, responsibility, and the like. See McNamara and Van De Putte (2025).

It is, nonetheless, more typical for imperatives in the letter bodies to be mitigated and this contrasts with the complete absence of mitigation in the Subject lines. The Message Recipients and Subject lines are not integrated into the letter bodies; they occur in the embedding emails and in the webpages in a small textbox, just above the pane in which the letters appear. Consequently, I do not know whether they are integrated into whatever form the letters take when they are forwarded to their Message Recipients. Because unmitigated imperatives are not uncommon on protest placards, the Subject lines may reflect the protest aspects of the appeal letters directly. However, as we do not know whether the Subject lines are ever transmitted to the Message Recipients, it is likely that they are directed at the AI volunteers as elements in AI's attempts to engage and motivate them. The imperatives implicate the appeal SENDers as Agents of directives, thus positioning them as powerful actors in the engagement with the Message Recipients. This conjecture is supported by the fact that many protest placards are addressed to other protestors and potential allies rather than to the powerful who can redress the protestors' concerns, for example, WITHOUT IMMIGRANTS TRUMP WOULD HAVE NO WIVES.[21]

The directives in the corpus are designed to get the Message Recipients to bring the appeal situation into compliance with universal human rights values. However, as directives are threats to their addressees' negative face (Brown and Levinson 1987), and even a mitigated imperative may be perceived as a serious face threat, the letters use other expression types to accomplish this communicative function, for example, declarative sentences in which various categories of deontic expression introduce the desired actions, for example, passive participles as in "The US government is obligated to …" (#7 Aamer, USA) and "The Salvadoran government has been ordered … by the Inter-American Court of Human Rights." (#8 Beatriz, El Salvador). The modal auxiliary *should* plays a similar role:

> If so, like any other Guantánamo detainee who is not to be charged, he *should* be immediately released. In Shaker Aamer's case, he should be released to the UK following repeated requests for his return made by the UK government.
>
> (#7 Aamer, USA; emphasis added)

As does *must*, though it expresses a stronger deontic stance:

> I call on you to ensure that Maria Alekhina and Nadezhda Tolokonnikova are immediately and unconditionally released. While they remain incarcerated, the two women *must* not be ill-treated by prison staff or inmates, and they *must* be allowed regular contact with their families and legal teams.
>
> (#11 Pussy Riot, Russia; emphasis added)

[21] https://digitalcollections.library.gsu.edu/digital/collection/marches/id/351 (accessed March 18, 2026).

Should occurs eleven times in the corpus; *must* occurs twenty-three times. Their potential face threat is mitigated, in the examples above, by their occurrence in passive sentences whose addressees are not mentioned and thus not directly implicated as responsible for the violative situation.

Other deontics include the directive speech act verbs *ask*, *call on*, and *urge*. These range in directive strength from weak to moderately strong. The distribution of these verbs implies that the letter writers and SENDers assume that they have the right to address appeals to the Message Recipients, but do not have the right or the authority to demand that they act. Other deontic items include the verbs *allow*, *ensure*, *grant*, and the noun *request*.

In addition to positive injunctions to redress situations, negative deontics enjoin addressees from various actions, for example, "I respectfully call on you to ensure that these men are not killed" (#4 Al-Qahtani, Iraq), or to contrast acceptable with unacceptable actions, for example, "[P]lease ensure they are dealt with under civil, not criminal, law" (#3 Satire as Crime, Egypt). *Not* occurs forty-five times in the corpus. As the letters comprise approximately 11,926 words, *not* occurs once in 265 words. This is somewhat less frequent than its approximately once in 200 words according to the *OED* online.[22] While this suggests that the letters devote more space and language to representing situations as they are, we should also take into account in any calculation of negation, expressions that imply negation without recourse to *not*, for example, *Stop X*, which presupposes that X is occurring at the utterance time. It can be paraphrased as *Do not do X from now on*.

Very few occurrences of *not* are directly addressed to the Message Recipients, for example,

> Immediately stop violating the rights of your own citizens, meet international standards for deportation (including judicial oversight, individualized assessment and right to appeal the deportation decision), and *do not expel* Dominicans of Haitian descent!
>
> (#22 Haitians, Dominican Republic; emphasis added)

Most occurrences of *not* are embedded in the complements of verbs such as *urge*, *call on*, and *ensure*:

> I urge you not only to ensure that this woman is not caned, but also to end the use of caning as a form of punishment and repeal the bylaws that allow it in Aceh province.
>
> (#17 Caning, Indonesia)

> - Ensure that pending their release, they are not tortured or otherwise ill-treated.
>
> (#28 PoC, Myanmar)

> Furthermore, we ask for you to stop investigating defamation cases as a criminal offense. If such cases are to go to court, please ensure they are dealt with under civil, not criminal, law.
>
> (#3 Satire as Crime, Egypt)

22 www.oed.com/dictionary/not_adv (accessed January 4, 2025).

The infrequency of direct and the much greater frequency of embedded injunctions is consistent with the letters' characteristic concern for the addressees' face wants in intensely intrusive communications.

Verschueren (2012: 156–157) emphasizes the dialogic nature of negation, claiming that it "always evokes a voice presenting its opposite."[23] The phrase, "not criminal law," in the extract just above evokes the voice(s) of Egyptian legislators, authorities, and law, while the rest of the extract represents the opposing voice(s) of AI and its members and volunteers. The dialogistic evocation of negation is consistent with the occasional direct invitation in the letters to the addressees to communicate with the SENDer, and with AI's request to volunteers to tell the organization about any responses they receive from letter addressees.

Deontics imply a possible world that is distinct from the actual one, in the case of the AI appeals, a world in which victims of human rights violations are set free and/or are no longer subject to torture and other forms of abuse. More generally, they evoke a world in which governments abide by their human and humanitarian obligations. Many letters include, in addition to the call for redress for an individual, an appeal that the governments refrain from a class of rights violations. For example, the Sudanese president is requested to drop charges against ten female Christian students for "indecent dress" for which they could be flogged and is additionally called on "to abolish the penalty of flogging, which violates the absolute prohibition of torture and other cruel, inhuman or degrading treatment or punishment" (#24 Indecent Dress, Sudan). The movement from the particular to the general is a frequent pattern in the letters and is typically supported by reference to human and other rights, or, as in the Sudanese case, by reference to a specific article in its constitution.

Besides being the main epistemic marker, the declarative mood is also the main marker of evidentiality, as it carries the implicature of the utterer's assurance of truth and evidence, per Grice's (1975) maxim of Quality, for example, "These programs are a violation of the human rights of people across the globe. They violate privacy on a massive scale and have a chilling effect on freedom of expression" (#23 Mass Surveillance, USA). These two sentences present the situations they represent as facts – no marker of evidentiality besides the declarative mood is included, though AI's reputation for accurate and evidenced reporting is implicated.

Other evidentials represent the sources of information, for example, medical expertise is invoked in "Her team of doctors have diagnosed her as …"

[23] For a comprehensive discussion of negation, see Horn (1989), reissued in 2001 by CSLI Publications and including a survey of research work on negation between initial and later versions.

(#8 Beatriz, El Salvador). Unnamed reports are invoked in "According to media reports …" (#26 PoCs, Vietnam), "Amnesty International received documented reports …" (#13 Women Protesters, Egypt). Non-specific authorities are invoked in "The US authorities made public …" (#7 Aamer, USA), though sometimes specific authoritative individuals are represented as sources, for example, "I am encouraged by recent statements from Health Minister María Isabel Rodríguez that Beatriz will receive the treatment that she needs" (#8 Beatriz, El Salvador). And appeals may be made to the addressees' knowledge, for example, "As you know …" (#8 Beatriz, El Salvador). Unsourced evidence is invoked in "Evidence suggests …" (#12 Wallace, Louisiana, USA). Complementarily, we find lack of evidence noted, for example, "No physical evidence ties Mr. Woodfox to Officer Miller's murder …" (#16 Woodfox, Louisiana, USA).

We also find reference to visual evidence, which is then entextualized, for example, "I have been shocked by images showing police actions against demonstrators in Istanbul and other Turkish cities" (#9 Police Action, Turkey). I presume that these are photographic images derived from various media sources. As the letter provides no indication of the source, nature, or reliability of these images, it appears to imply that images per se are reliable evidence for what they depict.[24]

Quote marks are used in a number of letters to indicate the writers' ironic distancing from a particular categorization or characterization, for example, "confession" (#4 Al-Qahtani, Iraq), though not all quoted expressions must be interpreted as ironic. Occasionally, expressions are marked to indicate that they are indeed quoted, but the sense of authorial distancing is still to be felt, for example, the quote marks around "global war" in "End claims that the USA is authorized by international law to use lethal force anywhere in the world under the theory that it is involved in a 'global war' against al-Qa'ida" (#1 Targeted Killings, USA). Likewise, the quote marks around "criticizing" and "misusing" in "[H]e's on trial for 'criticizing' the Interior Ministry and 'misusing' the Internet," and in the same letter, "Some have been charged with 'insulting the President'" (#3 Satire as Crime, Egypt), can all be read as direct quotes, though it is difficult to avoid assuming that the letter writers are calling into question the validity of the laws and policies indexed by the quoted expressions.

It is notable that the letters typically do not hedge their descriptions of the facts of a case or their claims that these facts violate or otherwise contravene international or other laws:

[24] A perilous assumption given the ubiquity of manipulated images online, especially given recent advances in artificial intelligence, though this peril may be moderated by acknowledging, even if reluctantly, AI's reputation for careful vetting of evidence.

The corporal punishment of up to 40 lashes is a *clear violation* of Article 33 of Sudan's 2005 Interim Constitution, Article 5 of the African Charter on Human and Peoples' Rights and Article 7 of the International Covenant on Civil and Political Rights (ICCPR), to which the Republic of Sudan is a state party.

(#24 Indecent Dress, Sudan; emphasis added)

Note particularly the booster expression "clear" modifying "violation" in this sentence.

The deontic, epistemic, and evidential get systematically integrated, with the epistemic providing the evidential support for the deontic, as in, "I urge you to end indiscriminate mass surveillance practices that are jeopardizing the privacy of millions of Americans and people around the world" (#23 Mass Surveillance, USA). Here, the main, deontic, clause expresses the directive while the relative clause, "that are ...," provides the evidence and rationale for the directive. This and similar patterns are found in many of the opening paragraphs of the letters and clearly reveal the tight connection AI makes between the facts of a case and their ideological evaluation and redress.

AI makes strong claims for the truth of the assertions it makes. Its website says, "Human rights change starts with the facts. Our experts do accurate, cross-checked research into human rights violations by governments and others worldwide."[25] This assertion, of course, inextricably entwines facts with their ideological evaluation.

AD 3.3.5: And still at the sentence level: What is the calibration between given, new, and accessible information and between highlighting/foregrounding and backgrounding? (Verschueren 2012: 157–159)

Citing Gundel and Fretheim (2002), Verschueren distinguishes between "referential givenness/newness and relational givenness/newness." The former "pertains to the relation between a linguistic expression and a non-linguistic entity (whether in the language user's mind, the discourse, or a real or a possible world)." The latter "distinguishes what the sentence is about (the 'given' part X, often coinciding with what could be called the 'theme' or 'topic') from what is predicated about X (i.e., the 'new information' or Y, the 'rheme' or 'comment')." To flesh out referential givenness/newness, Verschueren (2012: 158, fn. 65) distinguishes the following statuses and their relationships: "in focus > activated > familiar > uniquely identifiable > referential > type identifiable." These statuses are associated respectively with the following expression types: *it > that, this, this N > that N > the N > indefinite this N > a N*. In-focus expressions may be zero or unstressed pronouns (Gundel 2003: 128; Gundel et al. 1993: 279).

[25] www.amnestykenya.org/what-we-do/ (accessed August 8, 2025). See "How change happens RESEARCH."

Many of the letters contain proper nouns and NPs and because Gundel et al. (1993) do not discuss their status, I rely here on Lyons (1999), who claims (121) that "proper nouns show the general behavior of definite noun phrases," which exhaustively and identifiably represent their referents, and so are at least referential and uniquely identifiable, in Gundel et al.'s (1993) terms.

In the Message Recipients line or in the *To*-line, the addressees are uniquely identifiable as they are represented by their proper names and (generally) their titles, for example, "Vladimir Putin, President of the Russian Federation" (#14 Restrictive Legislation, Russia).

In the letter bodies, the letter SENDers and Message Recipients are represented by personal pronouns *I* and *you* respectively, which are definite and in focus, though this assignment understates the complexity involved in determining their referents, as discussed in Chapter 4.

When the subjects of the appeals are individuals, they are typically introduced by their proper names, for example, "I am writing with an urgent request on behalf of Abdullah 'Azzam Saleh Musfer al-Qahtani and 'Safa Ahmad 'Abul'aziz 'Abdullah" (#4 Al-Qahtani, Iraq), which are assumed to be referential. The subjects may be represented by indefinite NPs, for example, "a woman" and are therefore at least as type-identifiable. Subsequent mentions typically present them as definite NPs, for example, "the woman," "this woman" (#17 Caning, Indonesia). The definite NPs imply that their referent is uniquely identifiable, but in this appeal only as the woman who was accused of adultery and gang-raped. She may be individually identifiable to the source of AI's information, or to the Message Recipients and other Indonesian authorities, but not to the appeal SENDers. Though appeal subjects are typically named in the appeals, the woman in this appeal is not named, perhaps to protect her, perhaps because the AI staffers writing the letter do not know it. I have a strong impression that if she were named, she would have been more strongly represented as individually identifiable, suggesting that the hesitation in Lyons' claim that "proper nouns show the *general* behavior of definite noun phrases" is merited (emphasis added). I return to the interpretation of definite NPs in Chapter 6, where I provide a Relevance Theory analysis of the presuppositions they license.[26]

The subjects of the appeals are frequently represented by their proper names pre-modified by an attributive noun, for example, "satirist Bassem Youssef,

[26] According to Relevance Theory, a reader of (#17 Caning, Indonesia) may construct a "conceptual representation" of the woman that is based on and limited to the information provided in the appeal rather than being able to identify a specific known individual. The personal name of an otherwise unknown individual would provide even less information upon which to construct a conceptual representation of the individual, and would, on its own, provide none of the information specific to AI's concerns presented in the more descriptive NPs, thus distinguishing the "general behavior" of proper nouns from that of definite NPs.

comedian Ali Qandil, blogger Ahmed Anwar" (#3 Satire as Crime, Egypt). Huddleston and Pullum (2002: 519–520) refer to such attributives as "embellishments" that are "semantically non-restrictive," though they are obviously ideologically motivated in the context of the letters as they characterize rather than individually identify the individuals referred to as engaged in activities that should be legal under international civil and human rights law, but which are penalized by the countries' political regimes. Complementarily, and more frequently, the appeal subjects are represented by referential definite NPs with extensions that indicate the basis for the appeal, such as the relative clause modifying "the penalty of flogging" in:

> I also call on the Sudanese government to abolish the penalty of flogging, which violates the absolute prohibition of torture and other cruel, inhuman or degrading treatment or punishment.
>
> (#24 Indecent Dress, Sudan)

As my argument is that the letters serve (at least) two functions – informing and ideologically positioning AI volunteers and ideologically positioning and persuading addressees – we must distinguish what is given/accessible/new to the volunteers from that which might be given/new for the appeal addressees. The volunteers are provided with background information on the case in the embedding webpage and email along with exhortations to the addressees to act to redress the appeal situation, so little if any information in the letters is presumed to be new to them.

The letters typically present the appeal situation as accessible to the addressees, for example, "**Subject**: Please act now: Stop the execution of al-Qahtani and Abdulla" (#4 Al-Qahtani, Iraq). The referents of these proper names are presented as uniquely identifiable by the addressees. As the Message Recipients are the Iraqi Prime Minister (al-Maliki), the Justice Minister (al-Shammari), the Human Rights Minister (al-Sudani), and the Ambassador to the US (Jabir), it is most likely that at least some of them are familiar with the cases of the appeal subjects. Moreover, the definite NP, "the execution of," presents the execution as uniquely identifiable.

While some letters use proper NPs to refer to and identify specific legal documents and articles, for example, "Article 13 of the International Covenant on Civil and Political Rights and Article 22 of the American Convention on Human Rights" (#22 Haitians, Dominican Republic), the vast majority of references to such instruments is by generic NPs, that is, those that denote classes of entities rather than individuals, for example, "human rights" occurs sixty-eight times and "international law" nineteen times in the corpus; for example, "I urge you to ensure that the US government follows international law governing the use of lethal force: international human rights law and, in the exceptional circumstances where it applies, international humanitarian law as well" (#1 Targeted Killing, USA). According to Lyons (1999), "Both 'ordinary' generics and proper nouns behave much like definites, because they apparently meet both the basic semantic/pragmatic criteria for definite reference (inclusiveness and identifiability)" (198). Thus, these bodies of laws are presented as familiar to the AI members and Message Recipients, and therefore presented as universalized, naturalized, and thus ideological (Eagleton 2007: 45), and therefore "powered by an ulterior motive bound up with the legitimation of certain interests in a power struggle" (Eagleton 2007: 16).

The letters also exhibit ideologically relevant patterns of relational givenness/newness. To illustrate these patterns, I examine a short letter (#6 Guantanamo, USA).

> **Message Recipients**: President Barak [*sic*] Obama
>
> **Subject**: Close Guantanamo Detention Facility
>
> I support closing the Guantanamo detention facility and urge you to get the job done, today.
>
> The US government is obligated under international law to respect, protect and fulfill human rights. Each Guantanamo detainee must either be charged and fairly tried in federal court or be released to countries that will respect their human rights.
>
> Instead of justice for the September 11 attacks, Guantanamo has given the world torture, indefinite detention and unfair trials.
>
> It is well past time to change course and close the detention facility.

"[T]he Guantanamo detention facility" is a part of the military prison situated in the US Naval Base at Guantanamo Bay, Cuba. As of July 2025, it was still[27] being used to incarcerate individuals captured during and after the 2003 invasion of Iraq by the US and a number of its allies, and was also used to imprison immigrants to the US alleged to have committed crimes.[28] President Obama wanted to close the facility, but he was prevented from doing so by the US Congress, and Presidents Trump and Biden kept it open.[29] Obama must be assumed to have been familiar with the facility, thus licensing the definiteness of the definite description that first mentions it in the first paragraph. This richer description in turn licenses the one-word identifier, "Guantanamo," in the second and third paragraphs, as well as the reduced description, "the detention facility" in the last line.

[27] https://en.wikipedia.org/wiki/Guantanamo_Bay_detention_camp (accessed September 13, 2025).
[28] https://tinyurl.com/ytswsxxs (accessed September 13, 2025).
[29] https://responsiblestatecraft.org/biden-close-guantanamo/ (accessed September 13, 2025).

As "Guantanamo" is a detention facility, it can be inferred that it is used to incarcerate detainees, and this inference licenses the assumption underlying the NP "Each Guantanamo detainee," that there exist multiple detainees in Guantanamo. (At its maximum, Guantanamo officially held 779 detainees.)

The morphologically related words, "detain," "detainee," and "detention" have legal interpretations. To "detain" is "1 : to hold or keep in custody 2 : to restrain from proceeding." A "detainee" is "a person who is detained" and thus kept in custody and restrained. "Detention" is "1 : the act or fact of detaining or holding back; *esp* : a holding in custody 2 : the state of being detained" (Merriam-Webster's *Dictionary of Law*, 2011: 136–137). The definition of "detainee" includes the rider "*esp* : a person held in custody prior to trial or hearing," which suggests, but, crucially for the controversy regarding Guantanamo, does not entail, that detainees must be tried. Consequently, the use of the term and its morphological relatives in the political and legal context in which the letter was composed is freighted with ideological assumptions that get articulated in other elements of the sentences in which "Guantanamo" is mentioned.

Guantanamo's immediate closure is urged in the first paragraph. The second paragraph invokes the United States' obligations under international law and derives the conclusion from these obligations that each detainee must be fairly charged and tried or released. The third paragraph contrasts AI's ideologically desirable "justice" with the undesirable "torture, indefinite detention, and unfair trials." The fourth paragraph also presents an ideological contrast between the current unjust course of action and the just one of closing the facility and either charging and fairly trying the detainees or releasing them, as specified in the second paragraph.

Thus, the paragraphs, three of which consist of just single sentences, linguistically oscillate between the givenness of an undesirable situation and the newness of that situation's desirable redress.

A similar pattern in which a sentence subject/theme and its corresponding predicate/rheme both entail ideologically framed representations can be discerned in, "They are unable to travel, work, go to school, register their children, call the police for help, access healthcare, or even work, just because of their Haitian heritage" (#22 Haitians, Dominican Republic). The antecedent of "They" is "the tens of thousands of Dominicans of Haitian descent who are enduring the difficulties and humiliation of statelessness and who could face expulsion," mentioned in the immediately preceding sentence.

AD 3.3.6: At the suprasentential level: How is coherence/relevance established? (Verschueren 2012: 159)

Cohesion, coherence, and relevance have to do with connectedness in texts: cohesion refers to connectivity created by linguistic forms; coherence refers to connectivity created by the reader's construction of meaning; relevance has to do with the ways in which various informational elements jointly contribute to the understanding of (a portion of a) text.[30] At the level of genre meaning, the appeal letters incorporate problem/solution texts (Hoey 1983): they characterize a situation as a problem and urge its solution. Crucially, for the letters to be coherent, the solution must be relevant, indeed specific, to the problem. The appeal situation is evaluated as problematic by being conceptualized as a violation of human or other rights and the proposed solution as the redress of the rights violation. At the level of interaction, the letters are appeals to the Message Recipients to accept the evaluation of the appeal situation as problematic and to enact the solution proposed. The typical organization of the letters is laid out in my move and step analysis above.

Halliday and Hasan's (1976) conceptualization of textual cohesion, though problematic in many ways, provides a useful inventory of cohesive devices: reference, substitution, ellipsis, conjunction, and lexical cohesion (cf. Bublitz 1998; Martin 2015). Examples of each can be found in the letters.

Letter (#6 Guantanamo, USA), quoted above, provides clear, ideologically relevant instances of co-reference and lexical cohesion: "the Guantanamo detention facility," "Each Guantanamo detainee," "Guantanamo," "the detention facility," "detainee," "indefinite detention"; "closing the Guantanamo detention facility," "the job," "change course," and "close the detention facility." Each of the expressions refers to the facility itself, its detainees, and its proposed closure. The expressions occur throughout the letter, their mutual dependencies constitute the text as a "unified whole" (Halliday and Hasan 1976: 1) that characterizes "the Guantanamo detention facility" as the locus of violations of international human rights law and urges its closure and the legal disposition of its detainees.

Substitution involves the replacement of one expression with another, type-matched, shorter expression, somewhat akin to pronominalization, for example, "do so" in "Though the Dominican Republic has the right to control migration and deportation in its own borders, it must *do so* in compliance with international law and it cannot expel nationals" (#22 Haitians, Dominican Republic; emphasis added). This device is relatively infrequent in the letters as the writers are more likely to repeat an expression or to elaborate on it by using the resources available for lexical cohesion. This seems to be a genre characteristic as it allows the writers to vary and elaborate ideologically relevant references and evaluations. It is also consistent with the AI Letter Writing Guide's prescription that writers repeat appeal subjects' names in a letter.

Substitution and ellipsis, according to Halliday and Hasan (1976), are closely related. Ellipsis is "substitution by zero" such that the zero elements leave

[30] Verschueren (2012: 159, fn. 68) uses "relevance" in its ordinary, not in its technical Relevance Theory sense.

"specific structural slots to be filled from elsewhere" (143), but "understood nevertheless" (142), and thereby contributing to the elements of coherence and cohesion that constitute the textuality of an utterance. While ellipsis is ubiquitous in language use – it reduces redundancy and thus adds to relevance, in the Relevance Theory sense, of utterances – it has no inherent ideological import. Nonetheless, we do find instances of ellipsis with potential ideological significance: consider the omission of any reference to the basis for the obligation mentioned in:

> There are currently at least 60 million refugee [*sic*] and displaced persons worldwide. 19.5 million of them have sought sanctuary outside of their home countries. All countries have an obligation not to send refugees back into harm's way.
>
> (#36 Refugee-Bashing, USA)

The 1951 Refugee Convention and its 1967 Protocol define "refugee" and assign responsibility for refugee protection to the United Nations High Commissioner for Refugees (UNHCR). The Convention sets non-binding guidelines for governments to determine refugee status within their own legal systems. It is unlikely that ordinary AI members and volunteers are familiar with this background information and are thus unable to identify the bases for the obligation mentioned in the letter. Nonetheless, they may assume, and seem invited to assume, that such legal bases exist, and by so assuming, contribute to their ideological naturalization.

However, not all ellipses are "filled in from elsewhere." As I noted above in my discussion of the passive voice, there appears to be a pattern of eliding the agents of the actions that the letters frame as problems:

> Ahmed Anwar … [is] just one of the many targeted in a new crackdown on freedom of expression. Scores of Egyptians have faced interrogation for criticizing the authorities. They range from famous comedians such as Bassem Youssef to opposition activists. Some have been charged with "insulting the President"; others face trumped-up or politically motivated criminal charges.
>
> (#3 Satire as Crime, Egypt)

We are not told who "targeted," "interrogated," or "charged" Anwar nor who interrogated scores of Egyptians, nor who "trumped-up" the "criminal charges" against "others." Elision of the agents of passive and nominal constructions appears to be a genre characteristic, perhaps because, as I've noted, it politely avoids blaming any specific individuals for the violations. We might also see these types of elision as ideologically positioning the kinds of activities and situations described by these expression types as generally to be taken as human rights violations when mentioned in the AI documents.

The main conjunctive device is the coordinator *and*, which occurs 450 times in the corpus. Its typical use is in the construction of lists of people, events, situations, and directives, for example, "I call on you to stop arresting, charging, prosecuting and sentencing activists for simply exercising their rights to freedom of expression, association and assembly" (#18 Badawi, Saudi Arabia).

The adversative coordinating conjunction *but* occurs only seventeen times and is used to introduce restrictions or conditions on directives that are ideologically based, for example, "But in doing so, the US government must respect its obligations under international law." "Doing so" substitutes for "bring to justice perpetrators of crimes under international law" in the immediately preceding sentence (#1 Targeted Killings, USA).

The subordinating conjunction *however* occurs eight times. It indicates that an inference readily accessible from the preceding utterance or sentence is to be eliminated from the interpretation of the text and to be replaced by the proposition represented by the sentence within the scope of *however*:

> As you know, Beatriz, suffers from lupus and other serious health problems. Her team of doctors have diagnosed her as being at high risk of pregnancy-related death if she continues with this pregnancy. They have not provided the life-saving treatment she needs, *however*, as they fear prosecution under El Salvador's strict ban on abortion.
>
> (#8 Beatriz, El Salvador; emphasis added)

We might gloss "however" in this context as something like: contrary to what you might infer from Beatriz's illness and her medical team's diagnosis and prognosis, namely, that the team should have provided her with the life-saving treatment she needs, an abortion, they have not done so because they fear prosecution.

Consistent with this interpretation of *however*, we also find it introducing a rebuttal to a concession, for example, "The two men were sentenced to death … *However*, Abdullah al-Qahtani testified that his 'confession' was obtained through torture" (#4 Al-Qahtani, Iraq; emphasis added).

Both uses of *however* relate ideologically relevant positions, the first of which would lead us to expect a certain outcome which is eliminated and replaced by the second one.

AD 3.3.6.1: What discourse topics are established? (Verschueren 2012: 160 ff)

The following is a list of the letter topics (and the countries involved) based primarily on the Subject lines of the letters:

US government's targeted killings (USA)
Strong arms control treaty (USA)
Treating satire as a crime (Egypt)
The execution of al-Qahtani & Abdullah (Iraq)
Violence against LGBTQI people (South Africa)
Closing the Guantanamo Detention Facility (USA)
Transfer Shaker Aamer from Guantanamo (USA)
Urgently needed life-saving treatment (El Salvador)

Abusive police action and reveal extent of injuries [*sic*] (Turkey)
Drone wars (USA)
Mass surveillance (USA)
Free Herman Wallace from solitary confinement (USA)
Sexual harassment of Egyptian women protesters (Egypt)
Russian restrictions on the right to freedom of expression, association and peaceful assembly (Russia)
Overturning of Albert Woodfox's conviction (USA)
Prisoner of Conscience Yevgeniy Vitshko (Russia)
Public flogging of blogger, Raif Badawi (Saudi Arabia)
US Senate Torture Report (USA)
Creation of US National Crime and Justice Task Force (USA)
Citizenship revocation of Haitians in Dominican Republic (Dominican Republic)
No more mass surveillance by US government (USA)
Charges against 10 female Christians for "indecent dress" (Sudan)
Freedom for Nadezhda Tolokonnikova and Maria Alekhina (Russia)
Crackdown on human rights lawyers and activists in China (People's Republic of China)
Release of all Prisoners of Conscience in Vietnam (Vietnam)

The letter topics are laid out in more detail in my move and step analysis in Chapter 4 and more synoptically earlier in this chapter, but I very briefly reiterate them here.

The letters typically open with an expression of the writer's concern over the violation of the human rights of an individual, group, or class of individuals, and an expression of the exigency of the situation:

> I wish to express my deep concern about the nationwide crackdown on human rights lawyers and activists in China, which started on July 9 with the disappearance of prominent human rights lawyer Wang Yu.
>
> (#25 Missing, China)

They then direct the addressee(s) to redress the violation or take action to avoid violations:

> I am calling upon your government to include all prisoners of conscience, imprisoned because of their political, religious or other conscientiously held beliefs, among those released.
>
> (#26 PoCs, Vietnam)

They may offer concessions to the addressees based upon exigencies particular to the addressees' country:

> I am encouraged by the report produced by the President's Task Force on 21st Century Policing, which provides some *initial* best practices and offers recommendations for improving policing.
>
> (#21 Crime Task Force, USA; emphasis added)

They then rebut those concessions – note "initial" in the quote above and "finally" in:

> I join Amnesty International USA in respectfully urging the creation of a National Crime and Justice Task Force to *finally* address the widespread pattern of human rights abuses within the US criminal justice system, including the alarming use of lethal force nationwide.
>
> (#21 Crime Task Force, USA; emphasis added)

The letters often call for redress of situations related to the initial one and/or call for redress of a situation that is a generalization of that initial situation.

> I call on your Government to immediately and unconditionally release all those detained solely for their work defending human rights.
>
> (#25 Missing, China)

Occasionally, the letters invite the addressees to engage in discussion or otherwise with the letter writers:

> I hope to hear back from you regarding the steps that you are taking to ensure that Beatriz is given the medical care she has requested.
>
> (#8 Beatriz, El Salvador)

> If you won't read the report, I will send it to you.
>
> (#19 Torture Report, USA)

And offer thanks for their attention to the addressees: "Thank you for your attention to this important matter" (#22 Haitians, Dominican Republic).

I have already discussed the ideological significance of these elements and will make only a few further remarks here about the ideological strategy that seems to underlie AI's use of these appeal letters.

AI, and many other organizations like it, are engaged in an exercise in counterpower, that is, "a capacity to challenge dominant ideologies" (Featherman 2015: 6). And power is

> the relational capacity that enables a social actor to influence asymmetrically the decisions of other social actor(s) in ways that favor the empowered actor's will, interests, and values. Power is exercised by means of coercion (or the possibility of it) and/or by the construction of meaning on the basis of discourses through which social actors guide their action.
>
> (Castells 2009: 10)

And

> the concept of ideology aims to disclose something of the relation between an utterance and its material conditions of possibility, when those conditions of possibility are viewed in the light of certain power-struggles central to the reproduction (or also, for some theories, contestation) of a whole form of social life.
>
> (Eagleton 2007: 223)

AI and similar organizations "campaign to end abuses of human rights,"[31] that is, for the "whole form of social life" encoded and legally enacted in various

[31] www.amnesty.org/en/ (accessed December 8, 2024).

rights documents such as the UN UDHR. These organizations operate in a world in which

> [p]ower is primarily exercised by the construction of meaning in the human mind through processes of communication enacted in global/local multimedia networks of mass communication, including mass self-communication.
>
> (Castells 2009: 416)

Even when that power is also exercised by violence.

The world in which AI operates is characterized by dense multimedia communications networks, and "in a network society, communication is a source of power and counterpower" (Featherman 2015: 6; citation omitted). And

> [a]ccording to the logics of networks, Castells has argued, the flow of power is replaced by the power of flows, and the presence or absence in the network is a significant source of social control and change.
>
> (Featherman 2015: 33)

It follows that AI's strategy of sending large numbers (in the tens of thousands) of letters represents an ideologically motivated "power of flows."

AD 3.3.6.2: How do central discourse topics relate to peripheral ones? (Verschueren 2012: 161)

Verschueren characterizes the central topics of the history textbooks as the historical events and their causes and the peripheral ones as the related circumstances or properties.

While the AI letters typically begin by raising a specific issue, for example, the violation of the human rights of a named individual and its redress or a critical situation, for example, "the global refugee crisis" (#36 Refugee Bashing, USA), or violative activity, for example, the US' "'targeted killing' program" (#1 Targeted Killings, USA), many of them then generalize from that single case to the entire class of individuals represented by the named individual, for example, from Yevgeniy Vitishko to "civil society activists, including members of Environmental Watch for North Caucasus" (#15 Vitishko, Russia). I will assume, following Grimes (1975, cited in Blommaert et al. 2007), that the central, most important topic of the letters is the one raised initially, and that the generalization is more peripheral. The initial topic in (#18 Badawi, Saudi Arabia) is the flogging of Raif Badawi, but the last move in the letter generalizes from Badawi to the treatment of other activists:

> I call on you to stop arresting, charging, prosecuting and sentencing activists for simply exercising their rights to freedom of expression, association and assembly.
>
> (#18 Badawi, Saudi Arabia)

Some letters begin by appealing for the release of one or a group of prisoners and then raising concerns about their whereabouts, health, treatment by guards and inmates, contact with lawyers and family members, and similarly related matters:

I am concerned that Yevgeniy Vitishko's whereabouts and final destination are still unknown, and call on you to inform his family and lawyer of his whereabouts without delay. Please also inform them of the state of his health, as there is serious concern about his condition following a recent hunger strike, and ensure that he receives all necessary medical support.

(#15 Vitishko, Russia)

Letters also raise concerns about the legal procedures by which individuals have been convicted, for example, "There are also serious concerns that the men might not have received a fair trial, in line with international standards" (#4 Al-Qahtani, Iraq). Letters criticize the refusal by authorities to act in accordance with specific legal rulings, for example, "More than a year has passed since Judge James Brady of the U.S. District Court overturned Albert Woodfox's conviction. Today, nearly 41 years after he was first placed in solitary confinement, Albert is still behind bars in isolation" (#16 Woodfox, Louisiana, USA) and "The Inter-American Court of Human Rights ruled on May 29 that the Salvadoran government is obligated under international law to ensure Beatriz's life and health – and it must comply with the IACtHR's order to provide her with the necessary treatment immediately" (#8 Beatriz, El Salvador).

Several letters begin with an expression of general concern and conclude with a list of specific actions the addressees are urged to take:

Message Recipients: President Barak [*sic*] Obama

Subject: No more mass surveillance

I urge you to end indiscriminate mass surveillance practices that are jeopardizing the privacy of millions of Americans and people around the world.

I also urge you and the other leaders of the Five Eyes Alliance to:

- End any existing indiscriminate mass surveillance programs and practices without further delay and ensure that all communications surveillance measures comply with international human rights law;
- Ensure that surveillance of communications is the exception and only happens when absolutely necessary, targeted, based on sufficient evidence of wrongdoing, and authorized by a strictly independent authority, such as a judge. All officials must respect these safeguards;
- Make the rules and policies governing surveillance practices publicly available, including with regard to the sharing of information with other states;
- Ensure that there is transparent and independent parliamentary and judicial oversight of surveillance powers;
- Protect people from indiscriminate or otherwise abusive surveillance of communications by other states;

- End intelligence sharing relationships with foreign states that subject individuals' communications to surveillance that contravenes international human rights law.

(#23 Mass Surveillance, USA)

The progression of the discourse is best represented by the move and step analysis of the typical appeal letter that I presented above. For example, the following illustrates a relatively typical pattern in which the opening expression of concern occurs immediately prior to the directive that indicates how that concern is to be allayed:

I am writing to express my concern about the global refugee crisis and to urge you to help the United States lead the global community in effectively addressing the crisis.
(#36 Refugees, USA)

This opening paragraph incorporates into a single sentence the situation of concern and its redress.

Other openings combine in a single sentence concern about a situation and its evaluation as a rights violation:

I am disappointed to learn that current state laws on the use of lethal force by law enforcement officers do not comply with international human rights law and standards and that the United States does not even keep track of how many lives are lost every year.
(#1 Targeted Killings, USA)

The letters occasionally open with expressions of concern combined with evidence for their claims of rights violations and directives for their redress:

I have been shocked by images showing police actions against demonstrators in Istanbul and other Turkish cities and call upon the Turkish government to immediately end the excessive use of force against peaceful demonstrators.
(#9 Police Action, Turkey)

In general, the situations of concern are represented factually, with the primary evidential being the declarative mood, as discussed above.

As the move and step analysis lays out, various elaborations of the initial concern occur, including generalizations of that situation, concessions to local exigencies, and their rebuttals by appeal to international standards or universal values.

AD 3.3.7: In a wider corpus: How do discourse topics and rhetorical patterns develop/change across different parts of the corpus? (Verschueren 2012: 164–166)

All the letters deal with violations of human and other universal rights. However, except for some very short letters, all the letters in the corpus are topically and rhetorically complex, as I hope my discussion has shown. I have, however, identified for each letter in the corpus what appears to me to be the most important topic of each letter. Below is a list of those topics along with the numbers of letters belonging to each topical group:

Abortion rights (#s 8, 33) [two]
Activism/activists (#s 3, 12, 13, 14, 15, 18, 25, 26, 37) [nine]
Arms sales/trade (#s 2, 34) [two]
Death penalty (#s 1, 4, 7, 12, 35) [five]
Deportation (#22) [one]
Discrimination against LGBTQ+ persons (#s 5, 14) [two]
Freedom of expression and assembly (#s 3, 5, 9, 11, 14, 15, 18, 23, 37) [nine]
Mass surveillance (#23) [one]
Prisoners of Conscience (#s 11, 15, 18, 26, 28, 37) [six]
Right to life (#s 1, 4, 9, 10, 21, 38) [six]
Solitary confinement (#s 12, 16, 17, 20, 28) [five]
Violence against women (#s 13, 32) [two]
Women (#s 11, 13, 17, 24, 32, 33) [six]
Torture (#s 4, 6, 16, 17, 18, 19, 24, 25, 26, 28, 29, 39) [twelve]

While it is clear from the numbers above that torture is by far the object of greatest concern, most of the letters are on behalf of the rights of individuals or classes of individuals, for example, PoC(s); some letters are on behalf of other classifications of people, for example, classifications based on gender or sexual orientation or ethnicity; still others are on behalf of individuals who have been unfairly sentenced, for example, on the basis of tainted evidence; or improperly imprisoned, for example, in solitary confinement; some are protests against violence perpetrated by agents of governments; and some others criticize specific laws, for example, Russian laws restricting freedom of expression and association.

Conclusion

This chapter applied Verschueren's Guideline 3 and its associated caveats and procedures. It investigated the "dynamics of meaning generation in relation to issues pertaining to social structures, processes, and relations." It examined the roles of grammatical voice and its interactions with semantic relations and particularly the identification of agents of violative and other actions and the ideological positioning of those agents relative to human rights evaluations of those actions. It also examined the language of the various moves and steps that constitute the appeals and the topics of the letters.

6 Implicit Meanings

This chapter follows Verschueren's Procedures 3.4 to 3.7, by exploring indicators of implicit meanings, of interaction, of metapragmatic activity, and of interactions between implicitly and explicitly communicated meanings.

> ***Procedure 3.4: Look systematically for carriers of implicit meaning (Verschueren 2012: 166–181).***

US Special counsel Robert S. Mueller III[1] was reported in the *Washington Post* (May 29, 2019) to have said, "If we had had confidence that the president clearly did not commit a crime, we would have said so." Mueller's remark was widely assumed to have implicated – in its linguistics rather than its legal use – that his team did not have confidence that President Trump clearly did not commit a crime, thereby suggesting that he had. Clearly, what's not said may be as potent as what is said, and as ideological meanings are often implied rather than explicitly asserted, it is important to identify the ideological potential of the indicators of such implicit meanings.

> ***AD 3.4.1: Find presupposition carrying expressions and constructions (e.g., definite descriptions, change-of-state verbs, factive verbs, implicative verbs, cleft constructions, scalar notions) (Verschueren 2012: 166–174).***

Presupposition is an effective device for inserting information into discourse as if it were uncontroversial, that is, as if it were accepted as true by speakers and addressees. The phenomenon has a long and stormy history in philosophy (Beaver and Geurts 2014) and linguistics (Huang 2014; Levinson 1983; McCawley 1981). I assume here that it is a pragmatic rather than a semantic matter and that the presupposed information may or may not be new to the discourse and/or to the addressees, and while generally presupposed information is backgrounded, it may on occasion be the "main" or "real" point of an

[1] Mueller was appointed in 2017 as Special Counsel to oversee the investigation into allegations of Russian interference in the 2016 US presidential election. See www.justice.gov/archives/sco-mueller (accessed August 8, 2025).

utterance (Simons 2005: 331). Simons offers a "sketch" of a theory of presupposition grounded in Relevance Theory (Sperber and Wilson 1995; Wilson 2017), arguing that presuppositions, like (in fact, as) implicatures, are "relevance establishers" for utterances – "for a speaker to presuppose *p* in uttering S is for the speaker to intend the addressee to accept *p* for the purposes of establishing the relevance of the utterance" (334). That is, presuppositions represent information to be assumed to be true by addressees as they identify the relevance of an utterance in its context as intended by the speaker (341). Presupposition is thus an important device for making information seem natural, an ideological prerequisite.

Presuppositions are typically taken to follow from the utterance of a positive declarative sentence, its negation, and its interrogation. That is, unlike entailments, presuppositions "survive" negation and interrogation. For example, my utterance of "The right to abortion is recognized in many countries," commits me to the assumption that the right to abortion exists (because definite noun phrases [NPs] are presupposition triggers), as does "The right to abortion is not recognized in many countries," and "Is the right to abortion recognized in many countries?" My utterance invites my communication partners to accept the existence of the right to abortion, though they might very well reject my invitation: "You are seriously wrong, there is no such thing as the right to abortion."[2]

Presuppositions are triggered by expressions in utterances. The items Verschueren mentions in AD 3.4.1 are all presupposition triggers. I discuss them in the order given in AD 3.4.1.

Definiteness

Definiteness is an important indicator of presupposition and definite descriptions are the most abundant presupposition triggers in the letters. They include proper nouns, for example, "Beatriz," and proper NPs, for example, "George Tenet, The Director of Central Intelligence" (#19 Torture Report, USA), NPs with definite articles, for example, "The theory that it is involved in a 'global war'" (#1 Targeted Killings, USA), "the right to life." In his substantive cross-linguistic and diachronic study of definiteness, Lyons (1999: 278) claims that "[d]efiniteness is the grammaticalization of what I have informally termed 'semantic/pragmatic definiteness identifiability.'" Lyons characterizes the Relevance Theory, and specifically Wilson's (1992), conceptualization of definiteness, as

[2] Presuppositions also fail in opaque contexts, which can be created by epistemic verbs such as *think*, *believe*, etc.: "I believe the UDHR exists" does not presuppose the existence of the UDHR as one's belief may be incorrect.

> a version of identifiability: interpreting a definite noun phrase means retrieving or constructing a conceptual representation which uniquely[3] identifies the referent. Kempson (1988) presents a similar view more fully. Definiteness amounts to a guarantee of accessibility: a speaker uses a definite noun phrase to indicate that a conceptual representation corresponding to the noun phrase is easily accessible to the hearer. The most straightforward cases are immediate situation and anaphoric uses, in which the relevant easily accessible information consists, respectively, of the hearer's perception of the scenario in which the utterance occurs and the content of the preceding discourse. Where the situation and the explicit content of the discourse do not provide the representation required, the hearer must assume that this representation can be easily inferred by way of the context. The concepts expressed by words are claimed to be stores of information, including associated information, and such information contributes to the context. (273)

Many of the expressions that include "right" or "rights" are definite, typically because they are modified by the definite article, for example, "the right to life." The conceptual representations of the various rights mentioned in the AI letters are not derivable from the immediate situation of the reading of the letters nor from the content of preceding discourse in the sense intended by "anaphoric." So, letter readers, whether AI volunteers or Message Recipients or their surrogates, are assumed to be able to construct relevant, if individually variable, representations from information they have stored concerning these rights. This assumption implies that letter writers and letter readers exist in a shared socio-cognitive world in which the mentioned rights should trump any local contingencies that might otherwise have legitimized the actions that are characterized as violations of those rights. This shared world is, of course, the legal world of treaties and conventions to which almost all the countries of this world are signatories and to which, consequently, all the citizens of those countries, however powerful, are subject.

However, definite descriptions are generally assumed to refer via the denotation of entities or classes of entities in their discourse world. Consequently, the definite "rights" phrases commit writers and readers to the existence of those rights, not merely to their cognitive representations. For example, the definiteness of the two NPs in "The death penalty violates the right to life" (#4 Al-Qahtani, Iraq) indicates that the writer assumes that an intended letter reader can readily access or construct mental representations of the penalty and the right that are similar to those of the writer. However, the existence of an easily accessible mental representation is in itself insufficient; the representation must be instantiated by referents in the relevant world, in the case of the AI letters, the world of internationally binding legal instruments and their

3 Jeff Kaplan, (p.c.) reports an example suggesting that definiteness need not imply uniqueness: In a hotel lobby, a person might be told that "the elevator" is around a corner, and upon going around that corner, the person discovers a bank of elevators.

violations. Definite descriptions such as those listed above are typically taken to trigger the pragmatic presupposition that their referents exist (Beaver and Geurts 2014; Levinson 1983), and thus commit letter SENDers and their recipients to their existence, and to the assumption that the identification of those referents is essential to the discovery of the intended relevance of the letters (Simons 2005). (For more fine-grained analyses of the information status of various types of referring expression, see Abbott 2019; Gundel et al. 1993; Huddleston and Pullum 2002: 368–373; and Prince 1981.)

In addition to implicating the existence of a referent, a definite description implicates that the description applies inclusively, that is, to every contextually relevant entity that fits the description (Lyons 1999: 11). Thus, the occurrence of "the rights guaranteed to Egyptians" (#3 Satire as Crime, Egypt) refers to everything that can be described as a right guaranteed to Egyptians.

A definite description may implicate the truth of a modifier. "[T]he horrific public flogging of blogger, Raif Badawi" (#18 Badawi, Saudi Arabia) presupposes the truth of the proposition that Badawi was a blogger who was flogged and that the flogging was public and horrific.

We also find NPs with categorizing attributive pre-modifiers, for example, "satirist, Bassem Youssef" (#3 Satire as Crime, Egypt), which suggests that the activity that brought Youssef (and others) to the attention of the Egyptian authorities was his satirizing members of the Egyptian government, an activity that should be protected by this right to freedom of expression. Other such examples of definite NPs include "the absolute prohibition of torture …" (#24 Indecent Dress, Sudan), which clearly presupposes the existence of this prohibition, and that it applies without exception. Similarly, "this important matter" (#22 Haitians, Dominican Republic) presupposes the existence of the matter of the letter and that it is important.

In (#18 Badawi, Saudi Arabia), we find Badawi characterized as "Saudi blogger Raif Badawi." As the letter is addressed to the King of Saudi Arabia and to the US ambassador to that Kingdom, it is odd that Badawi is characterized as a Saudi, as his nationality might reasonably be inferred by, if not already known to, the addressees. Most likely, the inclusion of "Saudi" in this phrase is directed toward the AI volunteers rather than to the Message Recipients, as it highlights Badawi's nationality and thus his connection to the state whose legal system sentenced him to "the horrific public flogging," and is consistent with my claim that the goal of the appeals may be as much for engaging AI members and volunteers as for persuading their Message Recipients.

We also find NPs with genitive modifiers: "Amnesty International's report documents adults and children as young as seven working in hazardous conditions in artisanal cobalt mines in the DRC" (#40 Cobalt, Apple Corporation), which presupposes the existence of the report, while the verb "documents" presupposes the truth of the proposition expressed by its complement clause.

Seven of the letters sign off by expressing thanks for, or the hope of, "your attention to" the matter of the letter, others are for "your time." When included as the complement of a thanking expression, these expressions project a presupposition into the future, viz., that the Message Recipients will in fact accord the matters of the letters their time or attention. Other examples include "their rights to freedom of expression, association and assembly" (#18 Badawi, Saudi Arabia), which presupposes the existence of the listed rights.

While many of the rights expressions are grammatically definite, others are grammatically indefinite, though they are nonetheless also typically referential, as can be demonstrated by the coreferential pronoun test (Huddleston and Pullum 2002: 400–401):

Such conditions violate minimum international standards for humane treatment. These are defined in Article X of Statute Y.

"These" is anaphoric to "minimum international standards for humane treatment" and because it is definite, it refers, implicating that its antecedent, though indefinite, also refers. Consequently, readers are positioned as accepting the existence of the characterized entities, in this case, the existence of minimum international standards for humane treatment (#16 Woodfox, Louisiana, USA).

These expressions, whether grammatically definite or not, are nonetheless vague, that is, they do not specify which international standards are being referenced nor how many of them constitute a minimum. Neither the death penalty nor the right to life exists except by virtue of the specific legal instruments that create and define them, and these instruments are only occasionally identified in the corpus. Nonetheless, these expressions and others like them are presented as sufficiently informative in their contexts and, thus, present their referents as unproblematically accessible to addressees.[4] These expressions thus naturalize and render commonsensical their referents by presenting them as assumed and unquestioned, perhaps even unquestionable, elements of context, familiar to both writers and addressees.

Change of State Expressions

Change of state verbs presuppose the existence of the events or truth of the propositions represented by their complements. Three that occur in the appeals are ideologically significant as they presuppose the existence of ideologically

[4] Relevance Theory entails that individual AI members and volunteers may informationally "enrich" these expressions to a degree determined by their preferences, their knowledge (of human rights), and their processing costs. Individuals who undertake the burden of these costs may have a deeper knowledge of, and commitment to, human rights and to AI's ideologies, goals, and methods than the AI members imagined to be typical by AI staffers.

relevant events and situations. *Stop* occurs twenty times, eight of which occur in subject lines, for example, "Stop killing people with Albinism" (#38 Albinism, Malawi). It presupposes that the addressees are killing people with Albinism; *quash* occurs once: "I call on you to quash Raif Badawi's flogging sentence immediately" (#18 Badawi, Saudi Arabia) presupposes that Badawi has been sentenced to be flogged; *overturn* occurs six times, for example, "I respectfully call on you to … overturn their sentences" (#4 Al-Qahtani, Iraq) presupposes the existence of sentences to be overturned.

Akin to change of state predicates like *stop* are temporal adverbs such as *still*, which occurs eight times in the corpus with the relevant meaning, for example, "Though you attempted to solve the problem with Law 169–14, the law is *still* discriminatory and ineffective" (#22 Haitians, Dominican Republic; emphasis added). *Still* licenses "the presupposition that the situation also obtained prior to the time referred to" and implies a contrast with what "might have been expected" (Huddleston and Pullum 2002: 711). "Still" in the Haitians example licenses the presupposition that Law 169–14 was discriminatory and ineffective before the time the appeal was written and sent and that this is unexpected and contrary to what the letter writer/senders might anticipate if Haitians' human rights were being honored.

Factive Predicates

The most important subclass of factive predicates are those that are systematically used to express the writers' feelings about the appeal situations and to embed a presupposed factual claim. These are primarily various morphological forms of *concern*, which occur twenty-five times, for example, "I am writing to express my deep concern about the global refugee crisis …" (#36 Refugee Bashing, USA); *disappoint*, which occurs once: "I am disappointed to learn that current state laws on the use of lethal force by law enforcement officers do not comply with international human rights law and standards" (#21 Crime Task Force, USA); and forms of *disturb*, which occur four times, for example, "a disturbing and increasing pattern of sexual violence" (#13 Women Protesters, Egypt). These examples are all analogous to "I am concerned that Yevgeniy Vitishko's whereabouts and final destination are still unknown" (#15 Vitishko, Russia), which presupposes that Vitishko's whereabouts and final destination have been and remain unknown.

Other factive predicates that occur are forms of *confession* (four times), one of these in scare quotes (#4 Al-Qahtani, Saudi Arabia), which, as I noted earlier, indicate the writer's ironic distancing to cast doubt on the reliability of the confession, which is alleged to have been obtained by torture. The scare quotes also have the effect of suspending the presupposition that *confession* would normally imply.

Implicative Expressions

Of the implicative verbs, *avoid* occurs once, "I urge you to respect international law and standards at all times during deportation proceedings, to establish adequate mechanisms to avoid the expulsion of Dominican-born people who were deprived of their Dominican nationality in September 2013" (#22 Haitians, Dominican Republic). "Avoid" here implicates that the expulsion of "Dominican-born people …" is to be expected unless the Dominican Republic takes action to stop it.

Cleft Constructions

One *it*-cleft occurs: "It is against that backdrop – the largest attack against the American homeland in our history – that the events described in this report were undertaken" (#19 Torture Report, USA). This sentence, from the first page of the Foreword to the US Senate's report, presupposes that the events described in the "Torture Report" were in fact undertaken.

Only one *wh*-cleft occurs: "There is much we do not know, but *what is clear is that the National Security Agency (NSA) is relying on this obscure executive order to justify expansive surveillance activities worldwide*" (#23 Mass Surveillance, USA; emphasis added). This *wh*-cleft highlights the contrast between what is not known and what is clearly known, and what is clearly known is also clearly ideologically significant, viz., that the NSA is relying on an obscure executive order – "Executive Order 12333, a presidential order that is shrouded in secrecy and has never been subject to meaningful oversight by Congress or a U.S. court" – to justify its global surveillance, which is "a violation of the human rights of people across the globe" as it violates "privacy on a massive scale and [has] a chilling effect on freedom of expression" (#23 Mass Surveillance, USA).

Presupposition Triggers in the Appeals

The presupposition triggers found in the letters are listed below. These and their category titles are derived from lists in Huang (2014: 86–87) and Levinson (1983: 181–184). (See references therein.)

FACTIVE AND SEMI-FACTIVE PREDICATES: *disturbed, concern/concerned, know, understand, realize, reject, uphold, disclose, recognize, respect, shocked, assault on, jeopardize, reveal, intercepted, sharing, violate, violation, surveillance, protect from, welcome, revelations, in accordance with, comply with, member of, unknown, disappointed, learn, highlight, find, aware, condemn, silence, even though, though, impose*

ASPECTUAL/CHANGE OF STATE PREDICATES: *stop, quash, drop, decriminalize, expand, slow down, end, re-open, re-criminalization, uphold, amend, contravene, stay (the executions), overturn, release, free, remedy, still, withdraw, remove, deprive of*

ITERATIVES: *ongoing, also, once again, retry, first, repeated, reintroduce, continue, another*

IMPLICATIVE PREDICATES: *remember, get, happen, take this opportunity*

NEGATIVE IMPLICATIVE VERBS (imply the falsity of their complements): *fail, avoid*

QUANTIFIERS: *one of, further, more, just one of, many of, no more, full extent of, furthermore, most of, some*

TEMPORAL ADVERBIALS/CLAUSES: *when blogger Ahmed Anwar posted a video ... on-line, while they remain incarcerated, after surviving 41 years of a nightmare*

VERBS/NOUNS OF JUDGING: *accused, criticize/criticism, justify, prosecute, sentence*

COMPARISONS AND CONTRASTS: *longer than, contrary to*

NON-RESTRICTIVE RELATIVE CLAUSES: *which started on July 9 ..., which require ..., which carry, which violates ...*

QUESTIONS: *Where are the missing?*[5]

The broad range and large number of these triggers is testament to the fundamental role of presupposition in the letters; that is, the various rights, their violations, and their appropriate redress are presented as to be taken for granted by AI, its members and volunteers, and the appeal Message Recipients. Presupposition in the appeals is, therefore, a potent device for ideologically positioning individuals and evaluating situations and events (see Sbisà 1999).

AD 3.4.2: Find logical implications and entailments (Verschueren 2012: 174–176).

Under this heading, Verschueren (2012) includes the relations of "(logical) implication, entailment, [and] conventional implicatures" (174). He discusses the implications licensed by the occurrence of *mais* "but," *comme* "since, because," *donc* "therefore," and *even*. I discuss the ideologically relevant uses of such conventional implicature triggers that occur in the corpus.

But occurs seventeen times in the letters, and six of these introduce rebuttals to concessions:

> I fully recognize the US government's duty to take robust action to protect the life and physical integrity of people within its jurisdiction, and to bring to justice perpetrators of crimes under international law. *But* in doing so, the US government must respect its obligations under international law.
>
> (#1 Targeted Killings USA; emphasis added)

However occurs eight times in the corpus and is similar to *but* in introducing a contrast, which can be used to introduce the rebuttal to a concession:

> Over the years, Louisiana authorities have often repeated that Brent Miller's family is due justice. I have no doubt that this is true, and I have tremendous sympathy for Officer

[5] Other triggers include counterfactual conditionals, implicit clefts with stressed constituents (Huang 2014; Levinson 1983). I found no examples of these in the letters.

Miller's family and friends. *However*, I do not believe that confining Albert Woodfox to a cell the size of a parking space is just.

(#16 Woodfox, Louisiana, USA; emphasis added)

Because occurs eight times in the corpus and introduces a clause that represents a cause of, or reason for, the situation represented by a related clause, for example, "Father Nguyen Van Ly is a Catholic priest who has spent twenty years in prison *because* of his peaceful human rights activism" (#26 PoCs, Vietnam; emphasis added); "They are unable to travel, work, go to school, register their children, call the police for help, access healthcare, or even work, just *because* of their Haitian heritage" (#22 Haitians, Dominican Republic; emphasis added). *Just because* occurs twice and may be glossed as "for no other reason than" (Calude and Delahunty 2020).

Therefore, which occurs just once in the corpus, is categorized as an "impure" connective by Huddleston and Pullum (2002: 777) as it both connects its "clause to the surrounding text" and indicates a reason or result (779). Rouchota (1996) glosses *therefore* as "as a result of this."

Each day that goes by without action brings increased danger for Beatriz.

I am *therefore* calling on you to allow Beatriz immediate and unfettered access to the lifesaving treatment she needs.

(#8 Beatriz, El Salvador; emphasis added)

In the extract just above, *therefore* indicates that the first sentence represents the reason for the writer's request in the second sentence, which complementarily represents the result of the writer's estimate of the danger to Beatriz. *Therefore* in this extract seems also to be glossable as "because of this," which may be a narrowing of the reason/result interpretations (Allan 2012: 228; Sperber and Wilson 2012: 105–107; Traugott 2012: 552).

As, which occurs seventy-two times in the corpus, functions in a variety of ways, and I focus here on just one, *as* used as an indicator of class membership.

Subject: Stop treating satire *as* a crime.

(#3 Satire as Crime, Egypt; emphasis added)

Shaker Aamer's designation by US authorities as "approved for transfer" implies that US authorities have no intention of charging him with criminal offenses

(#7 Aamer, USA; emphasis added).

In these two instances, *as* introduces the class to which certain types of actions have been assigned, problematically, according to the letters. In the first case, because treating satire as a crime violates the universal right to freedom of expression.[6] In the second case, designating Aamer as approved for transfer

[6] See Witczak-Plisiecka (2013) on "speech acts in legal contexts."

should mean that he is to be transferred to the UK, an obligation the US authorities refused to meet.

The fixed expression *as such* occurs once:

> I understand that your government has as an obligation to bring to [*sic*] those responsible for serious crimes to justice, and that Iraq must confront violence by armed group [*sic*]. However, I am deeply concerned about convictions that are based on forced confessions and trial proceedings that fall short of international standards. *As such*, I urge you to declare an official moratorium on executions, with a view to abolishing the death penalty.[7]
>
> (#4 Al-Qahtani, Iraq; emphasis added)

As such here appears to mean "given the situation I have just described" or "because the situation is as I have just described it," that is, the request is the result of the writer's evaluation of thc situation: "it falls short of international standards," which are based on internationally recognized human rights.

Persecute and *persecution* occur four times in the corpus, for example, "I urge you to stop the persecution of civil society activists, including members of Environmental Watch for North Caucasus" (#15 Vitishko, Russia). *Persecution* is defined as "punishment or harassment usually of a severe nature on the basis of race, religion, or political opinion in one's country of origin" (Merriam-Webster's *Dictionary of Law*: 358), to which the *American Heritage Dictionary* adds, "gender, sexual orientation, or beliefs" (1316). Google's online dictionary gives as "similar words": *oppress*, *abuse*, *victimize*, *ill-treat*, *mistreat*, *maltreat*, *punish*, *tyrannize*, *afflict*, *torment*, *torture*, *martyr*, and many others. These synonyms give a more comprehensive list of the injustices inflicted upon the subjects of the appeals than the dictionary definitions, and even though the actions characterized by the letters as persecution may be legal within the local legal systems, they are, from a universal human rights point of view, unjust and ultimately illegal.

Even, which occurs eleven times in the corpus, "evokes a *scalar contrast*" (Verschueren 2012: 176; emphasis in original). In the following example, "even under this law" suggests that other laws (or legal instruments) failed and this law was the one least likely to fail, presumably because it was an attempt to solve the citizenship/nationality problem of Haitian Dominicans, as described in:

> The Dominican Constitutional Court established that children of irregular migrants born in the Dominican Republic between 1929 and 2010 had never been entitled to Dominican nationality and have been stripped them [*sic*] of it, *even though* your constitution's provision had granted them citizenship. Though you attempted to solve the problem with Law 169–14, the law is still discriminatory and ineffective. Law 169–14 obliges Dominicans of foreign descent to register as foreigners, and *even* under this law

7 "[T]o those" in the first line of the extract seems to be an editing error; "by armed group" and "[a]s such" may indicate that the writer was not a native speaker of English. For uses of *as such*, see www.collinsdictionary.com/us/dictionary/english/as-such (accessed August 8, 2025).

you have failed to regularize the status of tens of thousands of Dominicans, most of whom are of Haitian descent.

(#22 Haitians, Dominican Republic; emphasis added)

Even though is also worthy of note here. *Though* introduces a concession; *even* here appears to mean something like "and especially"; *even though* indicates that given that concession, and especially that specific concession, it is unexpected that whatever the main clause represents would be the case. Applying this gloss pattern to the "even though" segment of the quote above we get:

Especially given that the constitution's provision granted people of Haitian descent citizenship, it is unexpected that the Dominican Constitutional Court established that children of irregular migrants born in the Dominican Republic between 1929 and 2010 had never been entitled to Dominican nationality and stripped them of their nationality.

Or

The Dominican Constitutional Court established that children of irregular migrants born in the Dominican Republic between 1929 and 2010 had never been entitled to Dominican nationality and stripped them of their citizenship, *in spite of the fact that* the Dominican constitution had granted them that citizenship.

While occurs eight times with at least two functions, the first and presumably most central one is an indication of temporal simultaneity, for example, "While they remain incarcerated, the two women must not be ill-treated by prison staff or inmates, and they must be allowed regular contact with their families and legal teams" (#11 Pussy Riot, Russia). With one exception, the *while*s in the corpus are of this type.

The second function of *while* is to indicate a discourse extension of the temporal reading. It indicates the discourse, rather than the temporal, simultaneity of (at least) two propositions, the second of which contrasts in some way with the first, typically by contrasting some members of a set with other members of the same set, and presenting the first as a concession:

While all sides have committed violations, a UN report found that Saudi Arabia-led coalition airstrikes were responsible for most of the civilian deaths in Yemen's conflict through the end of July of 2015.

(#34 Arms Sales, USA; emphasis added)

The violations mentioned in the first line must be interpreted to include the killing of civilians indicated in the second. Killing civilians during a war may be, and in this letter is claimed to be, a violation of the laws of war which have been articulated in multiple declarations and covenants. The Saudi Arabia-led coalition is characterized as the greater violator of those laws than other parties to the conflict.

While, like *but* and *however*, may be used to indicate a contrast between a situation that is ideologically more acceptable or less unacceptable to the writer than another.

AD 3.4.3: Find implicatures (Verschueren 2012: 176–178).

Though there are several competing theoretical approaches (e.g., Horn 2004; Huang 2017; Levinson 2000, Sperber and Wilson 1995; Wilson 2017) currently purporting to account for implicatures, Verschueren invokes the standard Gricean Cooperative Principle (CP) and its attendant maxims (or "principles," as he calls them) as the mechanisms underlying the derivation of implicatures (Grice 1975, 1989).

If we assume that the letter writers abide by the CP and thus make each letter "such as is required, at the stage at which it occurs, by the accepted purpose or direction of the talk exchange in which [they] are engaged," then we must also assume that they are abiding by the maxims of Quantity, Quality, Relation, and Manner.

The maxim of Quality expresses the expectation that speakers/writers will not say what they believe to be false nor say things for which they lack evidence. I discussed aspects of this above in my discussion of assertive speech acts. As I noted there, AI claims to be meticulous in its research and in its reporting of the specifics of cases. So, we can infer on the basis of AI's reputation and record and our assumption that the maxim of Quality is in effect that truth claims in the letters are not believed by AI staffers to be false and are well-evidenced. So, the truth and evidential sufficiency of assertions like the following are presented by AI and its appeal SENDers as to be accepted as true by all the relevant interlocutors:

> Over the past year, Russian authorities have passed a series of laws that restrict the right to freedom of expression, association and assembly. These laws obstruct the legitimate role of civil society in Russia and suppress initiative, creativity and development of non-governmental organizations.
>
> (#14 Restrictive Legislation, Russia)

The Russian authorities might well balk at the characterization of their series of laws as restricting rights or that they obstruct legitimate civil society activities. Just as AI's stance on the Russian laws is ideological, so too is a potential Russian response that reframes them as appropriate circumscriptions, legitimated by the Russian Duma, of behavior the authorities characterize as socially disruptive.

The maxim of Quantity leads us to expect that the letters contain enough but no more than enough information for their purposes. Scalar implicatures are an important class that are argued to derive from the maxim of Quantity (Levinson 1983: 132–136). One important trigger of scalar implicatures is the quantifier *some*. It occurs nine times in the corpus, eight of which license an implicature. For example, "Some have been charged with 'insulting the President'; others face trumped-up or politically motivated criminal charges." Here, "some" licenses the implicature that not all of the "[s]cores of Egyptians [who] have faced interrogation for criticizing the authorities" have been charged with the (dubious) crime of "insulting the President," which of course raises the question of what has happened to that remainder, which is immediately answered by the parallel juxtaposed clause, "others face …" (#3 Satire as Crime, Egypt).

More generally, if my argument is correct, and the letters have the primary purposes of persuading the Message Recipients to act to redress an injustice and of educating, engaging, and motivating the AI volunteers, then the amount of information required for the Message Recipients is likely to be less than that required for the volunteers. As the letters function partially as protests to the Message Recipients, who, as high-ranking government officials, may be assumed to have access to more or less detailed knowledge of the facts of the appeal situations, minimal reference to those facts and to their redress might be sufficient, though these addressees can reasonably expect some attempt at justification for the evaluation of the situation and for its redress (Forst 2012). An examination of the information included in the following letter will allow us to tease apart the information that seems to be aimed at each audience. I have numbered the paragraphs for ease of reference.

Message Recipients:[8] Ambassador Pham Quang Vinh, *Ambassador of Vietnam to the United States*

Subject: Release Prisoners of Conscience

[1] I am writing to you today with regard to the major prisoner amnesty that has been announced to mark Vietnam's National Day on 2 September 2015. According to media reports, up to 17,000 prisoners are expected to be released.

[2] I am calling upon your government to include all prisoners of conscience, imprisoned because of their political, religious or other conscientiously held beliefs, among those released. This includes prisoners of conscience Thich Quang Do, Ta Phong Tan, Tran Huynh Duy Thuc and Father Nguyen Van Ly.

[3] The Most Venerable Thich Quang Do is the head of the banned Unified Buddhist Church of Viet Nam (UBCV) and a leading advocate of religious freedom, human rights and democracy. He is confined to the Thanh Minh Zen monastery as a prisoner of conscience. Ta Phong Tan is a peaceful blogger sentenced to ten years' imprisonment, and suffers from several deteriorating medical conditions. Tran Huyn Duy Thuc is also a peaceful blogger and entrepreneur serving a sixteen-year sentence, and alleges that he was tortured while in detention. Father Nguyen Van Ly is a Catholic priest who has spent twenty years in prison because of his peaceful human rights activism.

[8] The plural "recipients" is used regardless of the number of Message Recipients identified, presumably because the appeal writers are using a template.

[4] I urge your government to comply with international human rights law and take this opportunity to show Vietnam's commitment to upholding human rights by releasing immediately and unconditionally these four individuals, along with all prisoners of conscience.[9]

(#26 PoCs, Vietnam)

It is quite conceivable that the names of the individuals for whose release the letter appeals would be sufficient to identify them to the Message Recipients, or at least to his staff. If this is the case, then much of the information about those individuals in the third paragraph is redundant for that audience. However, for the volunteers, this information, though a repetition of that in the email and embedding webpage, is not redundant as it reinforces what was said in the email, but also demonstrates to the Message Recipients what the volunteers know and their evaluation of that knowledge.

It is noteworthy that even though the Subject line indicates that the subjects of the appeal are Prisoners of Conscience (PoCs), paragraph 2 provides a synoptic definition of the category: "imprisoned because of their political, religious or other conscientiously held beliefs," which does not include the criterion that they have not used or advocated violence. However, in paragraph 3, three of the individual appeal subjects are characterized as "peaceful," and the remaining one is explicitly characterized as a PoC. This repetition is probably unnecessary for the AI volunteers, but for the Vietnamese authorities it emphasizes a specific characteristic of the four individual appeal subjects that seems to differentiate them from the "up to 17,000 prisoners" mentioned in paragraph 1, who may be released. This characteristic then provides the basis for the general appeal to the Vietnamese government with which the letter ends – to adhere to international human rights standards and to release all PoCs. If this interpretation is correct, then we have further evidence that the appeals are designed to engage AI volunteers and not solely to persuade their Message Recipients.

The maxim of Relation articulates the expectation that any information provided will be relevant to the communicative task at hand and so is at least partially redundant with the second maxim of Quantity: Do not make your contribution more informative than is required. I will discuss the information in the letter's third paragraph in terms of its sufficiency and relevance for the two audiences. The information that Thich Quang Do is a Most Venerable person, the head of the banned Unified Buddhist Church of Viet Nam,[10] a leading

[9] As we are deep in Gricean territory, it is worth noting, as an aside, the operation of Grice's submaxim of Manner: Be orderly: the order in which the individuals are mentioned in paragraph 2 is the same as that in paragraph 3.

[10] Note that the country's name is spelled in two ways in the letter – Vietnam and Viet Nam – suggesting that the third paragraph was cut and pasted in from another source and/or that editing

advocate of religious freedom, human rights, and democracy, and is confined to the Thanh Minh Zen monastery as a PoC is considerably more relevant to the purpose of convincing AI volunteers than in either informing or persuading the Vietnamese Ambassador to the US. Similar remarks can be made about the information provided in the letter about the other appeal subjects. It does, however, as I noted above, indicate to the Message Recipients the ideological assumptions upon which AI and its volunteers base their evaluations of the appeal situation and its redress.

My discussion of the roles of the maxims of Quantity and Relation might seem to contradict each other. This contradiction may be resolved if we accept what I have been arguing, viz., that the letters are designed for two audiences – the AI volunteers and their Message Recipients.

While Message Recipients are individuals who have the power to redress the appeal situation, ambassadors probably do not have the power to do this directly; however, they do have the responsibility to convey to their governments that a great many AI volunteers are concerned about the situation and wish it to be redressed, thus providing further support to the assumption that the appeals derive much if not all of their power from the numbers of people who send them, rather than to the persuasiveness of their arguments.

Grice's maxim of Manner subsumes four submaxims: Avoid obscurity of expression, Avoid ambiguity, Be brief (avoid unnecessary prolixity), and Be orderly. The submaxim Be brief is redundant with both Quantity and Relation, just as the submaxim Avoid ambiguity is: an ambiguous expression would give too much information, some of which would be irrelevant. Nonetheless, it is worth considering the letters from the perspective of the submaxims.

Generally speaking, the letters are as brief as their purposes allow, especially if information that might seem redundant from the point of view of one intended audience might not seem so from the other audience's point of view, and especially as a demonstration to the Message Recipients of what AI and its volunteers know of the cases and how they view them.

However, it is worth remembering here that the AI Letter Writing Guide advises its users to repeat the name(s) of the appeal subject(s) as often as practicable – the four appeal subjects of letter #26 are each named twice. Letter #26 also mentions "prisoner(s) of conscience" five times, and twice characterizes the four named prisoners as such, and then characterizes Thich Quang Do yet again as a PoC. In addition, these individuals are characterized as "a leading

for consistent and error-free prose is not a high priority. If the paragraph were cut and pasted, then at least a second utterer's voice is involved (see AD 2.2.1.2; Verschueren 2012: 89 ff). If editing is not a high priority, then, as I've noted elsewhere, we may have further evidence that the appeals are designed for AI members and volunteers.

advocate of religious freedom, human rights and democracy," as "a peaceful blogger," as "a peaceful blogger and entrepreneur serving a sixteen-year sentence" who "alleges that he was tortured while in detention," and as someone "who has spent twenty years in prison because of his peaceful human rights activism," characterizations that, except for "entrepreneur," are implied by AI's definition of PoC and that imply violations of their human rights.

If we assume that the CP and maxims are "guidelines for efficient and effective" communication (Levinson 1983: 101), then the redundancies we observed in the letters reduce their efficiency. However, if we consider the CP and maxims as guidelines for the conduct of "rational" discourse, then we might view these redundancies as purposeful reminders of the identities and ideologically relevant characteristics of the appeal individuals, so that "effective" trumps "efficient," in much the way that polite discourse tends to be more prolix than the mere communication of topical information might be (Brown 2017; Leech 1983; Terkourafi 2012).

The move and step analysis of the letters demonstrates their orderliness at a macro level. Their orderliness at the micro level can be illustrated by the licensing of inferences by the juxtapositioning of sentences. I have numbered the sentences in the following extract:

> [1] I am writing to express my deep concern about Nadezhda Tolokonnikova and Maria Alekhina, who were sentenced to two years in a penal colony for their participation in a February 2012 protest action by the feminist punk-rock group Pussy Riot at the Christ the Savior Cathedral in Moscow. [2] These two women, both mothers in their twenties, were detained solely for their peaceful expression of their beliefs. [3] They are Prisoners of Conscience.
>
> (#11 Pussy Riot, Russia)

The antecedent of the NP "These two women" in sentence [2] is to be found in the immediately preceding sentence, that is, within the minimally accessible context, thus minimizing the effort needed to identify the NP's referents.

More interesting from an ideological perspective is the juxtaposition of sentences [2] and [3]. As [2] provides the minimally accessible context in which to process [3], "they" may be taken to be anaphoric to "These two women." However, as there is no overt discourse or pragmatic marker (Fraser 1996) to indicate how to interpret [3] in the context of [2], one could claim, following Grice's maxim of Relation, that [3], merely by virtue of its juxtaposition to [2], is simply information added to that provided in [2], and indeed this might be a sufficiently rich interpretation for the purposes of the letter. However, a yet richer interpretation is possible and more likely, viz., that the two women have been declared PoCs as a result of their being "detained solely for the peaceful expression of their beliefs." Relevance Theory would lead us to infer this richer interpretation and provide us with a straightforward means of accounting for it.

RT's central assumption is the Communicative Principle of Relevance: Every act of overt communication conveys a presumption of its own optimal relevance; that is, that processing the communicative act will yield adequate positive cognitive effects for no undue processing costs. Deriving these cognitive effects requires the construction of an appropriate hypothesis about intended explicatures by developing the linguistically encoded logical form; constructing an appropriate hypothesis about the intended contextual assumptions (*implicated premises*); and constructing an appropriate hypothesis about the intended contextual implications (*implicated conclusions*) (Wilson and Sperber 2012: 13).

If we hypothesize that the propositions *Nadezhda Tolokonnikova and Maria Alekhina were detained solely for their peaceful expression of their beliefs* and *Nadezhda Tolokonnikova and Maria Alekhina are Prisoners of Conscience*, and the proposition expressed by AI's definition of PoC are all implicated premises, then we can derive the implicated conclusion that the two women are PoCs because they were detained solely for the peaceful expression of their beliefs. That is, RT articulates the mechanism that licenses us to inferentially enrich our interpretation of the two sentences from a mere accumulation of information to an explanation for the categorization of the two women as PoCs by contextualizing that categorization as a conclusion derived from the immediately prior sentence and the definition of PoC, thus justifying this categorization by reference to AI's ideological principles.

AD 3.4.4: Investigate tropes, i.e., cases of simile, metonymy, metaphor, irony, overstatement and understatement, rhetorical questions, (as well as cases of humor, politeness, and the like) (Verschueren 2012: 178–180).

In the following paragraphs, I discuss the occurrence of these tropes in the AI appeals in more or less the same order they are mentioned in AD 3.4.4.

My expectation was that I would find few if any instances of overstatement because of the danger that such statements would be taken literally and their falsity would undermine the credibility of the letters they occurred in and that of AI, which is jealous of its reputation as a careful and truthful researcher of the cases it acts on.

However, one might wonder whether the expressions of urgency and immediate necessity (emphasized) might not be tinged with overstatement:

> I am writing with an *urgent* request on behalf of Abdullah 'Azzam Saleh Musfer al-Qahtani and 'Safa Ahmad 'Abul'aziz 'Abdullah.
>
> (#4 Al-Qahtani, Iraq)

> I am writing to ask you to *immediately* and unconditionally release environmental activist Yevgeniy Vitishko.
>
> (#15 Vitishko, Russia)

Release Phyoe Phyoe Aung and all the detained peaceful student protesters *immediately* and unconditionally.

(#28 PoC, Myanmar)

Likewise, the characterization of the severity of the treatment of the subjects of appeals could be a locus for overstatement (emphasis added):

[Mustafa al-Hawsawi] is in *chronic extreme physical pain*, and has injuries sustained during torture and other ill-treatment he endured while in the custody of the Central Intelligence Agency (CIA) between 2003 and 2006.

(#39 Al-Hawsawi, USA)

[Flogging] is a *flagrant* violation of the prohibition on torture or other cruel, inhuman or degrading treatment under international law.

(#18 Badawi, Saudi Arabia)

It would be impossible to determine whether al-Hawsawi's pain is "extreme" or how "flagrant" Badawi's flogging was or just how urgent the urgent appeals are – *urgent* occurs five times in the corpus, though its relative *urge* occurs thirty-four times. Given AI's care in researching cases, I believe that these examples are not instances of overstatement, but of making the strongest rhetorical claim consistent with the facts.[11]

Nor did I expect to find instances of understatement. Though it may be a potent rhetorical device in some contexts, I did not expect to find instances in the appeals, as there seemed to be no rhetorical advantage to AI to understate its cases. Essential to the presentation of each case is its urgency and meiosis is likely to be taken literally and thus to undercut a letter's persuasiveness.

I looked for instances of simile by searching for instances of *like* and *as*. Though *like* occurred twice and *as* occurred seventy-two times in the corpus, none introduced a simile. The instances of *like* are used to narrow a general category by reference to members with defining characteristics:

Lawyers *like* Wang Yu, Zhou Shifeng, Sui Muqing and Li Heping should be able to do their work without being harassed, detained and criminally charged for protecting the rights of others.

(#25 Missing, China; emphasis added)

Wang Yu, Zhou Shifeng, Sui Muqing, and Li Heping are Chinese lawyers who have been "targeted" by the authorities for their human rights activities and are listed in the extract as defining a subcategory of lawyers needing to be protected from government harassment, detention, and charges.

As occurs in several more or less fixed expressions, most frequently in *as well as*, interpretable as *and*. It also occurs relatively frequently meaning *because*,

[11] "Extreme" and "flagrant" occupy positions on sets of scalar expressions. While they are high on those scales, it is not clear just how high, nor whether there are expressions that occupy higher positions on the scales. If there were, then those would be excluded by scalar implicatures. No such implicatures seem to be intended by these expressions.

for example, "as [her doctors] fear prosecution" (#6 Beatriz, El Salvador) and indicating simple comparisons, for example, "a jurisdiction as large as California" (#31 Death Penalty, California, USA), and categorizations, for example, "caning as a form of punishment" (#5 Caning, Indonesia).

My remarks about similes apply also to metaphors, and they are indeed as rare as hens' teeth in the corpus. However, we might regard "a … miscarriage of justice" (#4 Al-Qahtani, Iraq) as one, though it is probably a "dead" one; that is, it is a fixed phrase, an idiom interpreted directly rather than requiring the inferencing a "live" metaphor would require. "Assault" in "assault on freedom of expression" (#3 Satire as Crime, Egypt) seems just as moribund.

Relevance Theory provides an analysis of metaphor that might explain why they are rare in the texts. According to RT, metaphors are instances of "lexical broadening" and a type of "loose use" of language (Wilson 2017: 94–96). According to Carston (2012), "there is a loose use continuum, with literal use as the limiting case and metaphorical use as a case of radical loosening" (480). By choosing to speak literally, a language user's utterance has "the same propositional form as" her thought (Sperber and Wilson 1995: 233) and maximally constrains the hearer's interpretation. Loose uses allow the hearer greater freedom in the interpretation of the speaker's utterance. For example, in the context of a mathematical discussion of plane geometry, *square* would most likely be interpreted narrowly as denoting a plane figure with four equal sides subtending four right angles. In a less restrictive context, *square* might be taken to describe something that approximates the geometrical figure, as in *John has a square face*, and in the (old) metaphorical sense might be interpreted as old fashioned, out of touch, as in *John is so square he's never heard of Oasis*. As the letters' effectiveness depends upon their factuality, and as factuality is best represented literally – by imposing tight constraints on how the facts are represented and interpreted – it better serves the letters' purposes to eschew metaphor (and other loose uses such as hyperbole).

However, having said that, there are a couple of instances of apparently – and somewhat incongruously – playful uses of metaphor:

> We need a "bullet proof" arms trade treaty and we will need leadership of the United States to achieve that.
>
> (#2 Arms Trade, USA)

"Bullet proof" – in quotes in the original – occurs in a letter to President Obama in support of an arms control treaty. As the letter is about arms, "bullet proof" in this context is a pun, and possibly meant to be humorous, as it is clearly marked as an expression to be accorded special interpretive attention. As it seems impossible to interpret the expression literally in its context, the reader is accorded greater freedom of interpretation, presumably to the hope for an arms control treaty that would effectively "stop irresponsible and illegal arms transfers around the world." Arms control is a matter of continuing global legal and ideological discussion and dispute and an important AI goal.[12]

Double quote marks are used twenty-seven times in the letters, mainly to indicate that expressions are quoted from sources:

> End claims that the USA is authorized by international law to use lethal force anywhere in the world under the theory that it is involved in a "global war" against al-Qa'ida and other armed groups and individuals.
>
> (#1 Targeted Killings, USA)

The US has claimed that it is engaged in a global war on terrorism and that this licenses it to use drones and other such means in prosecuting that war.[13] Other examples include expressions apparently quoted from local statutes or other legal documents:

> When blogger Ahmed Anwar posted a video of belly-dancing policemen on-line, he expected to get some laughs. Instead, he's on trial for "criticizing" the Interior Ministry and "misusing" the Internet ... Some have been charged with "insulting the President."
>
> (#3 Satire as Crime, Egypt)

> Shaker Aamer's designation by US authorities as "approved for transfer" implies that US authorities have no intention of charging him with criminal offenses.
>
> (#7 Aamer, USA)

> Introduction of hefty fines for on those accused of promoting "propaganda of homosexuality among minors."
>
> (#14 Restrictive Legislation, Russia)

While the expressions in quotes above appear to be directly quoted from various sources, it is hard to avoid the impression that the particular expressions highlighted were not also chosen for their ironic potential. Irony, according to RT, is an echoic use of language (Sperber and Wilson 1995: 237–243): it deploys an expression that is attributable to someone with the implication of a critical attitude toward what the expression represents. From the perspective of AI's ideological commitment to freedom of expression, quote-marking the expressions in the letters implies that criminalizing criticism of an interior (or any) minister, insulting a president, or using the internet is of dubious validity, as is the US claim to be involved in a global war on terrorism. More clearly ironic is the expression "confession," indicating that the confession was of dubious legality as it "was obtained through torture and other ill-treatment" (#4 Al-Qahtani, Iraq), which are prohibited by international law.

In addition to indicating direct quotation and irony, double quotes are also used for nicknames, for example, "Angola 3," "Buddy" (#2 Woodfox,

[12] www.amnesty.org/en/what-we-do/arms-control/ (accessed August 9, 2025).
[13] https://2001-2009.state.gov/s/ct/rls/wh/6947.htm (accessed August 9, 2025).

Louisiana, USA), and proper names, for example, "Environment Watch for North Caucasus" (#15 Vitishko, Russia); "Senate torture report" (#19 Torture Report, USA); "This is what we die for"[14] (#40 Cobalt, Apple Corporation).

Verschueren (2012) only very briefly touches on the issue of (im)politeness in his texts, saying merely that "[t]he closest we come in written academic discourse to strategies for avoiding face threats or for supporting positive face is in the flattering ways in which the earlier acts of compatriots are described and the mitigating phrasing for possible points of criticism and blame" (180).[15] AI's Letter Writing Guide advises letter writers to "always be polite," and suggests how this is to be interpreted:

4. Be polite – Using offensive language is not effective. Assume the official is not informed but is willing to seek a remedy to the human rights violation.
5. Show respect – You will most likely keep the reader's attention by showing respect for his/her country's constitution and judicial procedures. If there have been positive developments in the country, these can be briefly recognized and welcomed (e.g. releases, an announcement of an official investigation into allegations of torture, etc.).[16]

The following letter (#11 Pussy Riot, Russia) illustrates the occurrence of (im)politeness in the letters.

Message Recipients: Yuri Yakovlevich Chaika – Prosecutor General

Subject: Free Nadezhda Tolokonnikova and Maria Alekhina

Dear Prosecutor General,

I am writing to express my deep concern about Nadezhda Tolokonnikova and Maria Alekhina, who were sentenced to two years in a penal colony for their participation in a February 2012 protest action by the feminist punk-rock group Pussy Riot at the Christ the Savior Cathedral in Moscow. These two women, both mothers in their twenties, were detained solely for their peaceful expression of their beliefs. They are Prisoners of Conscience.

I call on you to ensure that Maria Alekhina and Nadezhda Tolokonnikova are immediately and unconditionally released. While they remain incarcerated, the two women must not be ill-treated by prison staff or inmates, and they must be allowed regular contact with their families and legal teams.

In closing, I welcome the news of Ekaterina Samutsevich's freedom but remain concerned about the conditional status of the release. The three Pussy Riot members should not have been prosecuted in the first place. I call on you and all authorities to respect

[14] www.amnesty.org/en/documents/afr62/3183/2016/en/ (accessed August 9, 2025).
[15] The following discussion of (im)politeness in the appeals is derived from Delahunty (2013).
[16] https://tinyurl.com/3rhf55zd (accessed August 9, 2025).

and uphold the right to freedom of expression in the Russian Federation, and to remedy the unjust treatment of these young women immediately.

I thank you for your attention.

Yours sincerely,

I assume here the standard theory of politeness (Brown and Levinson 1987), though I recognize the burgeoning research on (im)politeness (Culpeper et al. 2017). I assume that there are two aspects to face – positive and negative. Positive face has to do with an individual's desire to be treated as they wish; negative face is the individual's desire not to be burdened. I assume utterers orient to their own and others' face wants and that all utterances index politeness choices. As I will show, AI letters orient to both writer's and addressee's positive and negative face.

The AI letters present the problems they refer to as ones that the addressee can solve and thus at least imply that the addressee and/or the government or other power group to which he/she belongs and/or represents is responsible for the problems and their solutions. To impute a problem to someone is an accusation and thus a threat to the addressee's positive face (Brown and Levinson 1987: 71).[17] It is also a potential threat to the accuser's positive face because they could be wrong about the details of the accusation or about the responsibility of the accused for the problem (Brown and Levinson 1987: 73). Gricean, neo-Gricean, and post-Gricean pragmaticists claim that assertors are responsible not only for the truth of the propositions expressed, but also for any inferences that must be derived in the interpretation of the utterance. Speakers must orient to these face threats and have the options of doing the face threatening act (FTA) with some redress, doing it bald-on-record (i.e., without any attempt to redress the FTA), or opting out and not doing the FTA. Clearly opting out is not an option for AI appeals.

Because making an assertion, and especially an accusation, may pose a threat to the asserter's positive face, assertions are frequently mitigated, particularly in conversation. Because imputing responsibility for human rights abuses threatens the addressee's positive face, it is inherently impolite. And because addressing a directive is a threat to the addressee's negative face (Brown and Levinson 1987), letter writers orient to these face threats while simultaneously indexing their rights to make these appeals, primarily by tacitly assuming the right without overtly orienting to it. (See Curl and Drew 2008 on callers' orientations to their rights to phone police and medical services.) As the letters never overtly claim a right to address their recipients, the right is implied to be uncontroversial and thus to be taken for granted. The Message Recipients or their surrogates may, of course, challenge that assumption, as the responses by

[17] I thank my late friend and colleague Inga Vassilieva for helpful discussion on this point.

Russian consular officials to AI USA's attempt to get them to accept petitions on behalf of the Pussy Riot members demonstrates, as described in Chapter 4.

The letters characteristically include mitigators of the statement of the problem, for which Caffi (1999, 2007, 2013) provides a useful typology. She distinguishes three mitigator types: *hedges* are expressions which operate on illocutionary force, for example, by indirection; *bushes* are expressions which operate on locutionary force, for example, by vagueness; and *shields* are expressions which operate on "the I-here-now of the utterance," that is, on the utterance's deictic origin (Caffi 2013: 272), for example, by omitting reference to the agents. This categorization provides us with a framework for characterizing the strategies adopted in the first paragraph.

In the Pussy Riot appeal, the problem is introduced via an expressive speech act, specifically by the writer's expression of feelings of concern for the two women. Characterizing a situation as an object of the writer's concern is less direct and therefore less threatening to the addressee than, for example, an accusation (recall Emile Zola's famous *J'accuse*). In Caffi's terms, it functions as a hedge.

The remainder of the first paragraph of the letter is an assertion embedded in the expressive. This assertion begins with a relative clause in the passive voice with no agent phrase, and thus with no direct indication of responsibility for the situation. This is followed by another truncated passive, which is followed by a simple, stative subject-complement clause, again with no attribution of responsibility. The vagueness of the impersonal, agentless passives and of the stative sentence serves to avoid any direct accusation that the Message Recipient is personally responsible for the problem. It is left to the reader to infer who is responsible for detaining and sentencing the members of Pussy Riot, thus mitigating the accusation using combinations of bushes and shields.

Two items that might strike us as mitigators in the paragraph are the remarks that the women are mothers in their twenties, that is, young people, who might be accorded leniency for youthful misjudgments, and young mothers, whose children are presumably also young and therefore most in need of their mothers' care. These do not fit neatly into Caffi's categories and are perhaps best seen as rhetorical appeals to pathos.[18] Recall my discussion in Chapter 5 of the ideologization of motherhood.

Additionally, by avoiding any claim that the addressee is personally responsible for the problem, the writer also avoids threats to their own positive face – if they haven't accused the addressee of wrong-doing, they can rebut any claim that they have falsely accused that addressee.

[18] Inga Vassilieva, (p.c.) suggested that the remark – "mothers in their twenties" – is not a typical mitigator because it is not a grammatical item, as mitigators characteristically are, but functions as an index of contextual assumptions that function as mitigating/attenuating factors in similar contexts (e.g., when someone faces a legal prosecution, as the Pussy Riot members did).

After the writer's expression of concern, the remainder of the first paragraph is for the most part a bald-on-record statement of fact, which commits the writer to its truth. The actual SENDers of the letters may feel a bit queasy about this and so are invited by AI in the embedding email to review AI's research on the problem. From a Gricean point of view, the SENDer has thus fulfilled both parts of the maxim of Quality; from a speech act point of view, the sender has fulfilled one of the preparatory conditions for making assertions – they have "evidence (reasons, etc.) for the truth of" their assertion (Searle 1969: 66).[19]

The solution to the problem is expressed differently. It is expressed as an explicit directive, *I call on you to* ... Note the form of this expression – it is a simple present tense active clause with a first-person subject and allows the insertion of the reflexive adverb *hereby*, the characteristics explicitly identified by Austin (1962) and many others as important heuristics for identifying explicit performatives. Note also the infinitival form of the complement, which proposes future actions by the addressee, a defining characteristic of directives.

Because directives "are attempts by the speaker to get the addressee to do something" (Levinson 1983: 240), they are threats to the addressee's negative face. In general, speakers may choose not to do the FTA, they may go bald-on-record, or they may redress to some degree the FTA.

There is evidence that the directive is mitigated. *Call on* is a relatively moderate performative verb. The *Cambridge Dictionary* online defines it as "to ask someone in a formal way to do something." In the email to AI members asking them to send appeals, the corresponding verb is the deontically stronger *demand*. In other letters, the performative verb is *ask*, the most neutral directive verb, or *urge*, whose relevant meanings are given in the *American Heritage Dictionary* (5th ed.: 1906) as "2. To entreat earnestly and often repeatedly; exhort. 3. To advocate earnestly the doing, consideration, or approval of; to press for." The speech acts of *asking*, *calling on*, *urging*, and *demanding* share felicity conditions because they are all directive, but they also differ in their strength, which Thaler (2012) theorizes as differences in their felicity conditions.

Other politeness indicators suggest a balder approach. The addressee is called upon to "ensure," a clear indicator of their power and responsibility; the women are to be released "immediately and unconditionally"; they "must" not be ill-treated, and they "must" be allowed regular contact; and the passive voice is no longer truncated and impersonal, the agents are specified – the "prison staff or inmates," over whom the Prosecutor General presumably has control.

[19] Searle's other preparatory condition for assertions, "it is not obvious to both *S* and *H* that *H* knows (does not need to be reminded of, etc.)," is not oriented to, though the expression of concern with which the letter begins presupposes its complement, thus indicating that the letter's SENDer assumes that the Message Recipient is aware of the basis for the writer's concern.

The final paragraph of the Pussy Riot appeal is also a melding of polite redressive and bald-on-record language. On the one hand, the writer "welcomes" the news of the release of one member of Pussy Riot, but does not attribute that release to the addressee. On the other hand, they remain concerned about the conditions of the release. The problem remains – the women "should" – the strongest modal possible in the context – not have been prosecuted. Again, the writer "calls on" – a muted directive – the addressee and "all authorities to respect and uphold the right of freedom of expression," implicating that the addressee and the Russian authorities have not been doing this and baldly characterizing the treatment of the Pussy Riot members as "unjust."

Searle (1979: 15) classifies *welcoming* as an expressive speech act that represents a speaker's psychological state. Searle and Vanderveken (1985: 216) say that "To welcome somebody is to receive him hospitably, and thus welcoming might be defined as an expression of pleasure or good feeling about the presence or arrival of someone. Welcoming, like greeting, is essentially hearer oriented." In the context of the Pussy Riot appeal, "welcome" expresses the writer's pleasure or good feeling about a situation, specifically "the news of Ekaterina Samutsevich's freedom," which is presented as presupposed. However, this welcome news is tempered by the writer's continuing concern about the conditional status of her release and presumably the continuing lack of "respect [for] the right to freedom of expression in the Russian Federation, and [the need] to remedy the unjust treatment of these young women immediately."

Approaching the appeals from a speech act perspective raises the issue of intentionality – utterances of speech acts are assumed to be intentional. However, if the words are not those of the appeal SENDers, who merely forward them on behalf of AI, then to whom can we attribute the intentionality of the speech acts embodied in the appeals? The SENDer is in the position of quoter of another's words or as a spokesperson for an organization. As far as I know, speech act theoreticians have not grappled with such issues, though relevance theorists have, under the rubric of echoic utterances.[20] The echoic utterer can have a range of possible attitudes to the uttered words, ranging from full endorsement to outright rejection. In the current case, we must assume endorsement if the volunteer opts to SEND the message and gives no indication of a different stance. Nonetheless, Message Recipients, if they consider the matter at all, may infer a lower level of endorsement on the basis that the SENDer has not gone to the trouble to write his/her own letter, and dismiss it as mere "clicktivism" or "slacktivism," as I noted earlier.

Procedure 3.5: Investigate interactional aspects (Verschueren 2012: 181–183).

[20] As have interactional sociologists, e.g., Goffman (1974; 1981) and pragmaticists, e.g., Levinson (1988), as discussed earlier.

The issue of whether the letters are interactional or not is problematic in ways similar to those in which the referents of *I* and *you* in the letters are; that is, while the letters are written as if they were intended to initiate a dialog between the writers and the addressees, it is unclear whether any of the letters are actually sent to the named Message Recipients, as opposed to simply counted toward AI's target number of electronic SENDs. So, any remarks about interactional aspects of the letters in response to Verschueren's ADs to Procedure 3.5 should be read with this context in mind.

AD 3.5.1: In the case of overtly interactional data (e.g., conversations, correspondence), investigate the sequential organization and patterns of mutual engagement (Verschueren 2012: 181–182).

As "correspondence," the appeals are "overtly" interactional. Many begin with the salutation "Dear ...," for example, "Dear President Putin," (#14 Restrictive Legislation, Russia), and in many the addressee's name appears to be added automatically. The first-person pronoun *I* occurs in all except one of the letters, but that exception uses "we," with AI as its referent. Forms of the second-person pronoun occur in all but three letters, though thirty-two have explicit imperative Subject lines, and thus have an understood second-person subject. In three letters, we find expressions inviting the addressee(s) to respond to the writers, for example, "I look forward to hearing from you regarding this matter" (#17 Caning, Indonesia). Every letter includes a directive in one form or another, for example, as explicit performatives, *I ask/call on/urge you to ...*, as imperatives, *Please ensure ...*, as strong deontic modals, *The US government must ...*, and as deontic adjectives, *It is essential that ...*

Nine of the letters include an expression of gratitude to the reader, typically for their attention to the subject of the letter: *(I) thank you for your (time and) consideration/attention (to this (important) matter).*

Politeness is an interactional factor, but as I discussed it at some length above, I say no more about it here, other than to point out that in concert with the AI Letter Writing Guide, the letters are unfailingly polite, even when their subjects are egregious violations of individuals' rights – *please* occurs fifteen times.

My move and step analysis (see Chapter 4) describes the typical "sequential organization" of the letters and need not be repeated here.

AD 3.5.2: In the case of covertly interactional data (anything that looks like it is purely "monologic"), look for aspects of dialogic organization, i.e., implicit patterns of interaction (Verschueren 2012: 182–183).

In this brief section, Verschueren identifies three "implicit patterns of interaction" and four sub-patterns of the third: "phenomena directly analogous to dialogic units" such as "interest-arousing openings" and "unmistakable closings"; "parallels to repair strategies"; and "interactional profiles" that include "the use of footnotes," unidentified sources of "opinions/views," contradictory voices, and voices "simply invoked."

Unlike Verschueren's history textbooks, the letters are overtly dialogic, so this AD might seem irrelevant to them. Nonetheless, we do find instances of Verschueren's categories of covert interaction.

As an example of an "interest arousing" opening, Verschueren (2012) provides the following piece of hyperbole (182):

> In May 1857 the great Indian Mutiny shook to its foundations the whole fabric of British rule in Hindostan.
>
> (McCarthy 1908: 170)

And its equally hyperbolic "unmistakable closing":

> On December 20, 1858, Lord Clyde, who had been Sir Colin Campbell, announced to the Governor-General that the rebellion was at an end, and on May 1, 1859, there was a public thanksgiving in England for the pacification of India.
>
> (McCarthy 1908: 193)

Given the exigent nature of the situations represented in the appeals, we should expect to find at least some openings that make aspects of the exigency particularly salient, even shocking. For example:

> **Subject**: Stop the horrific public flogging of blogger, Raif Badawi
>
> I am profoundly disturbed that Saudi blogger Raif Badawi was publicly flogged in front of al-Jafali mosque after Friday prayers.
>
> (#18 Badawi, Saudi Arabia)

And this letter's closing is typical of the genre:

> I call on you to stop arresting, charging, prosecuting and sentencing activists for simply exercising their rights to freedom of expression, association and assembly.

The following is especially "interest arousing":

> **Subject**: Stop the killing of people with Albinism
>
> I am writing with deep concern over the fate of David Fletcher, a 15-year-old boy with albinism who was found dead with his hands and feet cut off after having been abducted.
>
> It is profoundly troubling that thousands of people with albinism in your country live in fear of being abducted or killed, and that their body parts are being sold for use in rituals.
>
> (#38 Albinism, Malawi)

"Repair" is a construct from conversation analysis and refers to online attention to possible troubles in the interaction. Edited texts, especially written ones, are typically assumed to have had "repairables" corrected before publication, and indeed, while we find uncorrected errors in the letters, for example, the occasional misspellings of Barack Obama's first name, we find no repairs akin to those discussed in the conversation analysis research (see Kitzinger 2013).

We might, though, consider instances of *however* and *but* as introducing a repair to an immediately preceding repairable. *However* is used to introduce the rebuttal to a concession in several letters. From a conversation analysis point of view, we might regard the concession/rebuttal steps as an adjacency pair, a sequence of discourse actions such that the first makes the second expectable, similar to a question/answer sequence. Unlike a typical question/answer sequence, where the concession and rebuttal in the letters are produced by the same individual, the concession is presented as a claim that might be made by a Message Recipient, while the rebuttal is made by the appeal writer.[21] The dialogicality implicit in the concession/rebuttal pattern is consistent with the actual dialogicality invited by sign-offs such as "I look forward to hearing from you regarding this matter" (#17 Caning, Indonesia), with the concession/rebuttal pattern suggesting a template for how that actual dialog might proceed.

More generally, because the letters identify rights violations and specify how they are to be redressed, they belong to the problem/solution genres of discourse, and as such represent a repairable and a strategy for its repair. We might view the two occurrences of "failing"[22] in the following extracts as indicating just such a repairable.

> [An AI report] found that major electronics brands, including Apple, Samsung and Sony, are *failing* to do basic checks to ensure that cobalt mined by child labourers has not been used in their products …
>
> Amnesty International concludes that the big brands are *failing* to adequately investigate their supply chains for human rights abuses as required by international standards.
> (#40 Cobalt, Apple Corp.; emphasis added)

The letter sets out AI's criteria for repairs to these failures by Apple and other corporations:

> Amnesty International is calling on companies to investigate their cobalt supply chain and prove they are addressing human rights abuses …

Interestingly, the letter does not specify who the proof should be addressed to. AI is an obvious addressee as it is calling for the investigation. The companies named in the appeal must be other potential addressees (and perhaps still others identified by AI, but not mentioned) as these documents are to be internally generated as the appeal letter calls on the corporations to investigate their own

[21] Rhetorical questions and their answers are typically produced by the same speaker; they are self-initiated, self-repairs in conversation (Schegloff 2018: 352).

[22] "Fail" and its morphological relatives occur thirteen times in the corpus, typically describing governments' and other institutions' disregard for human rights.

cobalt supply chains. But the letter also mentions "my smartphone," and identifies the referent of "my" as "a customer of Apple." The referent of first-person pronouns in the letters is always problematic, and particularly so in this letter as "I," (GD) its SENDer, do(es) not own a smartphone, nor any other Apple, Samsung, or Sony products. Did AI members and volunteers who sent this letter lie to its Message Recipients, the Apple Supplier Responsibility Team, if they did not own Apple smartphones? Or did some AI volunteers and members opt not to SEND the appeal because they do not own one or other of these products? This letter is the only one in the corpus that characterizes its potential SENDers in such detail and represents a considerable degree of personalization of the appeal and consequent ideological commitment. The AI volunteers who do not own Apple, Samsung, or Sony products but who sent the letter anyway are misrepresenting one basis of their appeal: the inference that they do own one of these products, while the letter characterizes them as concerned that the manufacture of the product that the letter implies that they own does entail illegal cobalt mining.

This potential misrepresentation raises the question of whether there are other such potential misrepresentations in the appeals. Two are inherent in the design of the appeals. First is the representation of the appeal situation and its characterizations as a rights violation: the appeal SENDers are very unlikely to have any personal knowledge of the situations they purport to know by SENDing the letters. Second, because their knowledge of the situations represented in the letters is at best second hand, the expression of the SENDer's concern in each letter may be suspect. How are we to understand such possible misrepresentations? If we consider the context of the appeal – the email in which it is embedded addressed to an AI member – then we can solve this problem: we must assume that AI assumes that the email addressee will read the email first and thus become familiar with the appeal situation, thereby licensing the mere clicking of SEND without reading the appeal because it simply re-contextualizes and re-genrecizes the information in the email (and associated webpage).

We must also assume that the SENDers at least appear to trust AI's epistemic authority. More importantly, we must assume that the SENDers at least appear to trust AI's moral and ideological authority and that they accord AI the right to speak for them on the matters typical of the letters. If we accept this analysis as true of at least some of the AI letter SENDers, then we are led to the conclusion that sincere belief is not essential for commitment to an ideology and its activities. Acquiescence and action are all that are required, even where no coercion is involved. Merely clicking SEND is a ritual of identification. As Blaise Pascal is claimed to have said: "Kneel down, move your lips in prayer, and you will believe" (Althusser 2014: 186).[23]

[23] Maugham (2003 [1944]) poses a variant: "Our wise old Church," he said then, "has discovered that if you will act as if you believed belief will be granted to you; if you pray with doubt, but with sincerity, your doubt will be dispelled …" (253).

Verschueren provides four examples of "*interaction profiles*." The first of these is the use of footnotes to engage alternative voices while indicating their sources. Though the AI reports incorporate footnotes for this and other purposes, the webpages, emails, and appeals do not, though they can accommodate such voices in other ways. For example, the letters indicate such other voices by quoting them directly:

> On January 19, Amnesty International launched the report "This is what we die for: Human Rights Abuses in the Democratic Republic of the Congo (DRC) Power the Global Trade in Cobalt."
>
> (#40 Cobalt, Apple Corp.)

Other direct quotes, as I claimed earlier in this chapter, are at least tinged with irony, for example:

> Disclose further legal and factual details about U.S. policy and practices for so-called "targeted killings," "signature strikes," and "Terrorist Attack Disruption Strikes," including any secret Department of Justice legal memorandums, and specific information about who has been killed.
>
> (#10 Drone Wars, USA)

Verschueren's second interactional profile device also engages alternative voices whose source is unidentified, for example, "It is estimated that there are tens of thousands of children being used as soldiers in 19 countries" (#2 Arms Trade, USA). The impersonal construction allows the omission of the agent of "estimated." Whether to regard this omission as misleading or not depends on one's assumptions about AI's veracity.

Outside voices may be "simply invoked," and explicitly or implicitly contradicted, for example, by enclosing expressions in double quotes, as discussed above, or by indicating their semiotic modality, as "images" does in "I have been shocked by images showing police actions against demonstrators in Istanbul and other Turkish cities" (#9 Police Action, Turkey). This letter provides no indication of the source or reliability of these images. As Verschueren notes, such examples of covert interaction "take us back to the discussion of evidentiality" in AD 3.3.4.

Procedure 3.6: Investigate metapragmatic functioning (Verschueren 2012: 183–186).

By "metapragmatic functioning," Verschueren (2012) means "reflexive awareness of what one is doing when using language" (183), which may be influenced by language ideologies (Verschueren 1999: 197–198, 2000: 450–452) and identity construction (Verschueren 1999: 239; 2000: 452–453).

Languages provide us with the symbolic wherewithal to talk about language, and language and pragmatics provide us with the wherewithal to talk about discourse. It follows that our reflexive awareness of what we are doing when we engage in making the linguistic choices that constitute language use may be manifested explicitly or implicitly (see also Verschueren 1999: 187–198).

Verschueren (2012: 185) says that "[m]any of the formal features that have already passed the review rely for their proper interpretation on metapragmatic awareness and thus serve as indicators of such awareness." He then lists eight classes of these formal features along with the sections in which they are discussed (emphasis in original):[24]

- The *positioning of utterer and interpreter* (for instance, by means of certain types of person deixis, as discussed in [2.2.1.1], the appeal to voices [2.2.1.2] and interpreter roles [2.2.1.3], as well as placement in relation to institutional settings [2.3.3], time and space [2.2.4]).
- The use of supporting *graphic features* [2.2.5].
- Properties of the *linguistic context* (including choice of *channels* [2.3.1], the establishment of *intertextual links* [2.3.2, including *quotation and reported speech*] and contextual *cohesion* [2.3.4]).
- The definition of the *activity type* ([3.1, including a treatment of *hedges*], but also the general comments under [3.6] above).
- The choice of *languages, codes, and styles* [3.2].
- Choices related to *carriers of information structure* [3.3., including quite centrally patterns of word choice and the categorizations they imply, modality and evidentiality, foregrounding and backgrounding, and the establishment of coherence].
- All *carriers of implicit meaning* [3.4], as choices at that level depend crucially on an assessment of what an interpreter can be assumed to already know.
- All *interactional features* [3.5], as they require awareness of meanings or discourse one interacts with, and hence awareness of what one is doing communicatively (Verschueren 2012: 185).

I leave to my readers the task of revisiting my discussion of the sections listed above and turn to expression types that indicate explicit and implicit metapragmatic awareness identified in Verschueren (2000: 447, Table 2).

Explicit Metapragmatic Indicators

Metapragmatic descriptions (e.g., by means of metapragmatic lexical items such as speech act or performative expressions): Speech act verbs found in the letters include *ask*, *call on*, and *urge*. Related nominals include *request* and *ask*.

Self-referential expressions: All the letters are written in the first person, and this pervasive use of the first person (singular) must reflect AI's assumption that first-person appeals are more effective, perhaps because the occurrence of *I* implies the co-occurrence of *you*, and their deictic complementarity

[24] The numbers in parentheses refer to Verschueren's guidelines and procedures.

signals an apparent desire to personally engage the addressees in consideration of the merits of the case being appealed. This attempt at engagement is made explicit in several letters which include expressions of the writer's hope that the addressee will respond. (See also my comments below on the AI Letter Writing Guide's advice to "Consider using a personal, friendly comment in your letter" and my earlier remarks on the problems associated with identifying the referent of the *I* of the letters.) The use of *I* also invites the AI volunteer to identify with the *I*s of the letters, thus serving to engage the volunteers in AI's ideological work.

Quoted and reported speech: We find quotations of legal(istic) language, typically from unidentified sources, for example, "approved for transfer" (#7 Aamer, USA), "targeted killings" (#1 Targeted Killings, USA), "treason" (#14 Restrictive Legislation, Russia), "propaganda of homosexuality among minors" (#14 Restrictive Legislation, Russia), "Senate Torture Report" (#19 Torture Report, USA), "indecent dress" (#24 Indecent Dress, Sudan), and "rule of law" (#25 Missing, China).

"Mention" (vs. "use"): Though the use/mention distinction is deeply problematic (Cappelen et al. 2023), these problems need not detain us as the traditional definitions are sufficient for our purposes. To mention an expression is to quote it with the purpose of saying something about it, for example, "*mention* is a difficult word to define." The vast majority of the expressions in the appeals are merely used. However, there are, as I've mentioned, a non-trivial number of quoted expressions which appear to be intended to be interpreted as ironical, that is, "echoic use of language (i.e., a mention GD) in which the speaker tacitly dissociates herself from an attributed utterance or thought" (Wilson 2006: 1722). Examples include "global war" (#1 Targeted Killings, USA) and "'misusing' the Internet" (#3 Satire as Crime, Egypt). Identifying these items as ironic invites a critical evaluation of their use in their source contexts, for example, the calling into question of the legitimacy of the US claim to be involved in a "global war," which would – purportedly – legalize its targeted killings program. I discussed above the ironic character of a number of these marked expressions.

Discourse markers/particles or pragmatic markers/particles: *Simply*, *just*: "I call on you to stop arresting, charging, prosecuting and sentencing activists for *simply* exercising their rights to freedom of expression, association and assembly" (#18 Badawi, Saudi Arabia; emphasis added) and "Ahmed Anwar isn't alone. He's *just* one of the many targeted in a new crackdown on freedom of expression" (#3 Satire as Crime, Egypt; emphasis added). We might gloss *simply* as "no more than" with the implication that at least that minimal activity – exercising rights to freedom of expression – should be legal. *Just* is also a minimizer and may be glossed in the instance above as "only," and in modifying "one" contrasts it with and thus emphasizes "many." The construction, "just one of many," allows the letter writers to present the plight of one individual as an exemplar of a much broader, systemic problem affecting classes of people rather than individuals.

Sentence adverbs: *Unfortunately*, *shockingly*, *respectfully*, *particularly*. The first two represent the appeals SENDer's emotional reaction to aspects of the appeal situation. *Respectfully* is a conventional characterization of the relationship between a letter writer and addressee and attends to the AI Letter Writing Guide's directive to use respectful language. *Particularly* identifies an especially noteworthy member of a class of individuals, situations, or events: "I am deeply concerned about the widespread practice of early and forced marriage in Burkina Faso, and *particularly* the Sahel region" (#30 Forced Marriages, Burkina Faso; emphasis added). *Particularly* allows the appeal writers to highlight a specific instance of a more general situation, akin to the member-to-set relationship indexed by *just*.

The primary evidential used in the letters is the indicative mood. However, indicative sentences are frequently hedged by various devices, including adverbs: *presumably*, *reportedly*, *publicly*, *undoubtedly*, *images*, *documented reports*, *likely*, *nearly*, *essentially*.[25] And modals, for example, "There are also serious concerns that the men *might* not have received a fair trial" (#4 Al-Qahtani, Iraq; emphasis added). Complementary to hedges we find boosters, which enhance the utterer's commitment to a proposition: *solely*, *extremely*, *absolutely*, *strictly*, *fully*. We also find explicit intertextual links, for example, direct references to constitutions and laws, as well as to legal rulings and findings: the International Violence Against Women Act; Article 152 of the 1991 Criminal Act; Article 33 of Sudan's 2005 Interim Constitution; Article 5 of the African Charter on Human and Peoples' Rights; and Article 7 of the International Covenant on Civil and Political Rights (ICCPR).

Many of the items discussed just above can be regarded as contextualization cues: *criminal* occurs fifteen times in the corpus and cues legal frames of interpretation, for example, "criminal prosecution" (#8 Beatriz, El Salvador). *Rights* cues human and humanitarian rights frames, as well as the legal systems in which they are articulated. Legal frames are also invoked by reference to *justice, investigation, charges, trial*, and the like.

Implicit Metapragmatic Indicators

Most "shifters" (Jakobson 1971), deictic expressions (pronouns, tense, etc.), aspect, mood and modality, and (some) evidentials indicate metapragmatic

[25] The following notable use of *essentially* was reported in *The Guardian* (online), August 10, 2016: "Hillary wants to abolish, essentially abolish, the second amendment," said Trump, eliciting boos from the crowd. "Essentially abolish" may be downtoned from the just prior "abolish," presumably as a repair of the more egregious misrepresentation. On the other hand, "essentially" may, given the speaker's penchant for embellishment, be a booster.

usage. The primary deictic pronominals are *I*, *we*, and *you*, referring, problematically, to the individual appeal SENDers, AI, and the Message Recipients. The subjects of the appeals are referred to by their names and then by appropriate anaphoric pronouns.

The primary tense of the letters is the present. The simple present is used to express the writer's feelings about the appeal situation, for example, "I am deeply concerned about …" (e.g., #30 Forced Marriages, Burkina Faso); to describe the writer's current epistemic state, for example, "I know that …" (#4 Al-Qahtani, Iraq); to describe the current, exigent, state of the appeal subject(s), for example, "Right now, both men are at imminent risk of execution" (#4 Al-Qahtani, Iraq); to articulate various rights, for example, "The US government is obligated under international law to respect, protect and fulfill human rights" (#7 Aamer, USA); and, most importantly, in uttering performatives, for example, "I urge you …"

The present progressive is used to begin many letters, typically in the utterance of a performative, for example, "I am calling upon your government to …" (#26 PoCs, Vietnam). It is generally assumed that explicit performatives must be in the simple present tense; however, I believe that the three instances of "I am calling on X to Y" in the letters are explicit performatives, despite occurring in the present progressive. As evidence, consider that one important purpose of the letters is to persuade the addressees to act in certain ways, and that these three instances occur in the letters in precisely the position where explicit performatives in the canonical simple present occur and could be replaced by "I call on X to Y" without change in function. Additionally, these sentences in the present progressive pass the "hereby" test; compare "I hereby call on you to …" with "I am hereby calling on you to …"

The present progressive is also used to introduce an explicit metalinguistic expression, for example, "I am writing to …," a usage that deserves comment. If "I" is assumed to be the SENDer, then the statement is a lie: the SENDer is not writing and did not write the appeal. The simple present, *I write to …* is a possible alternative, though still perhaps mendacious. However, the choice of the present progressive has several benefits. It represents "a dynamic situation," which must be "temporally coextensive with the utterance." The simple present of dynamic verbs is typically interpreted as denoting a series of events (Huddleston and Pullum 2002: 128). For example, *I (frequently) write letters to powerful politicians*. This serial interpretation is not consistent with the textual context, a problem eliminated by the use of the progressive.

The simple present also seems out of place stylistically. It seems to represent AI volunteers as less actively engaged in the interaction than the progressive, which seems to represent the *I* as more deliberately agentive in making the appeal. The progressive represents the volunteers as personally active in contributing to the discourse and more committed to the appeal's representation of the violative situation and its redress, and thus representing themselves as actively engaged in AI's endeavors, thus fulfilling one of goals of the appeal – to integrate the SENDers into AI's activities. Recall that ideological discourse is action-orienting.

The present perfect is used to characterize a current situation as resulting from prior actions, for example, "the director, financial director and other staff members of this law firm have also been detained" (#25 Missing, China). It is also used to describe prior events that are relevant to the letters' current concerns, for example, "Scores of Egyptians have faced interrogation for criticizing the authorities" (#3 Satire as Crime, Egypt).

The simple past tense is used to describe events that led to the exigencies of the appeal situation, which is represented in the present tense, for example, "When blogger Ahmed Anwar posted a video of belly-dancing policemen online, he expected to get some laughs. Instead, he's on trial for 'criticizing' the Interior Ministry and 'misusing' the Internet" (#3 Satire as Crime, Egypt).

The strong deontic modals *must* and *should* are used in indirect directives, for example, "The US government must …" (followed by a list of items) (#1 Targeted Killings, USA); and "In Shaker Aamer's case, he should be released to the UK" (#7 Aamer, USA). The quasi-modal verb *need* is also used deontically, for example, "Moreover, there needs to be a prompt, independent and impartial investigation" (#9 Police Action, Turkey).

The indicative mood, which implicates the (writer's commitment to the) truth of the proposition the sentence represents, is shown in, for example, "Shaker Aamer was arrested by Afghan forces in late 2001 in Jalalabad, Afghanistan and subsequently transferred to US custody. Aamer is originally from Saudi Arabia, and his wife and four children are all British nationals and currently live in London" (#7 Aamer, USA).

Voices, as discussed in Chapter 4, may be explicitly or implicitly represented. Verschueren proposes "voice"

> as a cover term to distinguish different sources of the content of an utterance: the utterer may or may not be the source him- or herself; sources may be real or imagined; sources may be specified or remain vague; and so forth. To indicate the diversity of voices that may be involved in an utterance, the term "polyphony" is used.
>
> (Verschueren 2012: 89, fn. 30)

Of his history textbooks, Verschueren (2012: 89) says,

> [t]he discrepancy between the manifest reality of non-personally witnessed events and their manifold subsequent entextualizations on the one hand, and the discursively produced impression of mere factuality and immediate accessibility on the other, hiding modulations and calibrations introduced by intervening voices, results in a close connection between the investigated texts and a world view in which the author's (and the targeted readers') own temporal, geographical, and social deictic center abundantly prevails, thus making these materials eminently suitable for ideology research.

Like the history books authors, the writers and SENDers of the AI letters typically have not witnessed the events and situations they describe and so are dependent upon "intervening voices," whose "modulations and calibrations" are typically hidden, while "discursively" producing an "impression of mere factuality and immediate accessibility," thus creating "a world view in which the author's (and the targeted readers') own temporal, geographical, and social deictic center abundantly prevails," which makes the appeal letters "materials eminently suitable for ideology research."

The impression of factuality is typically created by sentences in the indicative mood and present tense:

> As I write you, 71-year-old Herman Wallace is being held in isolation in the infirmary in Hunt Correctional Center. After spending more than four decades held in cruel and unusual solitary confinement, he has been diagnosed with terminal liver cancer.
>
> (#12 Wallace, Louisiana, USA)

These two sentences, like a great many others in the letters, present the propositions they represent as facts, though nowhere in this letter is there to be found any indication of where the information (re-)entextualized in the sentences comes from. However, volunteers and readers are not entirely expected to take these assertions on faith: they may rely on AI's reputation for veracity, or they may verify the assertions themselves. Unlike the anticipated student readers of the history books, the Message Recipients may very well challenge the accuracy, veracity, and perspective of assertions in the letters, thus underscoring the need for reliable research from which truthful assertions can be derived, which, in turn, construct a world view in which universal human rights prevail over local exigencies and are available to rebut assertions to the contrary.

One interesting device that occurs three times in the letters is the modifier *so-called*. It occurs twice in (#1 Targeted Killings, USA),[26] modifying "targeted killing," in both instances marked by quotes, for example, "I am deeply concerned that US government's so-called 'targeted killing' program allows …" (#1 Targeted Killings, USA). *So-called* occurs also in (#32 Violence Against Women, USA): "condemning abuses such as so-called 'honor killings' …" The *American Heritage Dictionary* (1661) provides two definitions for this expression, "commonly called" and "incorrectly or falsely termed."[27] Thus, *so-called* appears to be a marker of ironic echoic use (Sperber and Wilson 1995).

[26] For a *New York Times* report on the effects of US airstrikes, see https://tinyurl.com/28exkt4b (accessed August 9, 2025).

[27] Intriguingly, the *AHD* adds a Usage Note for "so-called," which prescribes that "Quotation marks should not be used to set off descriptions that follow expressions such as *so-called* and *self-styled*, which themselves relieve the writer of responsibility for the attribution." Not everyone agrees with this advice; AI for one and Jeff Kaplan, (p.c.) for another.

Presumably, AI wants to cast doubt on one implication of "targeted," namely, that no one other than the targeted individuals are killed in these actions and that the individuals targeted are legitimately so. And in the case of "honor killings," it rejects the notion that there is any honor in killing women.

I briefly take up here two further metapragmatic issues mentioned in Verschueren (2012) and dealt with in greater detail in Verschueren (1999, 2000), viz., ideologies of language (2012: 184–185) and the relations between ideology and identity construction (Verschueren 2012: 5, 10, 49).

To focus my discussion of ideologies of language and of language use, I discuss a page of the AI Letter Writing Guide (Figure 5.1, p. 180), which embodies elements of an ideology of language use which are manifest in the letters.[28]

First, all the prescriptions are written as imperatives, always short, and without any rationale for why they should be imposed. A number of these prescriptions are clearly ideological, most notably the commandment, "Do not discuss political ideology or politics," which strongly implicates that the appeals themselves are neither political nor ideological. This proscription of political and ideological discussion in the letters is clearly a reflection of AI's "naturalizing" (Eagleton 2007: 58) its appeal letters, and is clearly presented as "commonsensical" as well as "normative" (Verschueren 2012: 10). It also appears to assume the traditional view that only powerful, hegemonic interests are ideological, while counterpower activities are not.

Several of the prescriptions can be gathered under the heading *Be polite*, and describe a number of ways in which letter writers can realize that goal: "Use respectful language throughout your letter," "Use the proper salutation," and, "Consider using a personal, friendly comment in your letter," though the assumption that the appeal SENDer has a personal and friendly relationship with a head of state such as Vladimir Putin or Barack Obama might be viewed as a threat to both the appeal SENDer's and Putin's and Obama's positive face. While the Message Recipients line in the appeal letters includes the proper salutation, the webpage provides no instructions on the choice of "respectful language," assuming, I presume, that knowledge of what is respectful is "commonsensical." These prescriptions are all directed at the Message Recipients' positive face (Brown and Levinson 1987), presumably as a counterbalance to the directives in the letters, of which there can be many in a single one, and which are all substantial threats to the Message Recipients' negative face. We can view Brown and Levinson's proposals (and a great many others) as attempts to articulate norms that are typically taken to be commonsensical and natural and so not to require articulation or even mention unless they are violated. (See AD 3.4.4 above.)

[28] On language ideologies, see Silverstein (1979); Woolard (2021); Woolard and Schieffelin (1994).

Several of the other prescriptions seem to reflect Grice's (1975) maxim of Manner, which, with his Cooperative Principle and other maxims, might be regarded as the rhetorical and linguistic ideology of a particular culture and tradition (Keenan 1976; Pratt 1986): "Keep your letter brief," "Write in English unless you are completely fluent in the language of the country concerned," "Use the victim's name throughout the letter," and "Wrap up by restating your concerns and expectations of the official." Alternatively, one might view these prescriptions as a manifestation of Relevance Theory's "presumption of optimal relevance," which enjoins a speaker to produce an "ostensive stimulus" that is (a) relevant enough to be worth the addressee's effort to process it and (b) the most relevant one compatible with communicator's abilities and preferences (Wilson and Sperber 1995: 270). That is, these prescriptions aim to keep the reader's processing burden as low as possible given the purposes of the letters. While Relevance Theory is a theory of the cognitive cost/benefit balance in communication, its practitioners are unlikely to consider it ideological. However, writing prescriptions such as those I've mentioned can certainly be considered to be ideologized articulations of an underlying cost/benefit calculation: they are genre prescriptions that can be legitimized, normativized, and rationalized within a Western rhetorical tradition that purports to value brevity and directness which the letter writers assume to be universal even though their addressees might belong to substantially different rhetorical traditions. (One might also assume RT's reduction of communication to cognition to be ideological, though I do not agree with critics of RT who claim that it provides no place for social aspects of communication: these can be adequately theorized as relevant encyclopedic information from which contextual premises and/or conclusions can be derived.)

I have characterized the AI volunteer who SENDs a letter as "inhabiting the *I*" of that letter. We can provide this very impressionistic characterization of the volunteer's role in SENDing the letter by reference to Verschueren's (2000: 452–453) discussion of ideology and its relation to identity construction. By clicking SEND, the volunteer adopts the (contingent) identity of an AI representative who is committed to the goals of the organization and whose evaluation of the appeal situation is consistent with that of AI and whose purpose in writing the letter is to attempt to persuade the addressees to adopt the letter's proposed redress. As all of these are ideologically infused actions and intentions, so is the identity "constructed" by the letter sender.

AD 3.6.1: Look for indicators of metapragmatic awareness (ranging from verba dicendi to sentence adverbs, question tags, hedges, quotations, and reported speech) (Verschueren 2012: 185–186).

The most unmarked speech act verb, *say*, occurs only once in the corpus: "In litigation the Justice Department has even *said* that its copies of the full report remain unread, in a sealed envelope" (#19 Torture Report, USA; emphasis added). *Say* can be used generically to include both spoken and written modes and implies no evaluation of the message, though the broader context may include evaluations.

Forms of *write* occur eighteen times, ten times in the formula "I am writing to …" and three times in "I write to …," forms I discussed above. These are typically complemented by an expression of concern or a directive such as *urge*.

Words denoting legal procedures, for example, *charge* (eight verb and ten noun occurrences, though six of these occur in one letter (#3 Satire as Crime, Egypt), *trial* (sixteen occurrences), and *tried* (four occurrences) generally co-occur with expressions denoting the standards of procedure to be met.

Forms of *comply* occur eleven times in the corpus. Though this is not a speech event verb, I include it here as it denotes a response to a directive such as *urge* and it denotes action in accord with verbally constructed formations, typically human rights obligations in the corpus:

> Ensuring that any use of lethal force outside of specific recognized zones of armed conflict *complies* fully with the USA's obligations under international human rights law, including by limiting the use of force in accordance with law enforcement standards.
>
> (#1 Targeted Killings, USA; emphasis added)

A number of categories of adverbs indicating metapragmatic awareness occur. In line with the expressions of the urgency that are characteristic of the appeals, we find "surely" in:

> Until the current free-for-all is stopped or slowed down, we will be consigned to trying to arrest those who recruit child soldiers after the fact, and after the harm has been inflicted on the children. *Surely* we must do better than this.
>
> (#34 Arms Sales, USA; emphasis added)

While the core meaning of *surely* is "with confidence, unhesitatingly," it also means "undoubtedly, certainly," and "without fail" (*AHD*, 5th ed.: 1753). In the context of the extract just above, it may be paraphrased with the metapragmatic adverbs *undoubtedly* or *certainly*, but it also adds an appeal to the addressee, an interrogative element not indicated by punctuation in the text, but nonetheless ideologically tinged by its context.

Other adverbs represent various stances adopted by the writers: "presumably" (#19 Torture Report, USA), "reportedly" (#23 Mass Surveillance, USA), "officially" (#19 Torture Report, USA), and "undoubtedly" (#25 Missing, China) represent epistemic stances; "unfortunately" (#13 Women Protesters, Egypt; #27 Syrian Refugees, USA) represents an affective stance; and "respectfully" (#4 Al-Qahtani, USA; #5 LGBTQI, South Africa; #17 Caning, Indonesia) an interpersonal one.

"Particularly" (#1 Targeted Killings, USA; #10 Drone Wars, USA; #16 Woodfox, Louisiana, USA; #30 Forced Marriages, Burkina Faso); "specifically" (#5 LGBTQI, South Africa; #17 Caning, Indonesia; #35 Executions,

California, USA); "lastly" (#39 Al-Hawsawi, USA), and "accordingly" (#40 Cobalt, Apple Corporation) are discourse or pragmatic markers indicating relationships between prior and following co-text. "Publicly" (#5 LGBTQI, South Africa; #14 Restrictive Legislation, Russia; #18 Badawi, Saudi Arabia; #23 Mass Surveillance, USA; #27 Syrian Refugees, USA; #40 Cobalt, Apple Corporation) denotes the manner in which information is made available, while "made public" (#4 Al-Qahtani, Iraq) denotes the result of that process.

Various hedges occur. Forms of *claim* occur three times, for example, "End claims that the USA is authorized by international law to use lethal force anywhere in the world under the theory that it is involved in a 'global war' against al-Qa'ida and other armed groups and individuals" (#1 Targeted Killings, USA). Notable is the co-occurrence of "maintains" and "claim" in "April 2015 will mark 43 years since Albert Woodfox was first placed solitary for a crime he *maintains* that he didn't commit – a *claim* that the available evidence supports" (#20 Woodfox, Louisiana, USA; emphasis added). According to Wierzbicka (1987: 324–325 and 327, respectively),

> *Claiming* is similar to *maintaining*, *asserting* and *affirming* in so far as it puts forward, confidently, a controversial view … The person who reports an act as *claiming* will often wish to dissociate himself [*sic*] from the original speaker, so much so that a sentence of the form "He claims that X" seems to convey the reporter's doubts, as well as the original speaker's confidence.

And

> *Maintaining* is closely related to *claiming* in being a somewhat defiant way of saying something: the speaker is aware that some other people might and probably would be sceptical about what he [*sic*] is saying, but he has no intention of wavering because of that.

Like *claim*, *allege* and its forms evaluate a report as unreliable because it is inadequately supported by evidence at the time of writing and that the writer therefore withholds endorsement of a proposition, for example, "Tran Huyn Duy Thuc … *alleges* that he was tortured while in detention" (#26 PoCs, Vietnam; emphasis added). It is very unlikely that AI would want to undermine the reliability of assertions by the subjects of their appeals, nonetheless, by using forms of *allege*, *claim*, and *maintain* it avoids fully committing itself to the truth of those assertions while implying that there is at least secondhand evidence to support them. The letters avoid undermining their subjects' veracity by making these hedged claims secondary rather than primary bases for the appeals. This evidentiary caution and backgrounding of hedged assertions comports with AI's concern for its reputation for veracity while allowing it to bolster its arguments on behalf of its appeal subjects.

Forms of *recognize* occur nine times in the corpus, most of them in two letters to US government officials regarding current US counter terrorism activities, for example, "I fully *recognize* the US government's duty to take robust action to protect the life and physical integrity of people within its jurisdiction" (#1 Targeted Killings, USA; emphasis added) and the directive, "*Recognize* the application of international human rights law to all US counterterrorism operations including those outside US territory" (#1 Targeted Killings, USA; emphasis added). *Recognize* is a mental or institutional action verb, which may be used performatively. "Recognize" in the first example above may be glossed as "acknowledge" or "accept," thus representing a mental action by the writer indicating their acceptance of the validity of the US government's duty. The imperative "[r]ecognize" in the second example represents a desired action on behalf of an institution, the US government, by individuals authorized to do so, in this case by the addressee, "President Barak [*sic*] Obama," committing the institution to international human rights law for the evaluation of its actions. The word may be being used in its legal sense in this instance, or at least, its use cues a legal context. The following represents the relevant senses:

> **1 :** to acknowledge formally: as **a :** to admit as being of a particular status <~ a precedent> <~ a union>; *specif* **:** to acknowledge (as a right, cause of action, or defense) as valid.
>
> (Merriam-Webster's *Dictionary of Law*, 2011: 405)

While an individual or an institution may recognize certain evaluations and their consequent obligations, they need not *comply* with them, a discrepancy the letters recognize when they direct addressees (and the states they represent) to uphold human rights by taking specific actions:

> I urge your government to comply with international human rights law and take this opportunity to show Vietnam's commitment to upholding human rights by releasing immediately and unconditionally these four individuals, along with all prisoners of conscience.
>
> (#26 PoCs, Vietnam)

One mode of compliance is to "release" or "disclose" information, which presupposes that the information has been concealed, thus invoking an interpretive frame of government secrecy and deception. "Disclose" re-formulates "release … information," and in doing so adds the implication that the information was improperly withheld.

> 3) Release more information
>
> • Disclose further legal and factual details about U.S. policy and practices for so-called "targeted killings," "signature strikes," and "Terrorist Attack Disruption Strikes," including any secret Department of Justice legal memorandums, and specific information about who has been killed.
>
> (#1 Targeted Killings, USA)

The quote marks in this extract have the dual roles of indicating that what they enclose is to be attributed to a source other than the writer and AI, while also serving to indicate a critical perspective on their referents.

Rulings by various courts and citings of various legal documents support appeals. Letter (#19 Torture Report, USA) takes the US Department of Justice to task for its failure to read, or even commit to reading, the US Senate's report on torture in the CIA's secret detention facilities. The appeal includes the text of the first page of the executive summary of the US Senate's report which was undertaken against the "backdrop" (from summary) of the attack on the World Trade Center on September 11, 2001, and prepared "in the hopes that it will prevent future coercive interrogation practices and inform the management of other covert action programs" (from summary). The AI appeal interprets the Department of Justice's refusal to read the report's "6,700 pages" as an indication of its unwillingness to bring any of the individuals responsible for the CIA's torture program to account, and to leave unpunished those who have violated human rights and international law. The letter includes the odd contradictory caution, "If you won't read the report, I will send it to you," and ends with strong directives and clear statements of the implications of international law:

> The Department of Justice must also re-open and expand its investigations into all CIA interrogations, detentions and renditions. It must bring to justice in fair trials all the persons, regardless of their level of office or former level of office, suspected of being involved in the commission of crimes under international law, such as torture and enforced disappearance.
>
> (#19 American Torture Story, USA)

Procedure 3.7: If possible, try to identify any strategies of meaning generation that may appear from any of the observations based on the foregoing procedural steps (Verschueren 2012: 186–191).

As the move and step analysis lays out and as the discussion above elaborates, the appeals can be characterized as personal expressions of concern addressed to specific individuals regarding situations or events evaluated as problematic by virtue of their violation of international human or humanitarian rights, laws, and covenants or treaties, and directives to the addressees to redress those violations. The appeal situations or events are described factually, typically without reference to sources of evidence; their evaluations are generally asserted without hedging; their redress is requested using neutral or moderate directive verbs and/or strong deontic modals. The overall intended effect is of polite discourse between rational people who subscribe to the values of human rights, which are typically presented generically and presupposed and thus as taken-for-granted by both parties. The letters thus avoid "political ideology or politics," which might alienate the AI volunteers who are asked to SEND the letters and/or the Message Recipients to whom they are directly addressed.

AD 3.7.1: Look for potentially strategic ways in which the interplay between the explicit and the implicit is exploited (Verschueren 2012: 187–191).

In his application of this guideline, Verschueren (2012) quotes a passage of twelve sentences from one of the textbooks in his corpus; he then creates "[a] schematic presentation of explicit and implicit information in this text" (Table 8, 188–190). I provide a similar analysis of the following, typical, appeal (#18 Badawi Flogging, Saudi Arabia); I number each sentence for ease of reference.

> **Message Recipients**: Salman bin Abdulaziz Al Saud, *King of Saudi Arabia*; Joseph Westphal, *United States Ambassador to Saudi Arabia*
>
> **Subject**: Stop the horrific public flogging of blogger, Raif Badawi
>
> [1] I am profoundly disturbed that Saudi blogger Raif Badawi was publicly flogged in front of al-Jafali mosque after Friday prayers.
> [2] I call on you to quash Raif Badawi's flogging sentence immediately, as it is a flagrant violation of the prohibition on torture or other cruel, inhuman or degrading treatment under international law.
> [3] Please ensure that he is not flogged again in the coming months.
> [4] I believe that Raif Badawi is a Prisoner of Conscience, held solely for peacefully exercising his right to freedom of expression.
> [5] Please drop all charges against Badawi and ensure that he is unconditionally released without further delay.
> [6] I am also deeply concerned about the number of activists in Saudi Arabia who, like Raif Badawi, are persecuted for openly expressing their views online.
> [7] I call on you to stop arresting, charging, prosecuting and sentencing activists for simply exercising their rights to freedom of expression, association and assembly.
> [8] Thank you for your attention to this important matter.

Explicit	Implicit
Subject: "Stop … Raif Badawi"	The aspectual verb "stop" presupposes the prior occurrence of "the horrific public flogging of blogger, Raif Badawi"; the definite NP "the flogging …" presupposes that the flogging occurred and that it was horrific and public and of Badawi; "blogger, Raif Badawi" characterizes Badawi as a blogger, which implicates in this context that Badawi's actions are verbal, and so should be protected under international freedom of expression law.
[1] "I am profoundly disturbed …"	"that … prayers" is presupposed by the factive verb *disturbed* and presented as uncontroversial knowledge shared by "I" and the Message Recipients.

(*cont.*)

Explicit	Implicit
[2] "I call on you to quash … law"	That Badawi was sentenced to be flogged is presupposed by "quash his flogging sentence."
[3] "Please ensure … months"	That Badawi was flogged at least once already is presupposed by "flogged again"; "ensure" implies that the Message Recipients have the power to prevent Badawi's being flogged again.
[4] "I believe … expression"	The belief is based on Grice's Quality maxim and AI's reputation for accuracy and truth; the causal relation between characterizing Badawi as a PoC and his being "held solely for peacefully exercising his right to freedom of expression" is implicated via Grice's maxim of Relation and RT's search for optimal relevance; the existence of Badawi's right to freedom of expression is presupposed by the definite NP "his right to freedom of expression."
[5] "Please drop … delay"	That there are charges against Badawi is presupposed by the factive "drop"; that Badawi is not currently free is implied by "ensure that he is unconditionally released"; that there have already been delays in dropping charges against him and/or in unconditionally releasing him is presupposed by "further."
[6] "I am also … online"	"also" implicates that the writer's current concern is an additional one; that a number of activists are persecuted in Saudi Arabia for openly expressing their views online is presupposed as the complement of "concerned about"; that the number of activists persecuted is not trivial is implicated by "the number" and its context, via Grice's maxim of Quantity and RT's "free enrichment" to reach optimal relevance; "persecuted" implies that Badawi and other activists were "oppress[ed] or harass[ed] with ill-treatment" (*AHD*, 5th ed.: 1316). It also suggests that the oppression was beyond what was sanctioned by law or was illegal and/or extrajudicial.
[7] "I call on you to … assembly"	"stop arresting" presupposes that "you" has arrested and continues to arrest, etc., "activists for simply exercising their rights to freedom of expression, association and assembly"; the definite NP "their rights to freedom of expression, association and assembly" presupposes the existence of these rights.
[8] "Thank you for … matter"	Expressions of thanks typically occur after the event for which the thanks are offered, so one interpretation is that the writer is offering thanks for the addressee's attention to the letter, which seems inadequate in the context, suggesting a second interpretation, viz., that the thanks are in anticipation of the addressees' acceding to the letter's requests, an interpretation supported by the occurrence in one letter (#5 LGBTQI, South Africa) of "in advance" with the expression of thanks; "this important matter" presupposes the existence of the matter and that it is important to both writer and addressees; "this … matter" anaphorically refers to the writer's two concerns articulated in the letter body; "your attention" presupposes the existence and the addressee's power to apply the required attention.

As with Verschueren's textbook corpus, much is communicated implicitly by the appeal letters. What is explicitly communicated are primarily the writers' concerns, directives, and expressions of thanks, which allow the objects of concern and the objectives of the directives, the situations and events, and their evaluations to be presented implicitly and thus as agreed upon by both appeal SENDers and Message Recipients and thus as uncontroversial. Additionally, given my argument that the letters are intended for two audiences (at least) – the AI volunteers who are urged to SEND them and their named Message Recipients – the existence of rights and the evaluation of events or situations as violations of those rights are implicitly endorsed by the volunteers when they hit SEND. They thus also implicitly identify themselves with the ideological bases upon which the appeal situations are evaluated, thereby enacting a particular identity affiliating them with AI, its staff and members, and the global human rights community in general. They thereby naturalize and legitimate the human rights ideology, the institutions that construct, enact, promulgate, and maintain it, and their own actions and those of others who engage in the practice of counterpower that sending AI appeal letters represents.

Guideline 4: For an overall interpretation, ask yourself whether the assembled observations can be seen to represent an identifiable pattern of meaning in relation to issues pertaining to social structures, processes, and relations (Verschueren 2012: 191 ff).

Guideline 4 invites a brief reprise of the main argument of the book, namely that the discourses of human rights, while intended to improve the human condition, are nonetheless ideological. The appeals are elements of AI's activism in support of human rights with the goals of persuading their Message Recipients to act in accord with the human rights articulated in various internationally binding declarations, treaties, and conventions; of ideologically engaging the AI members who receive the emails in which the appeals are embedded; and of identifying those members who have sent the appeals as likely to respond positively to a fundraising appeal.

The observations and the analyses presented in this and earlier chapters amply demonstrate the patterns of meaning described just above and their relations to social structures, processes, and relations. The analyses identified the rhetorical structure of the appeal letter genre, and how the evaluative stances toward explicitly and implicitly communicated propositions ideologically position the discourse participants.

The propositions represented in the appeals and their related stances index such social structures as activist organizations, their staffs, members, volunteers, and webpage visitors; local, national, and international authoritative institutions; (organizations of) nation-states, national and international laws, treaties and covenants, their associated judicial institutions; the nongovernmental organizations involved in collecting, curating, and distributing information regarding violations of human rights and appealing for their redress; and whatever media are available for their purposes.

The social processes identified include the drafting, ratification, and revision of human rights declarations, covenants, constitutions, and laws by international bodies such as the United Nations; the creation of activist organizations such as AI and Human Rights Watch; and the political, legal, and extra-legal activities in violation of, or support for, human rights.

The social relations represented are mediated by human rights discourses among staffers, members and volunteers of organizations like AI, and between them and the powerful government functionaries identified as Message Recipients, and among human rights proponents and opponents, academics of various stripes (philosophers, historians, political scientists, rhetoricians, and linguists), religious figures who engage in debate about human and humanitarian rights, and the activities and decisions made by individuals and organizations.

In his discussion of this last guideline, Verschueren (2012) advises us "to distinguish clearly between the *topical or informational content* of the discourse … under investigation, and the *involvement* or perspective that can be identified on the basis of careful analysis" and to attend to "the *legitimation* work" being accomplished by the discourse, notably by presenting claims and evaluations as "natural phenomena" thus potentially functioning as "strategies of *persuasion* or even *propaganda* and *manipulation*" (192–193; emphasis in original).

It is by no means clear that the topic and the perspectives adopted toward it can be distinguished. The topics of the appeals have to do with situations and actions whose descriptions and evaluations as violations of human and related rights and are typically integrated in a single sentence, for example, "I share Amnesty International's grave concern that the U.S. administration's policy on intentional use of lethal force appears to permit violations of the right to life" (#10 Drone Wars, USA) and "I am disappointed to learn that current state laws on the use of lethal force by law enforcement officers do not comply with international human rights law and standards" (#21 Crime Task Force, USA).

While some letters might appear to allow the separation of the appeal topic from the perspective from which they are viewed, for example, by characterizing an event merely as "flogging," "caning," or "closing the Guantanamo detention facility," in general the two cannot be disentangled. We do find occasional instances where the description and its evaluation are in separate sentences, though these are typically juxtaposed:

> I support closing the Guantanamo detention facility and urge you to get the job done, today.
>
> The US government is obligated under international law to respect, protect and fulfill human rights. Each Guantanamo detainee must either be charged and fairly tried in federal court, or be released to countries that will respect their human rights.
>
> (#6 Guantanamo, USA)

Or in adjacent paragraphs:

> Burkina Faso has one of the lowest rates of contraceptive use among women in the world: 17% at last count in 2014. It also has one of the highest maternal mortality rates in the world. By the time they are 19 years old, most girls are married, and nearly half of them are already mothers.
>
> Under the Universal Declaration of Human Rights, and Burkina Faso's Constitution, women and girls are entitled to the same human rights as men and boys. But in practice, they are discriminated against and denied their rights. They are too often unable to make decisions about who they can love, who they have intimate relations with, who they marry, and about whether to have children and how many.
>
> (#33 Contraception, Burkina Faso)

Typically, however, the topical description is embedded in an expression of the appeal sender's concern about the exigence and violative nature of the appeal situation.

Readers will recognize legitimation and naturalization as two of Verschueren's and Eagleton's characteristics of ideology. The others are normativizing, universalizing, rationalizing, action-orienting, unifying, and promoting the interests of a group. The previous chapters have demonstrated how the appeals entail all these processes and thus represent identifiable patterns of meaning and action that meet the criteria for an ideology proposed by Eagleton and Verschueren.

AI's strategy of writing letters as polite, factual, direct, first-person expressions of concern and appeal for the redress of violations of various rights is designed to engage AI members by persuading them of the truth of the descriptions, of the exigence of the situations, and of the rectitude of their concern. We can view this as a strategy of "*propaganda* and *manipulation*" (Verschueren 2012: 192–193; emphasis in original), or more neutrally, as action-orienting.

Conclusion

This chapter addressed Verschueren's Procedures 3.4 to 3.7 and his Guideline 4. These deal with implicit meanings, tropes, sequential ordering of genre and interactional elements, and metapragmatic indications in the AI appeals. It reviewed the overall interpretation of the data and its ideological significances, and presented some "unexpected findings" and conclusions derived from the analysis, as directed by Guideline 4.

7 Conclusions

In this final chapter, I provide a brief reprise of the discussion of the main findings of the analyses presented in the chapters above, reflections on the methodology employed, ideology, and suggestions for further research.

Chapter 1 briefly introduced ideology, Verschueren's (2012) guidelines for pragmatic ideological research, and his general rules and analytic dimensions for the analysis of ideological discourse. I introduced the data to be analyzed in this study and asked whether the AI appeals were in fact ideological. The remainder of the book demonstrated that the appeals fulfill the criteria defining ideological discourse proposed in Eagleton (2007) and in Verschueren (2012).

Chapter 2 explored conceptions of rights and provided a brief history of human rights and some of the arguments they evoke, as well as a short history of Amnesty International. It introduced the AI appeal letters that are the primary focus of this study and the AI documents most closely related to them. It provided a description of these documents, paying particular attention to the linguistic and visual resonances occasioned by their mutual contextualizations and proposed a Relevance Theory explanation for the intricate relations between the documents' linguistic and visual modes and argued for the ideological study of AI documents, particularly of the appeal letters.

Chapter 3 reviewed important understandings of ideology and concluded with a discussion of Verschueren's Theses 1 to 4, which articulate his characterization of ideology and its manifestations and roles in discourse. These theses, along with the attributes identified in Eagleton (2007), provided the bases for the arguments that the AI appeals and related documents are indeed elements of ideological discourse.

Chapter 4 addressed Verschueren's Caveat 1 through his Procedure 2.3. These deal with the data to be analyzed, its context, and "lines of vision" that connect it to its relevant contexts. The chapter investigated the ideological relevancies of the appeals' social, political, historical, geographical, and linguistic contexts. This investigation required that Verschueren's broad guidelines be complemented and implemented by a range of discourse analytic theoretical apparatuses: deixis; speech act theory; Gricean and post-Gricean pragmatics; contextualization cues; various theories of participant roles; positioning theory; theories of argumentation; move and step analysis; epistemic vigilance; and detailed discussion of the discourse implications of a number of linguistic devices.

Chapter 5 addressed Verschueren's Guideline 3 through his Procedure 3.3. It investigated the "dynamics of meaning generation in relation to issues pertaining to social structures, processes, and relations," the roles of grammatical relations and their interactions with semantic roles, particularly the identification of agents and experiencers of violative and other actions and the ideological positioning of those referents relative to human rights evaluations of the actions. It also examined the topics of the appeals and the language of the rhetorical moves and steps that constitute them.

Chapter 6 addressed Verschueren's Procedures 3.4 to 3.7 and his Guideline 4. These deal with implicit meanings, tropes, sequential ordering of genre and interactional elements, and metapragmatic indications in the AI appeals.

Overall, these chapters identified several essential characteristics of ideology and demonstrated that the appeals exhibit these characteristics and that the methods typically used for the analysis of nefarious ideologies can be profitably applied to more laudable ones. They augment Verschueren's analytic procedures with necessary technical and theoretical devices, for example, theories accounting for implicitly communicated propositions and referents, the interplay between implicit and explicit meanings, indices of discourse interaction, and metapragmatic activities.

While the primary focus of this work is the appeal letters, their analysis required study of documents closely related to them – AI's reports, emails, webpages, and appeals for donations. In this respect, the current work differs from Verschueren's analysis of the history textbooks in that he investigated only, and only briefly, one other related text, Ames' (1899) *An ABC for Baby Patriots* (194–197). He observed "the completely coherent faithfulness with which the patriotic stance of our history books can be found in children's books" (194), no doubt with the goal of instilling in impressionable minds the values of imperial colonization.

The other AI documents provided information included in the appeals, but were considerably more informative, and while the appeals are text only, the emails and reports are multi-modal. I can only speculate about why the appeals are mono-modal. If, as I argued, an important role of the appeals is to engage AI members and to prompt them to act by clicking SEND, then a minimal modality is sufficient, especially if the number of letters ostensibly sent to the Message Recipients is at least as important as their content. Alternatively, AI might assume that the technologically simple mono-modal format is more likely to be compatible with a broad variety of email and other electronic systems and thus more likely to reach the Message Recipients or their surrogates.

The analysis demonstrates that the appeal letters are designed for at least two audiences, the AI volunteers who receive them in an email or access them online and their Message Recipients, and for at least three functions: to persuade their Message Recipients by argument and by sheer numbers of appeals to redress one or more human rights violations; to engage, align, and motivate AI members; and to provide an opportunity for AI's fundraising – an appeal SENDer might reasonably be assumed to be favorably disposed to AI's mission and more likely to donate in support of the cause specified in the appeal. (Readers will recall that members receive a request for donations immediately after SENDing an appeal.)

I asked too what frames of reference are invoked by the appeals and what meanings they express. At Verschueren's "grand or global" level (198), AI discourses articulate variations on the ideology of human rights that are circulated in human rights documents of various sorts according to their roles in global institutions and politics. The activities of AI, its volunteers, and Message Recipients in the production and interpretation of the appeals constitute an intermediate level that mediates between the language of the appeals and the ideology of human rights as interpreted by AI.

At Verschueren's "local" level (198), AI's linguistic choices index relevant social structures, processes, and relationships: expressions of concern regarding situations and events; deictics of persons, times, and locations; expressions of evaluation and redress invoking human rights documents; deontic expressions directing AI members and appeal Message Recipients to act; general expressions referencing human rights; expressions presupposing the existence and local relevance of human rights; expressions of concession and rebuttal; and expressions of polite invitation to engage in dialog.

The AI appeals contain a broad range of presupposition triggers and other linguistic devices that index evaluations which are presented as to be regarded as valid by both authors and audiences, but which could and perhaps would be rejected by the Message Recipients, as indicated by the appeals' occasional concessions. That the presupposed evaluations are far more likely to be accepted as valid by AI members and volunteers suggests that the appeals are at least partially intended to engage those members/volunteers and to persuade them to continue their commitment to and actions and donations on behalf of human rights while AI acts in other ways on behalf of Prisoners of Conscience and other human rights goals, for example, as an organization that can "exert influence on the whole range of decision functions (intelligence, promoting, prescribing, invoking, applying, terminating, and appraising)" at organizations such as the UN (Chen 2015: 82, 79–89).

The non-technical, informal, and generic expressions used in the appeals (and other AI documents) to characterize human rights and their violations indicate that the letters are designed to engage, "action orient," AI members and volunteers by providing them with opportunities to join together virtually to protest human rights violations and appeal for their redress, rather than as individual efforts to persuade their apparent Message Recipients.

The meanings of the appeals can be viewed as a hierarchy of levels. At a considerable degree of abstraction, the appeals describe a situation and a proposed change to that situation. At less abstract levels, the situation and its change are evaluated as a problem and its solution. The problem is an injury to an individual, individuals, classes of individuals, and/or communities, and the solution is presented as a redress of that injury. The injury is argued to be a violation of the human rights of those individuals/communities and the redress to be a reinstatement of those rights. The violation and its redress are presented as matters of concern to the *I*s of the appeals and worthy of consideration and attention by the Message Recipients. The AI members who SEND the appeals "inhabit" the *I*, thus positioning them as human rights activists and identifying them as the experiencers of the concern and agents of the action of appealing. The Message Recipients are identified as agents of the proposed redress and persuadable by arguments based on concern and human rights.

The appeals are devices in an oppositional dialog. They are addressed to individuals who have far greater power in the communicative situation than AI and its members. Because of this power asymmetry, the appeals politely ask the Message Recipients to redress the violations. They acknowledge the concerns of the Message Recipients, but evaluate these from a human rights perspective. Some letters include an invitation to the Message Recipients to communicate with the letter sender about the case.

Remarks on Methodology

Verschueren (2012) suggests that "the most important theoretical contribution [his] book can make is an extremely practical one: providing theoretically justified tools for analysis," while arguing for a "linguistic pragmatics [that] may provide the perspective and tools for further advances in the social sciences, helping them to overcome the fruitless imitation of the natural sciences in attempts to produce cumulative and predictive knowledge by means of efforts at quantification in value-laden and essentially interpretive domains" (199).

Verschueren's theses and guidelines are based on various linguistic, pragmatic, and discourse analytic theories: of explicit and implicit communication; of textual coherence and cohesion; of information structuring; of linguistic interaction; of text and context relations; and, of course, of ideology. Verschueren's history textbooks and my AI documents are certainly value-laden and his analysis and mine are essentially interpretive, though I do not reject the value of a quantificational study of these documents and others like them: recall the Key Word analysis briefly described in Chapter 1. To reject quantificational studies would be to dismiss all the findings of, for example, quantificational corpus linguistics. Such a global rejection is untenable; there is room for both approaches and for their hybrids. I refer readers to the journal *Corpus Linguistics and Linguistic Theory*.[1]

Ideology/Ideologies

Verschueren (2012) notes and rejects claims that ideology has died. He "see[s] ideology not only in relation to grand political issues, but as much in relation to the working of institutions … and small scale 'local' contexts of practice" (198). I have shown in this work that AI's discourses perform all of the ideological functions identified by Verschueren and Eagleton, and that these range from the "grand political" in AI's engagement with international bodies such as the UN, while integrating the global with the local through its international organization, national affiliates, local organizations, and the individuals who receive and SEND its appeals.

Declarations that ideology is dead are particularly common in non-academic discourse (e.g., Borders 2018[2]; Eghagha 2018[3]; Shapiro 2018[4]); however, the chapters above have demonstrated conclusively that it thrives. And even though academic discussions of ideology claim that ideologies may be repressive or liberating, many, if not most, academic studies of ideology derive from aspects of their authors' moral and political stances and activities and have therefore focused on nefarious ones, for example, colonial, anti-immigrant, racist, and (Neo-)Nazi discourses. The current work has provided a convincing example of an ideological discourse designed to improve the lot of human beings. I say that this is an example of such an ideology because I anticipate that analyses of the discourses of organizations like AI, for example, Human Rights Watch, would reach the same conclusion, even if the activists engaged in these discourses would object to this characterization.

Because ideologies are designed to benefit their adherents and human rights are declared to be "universal," every human being should benefit from them. In contrast, racist ideologies, for example, benefit those who aim to create communities and institutions dominated by specific categories of people and to exclude other groups from those benefits. Obviously, as shown by the work of AI and similar organizations, a great many people and communities are deprived of their rights. And while the specific intended beneficiaries of the AI activities are primarily the individuals and groups on whose behalf the AI

1 www.degruyter.com/journal/key/CLLT/html (accessed August 11, 2025).
2 https://medium.com/social-evolution/the-death-of-political-theory-996f9bff369c (accessed August 11, 2025).
3 https://guardian.ng/opinion/the-death-of-ideology (accessed August 11, 2025).
4 https://geopoliticalfutures.com/ideology-is-dead/ (accessed August 11, 2025).

documents are created and distributed, the broader goal is to secure global observance of human rights treaties and legislation. The care taken in the preparation of the documents, particularly AI's reports, benefits AI by contributing to its reputation and influence in authoritative institutions such as the UN. Other beneficiaries are people who work for and are paid by AI. AI members and volunteers benefit by being engaged in activities that they and others view as morally, ethically, legally, and politically of great value. More abstractly we might say, as Sikkink (2017) has argued, that the global state of human rights has benefitted from the work of AI and similar organizations, though much remains to be done.

As ideologies are generally regarded as "hegemonic," we should ask whether the human rights movement is hegemonic. The word is glossed by Verschueren (2012: 12) as "the internalization of the authority one may be subjected to," and by Eagleton (2007: 112) as "the ways in which a governing power wins consent to its rule from those it subjugates," though he notes that Gramsci "occasionally uses the term to cover consent and coercion together." On these interpretations, hegemony is a result of "successful ideology." It is clear that the human rights ideology has not yet succeeded in establishing itself as an authority that is globally accepted and effective, but it should also be clear from my discussion that the ideology of human rights is driven by a hegemonic impulse in that its advocates seek to persuade those who need persuading that they should know and abide by norms such as those articulated in the UN UDHR and related legal instruments – to which their countries have committed to respecting – and to establish by such persuasion human rights as a global norm, globally observed.

The arguments above have shown that if we set aside the lay assumption that ideologies are devices created by and in support of the interests of ruling elites and are thus necessarily misleading or false and adopt a more neutral set of criteria for identifying discourses as ideological, then we can see that discourses of liberation and counterpower can also be ideological and can be profitably studied in the same ways as nefarious ideologies, while valuably discovering their similarities and differences. The examination of the discourse of the AI documents demonstrates that it is designed to ideologically position both the AI members/volunteers and the Message Recipients as, respectively, committed to, and governed by, the ideology of human rights as it is encoded in the United Nations Universal Declaration of Human Rights and its enabling covenants: the International Covenant on Civil and Political Rights and the International Covenant on Economic, Social and Cultural Rights, as well as The Hague and Geneva Conventions, which derive from the late nineteenth century.

Van Dijk (2013: 175) distinguishes between "ideologies of domination," like "racism, sexism, classism, or neoliberalism," and ideologies such as "anti-racism, feminism, socialism, pacifism, or environmentalism, among many others" that do not "function to found and legitimate domination." Presumably, van Dijk would include the ideology of human rights among the latter group. Nonetheless, we must also ask whether ideologies such as that of human rights are ideologies of domination. This, of course, depends upon what we mean by "domination," and crucially, whether we assume that it entails coercion. The *American Heritage Dictionary* is vague on this issue; it defines "domination" as "1a. Control or power over another or others. b. The exercise of such control or power" (534). The dominating ideologies in van Dijk's list all involve the power of one group of people over another – women by men, lower classes by higher classes – and to maintaining that domination by "consent and coercion," as required by their practitioners. Van Dijk's non-dominating ideologies seem to be assumed to seek to eliminate these asymmetries. However, strands of socialism have proposed the dominance of the working classes and in so far as socialist ideologies have the goal of inverting the power differentials, they can reasonably be thought to "function to found and legitimate domination," a supposition supported by the twentieth- and twenty-first-century history of countries such as China and confederations such as the Union of Soviet Socialist Republics (USSR), though the legitimacy of the resulting regimes might well be questioned. AI and other such organizations might also be thought to intend to invert the power relationship among individuals, institutions, and states that violate human rights. However, it is questionable whether human relations can ever be entirely egalitarian in all contexts, and so while human rights and similar movements seek to ameliorate and ideally eliminate the most harmful effects of autocracy, racism, sexism, and the like, they seek to accomplish these goals by persuasion, though they may have recourse to coercive institutions such as the International Criminal Court.[5]

Colonialism was "the dominant mainstream" ideology of the late nineteeth and early twentieth centuries; human rights is not the dominant mainstream ideology of the late twentieth and early twenty-first centuries, though its supporters argue that it should be and work to make it so. In fact, human rights are under severe threat not just in countries with few if any pretensions to democracy, but also in traditionally democratic countries such as the US, where right-wing politicians seek to limit minority populations' access to voting, thus violating Article 21 of the UDHR. These politicians

[5] "The International Criminal Court (ICC) investigates and, where warranted, tries individuals charged with the gravest crimes of concern to the international community: genocide, war crimes, crimes against humanity and the crime of aggression," www.icc-cpi.int/about. The ICC is empowered to sentence malefactors to prison and to order reparations to be paid to victims of HR abuses, as the case of Ahmad Al Faqi Al Mahdi illustrates, www.icc-cpi.int/mali/al-mahdi (sites accessed March 17, 2026).

are often supported by armed and militant extremist groups (Brownstein 2022[6]; Graham 2021[7]).

Verschueren's Theses 1 to 4 and their sub-theses, discussed in Chapter 3, claim that ideologies are "rarely questioned, in a given society or community" (Thesis 1.1) and that ideological meaning "is often … carried along implicitly rather than being formulated explicitly" (Thesis 1.2). These claims are partially supported by the frequent use of presupposition to represent human rights tenets, but are undercut by explicit references to human rights declarations and laws, as well as by the history of religions and political movements. Such movements are often riven by internal disputes about the interpretation of foundational documents and doctrines, often leading to mutually antagonistic schisms. Neither AI nor the human rights movement in general has been spared such debates, as Nickel and Etinson (2024) make clear.

The claim that ideological meaning is "often" communicated implicitly rather than expressed explicitly is also contradicted by the explicitness of foundational documents such as the UN UDHR and of AI's definition of Prisoner of Conscience. The appeal letters and other AI documents frequently, and in the case of AI reports characteristically, explicitly invoke these documents and categories. And nefarious ideologies may be explicit about at least some of their assumptions: (Neo-)Nazi manifestos are explicit about their exclusionary aims and AI discourses are explicit about their human rights commitments. Nonetheless, ideological discourses do often hide fundamental elements, which analysts can lay bare. For example, van Dijk's (2013) discussion of an anti-immigrant speech by a Conservative member of the British parliament revealed its underlying racist tenets. (See also van Dijk 1992.) AI discourses tend to elide the arguments and disagreements about the origins, reach, and applicability of human rights. More broadly, godly ideologies may be forged in ungodly places: human rights treaties, declarations, and conventions are crafted in intensely political, competitive, compromising, and nationalistic international fora such as the UN. Such decision processes cannot but be driven by competing ideologies at least some of whose tenets and beneficiaries may be obscured. One would like to know what rights have been proposed but left on the cutting-room floor, so to speak, a task beyond the scope of the current project.

Verschueren's (2012) argument that his history books left no room for fundamental criticism of colonization (194) prompts the question of whether the AI documents, and especially the appeals, leave room for a critique of the various rights they invoke. They do. Many of the appeals invite dialog between the Message Recipients or their surrogates and the appeal SENDers (or AI, which asks members to tell it if they receive communications from

[6] https://tinyurl.com/3xbd8rbs (accessed August 11, 2025).
[7] https://tinyurl.com/3jtejef5 (accessed August 11, 2025).

Message Recipients). The occasional concessions we find in the appeals may be seen as invitations to the Message Recipients to engage with the SENDers, while their rebuttals model the kinds of responses the Message Recipients may expect. Many appeals reference legal procedures and instruments of human rights, and as these are inevitably the outcome of political processes, they are open to the same kinds of critiques as all political outcomes – that they benefit some, but disadvantage others. For example, though Article 2 of the UDHR enjoins discrimination on the basis of sex, it does not distinguish sex and gender and so might be regarded as not (specifically) protecting LGBTQIA+ individuals (though some AI appeals attempt to do so). As shown in Chapter 2, AI documents and activities are typically – though not always – based on extensive research whose sources are explicitly identified in the AI reports on which the webpages, emails, and appeals may be based, and this concern for accountability may be seen as the recognition that the assertions and stances in those documents can be and often are disputed, with the possibility of undermining the human rights ideology and the devices that embody it. So, unlike Verschueren's history textbooks, the AI documents implicitly and explicitly anticipate critiques and take steps to forestall them.

Nazi Documents

Researchers' claim that ideologies may be "good" or "bad" is assumed throughout Verschueren's book, and to illustrate this contrast I provide a brief analytic comparison between the AI appeals and two Nazi documents: the American Nazi Party document "What we stand for"[8] and the American National Socialist 25 Points (25P).[9] The main take-away from this comparison is that while the AI appeals and the Nazi documents differ in many respects, they also share a number of characteristics.

The Nazi documents display a number of elements that we can characterize as mythic (recall Ruth Wodak's characterization of ideology discussed in Chapter 3) in that they presuppose (scientifically) undecidable concepts, among which those entailing "pure White blood" and "sacred White blood" are the most prominent and central. These concepts and (professed) belief in them function as tests for group membership and as the bases for legitimating individual and group action. And however members might apply the test of purity, it may be used to distinguish members of the "nation" from nonmembers, "us" vs. "them" (Frog 2018).

In contrast, the AI appeals are based on the presumption that human rights are universal. This presumption does not seem mythic to me. As I noted in

[8] www.americannaziparty.com/what-we-stand-for/ (accessed August 11, 2025).
[9] www.nsm88.org/25points/25pointsengl.html (accessed August 11, 2025).

Chapter 3, the phrase "the myth of human rights" seems contradictory, suggesting the possibility of a proof procedure to determine their actuality. The proof of their actuality lies in their genealogy and application. They derive from centuries of religious, philosophical, political, and legal argument, culminating in the declaration by the UN that a subset of the imaginable rights are to be universally binding, and their subsequent inclusion in the laws of individual countries and groups of countries. In contrast, "the myth of pure White blood" does not seem at all contradictory; in fact, it seems quite tautological.

Human rights apply to everyone, regardless of blood-type or any other such characteristic, and so cannot be used to exclude anyone. They can, as the appeals and other AI documents amply demonstrate, function as the basis for evaluating how individuals and groups are treated by powerful individuals, groups, or institutions, typically though not always, acting in the (apparent) interests of states. And on the basis of these evaluations, the AI documents can function to legitimate and motivate redressive actions on the part of AI and its members.

The two Nazi documents are manifestos looking to the establishment of states whose citizens will be limited to those of "sacred White blood." Their most salient discourse characteristic is their organization as a series of demands, some of which are supported by rationales or beliefs. Demands are directive utterances that attempt to oblige their addressees to make the world fit their propositions (Kissine 2013: 174). "Demand" implies an intensely desired future state of affairs, though it is unclear exactly who the audiences for these documents are, and who is obliged to bring about these states of affairs (Wierzbicka 1987: 39–41). I assume that this obligation is required of members of the Nazi organizations and especially of "the leaders of the movement" who "promise to work ruthlessly … to translate this program into action" (25P).

The 25P document consists of a series of directives many introduced by "We demand …" Because the document could have represented the same information if it had been introduced by a single occurrence of "We demand" followed by a numbered or bulleted list of the demands, this repetition appears to have been chosen for a particular rhetorical purpose. Repetition of linguistic and other elements is characteristic of rituals, which "affect the awareness of individual identity, by breaking it down, by providing alternative identities (for instance by role reversal), or by replacing it with an awareness of collective identity" (Koster 2003: 216), which is manipulated "for the sake of tribal loyalty" (217). Rituals, according to Koster, may be religious or secular, or characteristic of "political religions" such as "all the nationalisms of the 19th and 20th centuries (including Zionism) and, of course, fascism[10] and bolshevism" (217). Such rituals create a "sacred space," "a symbolic territory for 'us,' in

[10] On fascism, see Eatwell (2013) and many other Eatwell publications.

opposition to the claims of 'them'" (217), but "seek to extend their symbolic 'sacred space' to real territory" (217).

Ritual and myth are closely related: "[r]itual performance orchestrates mythic motifs, themes, and narrative patterns" (Frog 2018: 29). Ritual and myth are also associated with taboo. The Nazi documents declare those who do not have "pure/sacred White blood" to be taboo and thus to be excluded from the society the movement aims to establish.[11]

The UN UDHR, in contrast, is an authoritative declaration, which, though not legally binding, has been incorporated into various international treaties and legal codes. The Declaration's constituent rights have created an international order defined by the propositions representing those rights.[12] This is certainly not to say that these rights are universally adhered to, but they are regarded as having the force of international customary law in most countries that are members of the UN.[13]

The expression of rights and obligations differs in the two sets of documents. The Nazi documents locate these in the future by expressing them as complements of "demand," whereas the UN UDHR locates them in the enduring present by expressing them with simple, active, declarative, present tense sentences whose subjects, representing the beneficiaries of the rights, are universally quantified, for example, "Article 1. All human beings are born free and equal in dignity and rights."

The AI appeal letters and the Nazi documents are similar in describing desired states of affairs. However, where the Nazi documents posit benefits for individuals who are members of an exclusive and exclusionary group, the letters appeal for benefits to specific individuals on the basis of their membership in "mankind" (UDHR Preamble). The appeals, and other AI documents, as well as analogous documents and activities by other human rights organizations should be seen as responses to the exhortation in the UDHR Preamble that "every individual and every organ of society … shall strive … to secure their universal recognition and observance." The economic, social,

11 Myth and ritual are intimately related to purity, as "pure White blood" makes clear, though it is not the only criterion for admission to the proposed polity. Versions of the "What We Stand for" document demand "that steps be taken to halt the spread of heredity defects and racially impure blood within the gene pool of the racial community." Failure to halt these contaminants results in "race defilement" and racial "destruction." Echoing these grievances, on December 16, 2023, in Durham, New Hampshire, Donald Trump repeated his claim that undocumented immigrants to the US were "poisoning the blood of our country," thus echoing Hitler's vilification of Jews in *Mein Kampf*. See Douglas (1984 [1966]) on purity and taboo.

12 Searle's (1976) class of declaration/declarative speech acts "effect immediate changes to the institutional state of affairs and … tend to rely on elaborate extra-linguistic institutions" (cited in Levinson 1983: 240). They seem to have been subject to less research than other speech act types, but see discussion of them in Sbisà and Turner (2013).

13 www.un.org/en/about-us/udhr/foundation-of-international-human-rights-law (accessed August 11, 2025).

and cultural rights mentioned in the Declaration are presented as aspirational, as dependent upon the resources of the state, but nonetheless to be realized:

Article 22. Everyone, as a member of society, has the right to social security and is entitled to realization, through national effort and international cooperation and in accordance with the organization and resources of each State, of the economic, social and cultural rights indispensable for his [*sic*] dignity and the free development of his personality.

Unexpected Findings

Verschueren (2012) remarks (64) that "the best test for the validity of the proposed set of methods … would be to use them for the analysis of data one can feel aligned with, and then come up with unexpected findings." I am an AI member and am "aligned with" my data. Nonetheless, the analysis did uncover findings that I did not expect.

In Chapter 4, I offered an analysis of the complexities presented by the *I*s of the appeals, here I can reprise only the briefest hint of those complexities. Outside of the appeals, in the simplest cases, *I* is used to refer to the speaker/writer of an utterance; in the appeals *I* ostensibly refers to the AI member who receives the appeal in an email or finds it on an AI webpage. However, the member did not create the appeal and so is not the experiencer of its concern nor the agent of its request. Only when someone (sincerely?) SENDs an appeal can its *I* be said to refer to and to accrue these attributes. Second-person pronouns pose similar analytic gymnastics.

As discussed in Chapter 4 and briefly noted just above are the intriguing referential incommensurabilities presented by the first-person expressions in the appeals (and the emails and webpages), and to a lesser extent the second-person ones. The letters are at the intersections among the AI organization and the powerful people that it wants to influence and those it recruits in its influencing efforts. In essence, AI says to its volunteers who are asked to SEND appeals: "Here's what I want you to write to the Message Recipients, but I want you to pretend that you wrote it, even though the Message Recipients will be fully aware that you didn't." In this respect, they differ from, for example, fundraising appeals, protest signs, and electronically mediated person-to-person communication. The appeals are quoted texts masquerading as first-person utterances.

In Chapter 2, I briefly discussed the nature of rights, a concept that is complex and freighted with controversy. Somewhat surprisingly, none of these complexities and controversies is addressed in any of the AI documents reviewed for this work. Wenar and Cruft (2025) provide an overview of the concepts and controversies involved.

In Chapter 2 also, I briefly discussed human rights. These too entail complexities and controversies regarding what those rights should be, which of the conceivable rights and types of rights should exist, who should they apply to, how they should relate to legal and judicial systems, which should be enacted at various legal levels, and, perhaps most contentiously, what their sources are, for example, Western individualistic neo-colonialism, or should be, for example, Catholic or Islamic religious beliefs.

Just as rights are taken to be unproblematic notions in the AI documents, the category *human* is also unexamined, suggesting that it is to be taken as a transparent concept, unproblematically applicable, and causing no problems in determining its denotation. Definitional controversies indicate that "human" denotes a fuzzy category making it difficult to determine who or what may be included in its extension. A clear distinction between the human and the non-human would seem to be essential if we are to know who and what are owed human rights. It would appear that human rights discourse assumes that we know humans when we meet them. However, what counts as a human individual or community for the purposes of legislation has not always been as clear as the AI discourses would lead us to assume. While one might assume that deciding who is and who is not human might not be a problem at this point in history – note my "might" – it certainly was in the not-so-distant past, as even the most cursory glance at nineteenth- and twentieth-century characterizations of African, African-American, and Irish people will attest. These and other groups were represented as apes, a process referred to as "simianization."[14] And we should remember well Nazi treatment of physically and mentally disabled people up to and during World War II, as well as demands by today's Neo-Nazis:

A Better Race:

We demand that the state aggressively strive for the continual betterment of the Aryan Race through positive eugenic measures especially by encouraging propagation of the highest racial elements within the Aryan Republic. We also demand that steps be taken to halt the spread of hereditary defects and racially impure blood within the gene pool of the racial community.[15]

(American Nazi Party "What We Stand for")

For a glance at the issues involved, see Ereshefsky (2022), Roughley (2023), and Ward (2012).

In addition, there are movements to extend various rights to animals, despite Kant's claim that

[t]he fact that the human being can have the representation "I" raises him [*sic*] infinitely above all the other beings on earth. By this he is a person … that is, a being altogether

[14] https://tinyurl.com/58vxkjpr; https://tinyurl.com/b96vyy8e; https://tinyurl.com/4hm4sxtu (sites accessed August 11, 2025).

[15] Donald Trump has characterized immigrants as "vermin," https://tinyurl.com/54f3eep3, "animals," and "not people," https://tinyurl.com/msnxw74r (both accessed August 11, 2025).

different in rank and dignity from things, such as irrational animals,[16] with which one may deal and dispose at one's discretion.[17]

(Kant 2007 [1798]: 239 [Ak 7: 127])

None of the AI documents appeals for the redress of injuries done to animals, and we might view Kant's definition as an instance of "speciesism," a concept that invokes biological categorization, which challenges definition based on necessary and sufficient conditions. Rather, the contested boundaries between human and non-human imply yet other sites for ideological construal of those who are entitled to rights and of those who are not. See Gruen and Monsó (2024) on the moral status of animals.[18]

Change

Change is inevitable and AI has adapted to the broadening scope of human rights (Vašák 1977) and to evolving media possibilities and preferences. The appeals used as data for the current study were collected over a short period of time (March 7, 2013 to June 30, 2016) relative to the span of AI's human rights activism from 1961 to the present. In 1961, there were neither computerized word processing systems, nor email, nor internet, so appeal letters were written by hand or on typewriters and sent to their Message Recipients by regular mail and post. As the internet with its websites, webpages, and email developed, AI was able to more efficiently inform AI members about human rights violations and to deliver its appeals to their Message Recipients. In 1973, AI initiated its Urgent Action Network (UAN) with the goal of rapidly responding to particularly high-priority exigencies in which individuals were at imminent risk of serious harm.[19] And as the electronic devices we now take for granted became available and widespread, AI adapted nimbly and developed its current sophisticated, award-winning media presence.[20]

The forty analyzed appeals and additional forty collected for counter-screening represent an element of AI's activities during a particular period, and since then AI seems to have changed its mode of communicating with volunteers like me. The appeal letters now come to me in two modes. One is a development of the earlier mode: I receive an email that embeds an appeal letter, which members are invited to personalize. The second appears to be an adaptation of the UAN technique. The source identifier on these emails

[16] Readers mulling over Kant's characterization of animals as "irrational" might profitably take the matter up with my wife's and my cat, Téa.

[17] Many scholars view Kant's concept of human dignity as a secure basis for human rights.

[18] For a convincing argument that animals may entertain concepts that "are shared across species and were therefore present before language evolved and provided the precursors of more complex human concepts," see Fitch (2019: 6).

[19] https://tinyurl.com/484b3mww (accessed August 11, 2025).

[20] For example, a 2021 Webby award; see https://tinyurl.com/3ptew6wn (accessed August 11, 2025).

is "UAN at Amnesty International USA."[21] These invite the AI members to "[w]rite a letter in your own words or using the sample below as a guide to one or both government officials listed. You can also email, fax, call or Tweet them." The Urgent Action and appeal letters are much alike in structure and tenor.[22] In each case, I must identify myself as the appeal sender, presumably for authentication and fund-raising purposes. I am also asked to inform AI about my actions.

Counterscreening

Verschueren (2012: Rule 1, 22) requires that data should be analyzed and the analysis counterscreened to determine the reliability of the original analysis. To accommodate such counterscreening, I include in Appendix 3 an additional forty appeal letters. A further test of the reliability and generalizability of the current analysis would be to collect a corpus of more recent appeals and compare them with the current eighty. The focus of the current work is the appeal letters, and the analysis presented in Chapter 2 of an AI report and its associated webpage, email, and appeal could only be brief. A more detailed analysis of the re-contextualization and re-genrefication of a larger corpus of AI documents would provide an additional test of the current analysis and indicators of any changes that AI may be making to their documents and the ways in which the various ideologies are managed in them. This would require collecting a corpus of AI reports, and their associated webpages, emails, appeals, and a sample of AI's proliferating websites. While the webpage, emails, and appeals reflect just the human rights and legal ideologies, I suspect that the reports bring together a number of competing and complementary ideologies and the ways in which they are adapted in their re-contextualizations of AI's version of human rights, of the rhetoric of report writing, of the audiences for which the reports are designed, and of the legal and ideological participation frameworks in which all of these actors are positioned.

Our understanding of AI's discursive assumptions, goals, and strategies would benefit from ethnographic study of how AI gathers its information and how that is curated, re-contextualized and re-genrecized,[23] as it would from a comparison of AI documents and the discursive strategies, tactics, procedures, and ideologies of other global HR organizations such as Human Rights Watch (HRW), and with those of more local civil rights

21 For information on AI's UAN, see https://tinyurl.com/j3zw6t2s (accessed August 11, 2025).
22 For an example, go to https://tinyurl.com/3h6p7xrt (accessed September 15, 2025).
23 Hopgood (2006) provides an ethnographic account of the deliberations of AI's International Secretariat in London based on interviews with staff members and observations of meetings, along with study of AI's archives during 2002–03.

organizations such as the American Civil Liberties Union or the Southern Poverty Law Center (SPLC).[24, 25]

A further expansion of the focus of the analysis would be to examine the discourses of other oppositional activist organizations. This would provide for a comparative study of how AI and these organizations go about their activities. For example, I am a member of AI and of HRW, and while I receive emails and very occasional letters and cards from AI, I receive only letters from HRW. A recent card from AI notes the 511,000 actions taken to help free Guatemalan environmental human rights activists, the 5,100 emails sent to President Biden regarding the possible deportation of Cameroonian refugees in the US, the thousands of petitions sent to US Congress members to support reauthorizing the Violence Against Women Act, and the 765,000 actions taken to help free a South Sudanese man. Somewhat surprisingly, it does not ask for a donation. The letters from HRW are exclusively appeals for funds for lists of eleemosynary objectives. These letters might be compared with other fundraising appeals, as done, for example, in Mann and Thompson (1992) and Delahunty (2018b).

Given the potential for indefinite framing and re-framing of discourses, our understanding of inter-discursive strategies, practices, and arguments would benefit from the study of, for example, AI documents and (critical) responses they elicit, and responses to those responses, as far as temporal, institutional, and, especially, psychological resources allow.

[24] As of April 20, 2020, Margaret Huang is the president and CEO of the SPLC. She was Executive Director of AIUSA from December 2015 to April 2020, in which role she signed the example AI email presented in Chapter 1.

[25] Analysts who take the Discourse-Historical Approach adopt just such a broad-scale approach. See Reisigl and Wodak (2015).

References

Abbott, Barbara. 2019. The indefiniteness of definiteness. In Jeanette Gundel and Barbara Abbott (eds.), *The Oxford Handbook of Reference*. Oxford University Press, 130–145.

Agarwal, Kritika. 2019. Texas revises history education, again: How a "good faith" process became political. *Perspectives on History: The Newsmagazine of the American Historical Association*. Available at https://tinyurl.com/4b8jy4z6.

Allan, Keith. 2012. Pragmatics in the (English) lexicon. In Keith Allan and Kasia M. Jaszczolt (eds.), *The Cambridge Handbook of Pragmatics*. Cambridge University Press, 227–250.

Allen, Amy. 2022. "Feminist perspectives on power," *The Stanford Encyclopedia of Philosophy* (Fall 2022 Edition), Edward N. Zalta (ed.). Available at https://plato.stanford.edu/archives/fall2022/entries/feminist-power/.

Althusser, Louis. 2001 [1971]. Ideology and ideological state apparatuses (notes towards an investigation). In *Lenin and Philosophy and Other Essays*. Translation by Ben Brewster. New York: Monthly Review Press; NYU Press.

Althusser, Louis. 2014. *On the Reproduction of Capitalism: Ideology and Ideological State Apparatuses*. Translated by G. M. Goshgarian. London: Verso.

Ames, Mary Frances. 1899. *An ABC for Baby Patriots*. London: Dean & Son.

Amnesty International. 2015. *"Left to Die under Siege": War Crimes and Human Rights Abuses in Eastern Ghouta, Syria*. London: Amnesty International. Available at https://tinyurl.com/a4t6pd9e.

Andersen, Hanne and Brian Hepburn. 2021. "Scientific Method," *The Stanford Encyclopedia of Philosophy* (Summer 2021 Edition), Edward N. Zalta (ed.). Available at https://plato.stanford.edu/archives/sum2021/entries/scientific-method/.

Applebaum, Anne. 2020. The answer to extremism isn't more extremism: America's left and right are radicalizing each other. *The Atlantic*, October 30. Available at https://tinyurl.com/39z9ru8d.

Atiq, Emad, Andrei Marmor and Alexander Sarch. 2025. "The nature of law," *The Stanford Encyclopedia of Philosophy* (Summer 2025 Edition), Edward N. Zalta and Uri Nodelman (eds.). Available at https://plato.stanford.edu/entries/lawphil-nature/.

Atkin, Albert. 2023. "Peirce's Theory of Signs," *The Stanford Encyclopedia of Philosophy* (Summer 2–23 Edition), Edward N. Zalta (ed.). Available at https://plato.stanford.edu/archives/spr2023/entries/peirce-semiotics/.

Austin, John L. 1962. *How to Do Things with Words*. J. O. Urmson (ed.). Oxford University Press.

Baehr, Peter R. 2009. Amnesty International. In David P. Forsythe (ed.), *Encyclopedia of Human Rights*. Oxford University Press, 60–66.

Bartholomew, Amy and Jennifer Breakspear. 2004. Human rights as swords of empire. In Colin Leys and Leo Panitch (eds.), *The Socialist Register 2004: The New Imperial Challenge*. London: Merlin Press, 125–145.

Bateman, John A. 2018. Position paper on argument and multimodality: Untangling the connections. *International Review of Pragmatics*, 10(2), 294–308.

Beaver, David I. and Bart Geurts. 2014. "Presupposition," *The Stanford Encyclopedia of Philosophy* (Winter 2014 Edition), Edward N. Zalta (ed.). Available at https://plato.stanford.edu/archives/win2014/entries/presupposition/.

Bell, Alan. 1984. Language style as audience design. *Language in Society*, 13(2), 145–204.

Bell, Daniel. 1988 [1960]. *The End of Ideology: On the Exhaustion of Political Ideas in the Fifties*. Cambridge, MA: Harvard University Press.

Benedict, Ruth. 1946. *The Chrysanthemum and the Sword: Patterns of Japanese Culture*. Boston, MA/New York: Houghton Mifflin.

Bettinger-López, Caroline. 2018. The long arc of human rights: A case for optimism. *Foreign Affairs*, 97(3), 186–190.

Biber, Douglas and Edward Finegan. 1989. Styles of stance in English: Lexical and grammatical marking of evidentiality and affect. *Text*, 9(1), 93–124.

Biber, Douglas, Ulla Connor, and Thomas A. Upton. 2007. *Discourse on the Move: Using Corpus Analysis to Describe Discourse Structure*. Amsterdam: John Benjamins.

Biber, Douglas, Stig Johansson, Geoffrey Leech, Susan Conrad, and Edward Finegan. 1999. *Longman Grammar of Spoken and Written English*. Harlow, UK: Pearson Education.

Blakemore, Diane. 1989. Denial and contrast: A relevance theoretic analysis of *but*. *Linguistics and Philosophy*, 12(1), 15–37.

Blakemore, Diane. 2002. *Relevance and Linguistic Meaning: The Semantics and Pragmatics of Discourse Markers*. Cambridge University Press.

Blakemore, Diane. 2003. Re-visiting procedural meaning: "But," "however" & "nevertheless." Paper delivered at Georgetown University Round Table on Languages and Linguistics (GURT).

Blommaert, Jan. 2005. *Discourse: A Critical Introduction*. Cambridge University Press.

Blommaert, Jan and Jef Verschueren. 1998. *Debating Diversity: Analysing the Discourse of Tolerance*. London: Routledge.

Blommaert, Jan, Mary Bock, and Kay McCormick. 2007. Narrative inequality in the TRC hearings: On the hearability of hidden transcripts. In Christine Anthonisson and Jan Blommaert (eds.), *Discourse and Human Rights Violations*. Amsterdam: John Benjamins, 33–63.

Bonhoeffer, Dietrich. 1995. *The Cost of Discipleship*. New York: Touchstone.

Borders, Max. 2018. The death of political theory: Ideology dies one small experiment at a time. *Social Evolution*, March 6. Available at https://tinyurl.com/yck9catu.

Bourdieu, Pierre. 1977. *Outline of a Theory of Practice*. Cambridge University Press.

Bourdieu, Pierre. 1991. *Language and Symbolic Power*. Cambridge, UK: Polity Press.

Boyle, Michael J. 2008. The war on terror in American grand strategy. *International Affairs*, 84(2), 191–209.

Brown, Penelope. 2017. Politeness and impoliteness. In Yan Huang (ed.), *The Oxford Handbook of Pragmatics*. Oxford University Press, 383–399.

Brown, Penelope and Stephen Levinson. 1987. *Politeness: Some Universals in Language Usage*. Cambridge University Press.
Brownstein, Ronald. 2022. Republicans are trying to suppress more than votes. *The Atlantic*. Available at https://tinyurl.com/3xbd8rbs.
Bublitz, Wolfram. 1998. Cohesion and coherence. In Jan-Ola Östman and Jef Verschueren (eds.), *Handbook of Pragmatics* (7th annual installment). Amsterdam: John Benjamins, 37–49.
Buchanan, Tom. 2002. "The truth will set you free": The making of Amnesty International. *Journal of Contemporary History*, 37(4), 575–597.
Caffi, Claudia. 1999. On mitigation. *Journal of Pragmatics*, 31(7), 881–909.
Caffi, Claudia. 2007. *Mitigation*. Amsterdam/Tokyo: Elsevier.
Caffi, Claudia. 2013. Mitigation. In Marina Sbisà and Ken Turner (eds.), *Pragmatics of Speech Actions*. Berlin: De Gruyter Mouton, 257–285.
Calude, Andreea and Gerald Delahunty. 2020. Just because-constructions in spoken and written New Zealand English. *Journal of Linguistics and Language Teaching*, 10th Anniversary Issue, 29–51.
Cappelen, Herman, Ernest Lepore, and Matthew McKeever. 2023. "Quotation," *The Stanford Encyclopedia of Philosophy* (Summer 2023 Edition), Edward N. Zalta (ed.). Available at https://plato.stanford.edu/archives/sum2023/entries/quotation/.
Carston, Robyn. 2002. *Thoughts and Utterances: The Pragmatics of Explicit Communication*. Oxford, UK: Blackwell.
Carston, Robyn. 2010. Explicit communication and "free" pragmatic enrichment. In Belén Soria and Esther Romero (eds.), *Explicit Communication: Robyn Carston's Pragmatics*. Basingstoke, UK: Palgrave MacMillan, 217–285.
Carston, Robyn. 2012. Metaphor and the literal/non-literal distinction. In Keith Allan and Kasia M. Jaszcolt (eds.), *The Cambridge Handbook of Pragmatics*. Cambridge University Press, 469–492.
Castells, Manuel. 2009. *Communication Power*. Oxford University Press.
Castells, Manuel. 2013. *Communication Power*. 2nd ed. Oxford University Press.
Catalano, Theresa and Linda R. Waugh 2020. *Critical Discourse Analysis, Critical Discourse Studies and Beyond*. Boston, MA: Springer-Verlag.
Cave, Terence and Deirdre Wilson (eds.). 2018. *Reading beyond the Code: Literature and Relevance Theory*. Oxford University Press.
Chafe, Wallace. 2018. Constraining and guiding the flow of discourse. In Deborah Tannen, Heidi Hamilton, and Deborah Schiffrin (eds.), *The Handbook of Discourse Analysis*. 2nd ed. Oxford, UK: Wiley-Blackwell, 391–405.
Chamedes, Guilana. 2019. *A Twentieth-Century Crusade: The Vatican's Battle to Remake Christian Europe*. Cambridge, MA: Harvard University Press.
Chapman, Audrey 2023. An explicit right to abortion is needed in international human rights law. *Health and Human Rights Journal*, June 29. Available at www.hhrjournal.org/2023/06/29/an-explicit-right-to-abortion-is-needed-in-international-human-rights-law/.
Chen, Lung-Chu. 2015. *An Introduction to Contemporary International Law: A Policy-Oriented Perspective*. Oxford University Press.
Christov-Moore, Leonardo, Elizabeth A. Simpson, Gino Coudé, Kristina Grigaityte, Marco Iacoboni, and Pier Francesco Ferrari. 2014. Empathy: Gender effects in brain and behavior. *Neuroscience & Behavioral Reviews*, 46(4), 604–627.

Clark, Billy. 2013. *Relevance Theory*. Cambridge University Press.

Condoravdi, Cleo and Sven Lauer. 2012. Imperatives: Meaning and illocutionary force. In Christopher Piñón (ed.), *Empirical Issues in Syntax and Semantics* 9. Colloque de Syntaxe et Sémantique à Paris, 37–58.

Cooren, François. 2015. *Organizational Discourse: Communication and Constitution*. Malden, MA: Polity Press.

Cooren, François and Frédérik Matte. 2010. For a constitutive pragmatics: Obama, Médecins Sans Frontières and the measuring stick. *Pragmatics and Society*, 1(1), 9–31.

Costa, James. 2014. Review of Verschueren 2012. *Discourse Studies*, 16(2), 309–311.

Crystal, David. 2003. *English as a Global Language*. 2nd ed. Cambridge University Press.

Culpeper, Jonathan. 2011. *Impoliteness: Using Language to Cause Offence*. Cambridge University Press.

Culpeper, Jonathan, Michael Haugh, and Daniel Kádár (eds.). 2017. *The Palgrave Handbook of Linguistic (Im)politeness*. London: Palgrave Macmillan.

Curl, Traci S. and Paul Drew. 2008. Contingency and action: A comparison of two forms of requesting. *Research on Language and Social Interaction*, 41(2), 129–153.

Dagistanli, Selda, Adam Possamai, Bryan S. Turner, Malcolm Voyce, and Joshua Roose. 2018. The limits of multiculturalism in Australia? The Shari'a flogging case of R v. Raad, Fayed, Cifci, and Coskum. *The Sociological Review*, 66(6), 1258–1275.

Davidson, Donald. 2013. What metaphors mean. In Maite Ezcurdia and Robert J. Stainton (eds.), *The Semantics-Pragmatics Boundary in Philosophy*. Ontario: Broadview Press, 453–465.

Davies, Bronwyn and Rom Harré. 1990. Positioning: The discursive production of selves. *Journal for the Theory of Social Behaviour*, 20(1), 43–63.

de Gaay Fortman, Bas. 2011. Religion and human rights: A dialectical relationship. *E-International Relations*, December 5. Available at https://tinyurl.com/4ksvaepk.

Delahunty, Gerald. 2013. Speaking truth to power: Genre, speech acts, and (im)politeness in Amnesty International (AI) appeal letters to political and institutional leaders. 2013 PAMLA Conference, San Diego, CA. November 1–3.

Delahunty, Gerald. 2014. Stancetaking in Amnesty International (AI) appeal letters. 12th Annual Hawaii International Conference on Arts and Humanities. January 10–13.

Delahunty, Gerald. 2015. The linguistic and discursive management of ideological conflict in Amnesty International (AI) appeal letters on behalf of "Prisoners of Conscience." 5th New Zealand Discourse Conference. Auckland University of Technology. December 7–9.

Delahunty, Gerald. 2017. Linguistic Indexes of ideological positioning of multiple audiences in Amnesty International (AI) appeal letters on behalf of "Prisoners of Conscience." Seminar presentation. Waikato University, Hamilton, New Zealand, January.

Delahunty, Gerald. 2018a. Language, ideology, and participant positioning in Amnesty International appeal letters. *Journal of Linguistics and Language Teaching*, 9(2), 151–168.

Delahunty, Gerald. 2018b. Amnesty International (AI) and philanthropic fundraising (PF) appeals: A comparative move analysis. In Hans Götzsche (ed.), *The Meaning of Language: Proceedings of the 26th Scandinavian Conference of Linguistics*. Newcastle upon Tyne, UK: Cambridge Scholars Press, 127–147.

Delahunty, Gerald. 2021. Ideological positioning in Amnesty International human rights web-based documents. In Vijay Bhatia and Girolamo Tessuto (eds.), *Social Media in Legal Practice*. Routledge Series on Law, Language and Communication. London: Routledge, 63–77.

Delahunty, Gerald. 2023. Words, pictures, and arguments: A relevance theory synthesis. *Journal of Linguistics and Language Teaching*, 14(1), 11–33.

Dendale, Patrick. 2006. Three linguistic theories of polyphony/dialogism: An external point of view and comparison. *Sproglig Polyfoni: Arbejdspapirer*, 5, 3–32.

Devlin, F. Roger. 2012. Human rights between ideology & politics: Alain de Benoist's *Beyond Human Rights*. *Counter-Currents*, April 11. Available at https://counter-currents.com/2012/04/alain-de-benoists-beyond-human-rights/.

Dillon, Robin S. 2022. "Respect," *The Stanford Encyclopedia of Philosophy* (Fall 2023 Edition), Edward N. Zalta (ed.). Available at https://plato.stanford.edu/archives/fall2022/entries/respect/.

Domaradzki, Spasimir, Margaryta Khvostova, and David Pupovac. 2019. Karel Vašák's generations of rights and the contemporary human rights discourse. *Human Rights Review*, 20(4), 423–443.

Donnelly, Jack and Daniel J. Whelan. 2017. *International Human Rights*. 5th ed. New York: Westview Press.

Douglas, Mary. 1984 [1966]. *Purity and Danger: An Analysis of the Concepts of Pollution and Taboo*. London: Routledge.

Douven, Igor. 2025. "Abduction," *The Stanford Encyclopedia of Philosophy* (Winter 2025 Edition), Edward N. Zalta (ed.). Available at https://plato.stanford.edu/archives/win2025/entries/abduction/.

D'Souza, Dinesh. 1995. *The End of Racism: Principles for a Multiracial Society*. New York: Free Press.

Du Bois J. W. 2007. The stance triangle. In Robert Englebretson (ed.), *Stancetaking in Discourse: Subjectivity, Evaluation, Interaction*. Amsterdam: John Benjamins, 139–181.

Dupret, Baudouin. 2011. *Practices of Truth: An Ethnomethodological Inquiry into Arab Contexts*. Amsterdam: John Benjamins.

Dworkin, Ronald. 1984. Rights as Trumps. In J. Waldron (ed.), *Theories of Rights*. Oxford University Press, 153–167.

Eagleton, Terry. 2007. *Ideology: An Introduction*. 2nd ed. London: Verso.

Eatwell, Roger. 2013. Fascism. In Michael Freeden, Lyman Tower Sargent, and Marc Stears (eds.), *The Oxford Handbook of Political Ideologies*. Oxford University Press, 474–493.

Eggins, Suzanne. 1994. *An Introduction to Systemic Functional Linguistics*. London: Pinter.

Eghagha, Hope. 2018. The death of ideology. *The Guardian Nigeria News*. Available at https://guardian.ng/opinion/the-death-of-ideology/.

Englebretson, Robert (ed.). 2007. *Stancetaking in Discourse: Subjectivity, Evaluation, Interaction*. Amsterdam: John Benjamins.

Ereshefsky, Marc. 2022. "Species," *The Stanford Encyclopedia of Philosophy* (Summer 2022 Edition), Edward N. Zalta (ed.). Available at https://plato.stanford.edu/archives/sum2022/entries/species/.

Fairclough, Norman. 1989. *Language and Power*. London: Longman.

Fairclough, Norman. 1992. *Discourse and Social Change*. Cambridge: Polity Press.

Featherman, Chris. 2015. *Discourses of Ideology and Identity: Social Media and the Iranian Election Protests*. New York: Routledge.

Felski, Rita. 2015. *The Limits of Critique*. University of Chicago Press.

Fitch, W. Tecumseh. 2019. Animal cognition and the evolution of human language: Why we cannot focus solely on communication. *Philosophical Transactions of the Royal Society B* 375(1789): 20190046.

Forceville, Charles. 2014. Relevance theory as a model for analyzing visual and multimodal communication. In David Machin (ed.), *Visual Communication*. Berlin: Mouton de Gruyter, 51–70.

Forceville, Charles. 2017. Visual and multimodal metaphor in advertising: Cultural perspectives. *Styles of Communication*, 9(2), 26–41.

Forceville, Charles and Billy Clark. 2014. Can pictures have explicatures? *Linguagem em (Dis)curso*, 14(3), 451–472.

Forst, Rainer. 2012. *The Right to Justification*. Translated by Jeffrey Flynn. New York: Columbia University Press.

Forst, Rainer. 2015. Noumenal power. *Journal of Political Philosophy*, 23(2), 111–127.

Forst, Rainer. 2016. The justification of basic rights. *Netherlands Journal of Legal Philosophy*, 45(3), 7–28.

Foucault, Michel. 1980. *Power/Knowledge: Selected Interviews and Writings, 1972–1977*. New York: Pantheon.

Foucault, Michel. 1995. *Discipline and Punish: The Birth of the Prison*. Second Vintage Books ed. Translated from the French by Alan Sheridan. New York: Vintage Books.

Fraser, Bruce. 1996. Pragmatic markers. *Pragmatics*, 6(2), 167–190.

Friedman, Lawrence M. 2011. *The Human Rights Culture: A Study in History and Context*. New Orleans: Quid Pro Quo Books.

Frog. 2018. Myth. *Humanities*, 7(1), 14. https://doi.org/10.3390/h7010014.

Gee, Tim. 2011. *Counterpower: Making Change Happen*. Oxford: New Internationalist Publications.

Ghanea, Nazila. 2011. Religion, equality and non-discrimination. In John Witte, Jr. and M. Christian Green (eds.), *Religion and Human rights: An Introduction*. Oxford University Press, 204–217.

Gillespie, Liam. 2019. Pierre Bourdieu: Habitus. *Critical Legal Thinking: Law and the Political*. Available at https://criticallegalthinking.com/2019/08/06/pierre-bourdieu-habitus/.

Goffman, Erving. 1974. *Frame Analysis*. New York: Harper.

Goffman, Erving. 1981. *Forms of Talk*. Philadelphia, PA: University of Pennsylvania Press.

Gorman, Sara and Jack Gorman. 2021. *Denying to the Grave: Why We Ignore the Facts that Will Save Us*. Oxford University Press.

Graham, David A. 2021. The Republican party's irrational war on voting rights. *The Atlantic*, March 20. Available at https://tinyurl.com/4bk7jmzk.

Gregor, Mary. 1996. *Immanuel Kant: The Metaphysics of Morals*. Cambridge University Press.

Grice, H. Paul. 1971 [1957]. Meaning. In Danny D. Steinberg and Leon A. Jakobovits (eds.), *Semantics: An Interdisciplinary Reader in Philosophy, Linguistics, and Psychology*. Cambridge University Press, 53–59. [Reprinted from Philosophical Review 66(3), 377–388].

Grice, H. Paul. 1975. Logic and conversation. In Peter Cole and Jerry L. Morgan (eds.), *Syntax and Semantics, Volume 3: Speech Acts*. New York: Academic Press, 41–58.

Grice, H. Paul. 1989. *Studies in the Ways of Words*. Cambridge University Press.

Grimes, Joseph E. 1975. *The Thread of Discourse*. The Hague: Mouton.

Gruen, Lori and Susana Monsó. 2024. "The Moral Status of Animals," *The Stanford Encyclopedia of Philosophy* (Fall 2024 Edition), Edward N. Zalta (ed.). Available at https://plato.stanford.edu/entries/moral-animal/.

Gumperz, John J. 1982. *Discourse Strategies*. Cambridge University Press.

Gumperz, John J. 2018. Interactional sociolinguistics: A personal perspective. In Deborah Tannen, Heidi E. Hamilton, and Deborah Schiffrin (eds.), *The Handbook of Discourse Analysis*. 2nd ed. Oxford: Wiley-Blackwell, 309–323.

Gundel, Jeanette K. 2003. Information structure and referential givenness/newness: How much belongs in the grammar? In Stefan Müller (ed.), *Proceedings of the 10th International Conference on Head-Driven Phrase Structure Grammar*. Stanford, CA: CSLI Publications, 122–142.

Gundel, Jeanette K. and Thorstein Fretheim. 2002. Information structure. In Jan-Ola Östman and Jef Verschueren (eds.), *Handbook of Pragmatics* (7th annual installment). Amsterdam: John Benjamins, 146–160.

Gundel, Jeanette K., Nancy Hedberg, and Ron Zacharski. 1993. Cognitive status and the form of referring expressions in discourse. *Language*, 69(2), 274–307.

Gutmann, Amy (ed.). 2001. Introduction. In Michael Ignatieff, *Human Rights as Politics and Idolatry*. Princeton University Press, vii–xxviii.

Habermas, Jurgen. 2010. The concept of human dignity and the realistic utopia of human rights. *Metaphilosophy*, 41(4), 461–480.

Halliday, M. A. K. and Ruqaiya Hasan. 1976. *Cohesion in English*. London: Longman.

Harré, Rom and Fathali Moghaddam (eds.). 2003. *The Self and Others: Positioning Individuals and Groups in Personal, Political, and Cultural Contexts*. Westport, CT/London: Praeger.

Harré, Rom and Luk van Langenhove. 1999. *Positioning Theory: Moral Contexts of Intentional Action*. Oxford, UK: Blackwell.

Hawkes, David. 1996. *Ideology*. London: Routledge.

Hickey, Raymond. 2012. *Standards of English: Codified Varieties around the World*. Cambridge University Press.

Hobbs, Jerry R. 2004/06. Abduction in natural language understanding. In Laurence R. Horn and Gregory Ward (eds.), *The Handbook of Pragmatics*. Malden, MA: Blackwell, 724–741.

Hodge, Robert and Gunther Kress. 1993. *Language as Ideology*. 2nd ed. London: Routledge.

Hodges, Adam. 2018. Intertextuality in discourse. In Deborah Tannen, Heidi E. Hamilton, and Deborah Schiffrin. (eds.), *The Handbook of Discourse Analysis*. Oxford: Wiley-Blackwell, 42–60.

Hoey, Michael. 1983. *On the Surface of Discourse*. London: George Allen & Unwin.

Hoey, Michael. 1994. Signaling in discourse: A functional analysis of a common discourse pattern in written and spoken English. In Malcolm Coulthard (ed.), *Advances in Written Text Analysis*. London: Routledge, 26–45.

Hoey, Michael. 2001. *Textual Interaction: An Introduction to Written Text Analysis*. London: Routledge.

Hood, Bruce M. 2009. *Supersense: Why We Believe the Unbelievable*. New York: HarperCollins.

Hopgood, Stephen. 2006. *Keepers of the flame: Understanding Amnesty International*. Ithaca, NY and London: Cornell University Press.

Hopgood, Stephen. 2013. *The Endtimes of Human Rights*. Ithaca, NY: Cornell University Press.

Hopgood, Stephen, Jack Snyder, and Leslie Vinjamuri (eds.). 2017. *Human Rights Futures*. Cambridge University Press.

Horn, Laurence R. 1989. *A Natural History of Negation*. Chicago University Press. Reissued by CSLI Publications in 2001 with survey by author on research on negation from 1989 to 2001.

Horn, Laurence R. 2004. Implicature. In Laurence Horn and Gregory Ward (eds.), *The Handbook of Pragmatics*. Oxford, UK: Wiley-Blackwell, 3–28.

Huang, Yan. 2014. *Pragmatics*, 2nd ed. Oxford University Press.

Huang, Yan (ed.). 2017. *Oxford Handbook of Pragmatics*. Oxford University Press.

Huddleston, Rodney and Geoffrey K. Pullum. 2002. *The Cambridge Grammar of the English Language*. Cambridge University Press.

Hunston, Susan. 1994. Evaluation and organization in a sample of written academic discourse. In Malcolm Coulthard (ed.), *Advances in Written Text Analysis*. London: Routledge, 191–218.

Hunston, Susan. 2000. Evaluation and planes of discourse: Status and value in persuasive texts. In Susan Hunston and Geoff Thompson (eds.), *Evaluation in Text: Authorial Stance and the Construction of Discourse*. Oxford University Press, 176–207.

Hyland, Ken. 2005. Stance and engagement: A model of interaction in academic discourse. *Discourse Studies*, 7(2), 173–192.

Ignatieff, Michael. 2001. *Human Rights as Politics and Idolatry*. Princeton University Press.

Jackendoff, Ray. 1990. *Semantic Structures*. Cambridge, MA: MIT Press.

Jakobson, Roman. 1971. Shifters, verbal categories, and the Russian verb. In Roman Jakobson. *Selected Writings. Vol. 2: Word and Language*. The Hague/Paris: Mouton, 130–147.

Jary, Mark. 2020. Assertion and the declarative mood. In Sanford C. Goldberg (ed.), *The Oxford Handbook of Assertion*. Oxford University Press, 38–57.

Jewitt, Carey (ed.). 2009. *The Routledge Handbook of Multimodal Analysis*. London: Routledge.

Jewitt, Carey (ed.). 2014. *The Routledge Handbook of Multimodal Analysis*. 2nd ed. London: Routledge.

Jewitt, Carey (ed.). 2016. Multimodal analysis. In Alexandra Georgakopoulou and Tereza Spilioti (eds.), *The Routledge Handbook of Language and Digital Communication*. London: Routledge, 69–84.

Johnstone, Barbara. 2009. Stance, style, and the linguistic individual. In Alexandra Jaffe (ed.), *Stance: Sociolinguistic Perspectives*. Oxford University Press, 29–52.

Johnstone, Barbara. 2018. *Discourse Analysis*. 3rd ed. Oxford, UK: Wiley-Blackwell.

Kant, Immanuel. 2007 [1798]. Anthropology from a pragmatic point of view. In Robert Louden and Gunter Zoller (eds. and trans.), *Anthropology, History, and Education*. Cambridge Edition of the Works of Immanuel Kant. Cambridge University Press, 227–429. Original is *Anthropologie in Pragmatischer Hinsicht*, published in the standard Akademie der Wissenschaften edition, Vol. 7.

Kaplan, Jeffrey. 2020. *Linguistics and Law*. London: Routledge.

Kärkkäinen, Elise. 2003. *Epistemic Stance in English Conversation: A Description of Its Interactional Functions, with a Focus on I Think*. Pragmatics & Beyond New Series, 115. Amsterdam: John Benjamins.

Keenan, Elinor O. 1976. On the universality of conversational implicatures. *Language in Society*, 5(1), 67–80.

Kempson, Ruth. 1988. Grammar and conversational principles. In Frederick J. Newmeyer (ed.), *Linguistics: The Cambridge Survey, Vol. II: Linguistic Theory: Extensions and Implications*. Cambridge University Press, 139–163.

Kissine, Mikhail. 2013. Speech act classifications. In Marina Sbisà and Ken Turner (eds.), *Pragmatics of Speech Actions*. Berlin/Boston, MA: De Gruyter Mouton, 173–202.

Kitzinger, Celia. 2013. Repair. In Jack Sidnell and Tanya Stivers (eds.), *The Handbook of Conversation Analysis*. Malden, MA: Wiley-Blackwell, 229–256.

Klandermans, Bert. 2011. Who participates and why? In Wilco de Jonge, Brianne McGonigle Leyh, Anja Mihr, and Lars van Troost (eds.), *50 Years of Amnesty International: Reflections and Perspectives*. SIM (Netherlands Institute of Human Rights) Special No. 36. Utrecht, 221–240.

Kohn, Margaret and Kavita Reddy. 2024. "Colonialism," *The Stanford Encyclopedia of Philosophy* (Sumer 2024 Edition), Edward N. Zalta (ed.). Available at https://plato.stanford.edu/archives/sum2024/entries/colonialism/.

Kolbert, Elizabeth. 2017. Why facts don't change our minds. *New Yorker Magazine*, February 19. Available at www.newyorker.com/magazine/2017/02/27/why-facts-dont-change-our-minds.

Kolkmann, Julia. 2016. *The Pragmatics of Possession: Issues in the Interpretation of Pre-Nominal Possessives in English*. PhD dissertation, University of Manchester, Faculty of Humanities.

Koster, Jan. 2003. Ritual performance and the politics of identity: On the functions and uses of ritual. *Journal of Historical Pragmatics*, 4(2), 211–248.

Kristeva, Julia. 1986. *The Kristeva Reader*. Toril Moi (ed.). New York: Columbia University Press.

Lave, Jean and Etienne Wenger. 1991. *Situated Learning: Legitimate Peripheral Participation*. Cambridge University Press.

Lavisse, Ernest. 1902. *Histoire Générale: Notions sommaires d'histoire ancienne, du Moyen Âge et des temps modernes*. 17th ed. Paris: Libraire Armand Colin [1st ed. 1882].

Leech, Geoffrey. 1983. *Principles of Pragmatics*. London: Longman.

Levinson, Stephen C. 1983. *Pragmatics*. Cambridge University Press.

Levinson, Stephen C. 1988. Putting linguistics on a proper footing: Explorations in Goffman's concepts of participation. In Paul Drew and Anthony Wootton (eds.), *Erving Goffman: Exploring the Interaction Order*. Cambridge, UK: Polity Press, 161–227.

Levinson, Stephen C. 2000. *Presumptive Meanings*. Cambridge, MA: MIT Press.

Levi-Strauss, Claude. 1978. *Myth and Meaning*. University of Toronto Press.

Longacre, Robert E. 1992. The discourse strategy of an appeal letter. In William C. Mann and Sandra A. Thompson (eds.), *Discourse Description: Diverse Linguistic Analyses of a Fund-Raising Text*. Amsterdam: John Benjamins, 109–130.

Lyons, Christopher. 1999. *Definiteness*. Cambridge University Press.

Machin, David (ed.). 2014. *Visual Communication*. Berlin: De Gruyter Mouton.

Mackay, Rowan R. 2013. Multimodal legitimation: Looking at and listening to Obama's ads. In Piotr Cap and Urszula Oksulska (eds.), *Analyzing Genres in Political Communication*. Amsterdam: John Benjamins, 345–377.

Mann, William C. and Sandra A. Thompson (eds.). 1992. *Discourse Description: Diverse Linguistic Analyses of a Fund-Raising Text*. Amsterdam: John Benjamins.

Márquez, Xavier. 2020. The mechanisms of cult production. In Kirill Postoutenko and Darin Stephanov (eds.), *Ruler Personality Cults from Empires to Nation-States and beyond: Symbolic Patterns and Interactional Dynamics*. Milton Park, UK: Routledge, 21–45.

Martin, J. R. 2000. Beyond exchange: APPRAISAL systems in English. In Susan Hunston and Geoff Thompson (eds.), *Evaluation in Text: Authorial Stance and the Construction of Discourse*. Oxford University Press, 1–27.

Martin, J. R. 2015. Cohesion and texture. In Deborah Tannen, Heidi E. Hamilton, and Deborah Schiffrin (eds.), *The Handbook of Discourse Analysis*. 2nd ed. Chichester, UK; Malden, MA: Wiley-Blackwell, 61–81.

Maugham, W. Somerset. 2003 [1944]. *The Razor's Edge*. New York: Vintage Books.

McCarthy, Justin. 1908. *A Short History of Our Own Times, from the Accession of Queen Victoria to the Accession of King Edward VII*. London: Chatto & Windus.

McCawley, James. 1981. *Everything that Linguists Have Always Wanted to Know about Logic but Were Afraid to Ask*. University of Chicago Press.

McCawley, James. 1999. Participant roles, frames, and speech acts. *Linguistics and Philosophy*, 22(6), 595–619.

McLellan, David. 1995. *Ideology*. 2nd ed. Minneapolis, MN: University of Minnesota Press.

McNamara, Paul and Frederik Van De Putte, 2025. "Deontic Logic," *The Stanford Encyclopedia of Philosophy* (Winter 2025 Edition), Edward N. Zalta and Uri Nodelman (eds.). Available at https://plato.stanford.edu/archives/win2025/entries/logic-deontic/.

Menz, Florian. 1989. Manipulation strategies in newspapers: A program for critical linguistics. In Ruth Wodak (ed.), *Language, Power, and Ideology: Studies in Political Discourse*. Amsterdam: John Benjamins, 227–249.

Mercier, Hugo and Dan Sperber. 2011. Why do humans reason? Arguments for an argumentative theory. *Behavioral and Brain Sciences*, 34(2), 57–111.

Mercier, Hugo and Dan Sperber. 2017. *The Enigma of Reason*. Cambridge, MA: Harvard University Press.

Merriam-Webster, Inc. 2011. *Merriam-Webster's Dictionary of Law*. Springfield, MA: Merriam-Webster, Inc.

Merriman, John. 1996. *A History of Modern Europe, Vol. 2: From the French Revolution to the Present*. New York/London: W. W. Norton and Co.

Miola, Robert. 2004. Seven types of intertextuality. In Michele Marrapodi (ed.), *Shakespeare, Italy, and Intertextuality*. Manchester University Press.

Moka-Mubelo, Willy. 2017. *Reconciling Law and Morality in Human Rights Discourse: Beyond the Habermasian Account of Human Rights*. Cham, Switzerland: Springer Nature.

Morgan, Marcyliena. 2014. *Speech Communities*. Cambridge University Press.

Morris, Warren F. 2010. *Understanding Ideology*. Lanham, MD: University Press of America.

Muders, Sebastian. 2018. Dignity and human dignity. *Philosophy and Public Issues (New Series)*, 8(2), 109–138.

Mühlhäusler, Peter and Rom Harré. 1990. *Pronouns and People: The Linguistic Construction of Social and Personal Identity*. Oxford, UK: Basil Blackwell.

Mutua, Makau W. 1996. The ideology of human rights. *Virginia Journal of International Law*, 36, 589–657.

Neier, Aryeh. 2012. *The International Human Rights Movement*. Princeton University Press.

Nickel, James and Adam Etinson. 2024. "Human Rights," *The Stanford Encyclopedia of Philosophy* (Fall 2024 Edition), Edward N. Zalta and Uri Nodelman (eds.). Available at https://plato.stanford.edu/archives/fall2024/entries/rights-human/.

Ott, Brian and Cameron Walter. 2000. Intertextuality: Interpretive practice and textual strategy. *Critical Studies in Media Communication*, 17(4), 429–446.

Park, Joseph Sung-Yul and Mary Bucholz. 2009. Introduction: Public transcripts: Entextualization and linguistic representation in institutional contexts. *Text and Talk*, 29(5), 485–502.

Pinker, Stephen. 2011. *The Better Angels of Our Nature*. London: Viking.

Pinker, Stephen. 2019. *Enlightenment Now: The Case for Reason, Science, Humanism, and Progress*. New York: Penguin Books.

Posner, Eric A. 2014. *The Twilight of Human Rights*. Oxford University Press.

Power, Jonathan. 2001. *Like Water on Stone: The Story of Amnesty International*. Boston, MA: Northeastern University Press.

Pratt, Mary Louise. 1986. Ideology and speech-act theory. *Poetics Today*, 7(1), 59–72.

Prince, Ellen. 1981. On the inferencing of indefinite-this NPs. In Aravind K. Joshi, Bonnie L. Webber, and Ivan A. Sag (eds.), *Elements of Discourse Understanding*. Cambridge University Press, 231–250.

Quinlan, Michael. 2011. The sources of morality. *SSRN*. Available at http://doi.org/10.2139/ssrn.2970899.

Rashkin, Hannah, Eunsol Choi, Jin Yea Jang, Svitlana Volkova, and Yejin Choi. 2017. Truth of varying shades: Analyzing language in fake news and political fact-checking. In Martha Palmer, Rebecca Hwa, and Sebastian Riedel (eds.), *Proceedings of the 2017 Conference on Empirical Methods in Natural Language Processing*. Copenhagen: Association for Computational Linguistics, 2931–2937.

Reboul, Anne. 1992. How much am *I* I and how much is *she* I? *Lingua*, 87(1–2), 169–202.

Reese, Stephen D. and Seth C. Lewis. 2009. Framing the war on terror: The internalization of policy in the US press. *Journalism*, 10(6), 777–797.

Regilme, Salvador Santino F. 2019. The global politics of human rights: From human rights to human dignity? *International Political Science Review*, 40(2), 279–290.

Reisigl, Martin and Ruth Wodak. 2015. The discourse-historical approach (DHA). In Ruth Wodak and Michael Meyer (eds.), *Methods of Critical Discourse Studies*. Introducing Qualitative Methods Series. 3rd ed. London: SAGE Publications, 23–61.

Ricoeur, Paul. 2008 [1970]. *Freud and Philosophy: An Essay on Interpretation*. Translated by Denis Savage. New Haven, CT: Yale University Press.

Rohan, Olivia, Ryoko Sasamoto, and Rebecca Jackson. 2018. Argumentation, Relevance Theory, and persuasion. *International Review of Pragmatics*, 10(2), 219–242.

Roque, Georges. 2017. Rhetoric, argumentation, and persuasion in a multimodal perspective. In Assimakis Tseronis and Charles Forceville. (eds.), *Multimodal Argumentation and Rhetoric in Media Genres*. Amsterdam: John Benjamins, 25–50.

Rouchota, Villy. 1996. Discourse connectives: What do they link? UCL Working Papers in Linguistics 8.

Roughley, Neil, 2023. "Human Nature," *The Stanford Encyclopedia of Philosophy* (Winter 2023 Edition), Edward N. Zalta and Uri Nodelman (eds.). Available at https://plato.stanford.edu/archives/win2023/entries/human-nature/.

Roulet, Eddy. 2003. Polyphony. In Jan Zienkowski, Jan-Ola Östman, and Jef Verschueren (eds.), *Discursive Pragmatics: Handbook of Pragmatics* 8. Amsterdam: John Benjamins, 208–222.

Ryder, Andrew. 2015–16. Althusser's theory of ideology. *International Socialist Review*, 99. Available at https://tinyurl.com/mr3d4j5a.

Saeed, John. 2016. *Semantics*. 4th ed. Malden, MA: Wiley-Blackwell.

Sbisà, Marina. 1999. Ideology and the persuasive use of presupposition. In Jef Verschueren (ed.), *Language and Ideology: Selected Papers from the 6th International Pragmatics Conference*. Antwerp: International Pragmatics Association, Vol. 1, 492–509.

Sbisà, Marina and Ken Turner (eds.). 2013. *Pragmatics of Speech Actions*. Berlin: De Gruyter Mouton.

Schane, Sanford. 2012. Contract formation as a speech act. In Peter M. Tiersma and Laurence M. Solan (eds.), *The Oxford Handbook of Language and Law*. Oxford University Press, 100–113.

Schegloff, Emanuel A. 2007. *Sequence Organization in Interaction*. Cambridge University Press.

Schegloff, Emanuel A. 2018. Conversational interaction: The embodiment of human sociality. In Deborah Deborah Tannen, Heidi E. Hamilton, and Deborah Schiffrin (eds.), *The Handbook of Discourse Analysis*. 2nd ed. Oxford: Wiley-Blackwell, 346–366.

Searle, John. 1969. *Speech Acts: An Essay in the Philosophy of Language*. Cambridge University Press.

Searle, John. 1976. The classification of illocutionary acts. *Language in Society*, 5(1), 1–23.

Searle, John. 1979. *Expression and Meaning: Studies in the Theory of Speech Acts*. Cambridge University Press.

Searle, John and Daniel Vanderveken. 1985. *Foundations of Illocutionary Logic*. Cambridge University Press.

Shapiro, Jacob L. 2018. Ideology is dead: Reality check. *Geopolitical Futures*. Available at https://tinyurl.com/4fsjjeu2.

Sikkink, Kathryn. 2017. *Evidence for Hope: Making Human Rights Work in the 21st Century*. Princeton University Press.

Silverstein, Michael. 1979. Language structure and linguistic ideology. In Paul R. Clyne, William F. Hanks, and Carol L. Hofbauer (eds.), *The Elements: A Parasession on Linguistic Units and Levels*. Chicago Linguistics Society, 193–247.

Simmons, Beth A. and Anton Strezhnev. 2017. Human rights and human welfare: Looking for a "dark side" to international human rights law. In Stephen Hopgood, Jack Snyder, and Leslie Vinjamuri (eds.), *Human Rights Futures*. Cambridge University Press, 60–87.

Simons, Mandy. 2005. Presupposition and relevance. In Zoltán Gendler Szabó (ed.), *Semantics Versus Pragmatics*. Oxford, UK: Clarendon Press, 329–335.

Snyder, Ilana. 2015. Discourses of "curation" in digital times. In Rodney H. Jones, Alice Chik, and Christoph Hafner (eds.), *Discourse and Digital Practices: Doing Discourse Analysis in the Digital Age*. London: Routledge, 209–225.

Solan, Lawrence M. and Peter M. Tiersma. 2005. *Speaking of Crime*. University of Chicago Press.

Solin, Anna. 2011. Genre. In Jan Zienkowski, Jan-Ola Östman, and Jef Verschueren (eds.), *Discursive Pragmatics: Handbook of Pragmatics Highlights*. Amsterdam: John Benjamins, Vol. 8, 119–134.

Sperber, Dan and Deirdre Wilson. 1986. *Relevance: Communication and Cognition*. Cambridge, MA. Harvard University Press.

Sperber, Dan and Deirdre Wilson 1995. *Relevance: Communication and Cognition*. 2nd ed. Oxford, UK: Blackwell.

Sperber, Dan and Deirdre Wilson. 2012. A deflationary account of metaphors. In Deirdre Wilson and Dan Sperber (eds.), *Meaning and Relevance*. Cambridge University Press, 97–122.

Sperber, Dan and Deirdre Wilson. 2015. Beyond speaker's meaning. *Croatian Journal of Philosophy*, XV(44), 117–149.

Sperber, Dan, Fabrice Clément, Christophe Heintz, Olivier Mascaro, Hugo Mercier, Gloria Origgi, and Deirdre Wilson. 2010. Epistemic vigilance. *Mind & Language*, 25(4), 359–393.

Swales, J. M. 1981. *Aspects of Article Introductions*. Birmingham, AL: University of Aston.

Swales, J. M. 1990. *Genre Analysis: English for Academic and Research Purposes*. Cambridge University Press.

Sypnowich, Christine. 2024. "Law and Ideology," *The Stanford Encyclopedia of Philosophy* (Summer 2024 Edition), Edward N. Zalta (ed.). Available at https://plato.stanford.edu/archives/sum2024/entries/law-ideology/.

Tannen, Deborah. 1993. *Framing in Discourse*. Oxford University Press.

Tarver, Erin C. 2017. *The I in Team: Sports Fandom and the Reproduction of Identity*. University of Chicago Press.

Terkourafi, Marina. 2012. Politeness and pragmatics. In Keith Allan and Kasia M. Jaszczolt (eds.), *The Cambridge Handbook of Pragmatics*. Cambridge University Press, 617–637.

Thaler, Verena. 2012. Mitigation as modification of illocutionary force. *Journal of Pragmatics*, 44(6–7), 907–919.

Tharoor, Shashi. 1999/2000. Are human rights universal? *World Policy Journal*, XVI(4) (Winter). Available at https://ciaotest.cc.columbia.edu/olj/wpj/wpj_win00a.html.

Thompson, Geoff and Susan Hunston. 2000. Evaluation: An Introduction. In Susan Hunston and Geoff Thompson (eds.), *Evaluation in Text: Authorial Stance and the Construction of Discourse*. Oxford University Press, 1–27.

Tömmel, Tatjana and Maurizio Passerin d'Entreves. 2025. "Hannah Arendt," *The Stanford Encyclopedia of Philosophy* (Spring 2025 Edition), Edward N. Zalta and Uri Nodelman (eds.). Available at https://plato.stanford.edu/archives/spr2025/entries/arendt/.

Traugott, Elizabeth Closs. 2012. Pragmatics and language change. In Keith Allan and Kasia M. Jaszczolt (eds.), *The Cambridge Handbook of Pragmatics*. Cambridge University Press, 549–565.

Tseronis, Assimakis and Charles Forceville. 2017. Argumentation and rhetoric in visual and multimodal communication. In Assimakis Tseronis and Charles Forceville (eds.), *Multimodal Argumentation and Rhetoric in Media Genres*. Amsterdam: John Benjamins, 1–24.

Unger, Christoph. 2006. *Genre, Relevance and Global Coherence: The Pragmatics of Discourse Type*. Houndmills, UK: Palgrave Macmillan.

Unsworth, Len and Chris Cléirigh. 2014. Multimodality and reading: The construction of meaning through image-text interaction. In Carey Jewitt (ed.), *The Routledge Handbook of Multimodal Analysis*. 2nd ed. London: Routledge, 176–188.

Upton, Thomas A. and Mary Ann Cohen. 2009. An approach to corpus-based discourse analysis: The move analysis as example. *Discourse Studies*, 11(5), 585–605.

Van Dijk, Teun. 1992. Discourse and the denial of racism. *Discourse and Society*, 3(1), 87–118.

Van Dijk, Teun. 1995. Discourse analysis as ideology analysis. In Christina Schäffner and Anita L. Wenden (eds.), *Language & Peace*. Abingdon Park, UK: Routledge, 17–33.

Van Dijk, Teun. 1998. *Ideology: A Multidisciplinary Approach*. London: SAGE Publications.

Van Dijk, Teun. 2013. Ideology and discourse. In Michael Freeden and Marc Stears (eds.), *The Oxford Handbook of Political Ideologies*. Oxford University Press, 175–197.

Van Leeuwen, Theo. 2015. Multimodality. In Deborah Tannen, Heidi E. Hamilton, and Deborah Schiffrin (eds.), *The Handbook of Discourse Analysis*, 2nd ed. Oxford: Wiley-Blackwell, 447–465.

Varga, Somogy and Charles Guignon. 2020. "Authenticity," *The Stanford Encyclopedia of Philosophy* (Spring 2020 Edition), Edward N. Zalta (ed.). Available at https://plato.stanford.edu/archives/spr2020/entries/authenticity/.

Vašák, Karel. 1977. A 30-year struggle: The sustained efforts to give force of law to the Universal Declaration of Human Rights. *UNESCO Courier*, November, 29–32. Available at https://unesdoc.unesco.org/ark:/48223/pf0000048063.

Verschueren, Jef. 1999. *Understanding Pragmatics*. London: Edward Arnold.

Verschueren, Jef. 2000. Notes on the role of metapragmatic awareness in language use. *Pragmatics*, 10(4), 439–456.

Verschueren, Jef. 2012. *Ideology in Language Use: Pragmatic Guidelines for Empirical Research*. Cambridge University Press.

Wales, Katie M. 1980. Exophera re-examined: The uses of the personal pronoun *we* in present day English. *UAE Papers in Linguistics*, 12, 21–44.

Walton, Douglas. 1989. *Informal Logic: A Handbook for Critical Argumentation*. Cambridge University Press.

Walton, Douglas. 2009. Argumentation theory: A very short introduction. In Guillermo Simari and Iyad Rahwan (eds.), *Argumentation in Artificial Intelligence*. Boston, MA: Springer-Verlag, 1–22.

Ward, Adrian F. 2012. Scientists probe human nature – and discover we are good, after all. *Scientific American*, November 20. Available at https://tinyurl.com/2m8y2e6v.

Wason, P. C. 1968. Reasoning about a rule. *Quarterly Journal of Experimental Psychology*, 20(3), 273–281. https://doi.org/10.1080/14640746808400161

Waugh, Evelyn. 1945. *Brideshead Revisited: The Sacred & Profane Memories of Captain Charles Ryder*. Boston, MA: Little, Brown and Co.

Wenar, Leif and Rowan Cruft. 2025. "Rights," *The Stanford Encyclopedia of Philosophy* (Summer 2025 Edition), Edward N. Zalta and Uri Nodelman (eds.). Available at https://plato.stanford.edu/archives/sum2025/entries/rights/.

Wenger, Étienne. 1998. *Communities of Practice*. Cambridge University Press.

Wharton, Tim. 2009. *Pragmatics and Non-verbal Communication*. Cambridge University Press.

White, Peter R. R. 2011. Appraisal. In Jan Zienkowski, Jan-Ola Östman, and Jef Verschueren (eds.), *Discursive Pragmatics: Handbook of Pragmatics*. Vol. 8. Amsterdam: John Benjamins, 14–36.

Wierzbicka, Anna. 1987. *English Speech Act Verbs: A Semantic Dictionary.* Marrickville, NSW: Academic Press Australia.

Wilde, Oscar. 1982. *The Importance of Being Earnest.* In Richard Ellmann (ed.), *The Picture of Dorian Gray and Other Writings.* Toronto: Bantam Books.

Williams, Joseph M. and Gregory G. Colomb. 2001. *The Craft of Argument.* New York: Longman.

Williamson, Tricia, Danielle L. Wagstaff, Jane Goodwin, and Naomi Smith. 2023. Mothering ideology: A qualitative exploration of mothers' perceptions of navigating motherhood pressures and partner relationships. *Sex Roles*, 88(1–2), 101–117.

Wilson, Deirdre. 1992. Reference and relevance. *UCL Working papers in linguistics*, 4, 167–191.

Wilson, Deirdre. 2006. The pragmatics of verbal irony: Echo or pretense? *Lingua*, 116(10), 1722–1743.

Wilson, Deirdre. 2017. Relevance theory. In Yan Huang (ed.), *Oxford Handbook of Pragmatics.* Oxford University Press, 79–100.

Wilson, Deirdre and Robyn Carston. 2007. A unitary approach to lexical pragmatics: Relevance, inference and ad hoc concepts. In Noel Burton-Roberts (ed.), *Pragmatics.* Gordonsville, VA: Palgrave Macmillan, 230–259.

Wilson, Deirdre and Dan Sperber. 1988. Mood and the analysis of non-declarative sentences. In Jonathan Dancy, J. Moravcsik, and C. Taylor (eds.), *Human Agency: Language, Duty and Value: Philosophical Essays in Honor of J.O. Urmson.* Stanford University Press, 77–101.

Wilson, Deirdre and Dan Sperber. 2004. Relevance theory. In Laurence Horn and Gregory Ward (eds.), *The Handbook of Pragmatics.* Malden, MA: Blackwell, 607–632.

Wilson, Deirdre and Dan Sperber (eds.). 2012a. *Meaning and Relevance.* Cambridge University Press.

Wilson, Deirdre and Dan Sperber. 2012b. Truthfulness and relevance. In Deirdre Wilson and Dan Sperber (eds.), *Meaning and Relevance.* Cambridge University Press, 47–83.

Winter, Eugene. 1994. Clause relations as information structure: Two basic text structures in English. In Malcolm Coulthard (ed.), *Advances in Written Text Analysis.* London: Routledge, 46–68.

Witczak-Plisiecka, Iwona. 2013. Speech actions in legal contexts. In Marina Sbisà and Ken Turner (eds.), *Pragmatics of Speech Actions.* Berlin: De Gruyter Mouton, 613–658.

Witte, John Jr. and M. Christian Green (eds.), 2011. *Religion and Human Rights: An Introduction.* Oxford University Press.

Wodak, Ruth. 1989. 1968: The power of political jargon – A "Club-2" discussion. In Ruth Wodak (ed.), *Language, Power, and Ideology: Studies in Political Discourse.* Amsterdam: John Benjamins, 137–163.

Wodak, Ruth. 2007. History in the making/The making of history: The "German Wehrmacht" in collective and individual memories in Austria. In Christine Anthonissen and Jan Blommaert (eds.), *Discourse and Human Rights Violations.* Amsterdam: John Benjamins, 115–142.

Wodak, Ruth and Martin Reisigl. 2018. Discourse and racism. In Deborah Tannen, Heidi E. Hamilton, and Deborah Schiffrin (eds.), *The Handbook of Discourse Analysis.* 2nd ed. Oxford, UK: Wiley Blackwell, 576–596.

Woolard, Kathryn A. 2021. Language ideology. In James Stanlaw (ed.), *The International Encyclopedia of Linguistic Anthropology*. John Wiley and Sons, Inc. Available at https://tinyurl.com/5daepzr8.

Woolard, Kathryn A. and Bambi B. Schieffelin. 1994. Language ideology. *Annual Review of Anthropology*, 23(1), 55–82.

Wray, Allison. 2002. *Formulaic Language and the Lexicon*. Cambridge University Press.

Zuber, Valentine. 2019. Are human rights of religious origin? *SUR International Journal on Human Rights*, 16(29), 17–31.

Index

Printed in the United Kingdom by TJ Clays Ltd.